Luther H. Holton

A Founding Canadian Entrepreneur

HiST.233

Luther Hamilton Holton (1817-1880)

Luther H. Holton
A Founding Canadian Entrepreneur

HENRY C. KLASSEN

UNIVERSITY OF
CALGARY
PRESS

University of Calgary Press
2500 University Drive NW
Calgary, Alberta
Canada T2N 1N4

Canadian Cataloguing in Publication Data

Klassen, Henry C. (Henry Cornelius), 1931-
Luther H. Holton

    Includes bibliographical references and index.
    ISBN 1-55238-027-0

    1. Holton, Luther Hamilton, 1817-1880. 2. Businessmen—
Quebec (Province)—Montréal—Biography. 3. Politicians—
Quebec (Province)—Montréal—Biography. 4. Canada—
Politics and government—1867-1896.* I. Title.

FC516.H64K52 2000   971.05'1'092   C00-911367-3
F1033.H64K52 2000

 We acknowledge the financial support of the Government of Canada through the Book Publishing Industry Development Program (BPIDIP) for our publishing activities.

The Canada Council for the Arts
Le Conseil des Arts du Canada

Printed and bound in Canada by AGMV Marquis.

∞ This book is printed on acid-free paper.

In loving memory
of my wife,
Agnes Klassen

Contents

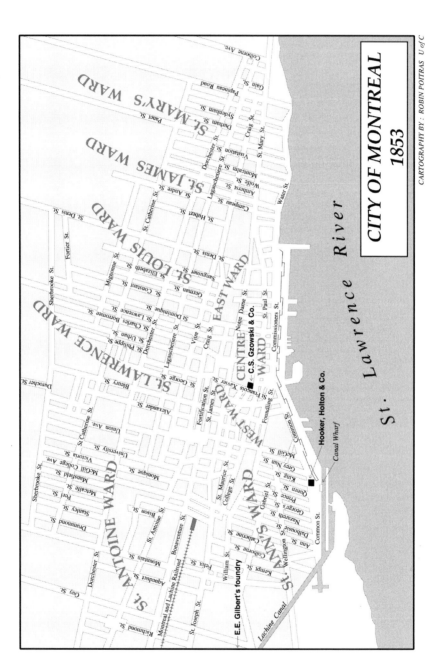

CITY OF MONTREAL
1853

St. Lawrence River

St. MARY'S WARD

St. JAMES WARD

St. LOUIS WARD

CENTRE WARD

EAST WARD

WEST WARD

St. LAWRENCE WARD

St. ANTOINE WARD

St. ANN'S WARD

C.S. Gzowski & Co.

Hooker, Holton & Co.

E.E. Gilbert's foundry

Canal Wharf

Lachine Canal

Montreal and Lachine Railroad

CARTOGRAPHY BY : ROBIN POITRAS   U of C

Preface

This book portrays a man who helped lead Canada through two of its great experiences in the nineteenth century: the transportation revolution and the completion of confederation. In the industrial exuberance of the early and mid-1850s, Luther Holton of Montreal was a prosperous businessman. He had the spirit of a generation of daring adventurers in an era when risk taking was celebrated and boldness frequently well rewarded. During his years as adviser to political leaders and government officials, Holton served as a crisis manager, grappling with the problems of cultural conflict and sectionalism that threatened to tear Canada apart. He saw that it was essential to sweep aside the suspicion and ill will caused by extreme views and to build better French–English relations. For Holton, success meant not only making suggestions to deal with the immediate tensions between English and French Canadians but also coming to grips with the long-term consequences, recognizing at the same time that failure could spell disaster for Canada.

Holton's life cannot be understood without an emphasis on the aspirations, achievements, and frustrations of a man who spoke English and French fluently. When we examine his business and politics, we see that his bilingualism gave full scope to the talents of a person who was able to cross cultural boundaries and to develop ties between cultures. The reputation established by Holton as a bilingual Canadian and maintained for more than half a century was an enviable one.

The story of Holton is a complex blend of traditions and transformations. Eventually, he entered steamboat, railway, iron, banking, and real estate businesses, struggling in them as a leader, as did other entrepreneurs in these industries. When Holton reflected on the histories of his firms toward the end of his life, he recognized that they had all maintained several important traditions in their longer or shorter histories. Most important, they had focussed on high-quality service, working to meet customers' needs. In addition, they had been diversified businesses, providing several different products and services. These traditions constitute one of the central themes in this exploration of the histories of the firms. Although relying on these traditions, Holton also took significant strategic courses over the decades that transformed his businesses. The transformation of his firms from relatively small ventures into larger businesses provides another theme in this examination of their histories. As they grew in size and complexity, they faced new problems of organizing marketing processes. Ideas about solving these problems often led the firms through transformations. Concern for continuity as well as change pervaded strategic thinking at the businesses with which he was associated and in which he provided leadership. In a period marked by transportation changes of a revolutionary magnitude, few individuals played as important roles in steamboats and railways as Luther Holton.

Leaders were essential – indeed, indispensable – to create and sustain a sense of direction and purpose in these business enterprises, and Holton was such a leader. Together with other men, he united and managed the components of the businesses. He invested capital in steamboats, land, buildings, railway equipment, marine engines, and banks, in addition to recruiting, organizing, motivating, and rewarding employees. Holton also helped arrange the distribution of goods and services. The breadth of his interest and his influence in transportation, commerce, manufacturing, and finance was truly remarkable. There developed a long tradition in his enterprises of taking the profits they earned and reinvesting them for the owners' long-term benefit. Founded in an area of Canada that was in the early stages of industrialization, his businesses faced many unforeseen problems and challenges. In leading Canada's transportation, commercial, industrial, and financial development together with other entrepreneurs, Holton was willing to assume huge responsibilities and take great risks.

My study analyzes Holton's life in business, but it examines as well the important roles he played in Montreal and Canadian politics. Holton consistently maintained two significant traditions in his long political career. First and last as a Liberal politician he was committed to taking the sharp edge off of conflict, to pulling together the many strands of colonial Canada's economic and social life in a way that might make the whole function smoothly. Most troublesome was cultural conflict, splits between the eastern and western sections of the united province of Canada, between French Canadians and English Canadians. Only with much difficulty could these divisions be combined, and any political alignment based on combination was almost certain to be fragile. Holton as a Liberal also toiled endlessly to promote business enterprise. In making the effort, he had long-term goals that went beyond the basic truism of earning a reasonable return on invested capital. Responding to a larger provincial need that had something to do with his own immediate interests, he made it clear that one of his main objectives was Canada's economic development. This allowed voters who elected Holton to the Canadian legislative assembly to believe, and with considerable reason, that their interests also were served by his success at the polls.

Besides attempting to maintain these traditions, Holton eventually followed new trends in strategic planning in the Canadian political community. Most important were ideas about the structure of the united province of Canada. The notion of transforming the legislative union into a federation had grown slowly at first from its origins in the 1840s. In Holton's case, too, this idea was slow to pervade his thinking. By the late 1850s, however, he had become a strong advocate of a federal union of Upper and Lower Canada. By this time, he was living in a political and social environment in which many Canadians had lost a sense of security in their political system. Holton wanted all people to feel secure in their province. Ideas about federation contributed to changes in his view of the future of Canada. In developing a strategy for a new Canada, Holton sought to clarify a vision of a province deeply rooted in its heritage. He believed that Canadians, both English and French, had preserved a particular orientation toward the united province that could provide guidance for the future. That orientation, he thought, included promoting a supportive political and economic environment for both cultures. As one whose strategic vision eventually became part of the planning process, Holton helped lead Canada through the most dramatic transformation of its history – the completion of confederation.

Holton held a key position in the inner councils of the Liberal party. But there were breaks in the pattern even then, moments when issues in provincial politics sparked problems for him. We see Holton the Liberal member for Montreal Centre, combining public and private life in the Canadian legislative assembly, but failing to get re-elected in the next general election; Holton the minister of finance, trying to bring order to the finance office, and then losing it to the Liberal-Conservatives in the often tumultuous politics of the Canadian union; Holton the Liberal politician, going on the offensive against the proposed federal union of British North America, but ultimately working out in his own mind a defence of confederation and becoming absolutely committed to preserving the Dominion of Canada.

This book is biographical, but it is not a complete biography of Luther Holton or a comprehensive history of his era. I have highlighted especially his business life and have paid close attention to his political life. In focussing on Holton the businessman, I have asked at every point in his career what problems he faced and how he tried to solve them. The route for advancement for him lay in finding solutions to these problems. In tracing his life as a politician, I have concentrated on what he knew when he had to take significant actions, why he made his decisions, and how he sought to put his ideas into practice. These are important topics, and they presented themselves to him in a practical manner. I have offered a broad discussion of how Holton's private life helped fashion his public career, how his absorption with Lower Canadian politics disrupted the Liberal party, and how his vaulting ambition enabled him to surmount one defeat after another. I have produced a portrait that reveals Holton's rise from comparatively humble origins in Ontario to prominent positions in business and political circles in Quebec. In these roles, Holton time and again demonstrated his phenomenal capacity for growth, which empowered the son of a poor farmer to become an important figure in Canadian business and politics.

The story of Luther Holton takes us back to an era when industrial capitalism was new and raw in Canada. Written rules were needed for the new industrial economy, but in the mid-nineteenth century they did not exist. As far as Holton is concerned, the historical record shows a man who usually charted a responsible course of action in the face of conflicting standards of business behaviour. But it also reveals a person who sometimes got drawn into business situations that proved to be questionable, if not illegal. The record discloses Holton's actions from the challenging time of his financial success in Montreal, operating a Canada-wide steamboat enterprise that enmeshed him in provincial and international trade, to a darker day when he found himself under attack, embroiled in a railway scandal in which he, John A. Macdonald, Alexander T. Galt, Casimir S. Gzowski, and David L. Macpherson were accused of making excessive profits. This was the dark side of Holton's fortune.

Holton could be ruthless, and the acquisitive side of his nature was well known, but among his business and political associates over the years he did not stand out as the villain. As a business manager, he was keenly attuned to the fundamental economics of his business enterprises. He knew that profit was an imperative in his business dealings. Without reasonable profits, his ventures could neither survive nor raise capital to offer goods and services, create jobs, and provide him and his family with a living. But rather than trying to maximize his own self-interest in each transaction without regard to the needs and interests of his customers, he usually exhibited a sense of fairness and self-restraint.

His reputation for treating people fairly, combined with his human warmth, allowed him to gain the trust and confidence not only of English

Canadians, but also of French Canadians. At the time of Holton's death in 1880, his long-time friend Wilfrid Laurier said: "All French Canadians today feel that the man who has just departed from us was the connecting link between the many discordant elements of our province (Quebec)." Holton saw the cultural conflict in Quebec and Canada as a challenge that had to be met. He believed that life would go better when English and French Canadians could count on each other for mutual respect and justice. His conciliatory approach and his ability to see things from various perspectives went a long way toward winning the good will of both French and English Canadians, permitting him to serve as a unifying force first in the Canadian union and then in the Dominion of Canada.

This study calls attention to a fundamental trait of character manifest throughout Holton's life: the essential flexibility of his nature. Holton himself recognized it in a letter he wrote on 5 May 1867 to George Brown, editor of the Toronto *Globe*, who wanted him to explain why he had shifted from his vow not to support the union of British North America to a policy of confederation. After relating how circumstances had caused him to change his mind – how confederation had become a political necessity – Holton concluded: the constitution "*has been* carried, and such as it is, *it is our constitution*. We must therefore live under it, work it, and if we can improve it."

From his earliest years, Holton had a sense that he needed to be open to change, to consider a fresh way of looking at things. This made for a pragmatic approach to difficulties, a ready capability to adapt to new or different requirements. From Holton's flexibility came some of his most attractive traits: his tolerance, his compassion, his willingness to forgive. Like many other Canadians who were optimistic about their future, Holton laboured constantly for a better world – for his family, for himself, and for his country. He was a defender of democracy, an ally of the poor, and a friend of black people. Like some of his Montreal contemporaries, he was a man of wealth, but for him wealth carried a social responsibility. In his Liberalism, he stressed the rights of the individual, but individualism in his life was tempered with a social conscience and concern for the larger community. Following this socially responsible course helped Holton to cope with the many setbacks he experienced and allowed him to continue a vigorous life of reaching high.

Acknowledgements

I owe my interest in Luther Holton to a fine seminar Maurice Careless gave at the University of Toronto. Inspired by his approach to history, I have been thinking about Holton off and on ever since those days in graduate studies. I offer special thanks to Maurice Careless and Carl Berger, who together directed my work on this subject as a dissertation. They provided both intellectual stimulation and encouragement. Special thanks go also to Gerald Tulchinsky at Queen's University, Kingston, Ontario, who generously shared his insights with me in our conversations and correspondence, as well as to Marcel Hamelin at the University of Ottawa for valuable help when I was his colleague.

I learned to care for history from Bill Morton when he was head of the department at the University of Manitoba and from Richard Glover and Tryggvi Oleson when they taught there. I learned to understand nineteenth-century central Canada from Maurice Careless and Donald Creighton when I studied at the University of Toronto. I am grateful to all of them for their lessons and for creating an atmosphere that enabled me to take my research in new and interesting directions.

In writing this book, I have also benefited from the work of numerous other scholars. Among them, I would like to mention Brian Young, Douglas McCalla, Andy den Otter, Michael Bliss, Jean-Paul Bernard, Dale C. Thomson, Michael J. Piva, Peter B. Waite, Yvan Lamonde, Joseph Schull, Bettina Bradbury, Ronald Rudin, Jacques Monet, Charles P. Stacey, Fernand Ouellet, John I. Cooper, Paul-André Linteau, Bruce W. Hodgins, Paul G. Cornell, Robin W. Winks, Peter A. Baskerville, J. E. Hodgetts, Ben Forster, Eric Ross, J. K. Johnson, Joseph Levitt, Craig Brown, Ramsay Cook, Peter G. Goheen, Suzanne Zeller, Donald Swainson, Margaret A. Evans, and Brian Osborne. I owe a special debt to Donald H. Akenson, John Zucchi, and Philip J. Cercone, all of whom encouraged me to complete this work.

As it became clear to me that the information on Holton could be found in a broad geographical area north and south of the border, I visited many archives and research libraries in Canada and the United States. A special debt of thanks is due to the numerous archivists and librarians who guided me to important sources and facilitated my research. They include the staffs at National Archives of Quebec in Montreal, Bank of Montreal Archives, Laurentian Bank of Canada Archives, National Archives of Canada in Ottawa, Baker Library at Harvard University, New York Public Library, Montreal Court House Archives, Montreal City Hall Archives, McGill University Archives, Montreal Board of Trade Archives, Montreal Unitarian Church Archives, Archives of Ontario, Queen's University Archives, Cincinnati Historical Society Archives, National Archives in Washington, D.C., CIGNA Archives at Philadelphia, Owen D. Young Library at St. Lawrence University in Canton, New York, Fraser-Hickson Institute at Montreal, Metropolitan Toronto Library, Toronto Public Library, Thomas Fisher Rare Book Library at University of Toronto, Ogdensburg Public Library, Cincinnati and Hamilton County Public Library, Western Reserve Historical Society Library in Cleveland, Ohio, Toledo-Lucas County Public Library, New York Historical Society Library, Stratford-Perth Archives, St. Mary's District Museum, Guelph Public Library, Guelph Civic Museum, and Hastings County Historical Society Archives in Belleville, Ontario.

A number of people performed valuable research tasks in archives and libraries I was unable to visit personally. I thank the staffs at Radcliffe College Archives in Cambridge, Massachusetts, Anglican Archives in Kingston, Lake Champlain Maritime Museum in Basin Harbor, Vermont, Yale University Library, and Windsor Public Library.

I was exceptionally fortunate to correspond or talk with Holton's relatives and with men and women who were linked to him in some way. Among those who generously provided data and insights were Thomas L. Brock and Geoffrey G. Gilbert in Victoria, British Columbia; Edna Holton Seaver in Cohasset, Massachusetts; Luther Hamilton Holton in New York City; Harriet Scofield in Cleveland, Ohio; Roberta Davies in Catonsville, Maryland; John Mullane in Cincinnati; Jean M. Smith in Port Ewen, New York; Anne K. Goodwill in Schenectady, New York; John B. Freeman in Palm Harbor, Florida; Phyllis Dodge in Pownal, Vermont; Elizabeth A. Knap in Ogdensburg, New York; J. H. Holton, Mrs. H. Y. Russel, Mrs. J. W. Nicoll, Isobel B. Dobell, Donald K. Roy, and Elliott A. Durnford in Montreal; Mrs. A. D. Holton and Bruce Holton in Belleville; Norma Shorey in Frankford, Ontario; Mark B. Holton in Halifax; Edith Jaques Coristine in Toronto; Mrs. R. W. Shepherd and Mrs. Margaret Peyton in Como,

Quebec; Mr. and Mrs. W. L. Howard in Delta, Ontario; Dr. and Mrs. W. O. Williams and Phyllis M. E. Stephenson in Prescott; and Mrs. A. N. St. John in Toronto. All of them were open, forthright, and extremely cooperative in helping me carry out the research for this study.

This book has been published with the help of a grant from the Humanities and Social Sciences Federation of Canada, using funds provided by the Social Sciences and Humanities Research Council of Canada. I gratefully acknowledge this generous grant.

I also thank the University of Ottawa and the University of Calgary for research grants that supported my early work on this project. Linda Toth, Wendy Amero, Joy Bowes, Barb Friesen, Marjory McLean, Joyce Woods, Karen McDermid, Carol Murray, Debra Isaac, Kelly Morris, and Jennifer Cooper responded to my repeated pleas for help with the typing, and I am indeed grateful to them. My colleagues in the Department of History at the University of Calgary deserve acknowledgement for their friendship and support – I trust that they will accept a collective thank you.

At the University of Calgary Press, I have been fortunate to work with Shirley Onn, Walter Hildebrandt, John King, Sharon Boyle, Joan Barton, Tim Au Yeung, and Kristina Schuring. They were uniformly supportive, and I truly appreciate their highly professional help. I owe special thanks to Kristina Schuring for designing the book cover, Joan Eadie for producing the index, and Kristina Schuring and Robin Poitras for preparing the maps. Special thanks are due as well to the anonymous readers for their helpful comments on the book.

Finally, my greatest support came from my wife, Agnes Klassen, who died after she had contributed to my work in many ways. This book would not have been possible without her constant love, friendship, and understanding.

A Note on Currency

In the text that follows, Halifax currency, based on pounds and shillings, is used during the years before 1858; Canadian decimal currency, based on dollars and cents, is employed from 1858 onward. During the 1820s, when the imperial government failed in its attempt to introduce British sterling currency in Lower and Upper Canada, the monetary system in these colonies came to be based on the Halifax standard. On 1 January 1858, the Province of Canada officially adopted a Canadian decimal currency. In the process, dollars replaced pounds.

Illustrations

Chapter 1

Work on the Harbourfront

Luther Hamilton Holton was interested in his ancestry. Drawing together the various strands of meaning in the lives of his ancestors, he demonstrated to those who listened to his stories that he cared about his family tree. In his later life, when relatives visited him in his Montreal home, Luther showed them a fascinating book, *A History of the Holton Family*, written by Dr. Holton of New York.[1]

Tourists now throng to his birthplace in summer. Luther Holton was born to Anner Phillips Holton and Ezra Holton on 22 January 1817 on a farm near Sheffield's Corners (now Soperton), a hamlet in the eastern part of Upper Canada, some twenty miles northwest of Brockville on the upper St. Lawrence River.[2] Although Luther spent his adult years far removed from the world of his childhood, knowledge of his place of birth shaped his life. Despite its occasional poverty, the Holton household became a favourite meeting place in the community. As his parents' reputation for hospitality and pleasant conversation spread, neighbours dropped by to visit and became interested in their background. The social values derived from this environment, austere in part, yet deeply indebted to enlightened behaviour, framed Luther Holton's outlook as the poor rural boy began his business career on the Montreal harbourfront, emerged as a successful entrepreneur, and won recognition as an influential Liberal politician. Luther's paternal grandfather was Lemuel Holton, a great-great-grandson of William Holton. From the family history, Luther had learned that William Holton and his descendants, including son William, had lived in the Connecticut Valley since the seventeenth century.

* * *

The first William Holton sailed from England in 1634, landed at Charlestown, became a farmer at Hartford, Connecticut on land along the Connecticut River, married Mary, possibly Mary Winche, and in 1653

1

THE HOLTON FAMILY

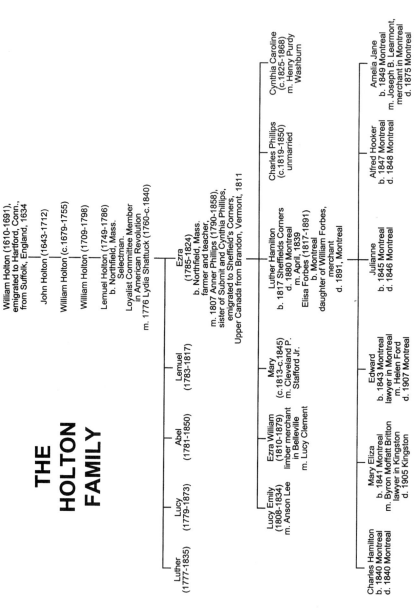

William Holton (1610-1691), emigrated to Hartford, Conn., from Suffolk, England, 1634

John Holton (1643-1712)

William Holton (c.1679-1755)

William Holton (1709-1798)

Lemuel Holton (1749-1786)
b. Northfield, Mass.
Selectman.
Loyalist Committee Member in American Revolution
m. 1776 Lydia Shattuck (1760-c.1840)

Luther (1777-1835)

Lucy (1779-1873)

Abel (1781-1850)

Lemuel (1783-1817)

Ezra (1785-1824)
b. Northfield, Mass.
farmer and teacher,
m. 1807 Anner Phillips (1790-1858), sister of Submit and Cynthia Phillips, emigrated to Sheffield's Corners, Upper Canada from Brandon, Vermont, 1811

Lucy Emily (1808-1834)
m. Anson Lee

Ezra William (1810-1879)
limber merchant in Belleville
m. Lucy Clement

Mary (c.1813-c.1845)
m. Cleveland P. Stafford Jr.

Luther Hamilton 1817 Sheffields Corners
d. 1880 Montreal
m. April, 1839
Elisa Forbes (1817-1891)
b. Montreal
daughter of William Forbes, merchant
d. 1891, Montreal

Charles Phillips (c.1819-1850)
unmarried

Cynthia Caroline (c.1825-1868)
m. Henry Purdy Washburn

Charles Hamilton
b. 1840 Montreal
d. 1840 Montreal

Mary Eliza
b. 1841 Montreal
m. Byron Moffatt Britton lawyer in Kingston
d. 1905 Kingston

Edward
b. 1843 Montreal lawyer in Montreal
m. Helen Ford
d. 1907 Montreal

Julianne
b. 1845 Montreal
d. 1846 Montreal

Alfred Hooker
b. 1847 Montreal
d. 1848 Montreal

Amelia Jane
b. 1849 Montreal
m. Joseph B. Learmont, merchant in Montreal
d. 1875 Montreal

Sources: Geoffrey Gilbert, "The Ancestry of Ezra Holton of Northfield, Mass. and Soperton, Ont., 1785-1824" (Victoria, 1953); Geoffrey Gilbert, "The Ancestry of William Forbes, Mass. and Montreal, Quebec, 1788-1833" (Victoria, 1953); Thos. B. Bower, "A Stafford Family Tree," (1948).

moved upstream to a new farm at Northampton, Massachusetts, the town which he helped to found.[3] Amidst endless agricultural activity, he found time to serve as a magistrate. For generations, the Holtons farmed their acres, first in the Northampton district and then farther upriver at Northfield, Massachusetts. Elected selectman at Northfield in 1780, grandfather Lemuel Holton participated in the revolutionary cause during the American Revolution. A pillar of the local church, Lemuel fathered six children who bore biblical names like Abel and Ezra and names harking back to the Protestant Reformation such as Luther and Calvin, which became traditional in the Holton family. A similar New England religious tradition was evident in the family of Luther Holton's mother, Anner Phillips, whose sister was called Submit. Although he never met his maternal grandmother Lydia Phillips, family legend holds that Luther heard a great deal of her resourcefulness from his mother.

A relative once remarked that Luther "was the son of parents of education and refinement."[4] His father, Ezra Holton, born at Northfield, Massachusetts, in 1785, was a man of considerable wit. Sensitive and patient, Anner Phillips was five years younger than her husband. She was born in 1790 at Ashfield, Massachusetts. Both Ezra and Anner left their hometowns to seek their fortune. They moved, at different times, to Brandon in west central Vermont, where they were married in 1807.[5] Here the couple settled on a farm. From the very first, Ezra and Anner tried to raise grains – barley, oats, and wheat – and livestock, but the discouraging results soon caused them to remove to Randolph, a central Vermont town, where their efforts at farming continued. Denied good crops over the next few years, Ezra and Anner Holton abandoned hope of doing well in Vermont but in 1811 decided to start again at Sheffield's Corners, Upper Canada. Ezra and Anner had two children when they moved to Sheffield's Corners: Lucy, born in Brandon; and Ezra William, born in Randolph. At Sheffield's Corners, Anner Holton soon gave birth to another daughter, Mary.

Sheffield's Corners was a growing community that afforded more opportunities than Randolph. The Holtons set up their first Canadian farm of 200 acres in the vicinity of Upper Beverley Lake.[6] Having only small means, they obtained the land on credit. They practised mixed farming, as in Vermont. One immediate source of support at Sheffield's Corners was Levi Soper, a farmer and country merchant who, together with his wife Lois Flint Soper, gave the Holtons all kinds of helpful information.[7] Former Vermonters themselves, the Sopers invited Ezra and Anner Holton into their home for visits. A cousin of Ezra, Lois Soper in particular made them feel comfortable. This friendship continued. During the War of 1812,

Ezra served in the second regiment of the Leeds militia under the command of Captain Levi Soper.[8] At the same time, the regular British troops in the upper St. Lawrence region supplied Ezra Holton with a ready market for his grain and livestock.

But shortly after the war everything began to go wrong. Ezra Holton fell upon lean days as the military market disappeared with the withdrawal of the troops. To make things worse, his efforts to profit from his contract to provide the garrison in Kingston with 3,000 cords of firewood were frustrated.[9] The major loss on the wood sales clearly hurt Ezra. There was room for further concern, for after the war the upper St. Lawrence region witnessed an acute economic depression. These were hard years in general for agriculture, as for other industries. Impoverished, Ezra lost his land to creditors but remained on the farm as a tenant.[10] His farming business almost collapsed. Despite the reverses he suffered, Ezra was willing to continue tilling the soil, and eventually the Upper Canadian government allowed him to occupy and possess 200 acres of free crown land in the Upper Beverly Lake area in recognition of his war service.[11]

Luther spent his early years on the farm, surrounded by the heavily wooded wilderness. On fine autumn days, the forest turned its colours. But the beauty of this countryside veiled difficult lives; Luther also saw the rugged terrain and the toil essential for survival. The farm generated only a little cash. Observing his parents' constant struggle to make ends meet and minister to the needs of their children, Luther learned the value of work and money. Ezra Holton also took a part-time position as the village schoolteacher, obtaining some additional income from this job.[12] He combined this task with much reading in history and literature. Both Ezra and Anner delighted in books, for which they had time particularly during the long winter evenings.[13] These were not years of isolation; Ezra and Anner kept in contact with the flowering of New England culture of the first quarter of the nineteenth century through books, correspondence, and visits. Born into a family devoted to learning, Luther Holton was always attracted to people who shared his father and mother's interest in reading. Perhaps he recalled how they taught him the alphabet when he was a little boy. Surely, to them he owed his good command of English. Already in the days of his youth, and certainly later, nobody could talk with Luther for five minutes without noticing that he was well-read, quick to observe, and well-spoken. For the rest of his life, Luther remembered his parents' love, prudence, and literary interests.

But life was also a season of great trials. On 12 August 1824, Ezra Holton died suddenly at the age of thirty-eight, leaving Luther the heritage of his New England character.[14] Luther was seven and a half years old.

There was a small funeral service, and Ezra was buried in the family plot at the old cemetery in Sheffield's Corners. The family was devastated by its loss. Ezra's death left his wife, Anner, to handle the farm and support six children. Anner, aged thirty-three, scrimped and saved. At the moment, she was able to cope with the uncertainties facing her. Luther gladly joined his older siblings in doing chores, and his attempt to bear burdens developed his character and bred independence. But it fell to Lucy, sixteen, and her younger sister Mary to help their mother keep the Holton household together. Fourteen-year-old Ezra, besides assisting his mother with the farm work and the management of the daily family economy, provided extra income by clerking in uncle Levi Soper's country store.

Within a few years of her husband's death, Anner recognized that she and her family could not go on alone. Anxious to have a father especially for her youngest children, Cynthia and Charles, she married local merchant Cleveland Stafford in 1829. This allowed Ezra to leave the family home in 1832 for Belleville, Upper Canada, where he found a job as a clerk with uncle Billa Flint, a merchant, who later took him into partnership and then backed him in opening his own general store in that town.[15] Meanwhile, Luther's affection for his mother grew, for he realized that her presence was helping him to bear the loss of his father. Anner Holton chose for Luther a better future than life on the farm could provide. In 1826, when he was nine years old, Anner sent him by steamboat down the St. Lawrence to Montreal to live with his uncle and aunt, Moses Haskell Gilbert and Cynthia Phillips Gilbert.[16] That Luther left Sheffield's Corners did not mean that he abandoned family ties. In later years, he visited his mother and siblings in Upper Canada as often as he could.

* * *

The arrival of Luther in Montreal marked a turning point in his life. Reassuring faces – Moses and Cynthia Gilbert – greeted the young traveller at the harbourfront. Less than an hour later, when he came to the Gilbert home, a modest structure on Grey Nun Street in the St. Ann's suburb, he was safe and sound in ways that mattered. From the beginning, he was treated like a member of the family by Moses and Cynthia, who was his mother's younger sister. Indeed, Luther's aunt and uncle took personal charge of his upbringing and made his career in business possible. The Gilberts' own children, Ebenezer, Luther's junior by six years, and Cynthia, a newborn baby girl in 1826, adjusted readily to the fact that they now had to share their parents' affection with their cousin.

When Luther Holton was growing up in Montreal, there was still a great deal of country in the city. Montreal, with a population of 22,500 in

1826, was a port and market centre 180 miles upstream from Quebec City, the capital of Lower Canada. Primitive outdoor toilets were common, and residents kept cows, pigs, and chickens, producing unsanitary conditions. In other respects, however, Montreal was changing. As a centre for increasingly diversified trade, the city experienced steady growth. Associated with the commercial expansion was the growth of industry, as Montreal businessmen set up artisan shops and manufactories. Young Luther marvelled at the harbour, thronged with steamboats, barges, Durham boats, and ships flying British flags, and was thrilled by the crowded warehouses, packed with a great variety of goods.

At the Gilbert fireside, Luther was fascinated by the tales about the family background. Born at Wilmington, Vermont in 1790, one year before the old British colony of Quebec became the new British colonies of Lower and Upper Canada, Moses Gilbert had moved to Montreal early in life. By 1819, the year he married Cynthia Phillips, Moses in partnership with his older brother Amasa had become a grocer and tavernkeeper.[17] But immense natural resources nearby offered new business opportunities. Large timber stands lay to the northwest, and by 1826 Moses Gilbert had struck out on his own account as a lumber dealer and commission merchant.[18] Cynthia, his wife, had grown up with her sisters, Submit, the oldest, and Luther Holton's mother Anner, at Ashfield, Massachusetts.

At the turn of the century, Submit, together with her husband William Forbes, a native of Rutland, Massachusetts, had migrated to Montreal.[19] The main skill William Forbes brought with him was brickmaking, and so he settled in the city as a brick manufacturer. Luther Holton was fondly regarded by aunt Submit and uncle William. Cousin Eliza Forbes, their daughter, was born at Montreal in 1817, making her Luther's age. Luther saw a good deal of Eliza and found he had much in common with her – among other things, they both had deep roots in New England.

Financially, Gilbert was in a position to do the right things for Luther Holton. Success in his business enabled him not only to feed and clothe his nephew, but also to provide him with an education. In 1826, when he was still nine, Luther entered the Union School at the corner of Nicolas and St. Sacrement streets in downtown Montreal. It was a private, elementary day school that took the education of young people seriously. Principal Benjamin Workman and the other teachers saw to it that Luther received a thorough grounding in English, arithmetic, spelling, and French as well as history and geography. Luther understood that teachers were not there to spoon-feed him but to guide him as he showed a willingness to learn. He had an excellent memory and an early grasp of mathematics.[20] The constant round of activities in the Gilbert household and at the nearby harbourfront had fired his imagination and curiosity. By the time he was in his late teens, he was truly bilingual, having mastered the ability to read and speak French fluently. Luther's four years at Union were enhanced by his association with his schoolmates like Theodore Hart, Thomas Workman, and Lewis Wallbridge. In the classroom, Luther Holton's thirst for knowledge was evident from the very start.

History fascinated Luther. "While yet a very young man," wrote the Toronto *Globe* many years later, Holton "became very well versed in the political and constitutional histories of Great Britain, the American Republic, and other countries." These histories remained permanently in his thought. "The great principles and issues that have drawn lines of demarcation between the Liberal and Tory parties all over the world" made an indelible mark on his mind. Besides reading history, Holton enjoyed biography, especially of prominent statesmen and leading businessmen.

But some of young Luther's classmates had not one favourable word to say about him. Offended by what they saw as his stealthy behaviour, they made scornful statements about Luther. Decades later, one of his critics claimed that he had been called a "sneak" in school.[21] Luther Holton could be secretive when someone posed a threat, then and later, but he was forthright in his dealings with those who placed their trust in him. Several of his former classmates, including Theodore Hart, defended his character by publicly stating that he "was distinguished among his school-fellows as an exemplary boy, studious, truthful and attentive. He was very ambitious to stand well in his classes, was highly esteemed by all the boys in school."[22] Benjamin Workman, who as a teacher learned to know Luther well at Union, recalled "that his schoolboy days were distinguished for veracity, honesty, a high sense of honor, a mild and deferential demeanor, attention to studies, and by talents far above mediocrity."[23] The respect for learning which uncle Moses Gilbert shared with young Luther helped create a natural sympathy between them; it also reinforced the priceless contribution Luther's parents had made to his life by their interest in books.

The intellectual kinship between Gilbert and his nephew flowed into Luther's concern for society and religious affairs. Gilbert was a Unitarian and helped provide Luther with philosophical ideas that shaped the spiritual and intellectual side of his life. Certainly one of those who was in close contact with the current Unitarian thought in New England, Gilbert gave his nephew the first opportunity to explore Unitarianism.[24] As the years passed, Unitarianism for Luther, as for many other Unitarians and liberal thinkers of the day, came to mean faith in God and progress, an interest in rationalism and science, and independent judgment. Such a code moved him to stress the ability of the individual to lay hold of the truth, to meet

Montreal harbour at the time Luther Holton began working as an apprentice clerk for his uncle, Moses Haskell Gilbert, in 1830.

obligations to society, to be tolerant, and to attach importance to written and oral debate. In later life, these traditions prompted Luther to aid the poor, work for democracy, and support McGill University financially and administratively. From the very outset, Holton gave to the Unitarian Church, founded in Montreal in 1842 and led by the Reverend John Cordner, both financially and through service on its managing and building committees.

In a different direction, Holton as a youth lived up to his duties in the Gilbert family. In addition to doing his share of the household work, he displayed an exuberant approach to life; he played with cousins Ebenezer and Cynthia, for he was like an older brother to them. A strong bond of friendship linked him to Ebenezer.[25] In later years, as their relationship matured, Ebenezer borrowed large sums of money from Luther to finance his marine engine works in Montreal. Now, in the late 1820s, Luther felt loved and understood by Ebenezer's parents and was grateful to them for sending him to Union.

The happy years of Holton's boyhood at Union were short, for he understood that he needed to go to work to support himself. It was not clear to him what career he might eventually follow. But in 1830, at age thirteen, this farmer's son, who had sparkling, alert eyes, climbed the first rung on the management ladder, becoming an apprentice clerk in Gilbert's lumberyard on Grey Nun Street in the St. Ann's suburb near the harbour.[26] Holton stayed until he was nineteen, in 1836, continuing to live in the Gilbert home. Exactly how much Gilbert agreed to pay Holton in unknown, but he probably withheld from his earnings enough cash to cover his board and room.

Holton's entrepreneurial flair exhibited itself early. With a quick mind, he learned everything his uncle taught him in his counting room. No one familiar with Holton's fine head for figures in school would be surprised that it did not take him long to become a competent bookkeeper.[27] Gradually, he mastered the task of writing a fine business letter, precise and logical, a skill that was to serve him well over the next fifty years.

Chances are good that Holton was soon chatting with Gilbert about the history of his firm, which sold mainly lumber but also carried on a modest trade in provisions such as cheese, salt, fish, bran, and flour. He learned, for instance, that in 1828 Gilbert had sold John Cliff, a Montreal builder, sufficient cedar, pine, and oak lumber to erect a new store for Pierre Beaudry, a local shopkeeper.[28] Holton also discovered that Gilbert's fear of fire had caused him to insure his lumberyard against fire at the Aetna Insurance Company of Hartford, Connecticut. Only a few months had passed since Holton started at the Gilbert firm when, on 1 August 1830, a terrible fire reduced a portion of his uncle's stock of lumber to ashes. Holton needed no urging to help Gilbert clean up and rebuild the lumberyard. Between 1830 and 1836, he left his mark there by assisting Gilbert in selling lumber and provisions and collecting debts from his customers, and he impressed his uncle with a sound judgment, a voice noted for persuasion, and an ability to provide good service and get to the crux of a problem without a lot of words.

Careful management of his resources helped Gilbert remain in business as a merchant until his death in 1843, at which time his assets exceeded his liabilities by £179.[29] The income from the business had only been sufficient to enable the Gilbert family to live in rented quarters on Grey Nun Street.[30] No one was more helpful to Cynthia, Moses Gilbert's wife, at this time than Luther Holton. He became one of the guardians for Cynthia Gilbert's children, and she often consulted him in the decisions concerning the finances of her family.[31] But seven years before Gilbert died, in 1836, Holton had chosen to leave the Gilbert firm while remaining a member of the Gilbert household.

* * *

Holton was simply too forceful and ambitious a personality to stay in the Gilbert enterprise. He now caught the rising tide with a more important position. While working for Gilbert, Holton came to the attention of James Henderson of Henderson, Hooker & Co., a relatively small Montreal forwarding and commission house, who hired him as a clerk in 1836 and

Steamboat wharf at Commissioners Street in Montreal in 1832, four years before Luther Holton became a clerk at Henderson, Hooker & Co. In that year, Montreal was made an official port of entry and the construction of a line of substantial wharves was undertaken. The *Queen*, a market steamer, brought people with produce from nearby parishes noted for their vegetable and fruit gardens. The gas lamp stood in the centre of the Custom House Square. Courtesy of the Metropolitan Library Board.

did much to promote his subsequent career. James Henderson was a bachelor and, unencumbered by a family, was prepared to take enough time to teach Luther the forwarding and commission business. He was willing not only to take this young man into the firm, but also to groom him to become a manager.

By this time, Holton had become a well-built man over six feet tall with dark, handsome features. He was amply endowed with the requisite qualities for success: intelligence, energy, resourcefulness, and a bold and adventurous spirit. Learning and doing were still his goals. Luther thought that working as a clerk for Henderson, Hooker & Co. would broaden his role in the business world.

Holton's future certainly looked very promising with the appearance of two forwarders in his life. The most substantial of the duet was Scottish-born James Henderson, the Montrealer who had a significant interest in the City Bank, an important force in the local capital market. Alfred Hooker, born in Connecticut and now living in Prescott, Upper Canada, with his wife Elvira and their two young daughters, also was a stockholder in the bank. These two men had migrated separately to Canada, where

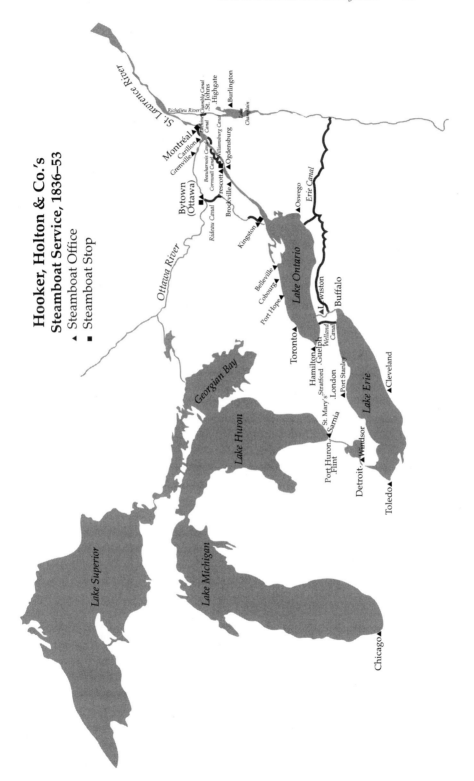

Hooker, Holton & Co.'s
Steamboat Service, 1836–53

▲ Steamboat Office
■ Steamboat Stop

Prescott, from the Ogdensburg harbour, on the upper St. Lawrence River in 1839. It was the home of Alfred Hooker, who established a Henderson, Hooker & Co. branch office here in 1825. Courtesy of the Metropolitan Toronto Library Board.

they had met in 1825 to found Henderson, Hooker & Co., with its Montreal head office on Common Street near the Canal Wharf and its Prescott branch office on Water Street at the bottom of Centre Street. Few entrepreneurs understood Canadian needs and aspirations better than James Henderson and Alfred Hooker did.

Holton's new job allowed him to widen his horizons immensely. The Gilbert firm concentrated on the local market, particularly on serving the Montreal building industry, and took little broader initiative. By contrast, Henderson, Hooker & Co. was an integral part of both local and regional commerce, as well as international trade. Money might be made out of developing steamboat services to the interior, and Henderson, Hooker & Co. had grasped this opportunity by making a substantial investment in shipping for the carriage of especially British goods to the interior and western agricultural produce to Montreal. Linked with this investment was the acquisition of a store, warehouse, and wharf on Common Street in Montreal, as well as the construction of store, warehouse, and wharf facilities on Water Street in Prescott. The partners, Henderson in Montreal and Hooker in Prescott, had a great deal of commercial experience. Like his employers, Holton could observe closely the transition in which Lower Canada responded to the decline of the old agricultural order by creating new facilities of transport and new industries.

* * *

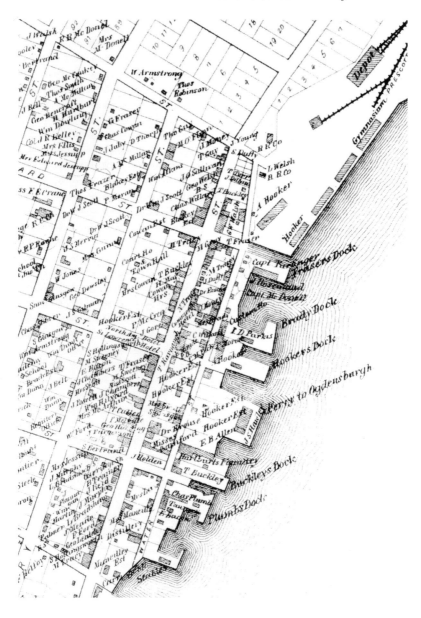

Prescott harbourfront in the 1850s and early 1860s, showing Alfred Hooker's Dock and his other properties. From Mika Publishing, ed., *Illustrated Historical Atlas of the Counties of Leeds and Grenville Canada West 1861-62*. Belleville, 1973. Courtesy of Mika Publishing.

Holton came to know intimately the first phase in the Canadian revolution in transportation – the increased use of steam power in upper St. Lawrence and Great Lakes commerce in the steamboat era. In these developments, as historian Gerald Tulchinsky has shown, Montreal occupied a vitally important place.[32] The city lay on an island on the principal east-west trade route at the junction of the St. Lawrence and Ottawa rivers, which tied it to the Great Lakes. These rivers and lakes were of great significance in the developing western and transatlantic shipping and trade of the city.

Improvements on the upper St. Lawrence, however, had failed to keep pace with the tremendous advances that had been made south of the border with the completion of the Erie Canal in 1825, which had given the port of New York freight rates to and from the West that were considerably lower than those which Montreal could offer. New York City had thus been more successful in extending its reach toward the farmlands of the mid-continent than Montreal. But the opening of the Lachine Canal above Montreal in 1825 had been a step in the right direction, for this had enhanced the viability of the city's route to the West, although it remained more expensive than New York City's.[33]

Montreal also had relatively viable trade routes to its own immediate hinterland and to the American states of New York and Vermont. Waterways radiated from Montreal, all of them serving as conduits for goods coming to and from the river port – the upper St. Lawrence and Ottawa rivers to eastern Upper Canada and the Ottawa Valley, the lower St. Lawrence and Richelieu rivers east and south to the Richelieu River Valley and Vermont. South of Montreal, an indirect route to New York City was available via the lower St. Lawrence, the Richelieu, Lake Champlain, and the Hudson River. Montreal's river location thus contributed to its growth as a major regional distribution centre. Accelerating this commercial expansion was an increase in the city's population from about 22,000 in 1825 to 27,000 in 1831 to 58,000 in 1851.[34] No one considered Montreal a factory city, but by 1836 an overall consequence of the advance in population, trade and shipping was the city's significant growth in the production of industrial and consumer goods.

Holton came to know many businessmen, in both English-language and French-language firms, as he dealt with them on behalf of Henderson, Hooker & Co. In these dealings, his energy and business judgment, coupled with his bilingualism, proved to be invaluable assets. Holton's language, economic, and social skills were intimately related. His story cannot be comprehended without giving his bilingualism an important place in it. At a time when the social and economic air in Montreal was filled with tensions between English and French Canadians, Holton became steadfast in his respect for both cultures. Among Holton's circle of friends in these days was John McEwan, who also served as a clerk in Henderson, Hooker & Co.'s Montreal office. In later life, when he was sheriff of Windsor, Ontario, McEwan remembered that Holton "was a youth of model habits."[35] There was in Holton as a young person a remarkably mature outlook on life, a quality that impressed businessmen of standing.

Holton quickly recognised that one major activity dominated Henderson, Hooker & Co.'s operations: the forwarding business. He understood as well that the firm followed a policy of diversified services from the start. Relying on a strategy that was common among Montreal forwarders, Henderson, Hooker & Co. spurned excessive specialization and entered more than one area of service. In addition to investing in steamboats and other vessels and engaging in the carrying trade, the firm served as a commission house. As a forwarding and commission concern, Henderson, Hooker & Co., acting sometimes as an agent for other business firms and sometimes on its own account, transported the goods in which it and others traded. Western flour millers, storekeepers, and pork packers often relied on Henderson, Hooker & Co. to market their products at home and especially in Great Britain. British imports frequently passed through this house for distribution in Montreal and the interior.

One can imagine Holton working as a clerk at Montreal's harbourfront from the time he rose early in the morning until sunset, particularly during the navigation season from May to November.[36] The streets that he walked to do business were filled with men and boys, horses, wagons, mud, dust, and manure. Whether he moved Henderson, Hooker & Co.'s goods from ocean-going ships or its own vessels to wagons to its store on Common Street, or back again, he always paid careful attention to fresh commercial information and additional business opportunities. Frustrated by the occasional lack of business, Holton surely felt unhappy from time to time during his early years at the firm. But the exhilaration of new trade soon replaced all the worries about a weak forwarding market.

The size of Henderson, Hooker & Co.'s fleet in the early and mid-1830s is not known, but the available evidence indicates that in this period the firm had about two steamboats, a few schooners, a number of barges, and some bateaux – flat-bottomed boats. With the completion of the Rideau Canal in 1832, Henderson, Hooker & Co.'s vessels met the challenge of the largely unimproved upper St. Lawrence by ascending to Lake Ontario, and sometimes even to Lake Erie, via the Ottawa River and the Rideau Canal and by running the St. Lawrence rapids on the downward trip to Montreal wherever the canals were incomplete. The original interior service established in 1825 soon grew from its initial simple run between Montreal and Prescott, taking in additional ports such as Kingston, Toronto, and Hamilton. Henderson, Hooker & Co. was quick to use the Welland Canal route, and by 1831 the firm's vessels were carrying goods right through to Port Stanley and Cleveland on Lake Erie. By 1836, Henderson, Hooker & Co. had established a profitable business. Profits on a steamboat's operations for a navigation season were calculated by subtracting from the freights the costs such as fuel (wood), labour, repairs, and insurance. The firm's profits are difficult to determine, for its account books have not survived. But the slowly growing volume of its carrying trade suggests that its earnings were moderate.

Business practices were a key success factor in the development of Henderson, Hooker & Co. For the most part, the firm's strategy – diversification and a great emphasis on high-quality service – led to an expanding enterprise. In financing its profitable growth, the firm relied especially on retained earnings. Rather than taking substantial funds from the business for their personal use, the owners of the firm put most of the profits back into it for expansion purposes. While they obtained some bank credit, they preferred a program of internally funded growth. In addition, they built up their investments in steamboats and other vessels slowly but soundly. By developing a proper system of bookkeeping, they demonstrated that they had learned one of the secrets of economic success.

* * *

In this milieu, Holton gave his undivided attention to Henderson, Hooker & Co., serving the firm at head office in a variety of ways. He kept the books, assisted in the writing and copying of business letters, toiled over the letterpress, and helped in receiving and forwarding of goods. As well, he lent a hand with the Montreal store's operations, stocking the shelves and selling to customers. Much of Holton's sales work was combined with banking transactions, especially discounting Henderson, Hooker & Co.'s own notes and those of its customers at the City Bank.[37]

To his lasting credit with his employers, Holton soon knew every detail of activity in Henderson, Hooker & Co.'s business from watching James Henderson at work, including the relations he built up with correspondents abroad. The history of the firm was intertwined with that of its correspondents. Characteristic of the firm's development was its close and long-standing relations with its main correspondents, such as Phelps Dodge & Co. in New York City, a major commission house and leading tin importer in America. James Henderson considered his relations with Phelps Dodge & Co. to be of utmost importance and made a major effort to cultivate mutual confidence with this company. Phelps Dodge & Co.'s

Liverpool office handled Henderson's valuable tin import trade, for example, the 610 boxes of tin he imported on commission from South Wales in 1836 for Edward Jackson & Co., Hamilton tin merchants and manufacturers. The contract in this case was typical: James Henderson received 2½ percent commission on the tin he purchased for Edward Jackson & Co. The Henderson, Hooker & Co. steamboat that successfully carried this shipment of tin upstream from Montreal had long been a familiar sight in Hamilton.[38]

But the depression of 1837 raised challenges for Henderson, Hooker & Co. owners and employees – the firm had difficulty collecting its debts in Montreal. As a clerk, Holton had to help address the issue of customers' failure to pay for the firm's forwarding services, the carriage of cargoes of British manufactured goods to the interior with return cargoes of wheat and flour. Acting on James Henderson's instructions, he pushed collections. For instance, Holton pressed William Bradbury, a local merchant, to pay the freight on 100 barrels of flour he owed Henderson, Hooker & Co. since the previous year. But the deepening of the depression shattered any hope that Bradbury would meet his obligations in the near future.[39]

To make matters worse, Henderson, Hooker & Co. was losing business in the trying circumstances of rebellion in Lower Canada in November 1837. The raw social and economic tensions in Lower Canadian society, largely between the ruling English-speaking elements and the French-speaking middle class and habitants, had erupted into violence and racial and class struggles. In Montreal, the destruction and confusion brought on by the rebellion damaged Henderson, Hooker & Co.'s trade.

Holton was doubtless nudged in the direction of taking a stand against the rebels by the problems Henderson, Hooker & Co. faced. On 28 November, he joined eighty-four other citizens of American origin, including City Bank directors John Frothingham and Samuel S. Ward, at the Exchange Coffee House to encourage loyalty to the Crown.[40] Like others present at the meeting, Holton aligned himself with the existing Lower Canadian government and sought to preserve the influence of the imperial connection. As a member of a group dedicated to the maintenance of law and order, he was anything but passive, showing that he favoured a decisive assertion of constituted authority. But the rebellion, as Holton could well see, continued to hurt nearly all Montreal commerce and severely limited available choices for business leaders. With the threat of violence looming continuously, Henderson, Hooker & Co. could not do business freely.

* * *

Not all was bleak in the late 1830s, however. Away from work, Holton lived in a world with relatives. For a long time, there had been a number of people about, his uncles and aunts, as well as his cousins. Holton still lodged in the Gilbert home, and uncle Moses and aunt Cynthia continued to give him a sense of belonging. By nature gregarious and known for his good-natured friendliness, Holton greatly enjoyed the company of young and older persons, both men and women.

With the passing years, Holton grew attached to his first cousin Eliza Forbes and was genuinely interested in her feelings and thoughts. A cheerful disposition made her always ready for conversation and amusement. But the year 1833 was a particularly difficult one for Eliza, for on 3 March her mother Submit Forbes died and, on 14 December, her father William Forbes died after a long and successful career as a small brick manufacturer in Montreal.[41] Eliza was touched by Holton's sympathy for her and her siblings. Four years later, on 9 May 1837, Holton, acting on the advice of relatives and friends, became one of the guardians of Eliza's younger brother, Benjamin, and her younger sisters, Sophronia and Julia.[42] The other guardian was Holton's cousin, James Wait, who was married to Eliza's older sister, Emma.[43] Eliza and Emma, who became the acknowledged leaders of the Forbes family, had confidence in Holton and Wait. From time to time, Eliza consulted Holton in the decisions involving the needs of her younger siblings.

Holton won Eliza's heart. A Presbyterian, she knew that he was a Unitarian, but religion did not drive them apart. They planned to be married on 27 April 1839. At that time, Luther was twenty-two, as was Eliza. Perhaps because Eliza and Luther were first cousins, some relatives may have had reservations about the wisdom of the forthcoming marriage, but their immediate families approved. After the Presbyterian ceremony, performed by the Reverend William Taylor in Erskine Church, the Holtons probably held a modest reception.[44] The new relationship matured rapidly into a solid marriage that became the most important source of happiness in Luther Holton's private life.

The newlyweds found easy acceptance on Queen Street, in Montreal's St. Ann's suburb near the wharves, where they rented a tiny frame house. Initially, Luther and Eliza's income was small, stretched by rental payments and the cost of food and fuel. The readings and lectures they attended at the Mercantile Library helped soften the rigors of life in this port city.[45] Luther's reading at home reflected a never-ending desire to broaden his understanding of economic and cultural affairs. As clear-sighted in the ways of business as Luther, Eliza was an intelligent and gentle woman. She gave him personal security, a sincere and constant love from which he drew tremendous strength. A relative once observed that Eliza was "the Queen of all womankind." Luther was capable of driving hard bargains in the marketplace, but at home he placed common needs above his own wishes and provided the warmth and affection that Eliza wanted.

Luther Holton's twin passions were ongoing self-education and earning money. From the days of his youth, hard work and learning were closely intertwined. Over the years, he acquired most of the education he had on his own initiative; school played only a relatively small part in the process. Fortunately, now, as a newly married man he still had a full-time job at Henderson, Hooker & Co. that gave him a modest but regular income. Luther was a capable clerk who trusted his own judgment. He nevertheless was content to let his chief, James Henderson, a principal owner of the business, make the major decisions. For example, one day in July 1840, when Holton was alone in the firm's Common Street office, the executor of deceased shipbuilder Andrew Yale came to demand that it pay for two barges it had recently purchased. Holton knew that Henderson was dissatisfied with the workmanship on the barges, but he did not discuss this problem with the executor. Instead, he correctly said that he had no authority to respond to the demand for payment in the absence of Henderson. Later, Henderson sorted matters out, agreeing to use arbitration as a mechanism to resolve the dispute.[46] The arbitration ended with a payment by Henderson, Hooker & Co. of £731 to the estate of Andrew Yale. As this incident shows, Holton understood his proper role in the firm. The need for the development of clear lines of authority was routine, and Holton recognized the necessity of leaving decisions about important financial questions in Henderson's hands.

Even then, however, Holton was eager to rise in the firm. His years with Henderson, Hooker & Co. had provided a critical learning experience. Despite its promise, Holton saw that the forwarding business was no easy road to quick riches. But having done well as a clerk, he believed that he could do even better as a partner.

Chapter 2

In a Plain Office
Down by the River Side

In Luther Holton, James Henderson saw qualities he admired – a youthful version of his own stable and vibrant personality. He treated Holton as his friend and protégé. Consequently, Holton's career advanced. He joined Henderson, Hooker & Co. as a junior partner on 1 April 1841, at the age of twenty-four. At the same time, Holton was promoted to manager of the firm in Montreal, a position he held until Henderson's death in the spring of 1845. This was the outcome of Henderson's decision back in 1836 to take into the enterprise a promising young man and to groom him to become a manager.

Putting in long hours "in a plain office down by the river side," Holton managed the Common Street headquarters in the city.[1] It was a challenging job, since the sixteen-year-old firm by now had a branch not only in Prescott on Water Street but also in Kingston on Ontario Street at the bottom of Princess Street, where James Henderson's younger brother and junior partner Francis was in charge of the enterprise's business. As a man whose previous work as clerk had confirmed his business qualities, Holton soon proved to be a valuable member of the partnership. Besides working well together with James Henderson at head office, he showed a strong interest in maintaining channels of communication with Alfred Hooker in Prescott and Francis Henderson in Kingston. To all his partners, Holton conveyed his optimism and loyalty. His job was to deliver forwarding and commission services, and he directed all his time and energy to that end. Although geographically dispersed, the firm remained tight-knit by any standard. Rare was the month during the navigation season that one of the partners did not make the trip between Montreal, Prescott, and Kingston by steamboat. As head office manager, Holton did his share of the travelling in an effort to acquire on-the-spot knowledge of the firm's business not only in Montreal but also in Kingston and Prescott and to co-ordinate its operations through face-to-face contact, in addition to discussing them in

Kingston, from Fort Henry, in 1849. Francis Henderson, brother of James Henderson, managed Henderson, Hooker & Co.'s Kingston branch office. Courtesy of the Metropolitan Toronto Library Board.

regular correspondence. With the partners' co-operation and persistent entrepreneurship, the firm was transformed into a substantial regional forwarding and commission house by 1845.

In setting the course of their firm, the owners of Henderson, Hooker & Co. sought to balance a quest for growth with a desire to develop a sound business. The strategy first adopted by James Henderson and Alfred Hooker of using their assets to diversify – to enter the forwarding as well as the commission trade – and to provide high-quality service turned out to be a viable formula for success in the long run. As owner-managers, the firm's partners presided over an expanding and prosperous enterprise. The moderate profits, which came especially from the carrying trade but also from the commission business, allowed the partners to gradually increase their firm's transport facilities. In classic risk-taking fashion, these entrepreneurs all had a direct, personal stake in their firm's success. James Henderson had a 50 percent interest in the firm, Alfred Hooker 40 percent, and Luther Holton and Francis Henderson each 5 percent.[2]

* * *

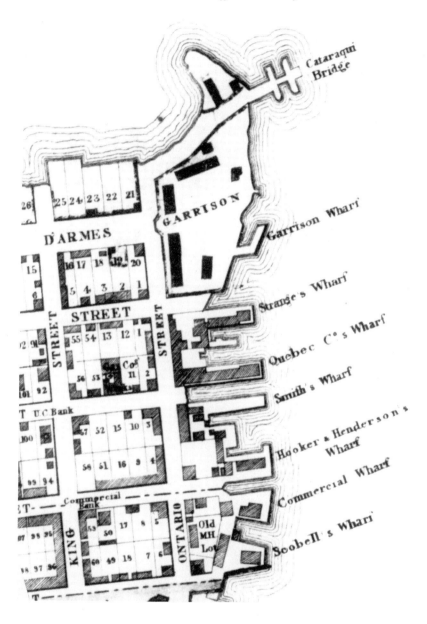

Kingston harbourfront in 1850, showing Hooker & Henderson's Wharf. In Kingston, the firm Luther Holton and his partners owned and ran was known as Hooker & Henderson. Courtesy of the National Archives of Canada.

Holton's success resulted partly from his abilities, but the nature of the forwarding business magnified them to some degree. He had entered a trade organized by relatively few forwarders, one that was quick to reward a number of them. His rise was helped considerably by conditions in the St. Lawrence and Great Lakes region, where important political changes occurred. The new united province of Canada was just beginning to take shape. On 10 February 1841, Governor General Lord Sydenham's goal to unite Lower and Upper Canada had been achieved. Although the new seat of government for the united province was to be in Kingston, Sydenham chose to be sworn in as first governor of the new Canada in Montreal, at the Château de Ramezay, his official residence at this point. Canada was still a relatively underdeveloped province, and Montreal was still the province's pre-eminent commercial centre. Although trade still drove the city's growth, manufacturing increased in importance as the decade progressed. Foundries and factories sprang up on the Lachine Canal, transforming Montreal into a modest but ambitious industrial city. Steamboats, the united province's first substantial carriers, constituted the most important transportation link between Lower Canada (Canada East) and Upper Canada (Canada West). The steamboat in fact still ruled inland transportation in the united province of Canada in 1841. At this time, Montreal was still fifteen years away from a rail connection with Toronto. The 1840s, therefore, marked the peak of the steamboat era, and this gave Holton and his partners an advantage.

Holton's ambition kept pace with his growing experience in the forwarding trade, motivated to some extent by family responsibilities. In 1840, Eliza gave birth to their first child, a boy they named Charles after Luther's younger brother. But Charles fell victim to an unknown ailment and soon died. The loss of one child led to a desire for another, and in 1841 Luther and Eliza welcomed their first daughter, Mary, whom they named after Luther's older sister. In the same year, Holton saw his firm's forwarding facilities expand to five steamboats, a few schooners, and twenty-six barges and its workforce grow to about 300 during the navigation season. By this time, he had hired a new senior clerk at head office, English-born George Edward Jaques.[3]

All of this Holton achieved in a way that showed his genius for management. He had certainly mastered the forwarder's skill of organizing, and he had enhanced it with the personality traits and intuition of the successful manager. Above all else, he demonstrated a clear sense of purpose. Holton's idea of administration was to help those who were actually serving customers. One of his outstanding skills was his ability to inspire others. He encouraged steamboat and schooner captains and barge masters in their work, instructing them to provide top-quality service. In other ways, his understanding affected those around him. He undoubtedly assured employees who were sick that their jobs would be waiting for them when they got back to work. He talked with workers to boost morale. At times, he could become irritable and snap at employees. But this was not the Luther Holton of their common experience. Those who worked closely with him rated his methods as nothing less than reasonable.[4] After a while, providing imaginative and humane leadership became second nature to him.

For Holton, the solution to Henderson, Hooker & Co.'s operating problems did not lie in establishing a formal management structure for the business. Instead, he concentrated on meeting the particular needs of the firm as they arose. Entrepreneurial leadership demands flexibility, and Holton showed the flexibility the firm needed. Management at Henderson, Hooker & Co., which permitted wide-ranging authority and responsibilities to Holton, gave a good deal of scope to his strengths and weaknesses. He made mistakes, and there were some disagreements between him and his boss. Despite occasional surface tension and disagreement, mostly stemming from pressures created by economic troubles, relations between the two men remained friendly. By working closely with James Henderson, Holton quickly learned more and more about effective leadership. A man of considerable commercial experience, a director of the City Bank, a director of the Montreal Fire, Life, and Inland Navigation Assurance Company, a Montreal Board of Trade council member, and the chief owner of Henderson, Hooker & Co., James Henderson had access to capital and credit and important business information.[5] Henderson had the wisdom to share all decisions about the business with Holton. By virtue of his seniority, Henderson was the dominant voice in the firm and had the final say, but there was plenty of room for Holton's input.

Holton's career as head office manager largely turned out as he had hoped. With the improvement in the general economic conditions in 1840-1841, and with population growth especially through the coming of a large wave of British immigrants to Lower and Upper Canada, the forwarding industry continued to expand. This provided new shipping opportunities for Henderson, Hooker & Co. With characteristic energy, Luther responded by taking advantage of them. The economy of the united province of Canada was still closely linked to that of Great Britain. Wheat grown and flour produced in the southwestern part of the province found markets in Liverpool, London, and Glasgow, among other British centres. In return, these and other British cities supplied the colony with most of its imports. Colonial firms such as Henderson, Hooker & Co., whose vessels carried goods between Montreal and the interior, held this transatlantic economy together.

The development of the firm's forwarding business was, however, not without its reverses. Accidents were common at Henderson, Hooker & Co.'s steamboat line, as they were at Montreal's other steamboat lines. In the winter of 1841, for instance, fire utterly destroyed Henderson, Hooker & Co.'s steamboat, *Burlington*, at Toronto.[6] The loss of the vessel amounted to about £2,000. This was a serious blow to the firm, but by May 1841 Holton had made arrangements to have a new steamboat built at Prescott to meet the growing demand for forwarding services.

Holton also had to deal with accidents on the upper St. Lawrence above Montreal. Many rapids, strong currents, and numerous eddies made navigation hazardous on this section of the river. In July 1842, Henderson, Hooker & Co.'s barge, *Highlander*, piled high with flour and pork, crashed into rocks at the Long Sault Rapids on its trip down to the city.[7] Damage was done to the vessel and its cargo, which greatly added to the costs of the firm. Later, in November 1843, two other barges owned by Henderson, Hooker & Co. and laden with wheat and flour met with costly accidents farther down the river near Montreal.[8] With the hazards of the route so great and with so much money tied up in his vessels, Holton kept them fully insured at the Montreal Fire, Life and Inland Navigation Assurance Company. But even with full coverage, which was about seventy-five percent of the vessel's estimated value, accidents led to considerable losses to his firm. Despite Holton's efforts to control navigation costs on the upper St. Lawrence through insurance and by hiring the best captains to operate his firm's steamboats such as the *Lily*, *Grenville*, and *Prince Albert*, he could not make much progress as long as this part of the river remained unimproved.

* * *

While Holton continued to be worried about the safe and trouble-free passage of the firm's vessels, he was also concerned about acquiring freight in the distant interior. Cooperation was his ultimate method of achieving success. He treated steamboat captains with respect and cooperation. He bolstered their confidence and gave them considerable latitude, for he had seen how often their ingenuity and enterprise made the difference between a successful and unsuccessful voyage. The overall results of the voyages to the interior in 1841 were most satisfactory, with over fifty percent of the eastward freight coming from Ohio and other American sources and most of the rest originating in southwestern Upper Canada.

The success of these voyages prompted Holton to increase Henderson, Hooker & Co.'s forwarding facilities. Plentiful evidence of Henderson, Hooker & Co.'s growing involvement in carrying Upper Canadian and American agricultural produce from the interior to Montreal can be found in the *Montreal Gazette*.[9] There is a gap in the data, however, because the newspaper reported only the shipments that came to the city through the Lachine Canal. Information on those shipments that arrived on the firm's vessels that ran the Lachine Rapids was not available. The firm's Lachine Canal flour shipments increased considerably between 1841 and 1842, from 18,221 barrels to 28,327 barrels. This figure dropped to 18,732 barrels in 1843, rose slightly to 19,884 barrels in 1844 and, then, with the beginning of the economic boom in Canada in that year, jumped to 36,216 barrels in 1845. Between 1841 and 1845, the firm's Lachine Canal flour shipments formed 42 percent of all the flour that arrived in Montreal via this canal. The vicissitudes of the business cycle meant that the freights of individual vessels fluctuated in both quantity and value. But the firm's substantial volume of trade helped alert the Montreal business community to Holton's abilities as a manager. Luther Holton was clearly a young man on the make, an adventurous entrepreneur seeking out opportunities in the carrying trade.

Holton rightly foresaw that the prosperity of the early and mid-1840s would open a new era for Montreal's overseas import trade. And he realised, too, that this period represented a new era for Henderson, Hooker & Co.'s import business. Holton's speedy and wholehearted move to expand the firm's import trade met with considerable success. Complete statistics have survived in the Montreal port records for Henderson, Hooker & Co.'s imports from Great Britain in the mid-1840s.[10] Liverpool figured most prominently in the firm's growing import business. Aided by his correspondent in New York City, Phelps Dodge & Co., which worked through its Liverpool house, Holton took in hardware, tinplate, bar iron, and a wide range of other British manufactures. He also maintained correspondents in London and Glasgow, who sent him a varied assortment of goods, including linens, clothing, hardware, books, wine, sugar, and tea. Henderson, Hooker & Co.'s own vessels carried a large proportion of these imports from Montreal to its customers in Upper Canada. The value of the firm's British imports more than tripled between 1843 and 1844, rising from £11,522 to £35,534. The following year, in 1845, the value of its imports from Britain soared to £66,269. Holton's basic strategy in the import business was to portray Henderson, Hooker & Co. as a responsible firm capable of providing top-quality services. His relations with correspondents such as Phelps Dodge & Co. were characterized by mutual trust and respect.[11] In his study of Phelps Dodge & Co., historian Richard Lowitt concluded that "the best customer of the company in Canada was Henderson, Hooker & Co."[12] The New York City firm was clearly impressed by Holton's business expertise and trustworthiness. To James Henderson, Holton was a highly competent manager. At the end of the day, Holton had much to show of concrete accomplishment. His efforts in the import arena helped leave Henderson, Hooker & Co. in a prosperous and confident position by 1845.

Imports remained the most important of Henderson, Hooker & Co.'s overseas operations, but western wheat and flour exports also attracted Holton's attention. The business he handled for other exporters is not well documented, but from Montreal newspapers in the early and mid-1840s we learn that his export trade on Henderson, Hooker & Co.'s account included especially flour. In June 1841, for example, Holton sent 1,000 barrels of flour aboard the ship *Robert Watson* to Newcastle upon Tyne.[13] Three years later, in June 1844, Holton shipped 1,100 barrels aboard the carrier, *Avon*, to Glasgow.[14] Like most other Montreal commission houses involved in the flour export business, Henderson, Hooker & Co. possessed the minimum capital needed to participate in this trade.

As Holton saw it, there was a need to keep on building up the firm. His eye for detail and his desire to foster sound expansion served him well throughout his years as manager at head office. By the end of 1844, the value of Henderson, Hooker & Co.'s assets had grown to £66,800.[15] Most of these assets consisted of steamboats, schooners, barges, wagons, horses, offices, stores, warehouses, and wharves. This figure, however, underestimates the real value of the firm. Additional assets included market connections, labour force loyalty, and the goodwill reflected in Henderson, Hooker & Co.'s growing reputation as a successful financial operation.

Holton's understanding of the need to protect the concern's credit by handling its financial affairs efficiently was one of the qualities James Henderson and Alfred Hooker had looked for in a partner to manage their business. They not only found themselves in fundamental approval of the way Holton secured business for the firm, but also strongly supported his efforts to monitor its bills receivable and payable. From the beginning, Holton had demonstrated to his senior partners an extraordinary grasp of the finances of their firm. He was acutely aware that in large part Henderson, Hooker & Co. had to finance growth internally through retained profits. During the years between 1841 and 1845, he ploughed most of the firm's earnings back into the enterprise.

At the same time, Holton continued to depend upon bank credit to fund Henderson, Hooker & Co.'s operations. Careful financing over the years at the firm had led to a long-lasting relationship with the City Bank in Montreal and, like other businessmen who tended to look to the same bankers who had assisted them before, Holton continued to borrow money at this bank.[16] Personal connections were also of considerable importance in obtaining this financing. James Henderson was vice-president of the City Bank in the years 1842-43, and he remained a director of the institution until his death in 1845.[17] Critics of insider borrowing might have argued that it promoted inefficiency and complacency. But defenders of the method could point out that, in fact, the City Bank provided competitive service and helped satisfy the credit needs not only of Henderson, Hooker & Co., but also of the wider business community. With the growth of the firm, however,

City Bank in Montreal in 1845. Vice-president of the bank from 1842 to 1843, James Henderson remained a director until his death. In 1847, Luther Holton became a director of the bank. From *Montreal Pocket Almanack for 1845*.

there was a need for added outside sources of funding. By 1844, Holton was able to broaden the firm's financial base by borrowing at the Commercial Bank of the Midland District.[18]

The story of Holton shows the role of an influential merchant, improving and integrative, successful by nineteenth-century standards, commercially as well as socially. He was a broad-minded man, who actively adapted his decisions and actions to the commercial and cultural imperatives of the moment. His bilingualism continued to allow him to make and maintain contact with both English-speaking and French-speaking entrepreneurs. He recognised early the importance of the need for Henderson, Hooker & Co. to form links with prominent houses in Montreal's merchant community, notably Gillespie, Moffatt & Co., John Torrance & Co., Stephens, Young & Co., Richardson & Co., Orlin, Bostwick & Co., and Kennedy, Parker & Co..[19] A substantial share of Montreal's trade with the West was in the hands of these major produce dealers. Year after year in the early and mid-1840s, Holton put Henderson, Hooker & Co.'s steamboats, schooners, and barges into service for Montreal firms, shipping large quantities of flour, wheat, and pork from the interior to the city. Holton's eastward shipments of wheat, flour, pork, lard, beef, butter, cheese, oatmeal, and whisky for other Montreal businesses such as Robertson, Masson & Co., Cuvillier & Sons, Bagg & Campbell, B. Hart

& Co., Kay, Whitehead & Co., Birss & Co, and Tobin & Murison were smaller by comparison, but they were also of considerable significance in Henderson, Hooker & Co.'s development.[20]

In this bicultural atmosphere, Holton possessed a feeling of identification with firms that consisted of English-Canadian partners like Stephens, Young & Co. and Bagg & Campbell, as well as with those that were made up of or included French-Canadian partners like Robertson, Masson & Co. and Cuvillier & Sons. Holton's bilingualism and his understanding of the complexities of French-English relations remained a major asset to Henderson, Hooker & Co. His ability to speak French with French-Canadian Joseph Masson of Robertson, Masson & Co., coupled with his capacity to switch to English when he communicated with English-Canadian John Young of Stephens, Young & Co., made for an excellent business situation in Montreal.

* * *

Holton nevertheless faced problems. More than anything else, cut-throat competition plagued Henderson, Hooker & Co. in the upper St. Lawrence forwarding industry. The most important competitors were Macpherson, Crane & Co., H. Jones & Co., and Murray & Sanderson. Holton proved to be a formidable rival. But rather than pour money into new vessels, which might have allowed him to compete more effectively, he sought through agreements to deal with his competitors. To lessen competition and protect his firm's profits, Holton planned to co-operate with H. Jones & Co. The two firms soon worked together informally to gain better access to the Ottawa River, an indispensable part of the steamboat route from Montreal to the interior. Ever since 1839 Macpherson, Crane & Co.'s control of the Montreal-based Ottawa and Rideau Forwarding Company had given it control of the privately owned lock at the St. Anne's Rapids, the best entryway to the Ottawa River from the St. Lawrence.[21] In the spring of 1841, at the opening of the navigation season, Macpherson, Crane & Co. refused to allow the vessels of Henderson, Hooker & Co. as well as those of H. Jones & Co. to pass through this lock.[22] These two smaller firms had no choice but to tow their barges over the St. Anne's Rapids as they entered the Ottawa River. But by the end of July, the level of the water at these rapids was so low that their steamboats could no longer tow their barges over them. Consequently, further navigation for their vessels on the Ottawa River-Rideau Canal route seemed impossible. This turn of events came at the worst possible moment, for it meant the interruption of their large volume of trade during the spring and summer months.

Holton, however, got around this problem by joining Sidney Jones, the Montreal partner in H. Jones & Co., and Robert H. Shepherd, one of that firm's steamboat captains, in marking out a new channel at the Vaudreuil Rapids for the passage of Henderson, Hooker & Co. and H. Jones & Co.'s steamboats and barges from the St. Lawrence to the Ottawa River.[23] There were some turns in the channel, but the two barges that Holton and Sidney Jones personally brought from Montreal for the trial run were moved through without any difficulty. By the beginning of August, it was clear that the experiment was a success. Unable to prolong its advantage, Macpherson, Crane & Co. now permitted the two smaller firms to tow their barges through its lock at the St. Anne's Rapids.

Holton wasted no time in seeking further co-operation with his counterparts in the other forwarding companies. Like the other forwarders, he looked to combinations as one way to stabilise his business and make it more profitable. James Henderson gave Holton full authority to commit their firm to an agreement that would be in its best interest. In mid-August 1841, a combination emerged. There was a pooling of resources to the extent that Henderson, Hooker & Co. and H. Jones & Co. became responsible for towing the barges for all three concerns between Lachine and Vaudreuil, while Macpherson, Crane & Co. undertook to tow them between Vaudreuil and Carillon.[24] Through their co-operative work, Luther Holton and James Henderson were able partially to protect their firm's profits.

All the while, Holton was enmeshed in emergency management: endless meetings, letters, and decisions. Customers made emergency appeals for credit, and he had to determine if they were creditworthy; meetings with partners in Prescott and Kingston called him out of town; steamboat captains had difficulty in securing freight or needed to be advised how to match their facilities with urgent requests for service. He responded to it all, and with the characteristic Holton touch – helpful, prudent, reassuring. For example, Robert Shepherd, the able captain of the steamboat *Oldfield*, which provided service on the Lachine-Vaudreuil run, called in November 1841 at the Common Street office to tell him that he desperately needed a job for the following season. Holton put him in touch with James Henderson and Shepherd was re-appointed as captain.[25] Even when a well-to-do passenger later grumbled loudly about the service on the steamboat, Holton conveyed a reassuring sympathy to Shepherd. "We are quite satisfied with your management," Holton told Shepherd, "and as long as that is the case you need not be afraid of any complaint coming from such quarters." Many years later, Shepherd recalled that "Holton was always a friend of mine."[26]

Holton also had to attack problems before they spread, for instance noting that rumours about excessive freight rates were false. This was a task for a top-flight manager who knew how to make decisions and had the mettle to follow through. Holton fully supported Francis Henderson when a select committee of the legislative assembly summoned him to its hearings in Kingston, Canada's capital, on 7 July 1841 concerning criticism from shippers on forwarders' freight rates on the Ottawa River–Rideau Canal route. Henderson argued that the absence of a public towing path on this route led to high transportation costs, causing forwarders to charge rates of £3 per ton from Montreal to Kingston. Without government regulation, forwarders could develop rate structures as they pleased, and if Henderson, Hooker & Co. vessels had to raise rates to cover costs, there was no way that the bitter pill for shippers could be sweetened. The select committee immediately accepted Francis Henderson's argument, thus settling the issue as far as the Canadian government was concerned.[27]

But the basic issue of forwarders' freight rates was complex, and it repeatedly occurred throughout the steamboat age. Holton faced constant pressure from shippers to lower rates. Henderson, Hooker & Co. could prosper, however, only if it charged 2s per barrel of flour from Kingston to Montreal. The firm felt that it had to maintain this rate or be swallowed up by rivals. In the business world, everyone knew that all Montreal steamboat lines from time to time attracted business by cutting freight rates. To moderate the swings in rates and limit competition, Holton seriously considered co-operating with other forwarding firms. In 1842, Henderson, Hooker & Co. joined five other Montreal forwarders in forming a combination to set the rate at 1s 6d per barrel of flour from Kingston to Montreal for July and August and at 2s for the rest of the navigation season.[28] In their fight for business, individual forwarders nevertheless abandoned these rates. In 1843, the idea of combination resurfaced. Holton committed his firm to the new combination of forwarders, but intense competition caused it to fall apart well before the navigation season was over. Despite these setbacks, Henderson, Hooker & Co. was profitable and the partners made money.

But the largely unimproved waterway above Montreal raised perennial challenges for Holton. His response was to co-operate with other forwarders in urging officials in the Canadian government to make the interior river system more navigable, thereby heightening the importance of governmental actions for his firm's development. In particular, Holton backed the efforts of Sydney Jones to have the government complete the public lock at the St. Anne's Rapids and replace the low arched bridges on the Lachine Canal with swing bridges so as to permit all kinds of craft to pass through these facilities and thus reduce forwarders' expenses.[29] The relations between Holton and Sydney Jones were usually cordial and

Brockville in 1852, an important steamboat stop for Henderson, Hooker & Co. since the 1830s.
Courtesy of the Metropolitan Toronto Library Board.

co-operative. By 1843, the improvements they called for proved successful in helping Henderson, Hooker & Co. remain a viable enterprise.

Operating costs had to be held down. Holton did not propose to run the firm on a shoestring, but he believed that it was important to cut costs wherever possible. In no instance, however, were the employees and quality service to be sacrificed to economy. After learning that bigger government canal tolls might soon swell the operating costs, Holton concluded that Henderson, Hooker & Co. could not live with a large increase in tolls. But suddenly, on 5 March 1842, the tolls on the Rideau Canal were raised sharply. For example, on an eighty-ton barge with a cargo of twenty tons, the toll more than tripled, rising from £9 18s to £31 4s. Convinced that this would injure his firm's interests in the Montreal-Kingston market, Holton conferred with other forwarders to see what could be done to force the government to abandon the new tolls. Common sense recommended fast action. In early April, Henderson, Hooker & Co. and several other Montreal forwarders, including Macpherson, Crane & Co. and H. Jones & Co., memorialized Governor General Sir Charles Bagot, Sydenham's successor, protesting the toll increase.[30] With similar memorials from the Montreal Board of Trade, the Kingston Board of Trade, the Kingston City Council, and the Immigrant Committee of the City of Montreal landing on Bagot's desk, it was plain that the forwarders had widespread support.

Holton was clearly wrestling with a financial dilemma. On the basis of the old tolls, Henderson, Hooker & Co. had over the winter already entered into contracts with numerous Upper Canadian merchants to deliver their imports upon the opening of the navigation season. Holton had allocated money to his operations in a sum large enough to cover the old tolls, but he did not know where he might readily find sufficient funds to pay the new toll charges. Even more frustrating for him was the fear that the new rates would wipe out Henderson, Hooker & Co.'s anticipated profits. Holton had every intention of making good on the firm's contracts, but he was certain that the new rates contained the seeds of serious problems in the future.

It looked as if Henderson, Hooker & Co. and their fellow forwarders were going to lose, until Bagot decided to revise the new Rideau Canal tolls downward on 16 April. If Holton had any question about where the governor general stood, he had none now. The move to raise the tolls struck Bagot as an economically dangerous policy, one that might choke off trade on the Ottawa-Rideau Canal–upper St. Lawrence route at a time when the Canadian economy was still very precarious and drive commerce into the United States by way of the Erie Canal. The revised tolls were in Holton's judgment a reasonable compromise, making it easier for him to control his firm's shipping costs.

* * *

The summer of 1843 found Luther Holton in an optimistic mood, for he thought that the Canada Corn Act just passed by the British parliament would have a salutary effect on Henderson, Hooker & Co.'s forwarding and commission business. The new law reduced the duty on Canadian wheat to the token amount of one shilling per quarter (480 pounds, or eight bushels) and on flour milled in Canada to a proportionate amount per barrel.[31] Under this law Canada, in addition to exporting an increasing volume of her own wheat and flour to the burgeoning British market, received significant amounts of wheat from the United States to be ground into flour for export to the same market. As Montreal forwarders took advantage of the new economic climate created by the legislation, there was quite a phenomenal boom in the city's forwarding industry.

Buoyed by the rising wheat and flour trade between Canada and Britain, Holton sought to become more heavily involved in the carriage of these products through an increase in Henderson, Hooker & Co.'s forwarding facilities. He added one steamboat, several schooners, and one barge to its fleet. In his Common Street office, Holton was formulating Henderson, Hooker & Co.'s response to the rapidly growing importance of wheat and flour exports for British markets. He was determined to seize the new opportunities in forwarding. The firm's Brockville, Kingston, Toronto, Hamilton, and Port Stanley loadings of flour and wheat began to grow larger in 1844. Like Montreal's other forwarding companies, Henderson,

Hooker & Co.'s vessels carried most of its wheat and flour shipments to the city via the Lachine Rapids, but only its carryings by the Lachine Canal are known. For instance, on 1 May, its barges arrived in Montreal by the canal carrying 9,000 bushels of wheat and 333 barrels of flour.[32] A month and a half later, on 18 June, the firm's steamboat *Grenville* with its barges brought 9,533 bushels of wheat and 1,759 barrels of flour through the canal.[33] In mid-November 1844, at the close of the navigation season, Henderson, Hooker & Co.'s steamboat *Lily* alone carried 950 barrels of flour as it made its way through the canal to the city.[34] Upon the opening of navigation, on 6 May 1845, the concern's barges *Mohawk*, *Pontiac*, *Brunette*, *Alice*, *Jet*, and *Canada* brought 4,077 barrels of flour to Montreal by the canal.[35] Even as these and many other such cargoes arrived by means of the canal, the bulk of the firm's flour and wheat shipments continued to reach the city via the Lachine Rapids in these years.

Holton's career in forwarding taught him that management meant co-ordinating transportation and commission services by providing information, advice, and encouragement to steamboat captains, barge masters, clerks, and other employees. He also saw the need for closer co-operation with other steamboat lines. But if this line of thinking made sense to Holton, it did not always do so to other Montreal forwarders. There was more to his personal brand of management. He was constantly walking here and there on the harbourfront, purposefully active, intense. In his office he was busy writing letters, often extending credit to merchants and flour millers in the interior and Montreal. The contracts he made with businesses to ship, handle, store, and sell produce in the city or British markets specified freight and commission charges. Unpaid accounts were a source of worry, but enough of them were settled to allow Holton to promptly repay the loans he had secured from the City Bank and the Commercial Bank to finance his operations. Among his partners, Holton's methods generated a sense of common purpose and co-operation. He and James Henderson conferred frequently, and they developed a special friendship. Henderson appreciated Holton's ability to put policies into action, but he also came to see other personal qualities in him. He enjoyed his straightforwardness, sense of humour, and optimism. He realised as well that Holton shared his sensitivity to other people.

* * *

Luther Holton needed the satisfactions of his business accomplishments to balance the problems he faced at head office. He sometimes had to deal with the differences that arose between his firm and other Montreal forwarders. For instance, in June 1842, Macpherson, Crane & Co. brought suit against Henderson, Hooker & Co. in the Court of Queen's Bench in Montreal. The case involved a claim for damages resulting from a breakdown in a forwarding agreement between the two firms. After James Henderson filed an answer disavowing all responsibility for the problem, Holton reviewed their firm's strategy with determination, confidence and, above all, optimism that with the aid of their lawyer William Walker they could win the case. The litigation dragged on for nine months. Perhaps Macpherson, Crane & Co. wondered whether Holton was tough enough to keep on fighting when he took the witness stand on 14 March 1843.[36] But Holton passed this test with flying colours; indeed, his toughness almost ran the plaintiffs into the ground. The jury, however, gave a verdict for Macpherson, Crane & Co. for £175. In James Henderson's eyes, Holton had nevertheless measured up.

Holton's closeness to James Henderson had made him more friends in Montreal, including Charles H. Castle, cashier of the City Bank. Castle and Holton co-operated well in arranging a supply of credit for Henderson, Hooker & Co.'s forwarding and commission services during the early and mid-1840s. But for both men, the year 1845 was also a time for a painful farewell. At ten o'clock Saturday morning, 22 March, James Henderson suddenly died of gout at his home on Bleury Street.[37]

A host of Henderson's friends attended the memorial service and followed the hearse to the Old Burying Ground on Dorchester Street. There were the officers and members of St. Andrew's Society, of which Henderson was vice-president; relatives; current business associates; and business friends. Alfred Hooker and Francis Henderson had come from Upper Canada to pay their respects. As Luther Holton stood at the Old Burying Ground, his mind must have been full of thoughts of the man who had shown him the way.

James Henderson had become a historic figure to him, a friend who was forty-seven years old at the time of his death. During his comparatively short life, he had pioneered in the development of forwarding on the upper St. Lawrence and the lower Great Lakes. The editor of the *Montreal Gazette* observed that "the number of gentlemen constituting the procession was certainly not less than four hundred, amongst whom was a large portion of the wealth and respectability of the city." It was "the high and deserved esteem which the deceased, whilst living, enjoyed from all who knew him" that "caused his remains to be followed to the grave by a large concourse of friends."[38]

The death of the Montreal founder of Henderson, Hooker & Co. was a personal loss to Holton, and it dissolved the firm, but it was not a business crisis. At the time of its dissolution, the firm was stable and profitable.

Holton carried memories of James Henderson leading him along in the business, step by step. If Holton felt something ought to be done, he could take his ideas to him. Henderson was always ready to hear what he had to say. Things, of course, could never be the same. James Henderson was dead, and Holton seemed to have gained a chance for a fresh role.

Henderson's death marked the close of an era for the firm, for it had removed from the world the oldest senior founding partner in the concern. Two decades of experience with the development of the forwarding and commission business had gone by when he passed from the scene. By the end of this period, health was certainly on James Henderson's mind. "This gentleman," wrote the *Montreal Gazette*, "had been suffering for some time from the effects of rheumatism, and it was his intention to have taken his departure in a few weeks for some more genial climate; but a week since he experienced a severe attack of this malady, which in a few days changed into one more serious – gout; and after suffering severely for a couple of days, he was relieved from his earthly pains by the hand of Death."[39] With James Henderson's health in an extremely precarious state by mid-March 1845, it was fortunate that Holton's role had become so important. He was truly the key person in management.

Making a living as a forwarder and commission merchant was still Luther Holton's objective. He wanted to form a new partnership with Alfred Hooker and Francis Henderson. For Luther, they represented a healthy link with his past, and together with them he intended to continue his business career.

Chapter 3

Developing Steamboat Services

In the last days of March 1845, Luther Holton carefully examined Henderson, Hooker & Co.'s books in the Common Street office and found the firm to be in a strong financial position. The company was making a profit, and its owners were ready to invest more money in it. In discussions with his remaining partners Alfred Hooker and Francis Henderson, Holton heard in detail about their operations in Prescott and Kingston. Besides the financial rewards associated with their venture, all three partners took immense satisfaction in continuing to provide forwarding and commission services. Their firm now stood on the brink of another change, but succession was not a problem. Management succession at the enterprise proceeded smoothly, as it continued to be led by a closely held group of owner-managers.

The death of James Henderson, rather than creating a hiatus as it might have done in other companies, was a special impetus to re-organization at the firm. In Montreal, the business was reconstituted as Hooker, Holton & Co. on 1 April, making Alfred Hooker of Prescott its senior, Francis Henderson its Kingston manager, and Luther Holton its managing head, and by that name it was known for the next nine years.[1] Both Hooker and Francis Henderson retained a great deal of respect for Holton's financial judgement. Now, as before, the firm was under the direction of one of the most capable forwarders in Canada. At twenty-eight, less than a decade after he had begun work at the enterprise as a clerk, Holton was thus at the helm of a major Montreal forwarding and commission house.

Like many of his contemporaries in Montreal, Holton liked the city with all its entrepreneurial opportunities, but he was not parochial. Instead, he thought in provincial and, indeed, in international terms. With his business career progressing by leaps and bounds, he shrewdly recognized the steamboat as a key to Montreal's and Canada's economic development. He wanted the city to benefit fully from steamboat technology. The steamboat had a fundamental impact on the inland water transport network and on general

Canadian transportation – it penetrated every nook of the provincial economy and affected every citizen's interests. On the steamboat moved everything imaginable, from agricultural produce to a wide range of manufactured goods to all classes of people. The steamboat landing shaped the daily rhythm of countless people in cities, towns, and villages in the 1840s.

James Henderson, Holton's first friend and mentor in the forwarding industry, had made it possible for him to continue in the steamboat business. In accordance with an offer Henderson had made shortly before his death, and confirmed by the will he left, Holton at this time purchased close to a one-third interest in the firm for £3,512 on a reasonable instalment plan. The other changes in the firm's ownership structure left Alfred Hooker with a two-fifths interest and Francis Henderson with a one-third interest.[2] Holton was to pay off the amount he now owed the James Henderson estate in quarterly instalments over a three-year period. As a substantial shareholder in the Montreal forwarding and commission house, Holton was well positioned to profit from the city's growing trade.

* * *

As always, whenever he felt highly motivated, Holton accepted the challenge of the new role. Under his leadership, Hooker, Holton & Co. remained among Montreal's most highly regarded employers, and enjoyed in the city as well as in Kingston and Prescott a reputation as a conscientious and fair employer. As a result, the firm continued to attract able steamboat and schooner captains and barge masters. The high calibre of the captains and masters reinforced Hooker, Holton & Co.'s standing especially within Montreal and this, in turn, helped to safeguard its effectiveness in the broader business environment across Canada.

Luther Holton was certainly a child of his age. The progress of Hooker, Holton & Co. under his inspiration moved with powerful currents already flowing in Canada. Included among these were the extension of steamboat navigation to increasingly long-distance trade in the interior, as advances in marine engine and boat construction made this possible over the years. Continuing to demonstrate his extraordinary levels of effort and commitment, Holton now plunged into the task of developing Hooker, Holton & Co.'s steamboat services. The main service remained as it had begun many years ago, Montreal via the Ottawa River and Rideau Canal to Kingston, with calls at Brockville and Prescott as well as deeper into the interior at Toronto, Hamilton, St. Catharines, and Port Stanley.

By the end of March 1845, Holton was instructing steamboat and schooner captains to prepare their vessels for the approaching navigation season.[3] At this time, the vessels were still at their winter quarters in various ports throughout Canada.[4] Around the end of April, the steamboats *Prince*

Albert and *Grenville* loaded agricultural produce in Kingston for Montreal, while the steamboat *Lily* took on the same type of cargo in Prescott.[5] The schooners *Sir Charles Bagot* and *Maid of the Mill* loaded similar cargoes at St. Catharines and Toronto for Kingston. This produce was to be unloaded at Kingston, to go forward to Montreal by steamboats adapted to river navigation. A few weeks later, the schooner *Sarnia*, which had been lying at Kingston with its cargo of manufactured goods, headed for ports on the western end of Lake Ontario as well as on Lake Erie. The steamboat *Oldfield* left Lachine with passengers for Carillon on the Ottawa, from where they could move to their destinations by other boats. In addition to getting the firm's steamboats and schooners underway, Holton put its twenty-six barges on the Montreal-Bytown-Kingston triangle for the delivery and receipt of cargoes.

While Holton was efficiently organizing the services of Hooker, Holton & Co.'s vessels, he was at the same time trying to reduce the economic uncertainties that faced the firm. The Canadian forwarding industry was highly vulnerable to every economic crisis, and this situation worried Holton. Growth in the forwarding trade depended to a considerable degree on factors beyond his control, namely the volume of shipments of both manufactured goods and agricultural products on the upper St. Lawrence and the Great Lakes. The American drawback laws affected his steamboat services, especially through a decrease in freight traffic and shrinking profits. In March 1845, Congress passed a drawback law, which provided that all British or other foreign goods imported into the United States for re-export to Canada could be shipped through American territory duty free. Fifteen months later, in June 1846, Congress acted decisively to direct Canadian produce destined for the British market through the United States.[6] By the terms of this law, all Canadian exports carried to Great Britain across American territory, say along the Erie Canal and through New York City, enjoyed the benefit of no United States duties. New York City's ocean-going rates to Britain were significantly lower than Montreal's. All this change caused Hooker, Holton & Co.'s vessels to lose business.

To make matters worse for Holton, the British parliament passed the Corn Law Act in June 1846, dismantling the imperial protective system and establishing free trade throughout the British Empire.[7] One of the provisions of the act was the gradual reduction of duties on foreign foodstuffs, including American ones, so that by 1849 wheat that was landed directly in Britain from the United States paid a token duty of one shilling a quarter. In practical terms, this meant that wheat from the United States entered Britain just as cheaply as did that from Canada. Now New York City cut even deeper not only into Montreal's grain trade with Britain, but also into this Canadian city's entire inland shipping which was the lifeblood of Hooker, Holton & Co.'s trade. The firm's vessels received reduced orders for the shipment of freight, and other orders were cancelled. A shipper who had used its services in one year might turn to shipping on the Erie Canal the next. In the mid-1840s, the trans-Atlantic world was thus fast changing, a world that left Montreal forwarders like Holton reeling.

Holton, however, refused to accept this situation. He tried to minimize the impact of the erratic swings in demand which plagued the Canadian forwarding industry. With his partners' approval, in good times Holton did not pay out profits in the form of substantial dividends. Instead, he took a long-range view, retaining most of the profits in order to ride out periods of provincial economic crisis in the future. The plan was partially successful, as events in the late 1840s would show. The demand for forwarding services generally rose between 1846 and 1847, as the Canadian economy grew. Holton nevertheless sensed potential trouble around the corner. In preparing for the future, he also became a force behind the free trade movement. As vice-chairman of the Montreal Free Trade Association in 1846-47, he sought to make a good case for free trade between Canada and the United States as a way to draw a larger volume of American grain exports into Montreal's overseas commerce.[8] His dream of free trade never had a chance in the mid- and late 1840s, however; lacking support in Montreal and Canada, he abandoned his idea for the time being.

* * *

But Holton could properly claim credit for innovative business techniques; he spent money to improve the efficiency of his steamboat services and thus reduced Hooker, Holton & Co.'s operating costs. Few businessmen were more eager to seize business or technological opportunities than Holton. By the end of May 1845, he had added the Ericsson screw propeller *London* to his fleet for service in the Montreal-Bytown-Kingston trade.[9] The new technology of the *London* pleased Holton and, in May 1846, with a growing demand for shipping in the Montreal-Bytown-Kingston triangle, he purchased three more screw propellers, *Traveler*, *Adventure*, and *Dickson*.[10]

The Ericsson steamboats were small craft, powered by high-pressure engines and designed to pass through fairly narrow canals.[11] The screw propellers gained particular significance in Hooker, Holton & Co.'s Montreal-Bytown-Kingston trade. Having no side-paddles, these narrow-beamed boats could pass safely through the locks of the St. Lawrence, Ottawa, and Rideau canals. Safety was, in fact, one of their most attractive features. Inasmuch as

Holton put the screw propellers to good use, he made an important contribution to the development of new technologies.

Holton faced a problem, however: he found it hard to reduce labour costs in loading and unloading his steamboats and barges. The use of men and boys to perform these tasks often brought difficulties that escalated costs considerably. But cost was not Holton's only concern; he wanted to speed up work and make it physically less taxing. He had the insight and motivation to get inside the skin of those who had to do more manual labour than he did. Fortunately, he could look to cousin Ebenezer Gilbert, who had been a clerk at Hooker, Holton & Co. since 1840, for a solution to the problem. Gilbert was clearly full of ideas and technical skills.[12] Encouraged by Holton, in 1845 Gilbert invented what the Canadian Patent Office described as "a new method of constructing counter balance machines for raising and lowering casks or other weights;" it was a hoisting apparatus for loading and unloading Hooker, Holton & Co.'s vessels.[13] This new, labour-saving device speeded cargo handling and enhanced the firm's ability to compete in the forwarding industry.

Time and again, Holton displayed a passion for innovation. With his experience on steamboats, barges, and canals, he realized that inland transportation was still primitive. No one was more willing to stress the need to construct canals and locks than Holton. With the completion of the Beauharnois Canal on the upper St. Lawrence above Lachine at the end of 1845, he soon became involved in innovative activity. In March 1846, he increased the towing capacity of the *Prince Albert*, one of his firm's old steamboats, by overhauling the vessel's machinery, installing a new boiler, and making other necessary alterations.[14] The results delighted Holton.

Despite Holton's euphoria, there was a great deal to cause him – and Alfred Hooker and Francis Henderson – much anxiety. Because their competitors in the forwarding industry were just as aggressive as they were, the partners felt threatened. As competition intensified, Holton sought to protect his market from rival firms. Rather than competition, he preferred co-operation. The co-operation he obtained was based on oral promises, a gentlemen's market-sharing agreement. In the process, in the spring of 1846, the *Prince Albert* became an essential element in what the *Kingston News* called "the great experiment" of towing barges heavily laden with merchandise from Montreal up the St. Lawrence and through its canals to Kingston.[15] Macpherson, Crane & Co. and H. Jones & Co., the two forwarding houses that had built similar towboats, agreed to co-operate with Hooker, Holton & Co. in this experiment. To carry out the undertaking, one of H. Jones & Co.'s steamboats towed the barges of the three firms from Lachine up to the Beauharnois Canal, from where Hooker, Holton & Co.'s *Prince Albert* brought them to the Cornwall Canal, at which point a Macpherson, Crane & Co. steamboat took them in tow and tugged them to Prescott. It was left to another one of Macpherson, Crane & Co.'s steamboats to tow the barges to Brockville and finally to Kingston. A similar arrangement existed among these three concerns for the shipment of agricultural produce downstream to Montreal. The St. Lawrence experiment proved so successful that, like the other two firms, Hooker, Holton & Co. shifted a substantial portion of its westbound freight from the Ottawa-Rideau Canal route to the shorter and cheaper St. Lawrence waterway.

Particularly striking among Holton's qualities were his flexibility and open-mindedness. When the market-sharing agreement broke down at the end of the navigation season in 1846, he was flexible enough to find a way for Hooker, Holton & Co. to do well on its own. Holton and his partners decided to push ahead with plans to expand, pouring retained earnings into new vessels, which allowed them to compete effectively with rival companies. By May 1847, Holton had added a powerful new steamboat and several new barges to Hooker, Holton & Co.'s fleet. The expanded fleet operated smoothly, enabling the firm to flourish on the upper St. Lawrence route.

* * *

By 1848, Hooker, Holton & Co.'s position on the upper St. Lawrence, as well as in the western interior, had been further enhanced. The completion of the Williamsburg Canals on the upper St. Lawrence in 1847, combined with the opening of the renovated Lachine Canal the next year, helped Montreal build stronger links to Upper Canada and the American midwest and grow larger and wealthier in the process. With the improvement of the canal system, freight rates dropped to 1s 6d per barrel of flour and bigger steamboats came into use. Under Holton's direction, Hooker, Holton & Co.'s fleet continued to carry eastward shipments of produce from the interior to Montreal for important French-Canadian firms such as Cuvillier & Sons, as well as for major English-Canadian businesses such as Gillespie, Moffatt & Co.[16] Holton also recognized the important alterations that were taking place, and he was willing to assume major responsibilities and incur great risks in order to take advantage of these changes. Drawing on profits he had retained in good years, he used the depression that began in 1848 to expand.

Supported by Alfred Hooker and Francis Henderson, Holton transformed their firm into a long-distance shipping enterprise by acquiring a new steamboat, the *Free Trader*, Hooker, Holton & Co.'s largest to date, which became operational in the spring of 1848, at the onset of the depression.[17] Holton chose this name for the steamboat at a time when the idea of free trade with the United States still held considerable fascination for him. Built by Augustin Cantin in Montreal, it was a 134-ton screw propeller that travelled at the rate of ten miles per hour. Costing about £4,000, this vessel was 136 feet long, had a 24-foot beam, and was capable of carrying about 3,000 barrels of flour.[18] By the standards of cargo capacity, economy, and speed of its day, the *Free Trader* was a superior steamboat, swifter than any boat Hooker, Holton & Co. had ever owned.

For Toronto and Hamilton.

THE Steamer FREE TRADER will LEAVE the Subscribers' Wharf, for the above Ports, THIS EVENING (Tuesday), the 5th instant.

For Freight, apply to
HOOKER, HOLTON & Co.
Canal Wharf,
June 5, 1849.   15

Hooker, Holton & Co. advertised its services in Montreal newspapers. On Tuesday evening, 5 June 1849, after loading the steamer *Free Trader* with goods for the interior at the Canal Wharf in Montreal, Luther Holton sent it to Toronto and Hamilton. From Montreal *Pilot*, 5 June 1849.

In his continuing search for cargoes of agricultural produce, Holton now extended Hooker, Holton & Co.'s services to ports in the American midwest, with calls at Toledo and Chicago. He followed a policy designed to attract an ambitious young man to command the *Free Trader* and to implement his over-all business strategy. He was particularly anxious to encourage someone who showed initiative and who shared his passion for growth. Neil McMillan was one such man, and Holton appointed him captain of the new steamboat.[19] After making her maiden voyage to Toledo and returning to Montreal with corn, corn meal, pork, tallow, and lard, the vessel left for Chicago with a cargo of salt, fish, oil, and pig iron. The steamboat completed the round trip between Montreal and Chicago in thirty days; the eastbound cargo consisted of 11,000 bushels of wheat. "The first adventure" in Chicago commerce "has been remunerative" for Hooker, Holton & Co., observed the *Montreal Herald* on 19 July.[20] Under Holton's direction, Neil McMillan continued to command the vessel, developing the firm's long-distance service with occasional voyages to ports in the American midwest as well as to Canadian ports on Lake Ontario and Lake Erie.

Although Hooker, Holton & Co. derived its main revenues from produce and merchandise traffic, it was not the only source of the firm's transportation profits. Its vessels also carried passengers. Luther Holton and his partners were renowned for the high quality of their steamboats and crews, careful attention to standards of safety, efficient handling of cargoes, and courteous treatment of passengers. Once passengers saw that captains and masters carried them in a responsible manner, the passenger trade grew. The steamboats had cabin space for a limited number of travellers, but all vessels were planned to passenger standards and could take a substantial number of deck passengers. In 1849, deck passage between Montreal and Kingston cost 7s 6d, while cabin passage cost 15s 6d.[21] The carriage of immigrants, merchants, workers, and politicians – the firm's core passenger service – proved a moderate source of profit.

At head office, Holton competed aggressively especially for the immigrant business in the mid- and late 1840s, for this was a period of rapidly expanding British immigration. By this time, Montreal had become a focal point for immigration westbound. Every year, thousands of immigrants passed through the port, and hundreds of them travelled to the interior aboard Hooker, Holton & Co.'s steamboats and barges by way of the Ottawa-Rideau Canal route. Each of the firm's small steamboats was designed to carry thirty cabin passengers and numerous deck passengers; many deck passengers could also be carried aboard its barges.[22] A particular problem for Holton, however, was the fluctuating nature of the immigrant trade. In months of rising immigration, passenger space was often short and overcrowding was common. By contrast, in months of falling immigration there was usually surplus capacity and Holton was faced with shrinking receipts. There was also a backhaul problem, for the natural movement of people was from Montreal to the West, and finding eastbound passengers became a challenge.

Holton sought to address the backhaul problem by developing eastbound passenger traffic with merchants, workers, and politicians. Fortunately, between 1844 and 1849, when Montreal served as the seat of government for the united province of Canada, the opening and closing of parliament generated a seasonal demand for passenger space in Hooker, Holton & Co.'s steamboats as Upper Canadian politicians travelled to and from the capital. Other Upper Canadians, especially merchants carrying on trade with Montreal and workers looking for jobs in the city, also made use of the firm's eastbound steamboats on the St. Lawrence. Together all these downstream travellers became a significant element in establishing Hooker, Holton & Co.'s passenger trade.

While remaining committed to the firm's core passenger service – the carriage of immigrants, workers, merchants, and politicians – Holton was flexible in the passenger business. In the mid-1840s, he diversified into carrying a growing number of recreation seekers, particularly Montreal and Bytown visitors to the Caledonia Springs at L'Orignal, Upper Canada eight miles inland from the Ottawa. In addition to the hot sulphur baths at the Caledonia spa, there were hotels and ball alleys.[23] For years, the spa had fascinated recreation seekers. The problem was that they were unhappy about having to spend one night aboard a steamboat to get there. In an innovative step, Holton provided a solution to the problem in June 1845. By arranging to have Hooker, Holton & Co.'s steamboats leave Montreal and Bytown at five o'clock in the morning, he ensured that visitors would reach the Caledonia Springs the same day, in time for a late dinner at a hotel.[24] Before long, the firm's steamboats became very popular with spa visitors.

* * *

Holton had a shrewd business sense and a remarkable perception of individuals. In the conduct of his trade, he built up important relationships in order to expand. Time and again, he made a decision to entrust part of his business to particular men and rarely was his trust misplaced. For instance, in 1847, Holton, Alfred Hooker, and Francis Henderson formed a partnership with Edward Smith, a Bytown merchant, to develop their steamboat service in Bytown and along the Rideau Canal. Smith is a young businessman of "good habits, prudent, cautious & ... perfectly responsible," reported the R. G. Dun & Co. credit correspondent.[25] The partnership lasted only one year, but during that time, its Bytown and Rideau Canal business flourished under the direction of Edward Smith. Through Hooker in Prescott, in the mid-1840s Holton established a close and mutually supportive relationship with James Averell, a leading Ogdensburg merchant and president of the Ogdensburg Bank, to develop trade with upstate New York.[26] The joint venture with Averell operated for a number of years and proved profitable for Hooker, Holton & Co.'s steamboat service on the upper St. Lawrence, the route to which Holton had shifted most of the firm's operations by the late 1840s.

Holton's cordial relationships with bankers in Montreal yielded personal benefits for many years. They brought direct benefits for Hooker, Holton & Co. immediately. In 1845, the Montreal branch of the Commercial Bank of the Midland District extended a credit line of £10,000 to the firm; the bank's Kingston head office provided the firm with an additional credit line of £5,000.[27] By agreeing to serve as a director of the bank in 1847, Francis Henderson reinforced its connection with the firm. In the same year, Holton became a director of the City Bank in Montreal, which continued to provide Hooker, Holton & Co. with credit.[28] In putting these financial resources to work to develop the firm's steamboat services, Holton helped to lay the foundations of Montreal's economic infrastructure and to build the city's links to its western hinterland.

During the mid-1840s Holton's ties to the interior economy gradually became more complex and rewarding. Besides remaining active in the City Bank, he was elected to the Montreal Board of Trade council in April 1846. By this time, Montreal had about fifty thousand residents. Much of the city's success was due to its business leaders. Overlapping spheres of influence, composed of merchants, bankers, and politicians, had seized the advantages brought by inland steamboat connections. Hooker, Holton & Co. formed an important segment of this business leadership.

As head of the firm, Holton certainly exemplified leadership in action. His numerous connections to banks and local and regional businesses made him one of the most respected and best known men in the city. In manner and speech, Holton epitomized the successful Montreal entrepreneur of the mid-nineteenth century. His well-chosen words, large face, and level, sometimes piercing, gaze indicated an alert, confident mind. A man rooted firmly in the age of growing industrialization, he was willing to adjust himself and his firm as the changing times demanded. Outgoing and by nature a booster and joiner, Holton was able to relate to people of various ethnic backgrounds and of different classes. But those who mistook his readiness to cooperate and listen to others for signs of softness were surprised when he showed himself to be a fierce competitor.

Holton's banking ties gave him and his partners a vehicle with which to direct credit into a dynamic sector of the local economy – the forwarding industry – as well as into western regional development. Hooker, Holton & Co. kept substantial deposits in the Commercial Bank of the Midland District and the City Bank. These deposits helped the banks fund the firm's steamboat operations and provide it with money needed to supply credit to its customers in Montreal and the interior. The Commercial Bank was the largest source of capital available to the firm for funding the activities of Upper Canadian produce merchants. Among the firm's many important customers in Upper Canada in the years 1845-49 were Archibald MacFaul of Picton, William Gamble of Milton Mills near Toronto, John W. Gamble of Pine Grove, Mair & Benty of Chatham, J. W. Wilson of Grimsby, Thomas Rigney & Co. of Toronto; C. Phelps of St. Catharines, and Malcolm Cameron of Sarnia.[29]

The experience of William Gamble, a Milton Mills general merchant and flour miller, offers an excellent example of how Upper Canadian produce merchants were able to operate with the aid of Hooker, Holton & Co. In August 1845, Luther Holton advanced Gamble £5,000 to buy wheat in Upper Canada on the security of his flourmill and its machinery. Holton provided this credit by asking the Commercial Bank to cash Gamble's drafts and give him bank notes for them. At the same time, Gamble put into Holton's hands promissory notes to cover this sum, payable in three months at the bank's Montreal branch. Fortunately for Holton, there was no delay in Gamble's repayment of this loan.[30]

On the strength of Hooker, Holton Co.'s credit at the Commercial Bank, Luther also provided his older brother Ezra Holton, a Belleville storekeeper and produce merchant, with short-term finance. Supportive and generous with family and friends, Luther encouraged Ezra, who like many other Upper Canadian merchants was short of working capital, to seek assistance from Hooker, Holton & Co. In November 1846, Ezra requested an advance of £1,000 to purchase farm produce.[31] Luther immediately responded by securing a commitment from the Commercial Bank to supply Ezra with the cash he needed. Ezra promptly settled the debt and, therefore, had no difficulty in obtaining further loans over the next few years. This arrangement, tied by kinship, loyalty, and credit, was not unusual for its time and place. Rather, it was typical of the pragmatic way in which many nineteenth-century Canadian businesses created cash and credit.

As Luther Holton was developing Hooker, Holton & Co.'s steamboat services, his private life was shattered by tragedy. He and his family, which in 1844 had grown to two children with the birth of Edward Holton, still lived in a rented house on Queen Street near the wharves. In July 1845, Eliza gave birth to their fourth child, a girl they named Julia after Eliza's sister. But Julia became ill within a year and died in September 1846. Grief overcame Luther and Eliza, but they did not draw inward in self-pity. Messages of sympathy arrived by the dozens. Luther's partner Alfred Hooker came down from Prescott to offer his condolences. Hooker was the kind of person one could trust and liked to sit up with, talking about the day's developments or reminiscing about past events. Luther genuinely enjoyed his relationship with Hooker, and vice versa. When Eliza gave birth to their third son in June 1847, they named him Alfred Hooker after Luther's Prescott partner. But baby Alfred also suffered from poor health and died in September 1848. Again Eliza and Luther sorrowed, but they were not beyond consolation. In August 1849, they celebrated the birth of their third daughter, Amelia Jane, a healthy girl, who brought them hope.[32]

* * *

While Luther rejoiced over the health of Amelia, the depression of 1849 destroyed his hopes for expanding Hooker, Holton & Co.'s steamboat services. Between 1848 and 1849, the value of Canada's imports and exports dropped from £4,931,464 to £4,662,208. The slump slowed the development of Canada's forwarding industry.[33]

As the depression spread across Canada, the economic downturn hurt Hooker, Holton & Co. The firm nevertheless was still stable. In September

1849, an R. G. Dun & Co. credit reporter explained the situation succinctly: the concern is "quite good, wealthy."[34] Holton, however, faced problems. The difficulties of other enterprises affected his business. The value of Hooker, Holton & Co.'s imports was £3,039 between October and December in 1848 and plunged to £304 during the same period in 1849. Some of Luther Holton's customers, including Montreal merchant Richard Latham, were among the first victims of the depression. Upper Canadian produce merchants, such as William and John Gamble, delayed payments. A number of customers defaulted. The banks, desperate for cash themselves, pressed Holton for payments on loans.[35] In the midst of the economic crisis the City Bank teetered on the brink of failure; only through assistance from Holton and other directors was the bank able to continue in business.

By October 1849, Montreal forwarders sensed the chill of potential disaster – Holton was no exception. He had gained a reputation for quality steamboat services in Montreal and the interior, but now the forwarding trade brought only headaches to him. In normal times, he might have been lining up captains and steamboats for the following year. But these were hardly normal times. Holton felt enormous pressure to keep funds flowing into Hooker, Holton & Co., yet this was no easy task. In previous bad years, he had pursued the policy of using retained profits for expansion. But this policy was no longer feasible, because the profits had already been spent for developing the firm's business.

Luther Holton hoped to revive Hooker, Holton & Co.'s sagging fortunes as the depression deepened, and he believed that his vision of a political union of Canada and the United States would provide a solution to the problem and would also appeal to other desperate Montrealers. When he joined the Annexation Association of Montreal in mid-October, which attracted over 300 other men, twenty of whom were bankrupt merchants, the city was in low spirits.[36] Montreal presented a bleak picture that mocked its previous reputation as an economic showplace. No city in Canada was a rival for Montreal when it came to cosmopolitan atmosphere, but it had few marks of prosperity. Several years earlier, it had been the province's busiest port; its harbour had teemed with steamboats, barges, and towering masts of sailing vessels flying British flags. Now there was relatively little activity at the waterfront.

Events rushed forward. Holton was elected a vice-president of the Annexation Association, an organization whose message was stridently economic in its tone and thrust.[37] The annexation manifesto he signed also bore the signatures of many other prominent Montreal businessmen, including Sidney Jones, his competitor in the forwarding industry, and John Redpath. All three men were aware that the financial underpinnings of the Montreal business community seemed to be verging on the disastrous. Hence, Luther Holton made his plea for peaceful separation from Great Britain and union with the United States to save Montreal from an imminent bankruptcy. He needed only to look around the downtown business district to see that conditions were deteriorating and had been going downhill since the euphoric days of 1847. Perhaps Holton, who was always conscious that his parents had come from the United States, thought the republic might provide him with a second chance. He expressed his feelings on annexation in a public letter, but he did so in a very restrained fashion.

Canada was lurching from one crisis to another. The scenes of the spring of 1849 were still fresh in Holton's mind when he recalled the fragile threads holding the Canadian union together as the assemblymen gathered in Montreal. Looking back on the days of the LaFontaine-Baldwin Reform ministry's Rebellion Losses Bill, he remembered clearly the atmosphere of crisis then prevailing in the city.

Louis-Hippolyte LaFontaine. An advocate of responsible government, Luther Holton threw his support behind the LaFontaine-Baldwin ministry and Lord Elgin during the Rebellion Losses Bill crisis in Montreal in 1849. Courtesy of the McCord Museum of Canadian History, Montreal.

The bill was designed to compensate Lower Canadians – along the same lines upon which Upper Canadians had received compensation earlier – for losses suffered during the Rebellion of 1837. Responsible to parliament and enjoying a strong majority, the ministry shepherded the bill through the legislature. Governor General Lord Elgin correctly viewed the bill as the ministry's policy and, acting in the spirit of responsible government, gave his assent despite the Montreal Tories' efforts to kill the measure. As a keen observer outside parliament, Holton spoke his mind among his friends and left no doubt where he stood. The bill, he remarked, was based on justice, for it positively affirmed especially French Canadians in Lower Canada and their important place within the social order.[38] Hoping to strike a balance between French and English Canadians, he challenged the convictions of the Tory elite. Earlier, just after the LaFontaine-Baldwin ministry had been formed in March

1847, Holton came to understand the degree to which he helped sustain Canada's hopes for responsible government. He took pride in knowing he inspirited his fellow citizens as well as government officials. "My personal advisor is Holton, a very sincere friend, and one willing to do his part most cheerfully," Francis Hincks, the new inspector general and editor of the *Montreal Pilot*, told Robert Baldwin.[39]

Reacting to the bill, the Tories burned the parliament house including its valuable library, pelted Elgin with stones and rotten eggs, smashed the windows in the *Pilot* office, and trashed the furniture in Louis LaFontaine's house. All the energies of Holton went in an entirely different direction propelled by the urgent need to recognize responsible government. He aligned himself with the moderate forces in the city and co-operated with other Montrealers such as Benjamin Workman and George-Étienne Cartier in getting up a giant petition in support of Elgin, LaFontaine, and Baldwin.[40] Well before the end of the crisis, Holton and his friends had come to embody a democratic Canada in the minds of many Montrealers. Related to this, Holton's widely applauded respect for French Canadians struck emotional chords among fellow liberals, including Cartier's law partner Joseph-Amable Berthelot. Many years later, Holton wrote: "I know Berthelot very well indeed. We were both followers and ardent admirers of LaFontaine in our youth."[41]

Almost six months had passed since Holton had exercised his moderate influence during the Rebellion Losses Bill crisis. Now, in November 1849, he, along with other influential annexationists, met in the Temperance Hall on St. Maurice Street, advocating union with the United States and thereby adding to the depression a political crisis in Montreal and Canada.[42] Annexationists were viewed by provincial government officials as intriguers, more concerned about feathering their own nests than about looking out for the interest of the general public. The commitment of Holton and others to annexation sharply altered the tone of politics, and it was denounced by inspector general Francis Hincks, who urged Baldwin to dismiss all militia officers associated with the annexation cause. "I am strongly of the opinion that unless we dismiss these annexationists we are ruined," wrote Hincks to Baldwin.[43] Holton had served as a lieutenant in the local militia since March 1847, but he now felt the sting of government action. On 24 December 1849, one day before Christmas, he was dismissed from this position by a senior militia officer. Other annexationists who had signed the manifesto were also dismissed.

Holton had a fairly sophisticated understanding of how the Canadian political process worked and decided not to make a prolonged fight for annexation. Despite his dismissal from the militia, he remained amazingly restrained. Nothing he said in his public statements can be construed as encouraging an assault on the provincial government. Several years later, when Holton was reinstated in the militia, he confronted the question of patriotic sentiment and his loyalty to the Queen: "I am not conscious of having failed on any occasion in my duty as a faithful subject."[44] Although he always sought to protect his economic position, he at the same time continued to maintain a strong identification with Canada. When his effort to make Canada a part of the United States collapsed, he suffered few pangs of loss. As the Canadian economy began to recover in early 1850, Holton no longer found annexation interesting and preferred instead to pursue his business career and develop his steamboat interests.

* * *

Even now, however, Holton had to deal with the results of the depression for Hooker, Holton & Co. Despite its successful weathering of the depression, the firm remained cash-poor, a situation that brought changes to the company. Thoroughly discouraged, on 1 January 1850, Francis Henderson dropped out of the partnership, which was immediately re-organized but under the same name – Hooker, Holton & Co.[45] Alfred Hooker and Luther Holton were now the only partners, but they hired Elijah Hooker, possibly a relative of Alfred, to act as their agent in the firm's Kingston office. This shake-up did little to improve the forwarding company's finances, because in leaving the enterprise Henderson also withdrew his capital. But if Henderson considered the firm's future unpromising, he miscalculated, for its prospects were not as bleak as they appeared.

Holton's task was to reconstruct a firm that had suffered considerably during the two long depression years. An immediate problem facing him was ageing vessels. He now had to set Hooker, Holton & Co.'s face toward the future, to plan a major program of fleet reconstruction, and to adapt to the needs of a growing economy. Anticipating better times in Montreal and Canada, Holton was soon preparing to expand the firm's steamboat services. The dramatic transformation a buoyant economy would bring to Hooker, Holton & Co. could not have been forecast by the most perceptive observer. At the start of 1850, Holton began to repair or replace vessels. He also decided to extend the firm's carriage of agricultural produce to Burlington, Vermont, on Lake Champlain by way of the Richelieu River. But this first incursion into the Vermont trade was intended mainly to strengthen his firm's position on the upper St. Lawrence and the Great Lakes. As Holton explained to a Burlington business concern: "we wish to impress upon you that our principal business lies on the River & Lakes above this place [Montreal] and that our only object in extending our line to Lake Champlain was to promote that business."[46]

HOOKER & HOLTON'S
THROUGH LINE.

—

THE Steamer "ONTARIO," Armstrong, Master, will leave Subscribers' Wharf, for TORONTO, HAMILTON and Intermediate Ports, THIS DAY, (Thursday) at NOON.

For Freight, apply to
　　　　　　　　　HOOKER & HOLTON.
May 19.　　　　　　　　　　　　16

HOOKER & HOLTON'S
THROUGH LINE.

—

THE Steamer ENGLAND, Hannah, Master, will leave the Subscribers' Wharf, for TORONTO, HAMILTON and Intermediate Ports, THIS EVENING, THURSDAY, 20th instant, at SIX o'clock.

For Freight, apply to
　　　　　　　　　HOOKER & HOLTON.
May 20.　　　　　　　　　　　　17

Luther Holton's newspaper advertisement for Hooker, Holton & Co.'s new through line service attracted wide attention in the early 1850s. From Montreal *Pilot*, 1852.

The interior service via the upper St. Lawrence remained at the centre of Hooker, Holton & Co.'s operations. But Holton dramatically transformed this service by establishing a new through line for trade between Montreal and Toronto, or Hamilton, or Port Stanley, or Toledo without trans-shipment at Kingston. Historically, Hooker, Holton & Co. had usually relied on offloading especially at Kingston for schooner shipment to the interior, but trans-shipment at Kingston was time-consuming and expensive. Before 1850, Holton had sent the occasional steamboat to Toledo or Port Stanley to load with wheat and flour, returning to Montreal via Hamilton or Toronto. Now the upsurge in economic activity encouraged him to develop a more permanent interest in this trade.

For the new through line service, Holton committed two fairly new steamboats in the spring of 1850, the *Free Trader* and *Hibernia*. The service proved so popular that by 1853 the cargo between Montreal and western ports was being carried in seven Hooker, Holton & Co. steamboats. Like the first two vessels, the other five – *Britannia, England, Ontario, St. Lawrence,* and *Lord Elgin* – were large and built specifically for the through line.[47] Holton was particular in his choice of names for the steamboats, emphasizing his devotion to free trade and the British connection and his use of inland waterways. Each steamboat had space for about 2,500 barrels of flour, with additional room for numerous passengers. As Luther Holton was transforming Hooker, Holton & Co., he sought to preserve those aspects of the firm's tradition he thought valuable. Especially important, he continued to surround himself with competent, reliable steamboat captains, including not only Neil McMillan but also Alexander Pollard and John Graham. Holton showed himself willing to trust his captains' judgement, to distribute responsibility, and to provide the best advice he could. In some situations, his knowledge

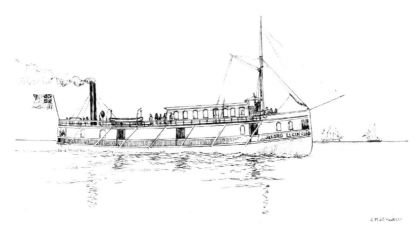

Hooker, Holton & Co.'s propeller *Lord Elgin*, shown here in an 1852 pen drawing by C. H. S. Snider. Built in Montreal in 1852, it was a 600-ton steamer in the firm's through line. Courtesy of the Metropolitan Toronto Library Board.

might be imperfect, but he was a forwarder who could make the decisions that fell to him without refusing to bear the consequences.

Even as Hooker, Holton & Co.'s through-line steamboats made regular voyages to the interior, Holton's presence was felt everywhere at the firm's facilities in Montreal. Observers must have noticed that he kept his eye on all operations, providing inspiring leadership for captains and other employees. As the economy picked up, Hooker, Holton & Co.'s Common Street office, warehouse, and wharf hummed with activity. During the navigation season, it was noisy on the wharf, where the loading and unloading of goods, rumbling wagons, and shouted directions and warnings all contributed to the constant racket. Despite Holton's efforts to provide a humane working environment, there probably were some complaints. Apparently good morale was nevertheless a key factor in allowing Hooker, Holton & Co. to maintain high-quality services.

A traditional challenge to Holton was intense competition from other forwarders. The conventional response was to cut freight and passenger rates, then make every effort to provide efficient transportation. But recognizing that cooperation had in the past allowed Hooker, Holton & Co. to protect its profits, Holton was again particularly interested in taking advantage of the opportunity to belong to an alliance. In the third week of April 1850, at the opening of navigation, Holton travelled by steamboat to Kingston to attend a forwarders' meeting. His plan was clear: he would try to maximize Hooker, Holton & Co.'s share of the forwarding trade, provide top-quality service, and operate at a reasonable profit. On 25 April,

Holton and five other forwarders on the upper St. Lawrence and Great Lakes signed an agreement.[48] The other firms were Macpherson, Crane & Co.; John Hamilton of Kingston; Donald Bethune & Co. and Thomas Dick of Toronto; and Sutherland & Jackson of Hamilton. Essentially, the agreement regulated the freight and passenger rates for all these firms.

Holton assessed his strategy with confidence, determination, and above all optimism that, with co-operation, Hooker, Holton & Co. would benefit. Gone were the sense of gloom, complaints about the recent depression, and fighting about Canada's political future. Holton's faith in co-operation was quickly justified and the agreement, after a break in 1851, was renewed in 1852, which in turn lasted only a few months. Frequent rate-cutting wars remained a problem. But between the wars, Holton was partially successful in protecting Hooker, Holton & Co.'s profits. Critics of this rate-fixing agreement might argue that it helped steamboat owners at the expense of shippers and that it promoted complacency among the large forwarders. Defenders of the agreement could, however, point out the advantage to shippers of stable freight rates. They could also argue that it did not prevent improved services, because each steamboat line could hardly maximize its share of the forwarding trade without providing a competitive service.

As Hooker, Holton & Co.'s operations grew in size and complexity, so did the firm's relationships with its competitors in the forwarding industry. Providing forwarding services became increasingly competitive. The growth of this competition led Holton to work together with some other forwarders informally, seeking to standardize services and divide markets.

* * *

But Holton also experienced other troubles in the steamboat business. In retrospect, difficulties might have been anticipated. Despite his image as a responsible merchant, some contemporaries criticized him for becoming involved in a questionable land transaction. One of his critics waited until many years later to strike. In the spring of 1871, Hector Langevin rose in the House of Commons to detail several charges against Holton. The most serious was that Holton had used his connections in Canadian government circles to secure some lots on the Lachine Canal at a public auction in 1851. Langevin charged that, although Holton knew that these lots were required for public use, he had purchased them from the government for Hooker, Holton & Co. and later sold them, "making a very handsome profit by the transaction."[49]

When Langevin aired his charges, Luther Holton was angry. The one kind of attack he could not abide was one against his integrity. Holton replied that "he strongly disapproved of the sale of those lots by government

Montreal from St. Helen's Island, shown here an 1852-53 watercolour by James Duncan. These were Luther Holton's last two years in the forwarding industry. Courtesy of the McCord Museum of Canadian History, Montreal.

in 1851 as a matter of public policy; but he attended the sale and purchased the lots as a merchant doing business in Montreal. He invested in them as a good speculation."[50] He made things worse for himself especially with part of his remarks, that "he strongly disapproved of the sale of those lots by government in 1851 as a matter of public policy," a statement many found incredible. After the initial salvos between Langevin and Holton, the two sides persisted in the war for about an hour. In the end, it was clear that there was some truth to Langevin's charges. The episode in 1851 was one of the low points of Holton's business career. His effort to present himself as a person who had done no wrong in the land transaction failed.

* * *

But Holton did not always operate this way. For the most part, as a forwarder his conduct in his relations with the Canadian government fell within the bounds of proper behaviour. Many Canadians associated the government with entrepreneurial opportunity – Holton himself believed that he owed some of his important opportunities to changes in government regulation. For instance, in August 1852, he sought to change the toll regulations on the St. Lawrence and Welland canals. He wrote to R.S.M.

Bouchette, commissioner of customs, complaining about the unjustness of the new policy of increasing the revenue from canals by making forwarders pay the same toll rate for a fraction of a ton of cargo as for a whole ton. Holton urged Bouchette "to set this matter right at once."[51] After considering Holton's letter, Bouchette ruled that the toll regulations should be interpreted more liberally, so that the rate on part of a ton would be less than that on one ton. Like other Canadian forwarders using the St. Lawrence and Welland canals, Hooker, Holton & Co.'s through line benefited from this ruling.

During the years 1850 to 1853, Holton built on earlier business practices. He continued to fully cover his fleet of steamboats with insurance, a policy that dictated the highest standards of steamboat maintenance and the best possible calibre of captains. For instance, in April 1851, he insured all his steamboats with the Montreal Fire, Life, and Inland Navigation Assurance Company.[52] As always, Holton took an intensely personal role in the management of Hooker, Holton & Co. His management style brought him into constant contact with many employees and numerous customers. Holton, in fact, knew the names of all the employees, and he was able to develop strong bonds of loyalty among them. He also continued to build up the firm through the traditional policy of dividend restraint and prudent husbandry of financial resources. Apparently net earnings rose substantially from 1850 onward, a sign of Hooker, Holton & Co.'s recovery from the depression of the late 1840s. The good conditions of the early 1850s led to significant gains in the firm's traditional carriage of merchandise and agricultural produce. Holton invested the profits he retained in new steamboats, barges, and warehouse facilities. By continuing to follow a policy of offering diversified services – forwarding and trading goods on commission – he never had to rely too much on one activity for profits. He also maintained traditional ties with banks, especially the Commercial Bank of the Midland District, to which Hooker, Holton & Co. never became dangerously indebted. On 13 September 1853, a R. G. Dun credit correspondent observed that Hooker, Holton & Co. is "very saving. Doing a very large business. Worth over 200M$ [$200,000]."[53]

Hooker, Holton & Co. had once been a relatively small steamboat firm; within a decade after Luther Holton became head, he had made it into the second largest forwarding company in Canada.[54] The steamboats, with their handsome lines, were part and parcel of the province's flourishing inland waterborne enterprise, familiar sights in the ports of Montreal, Upper Canada, Ohio, and New York. The years 1845-53 were the era of Luther Holton, but the era, too, of Alfred Hooker, both of whom served the firm well. Throughout the forwarding world, the firm had a reputation for efficient fleet management and the high calibre of its employees both on vessels and on shore. Led by Holton, the two exceptionally able partners sustained a Canada-wide enterprise with understanding and knowledge of all aspects of the business.

Against this background, one might expect Luther Holton to continue in the firm. But remarkably, he did not. Instead, on 1 January 1854, he withdrew from the firm and sold his share in it to Alfred Hooker.[55] To other entrepreneurs of the day, Hooker probably described Holton as a changed man. What he saw, perhaps more clearly than anyone else, was the awakening in Holton of a great interest in railway building. For some time, constructing railways had commanded part of Holton's attention, but now, as never before, he became convinced that the best opportunities for him lay in that direction. Now he was challenged to forge ahead, to take huge risks in an industry that promised more gain than the forwarding trade.

Chapter 4

Railway Builder

Already in the mid-1840s, Luther Holton's fertile imagination had been struck with the possibilities of railway development. At that time, he became a stockholder in the seven-mile Montreal & Lachine Railroad. Until the early 1850s, Holton as a forwarder sometimes used the line to carry goods between Montreal and Lachine.

The line was not particularly profitable and sometimes completely unrewarding. Holton craved bigger stakes, a more important railway, and larger profits. He realized that only large railway corporations could generate the earnings he needed to be in the same league as North America's great railwaymen. Constructing a railway was a complex business, but he believed that the cash provided by a big company's traffic would enable him to build part or all of a trans-provincial line.

* * *

Putting this theory into action, Holton sought to secure control of a trans-provincial railway route. In August 1852, having made a firsthand study of railway operations, he launched himself in the business. Holton and several associates bought a controlling interest in the Montreal & Kingston Railway with funds borrowed from the Commercial Bank of the Midland District.[1] This line had been incorporated in the previous year, but it was still no more than a paper railway. Holton's main associates were Alexander T. Galt, president of the Montreal-based St. Lawrence & Atlantic Railway, and David L. Macpherson of Macpherson, Crane & Co. The leadership of the Montreal & Kingston fell to Holton, who became president of the line. Holton, Galt, and Macpherson were prime examples of Canadian entrepreneurs who came to the railway world with big ideas and the desire to succeed in railway construction but lacked the capital to do so.

In the early 1850s, when the competitive trans-provincial rivalries began to develop, the group that seemed to be assured of success was headed by

Alexander T. Galt. Courtesy of the Ontario Archives.

capitalists associated with the British railway contracting firm Peto, Brassey, Jackson, and Betts. A monumental promotional campaign was carried out in the fall of 1852 under the leadership of William Jackson, who had the support of Francis Hincks, premier of Canada. The scope of the territorial ambition of Jackson's group was amazing, for it involved the entire trans-provincial route.

In his contest with Jackson to secure control of the trans-provincial railway route, Holton knew that speed was essential. Throwing considerations of financial safety and prudence to the winds, Holton and Galt made their first major move in the trans-provincial strategy by uniting the Montreal & Kingston and the St. Lawrence & Atlantic. They thereby succeeded in seizing control of about half of the strategic route. Holton did not work quietly. Rather, he bombarded the railway committee of the Canadian legislative assembly in Quebec City with letters to promote his cause.[2] He attracted province-wide publicity in his contest with Jackson over the trans-provincial route. Holton's relations with Jackson ranged from mutual distrust to open hostility. Even with the union of the St. Lawrence & Atlantic and the Montreal & Kingston, many thought Holton would fail. In the end, the legislative assembly rejected Holton's project. The pooled funds of Holton and his two principal associates were insufficient to meet the pressing needs of the trans-provincial system.

Far from discouraged, Holton continued to fight for a position on the trans-provincial route, seeking railway-building opportunities west of Toronto. In mid-October 1852, he initiated moves designed to secure a construction contract on the western section of the Grand Trunk Railway, the bill for the incorporation of which was now making its way through the Canadian parliament. Holton, Galt, Macpherson, and C. S. Gzowski, an engineer, formed a railway-building

David L. Macpherson. Courtesy of the Metropolitan Toronto Library Board.

partnership known as C. S. Gzowski & Co. Holton and Galt immediately travelled to Quebec City in an effort to work out a compromise with Francis Hincks and Jackson.[3] The four agreed to extend the Grand Trunk east from Montreal along the largely built but troubled St. Lawrence & Atlantic and all the way to Portland, Maine, and west from Toronto along the Toronto & Guelph Railway and right to Sarnia. Besides insisting that the construction of the Victoria Bridge across the St. Lawrence at Montreal should be part of the arrangement, Holton agreed to transfer all the stock in the Montreal & Kingston and its charter to the Grand Trunk in exchange for the contract to build the Toronto-Sarnia section. "The G.T.R.R. Co. obtained from" Holton and his associates the Montreal & Kingston "charter on condition of their securing to them a contract of about [172] miles of R. R. west of Toronto," observed the R. G. Dun & Co. credit correspondent for Toronto.[4] This contract was subject to the availability of funds for construction to Sarnia. Jackson committed himself to building both the Victoria Bridge and the section from Montreal to Toronto, as well as to buying the St. Lawrence & Atlantic and assuming its debts.

C. S. Gzowki & Co., led by Holton and Galt, immediately struck a bonanza by obtaining a £367,500 contract for the construction of the line between Toronto and Guelph.[5] This job dwarfed everything Holton had done previously. The Toronto-Guelph road was fifty miles long and was destined to become a part of the Grand Trunk. On 10 November 1852, the Canadian legislature chartered the Grand Trunk, with Holton and Galt as two of its directors. It also authorized the Toronto & Guelph to extend its line to Sarnia. Two weeks later, Holton and Galt finalized their contract with the Toronto & Guelph, which at the same time accepted their proposal to drive the tracks forward to Sarnia as soon as possible. Shortly afterward, Holton and his partners gained control of the Toronto & Guelph by purchasing a large amount of its capital stock – they would sell this stock to the Grand Trunk at cost,

Casimir S. Gzowski. Courtesy of the Ontario Archives.

once the Grand Trunk contract to build to Sarnia was safely in their hands. In the process, they transformed their relatively small railway building firm into a major enterprise.

Public opinion reflected the growing power of Holton and his associates, expressing both confidence and fear, depending on the economic interests involved. Their success would bring more business to Montreal and less to Toronto. Toronto would have benefited more if local railway building contractors had obtained the contract to build to Guelph. To the Toronto area, the moves of Gzowski & Co. were thus looked upon with a critical eye. The Toronto *Globe* referred to the firm as "strangers."[6] Most financiers were impressed by the clarity of the firm's reports, but some Toronto aldermen were outraged, and bent upon revenge. According to one source, a searching investigation revealed several rebate arrangements from which a few Toronto aldermen and Gzowski & Co. had profited at the expense of the City of Toronto.[7] In Montreal, however, the opinion was different. A leading Montreal daily described Holton and his associates as "spirited" entrepreneurs.[8] Holton had helped put the Grand Trunk especially at the service of Montreal, the headquarters of the great line. He fully appreciated the importance of Montreal as the emerging rail capital of Canada. The

C.S. Gzowski & Co.'s
Railway Construction Contracts, 1852–57

① Grand Trunk Railway: Toronto & Sarnia section
①A Grand Trunk Railway: St. Mary's & London section
② Port Huron & Lake Michigan Railroad
③ Toronto Esplanade
④ Montreal & Vermont Junction Railroad
--- Construction completed by July, 1857

building of the Victoria Bridge would not only open the St. Lawrence & Atlantic's way into Montreal, but also link the city through the Grand Trunk to Sarnia and Chicago. Holton foresaw Montreal, as Canada's rail hub, using the Grand Trunk to tap the burgeoning trade in Upper Canada and the American midwest and thereby fuel the city's economy.

* * *

By the early 1850s, the steam locomotive had become the symbol of growth in the pace and size of business in Montreal, and of the second stage in the transportation revolution that had begun with the advent of the steamboat. On the upper St. Lawrence and the Great Lakes, the heyday of steamboat transportation lasted from the 1820s to the mid-1850s. In the next two decades, the volume of steamboat shipping continued to grow, but the forwarding industry faced increasing competition from railways that provided year-round service, summer and winter. Ice covered the Montreal harbour, and the interior waterways were ice-edged in the winter months, making steamboat navigation impossible in that period, and this helped reinforce the railway's grip upon inland transportation. In the popular mind, Holton's name was connected as much with the new railway era as it had been with the steamboat age.

Breaking up the ice in the St. Lawrence River at Montreal. As Canadians knew, steamboats did not move at all in winter, but trains did. From the *Illustrated London News*, March 1859.

In November 1852, Holton and his colleagues opened an office in the heart of Montreal's business district on St. François Xavier Street, and another one in downtown Toronto on Church Street. While Holton and Galt worked out of the Montreal office and plotted long-term strategy, Macpherson and Gzowski stayed in Toronto and managed day-to-day operations. The partners agreed to share profits and losses equally and retain most of their earnings for development purposes.[9] In addition to sharing with Galt the task of handling strategic decisions, Holton served as treasurer. The business plan the partners discussed at their meetings and in their correspondence would have appeared fanciful to less ambitious minds. They hoped to create a railway-building organization that would speedily construct a high-quality road. Such an enterprise would require thousands of pounds in start-up capital. Experienced and wealthy financiers willing to risk their funds for quick, and perhaps large, profits needed to be found. But first, it was necessary to begin construction of the road with money borrowed from the Commercial Bank of the Midland District. The stock Holton and his partners received from the Toronto & Guelph for their work was used as collateral for short-term loans.

Holton wanted to study the route between Toronto and Guelph. With a map of the terrain in hand, he and his partners became familiar with the details of the route in December 1852. The route was not easy. It crossed successive ridges and streams, including Black Creek, the Humber River,

Mimico and Etobicoke creeks, Georgetown Creek, and the Eramosa and Speed rivers, and thus required a number of expensive bridges. By this time, the Toronto and Guelph had located the fifty-mile line and had purchased the lands needed for the right-of-way.

As the general contractors for the line, Holton and his partners now advertised for and accepted bids from local sub-contractors for grading, culvert work, earth excavation, bridge building, ties, track laying, ballasting, and fencing. The sub-contractors, among whom were P. W. Dayfoot & Co., Young & Barber, John Worthington & Co., and Hutchison, Morrison & Wells, needed short-term credit at the banks. By endorsing their notes, Holton as treasurer of Gzowski & Co. helped them gain access to bank credit. In this way, for instance, Holton assisted Hutchison, Morrison & Wells in borrowing £6,000 from the Bank of Montreal in December 1852.[10]

Under Gzowski & Co.'s direction, the sub-contractors began construction west of Toronto in February 1853. By the end of April, more than 400 men and numerous horses were employed by the sub-contractors on the project. To meet the need for labour, Holton and his partners helped the sub-contractors recruit workers especially from Toronto and Montreal, but also from small-town and rural communities in Upper Canada as well as from Great Britain. The partners, however, were having difficulty in securing equipment for construction. Initially, they tried to solve this problem by importing the earth wagons required for building the road from Britain, but by the winter of 1853-54, they found it more economical to get them from the newly established Grand Trunk workshops in Toronto.[11]

* * *

Meanwhile, in February 1853, Holton was corresponding with Galt, who had gone to London, England, to raise funds to finance the construction of the road between Toronto and Sarnia and to seek the amalgamation of this road with the Grand Trunk. Newspapers expressed admiration for the speed with which the building of part of this route, the Toronto & Guelph, had been undertaken. But to Holton and his partners, even in this project, the problems became increasingly formidable. They had already raised substantial sums by pledging their Toronto & Guelph securities for bank loans, but the money was nowhere near enough to carry out their ambitions. They strained their personal resources in order to supplement the funds that had been raised through the credit of their construction company. In an attempt to secure additional financial help, Galt made an approach to powerful capitalists in London: William Jackson, Thomas Baring of Baring Brothers and chairman of the Grand Trunk's London Board, and George

Carr Glyn of Glyn, Mills & Co. These capitalists agreed to back the construction of the Toronto-Sarnia line and to make a determined effort to amalgamate it with the Grand Trunk.[12] The support of Baring Brothers and Glyn, Mills & Co., the two houses that served as the Grand Trunk's bankers in London, was especially important, for as large stable banking concerns, they were one key to the early as well as the long-term success of Holton and his associates.

Holton was exuberant about Galt's success in finding the necessary money. He dashed off to Toronto to make arrangements with the Toronto & Guelph directors for constructing the 172-mile road from Toronto to Sarnia, and to work out a plan with them that would allow the Grand Trunk to take over the entire road.[13] Upon his return to Montreal, Holton threw himself into the challenge of strengthening the road, paying particular attention to the question of striking an alliance with Jackson that would provide Gzowski & Co. with a contract from the Grand Trunk to build to Sarnia. Holton, however, agonized over possible trouble with Jackson. He feared that this British capitalist might threaten Gzowski & Co.'s Toronto-Sarnia project. "Desirable as it unquestionably is to secure the means of constructing the whole line," Holton wrote Galt, "don't let us illustrate the moral of the old fable and by grasping at *too much* jeopardize our snug and safe little Guelph contract.... In becoming contractors under the Grand Trunk Company, under Jackson substantially, we must have our position and rights very clearly defined and be protected at every possible point or we may get a *hug from the Bear* that will be any thing but agreeable."[14] With a great deal of his money at risk, Holton continued to discuss the matter with Galt to determine what, if any, precautionary steps could be taken to secure the Toronto-Sarnia enterprise. But even though the whole thing looked tenuous, Holton remained committed to the project.

Although Jackson, who had undertaken to build the Grand Trunk section between Montreal and Toronto, occupied a position of strategic power in Canadian railway territory, he did not actually pose a threat to Holton and his partners at this point. By mid-February 1853, Galt's letters from London chronicled his satisfaction with Jackson. Despite the earlier fight for a place on the trans-provincial route between Holton and Jackson, the new reality was that Jackson was one of Gzowski & Co.'s important financial backers. At this time, the firm desperately needed Jackson's name, international reputation, and financial contacts to push construction forward.

Holton now sensed a ripe opportunity to influence politicians in Quebec City, whose support was needed to pass the bill for the amalgamation of the Toronto-Sarnia line with the Grand Trunk. While Galt was busy with finance in London and Macpherson and Gzowski were preoccupied with the details of railway construction, Holton personally handled the lobbying chores at Quebec City. His gregariousness, charm, spontaneity, and humour were assets. Quick-witted, Holton enjoyed the give and take of the political arena. Knowing that he could sway public opinion, his partners used him for the necessary glad-handing and back-slapping. Working closely together with Hincks, Holton was guardedly optimistic about success. His efforts bore fruit. On 17 March 1853, the Canadian legislature passed the amalgamation bill.

Holton realized that his work in Quebec City and Galt's efforts in London with respect to the amalgamation strategy had to be co-ordinated. Otherwise, things could lurch along on a hit-or-miss basis. Holton was watching the situation in London – sometimes he became impatient and demanding, however. Privately he fretted about the lack of vital information in Galt's correspondence on the progress of the amalgamation plan in London. On 26 March, he penned a long letter to Galt:

> *You have not* (quite unwittingly I am sure) kept us as fully advised in regard to the progress of this momentous negotiation as men who had staked their all in the issue might reasonably expect. I have been schooled to self-reliance, am used to judging and acting for myself, and am generally prepared to face the worst that can come of any venture, but I want to know just what I am grappling with. Although I always aim at extending a generous confidence to all with whom I am in intimate relations of any kind, I can not consent to *go it blind* even with one in whose talents, judgement, and honour I have such unlimited confidence as I have in yours.[15]

For the next two weeks, Holton played the dutiful partner. But his mind was on the larger matter of coordinating strategy. At the beginning of April, Galt's letter came from London bringing the news that Holton had been waiting for. The London capitalists had approved the amalgamation scheme. Holton and his partners had obtained a Grand Trunk contract to build the road between Toronto and Sarnia – one of the biggest plums in railway construction of the day.[16] The railway allowed a little over four years to do the job.

With a £1,376,000 Grand Trunk contract for work on the section between Toronto and Sarnia in hand, Holton and his partners became a symbol of the early stages of industrial capitalism in Canada. But public knowledge of the Canadian government's role in this mammoth industrial enterprise tended to deflate their entrepreneurial reputation. The Grand Trunk, capitalized at £9,500,000, was the largest private corporate undertaking in Canada in the mid-nineteenth century. But because of the shortage of capital in the province and the availability of government financial assistance under the 1849 Guarantee Act and the 1851 Main Trunk Act, the Grand Trunk relied heavily on the Canadian government for support. Government aid for the Grand Trunk dramatically increased the opportunities for Holton and his colleagues as railway-building entrepreneurs.

Critics, however, might justifiably argue that Holton and Galt had personally profited from their affiliation with the Grand Trunk and their connection with government officials such as John Ross, Belleville lawyer and solicitor-general of Canada, who became the first president of the railway. Specifically, critics accused Galt and Holton of using their position as directors of the Grand Trunk to give themselves a potentially lucrative contract. Many stockholders who followed these developments in the newspapers suspected that there must be some substance to the charges. The gossip in Quebec City, Montreal, and Toronto focussed on political favouritism. Predictably, a sombre mood prevailed in the Holton and Galt households. Galt and Holton resigned their directorships after they got the contract, but there was still a feeling that they had abused their power.

Other circumstances, however, brightened the picture. Many Canadians, who favoured the amalgamation of the Toronto & Guelph with the Grand Trunk, not only had confidence in the ability of Holton and his partners to build a quality road from Toronto to Sarnia, but also were pleased with the relationships they had established with British capitalists. The *Montreal Gazette* observed that "it was with much pleasure that we learned that the Toronto & Guelph Company had come into the amalgamation with the unanimous consent of the city of Toronto, which holds a large amount of their stock. We thought that it was hardly possible for the sharp-sighted Upper Canadians not to see the benefits likely to arise from allowing the influx of British capital to come in freely upon this country, especially as there will be no after demand for the return of it."[17]

* * *

Besides recognizing the importance of the support of British capitalists, Holton was sanguine about achieving dramatic results. He also sought to maintain a close personal rapport with his partners. After discussing railway construction with Gzowski and Macpherson in Toronto at the end of March 1853, Holton wrote Galt: "Gzowski I take this occasion to report rises day by day in my estimation. His energy, his tact, his thorough knowledge of every detail of his business, combined with his nice sense of honour, render him in my judgment the most desirable associate we could have chosen."[18] Everyone recognized that Gzowski was a gifted engineer; he knew his business well. Holton was a big believer in defining the responsibilities of each partner, even though he was flexible enough to understand the need for all four to be jacks-of-all-trades from time to time. Gzowski remembered Holton's emphasis on the "principles of division of labour."[19] Holton's idea was to combine a degree of decentralized responsibility with centralized control. At Toronto, Gzowski and Macpherson were thus charged with looking after the day-to-day operations of railway construction – they made this part of the business strong and stable, giving them the feeling that they were running their own show. At the same time, in the Montreal office on St. François Xavier Street Holton and Galt retained enough authority to co-ordinate and control the organization as a whole.

Holton found he could rely on Gzowski and Macpherson's business savvy and offered them encouragement on his visit to Toronto. Energetic and fair-minded, they had the ability to overcome unforeseen and seemingly impossible difficulties of engineering on the road west of Toronto. Despite the rapid progress of the project, nagging problems had appeared. Holton reported to Galt that one difficulty was the engineering staff. While Alexander M. Ross had accepted the job as chief engineer on the entire Grand Trunk, Walter Shanly and his brother, Francis, had become the chief engineer and the principal assistant engineer on the Toronto-Sarnia section, respectively. Prior to the amalgamation, the Shanly brothers had held exactly the same positions on the Toronto & Guelph, and they had as well been directly responsible to the board of that road. They were, however, upset by a change in organization that the Canadian Grand Trunk board had instituted. In revising the structure, the board gave Gzowski & Co. full authority over the whole engineering corps on the Toronto-Sarnia line.[20] One aspect of the altered structure was that Gzowski & Co. agreed to pay for the engineering services on this road.

Holton knew precisely how to cut fat out of the railway construction process. He combed his budget, studying every operation, in quest of prospective cost cutting. He fully appreciated the efforts of the talented Shanly brothers, but as one who stressed cost control he thought that their staff was too large and overpaid. "One of the first things we have to do after the amalgamation," he wrote Galt in early April 1853, "is to reduce the engineering expenses of our Road which have been and are frightfully extravagant. Shanly has had a lot of useless fellows at high salaries thrust upon him by the favouritism of the members of the (Toronto & Guelph) Board."[21]

Prodded by Holton, Walter and Francis Shanly fired six men, including Francis Kerr and T. Steers, in the engineering department in June 1853.[22] The decision to downsize the engineering corps made sense in both the short and long run, but it infuriated the Shanly brothers. Another problem complicated the situation: initially, Gzowski & Co. tried to get away with inferior bridge work, but the Shanlys made the contractors do it right.[23] Holton admired the Shanlys' earlier accomplishment in finding a feasible route to Guelph, and he now helped ease the tensions between them and Gzowski & Co.

Of all the parties involved, Holton was perhaps best positioned to assume a mediator's role. A trusted business associate of Galt, Macpherson, and Gzowski, he was also on good terms with the Shanlys. Holton was a tough bargainer, but he dealt in a friendly way. He never made long speeches, but in man-to-man talks he was remarkable. Holton was not an engineer and never pretended to be one, but he was charged with administering the financial affairs of Gzowski & Co. And he was not reluctant to accept this responsibility, for one of his most regular and responsible traits was sound money management. At the same time, he knew that Gzowski was an expert in engineering, and he stood as one with him, as he did with Galt and Macpherson. The partners' faith in each other, along with their recognition of the abilities of the Shanly brothers, helped them overcome organizational problems.

Throughout his business career, Holton demonstrated his uncanny ability to surround himself with loyal and exceptionally able men and to work with them an atmosphere of joint effort toward a common goal. Once the Shanlys sensed that the structural adjustments did not threaten their own personal positions and their psychological security, they accepted the administrative changes. This led to a better working relationship between them and the contractors. For example, it made it easier for Gzowski & Co. to deal with the problem of precisely where the line between Guelph and Sarnia should be built. In the fall of 1853, Gzowski & Co. and the engineering department's survey crews mapped out a route through Stratford to Sarnia.[24] It was clear that the terrain east of Stratford was much more difficult than that west of the town.

Almost instinctively, Holton tended to think that Stratford, like most other centres along the line, was an agricultural town with a future. He could not predict the consequences of the railway for these communities, but he interacted positively with local ambition. Besides, he could provide entrepreneurial skills to build the line. From the beginning, Holton and his partners took pains to publicize their careful attention to the quality road they were building.

In the twists of history, however, their names are forever associated with the infamous Sarnia land scandal in which they and John A. Macdonald were accused of making excessive profits at the expense of Grand Trunk stockholders and Canadian taxpayers. The Gzowski & Co.

partners purchased lands for the right-of-way from Guelph to Sarnia on their personal accounts and later transferred the land titles to the Grand Trunk at cost, with one exception which tarnished their reputation. Holton, Galt, Macpherson, and Gzowski kept their eyes open for profitable land speculation opportunities on the spot chosen for the line's freight and passenger station at Sarnia, the western terminus. As Holton wrote Galt, "another matter that will require much attention is land for our line & stations. It strikes me that if rightly managed we ought not only to get what we want for nothing but make a good deal of money besides."[25] In his speech at Kingston, John A. Macdonald later recalled that in the summer of 1853,

> I began to think whether I could make a profitable land purchase myself. I went west to different portions of Upper Canada, and, amongst other places, to Sarnia. There I was joined by Holton, and we discovered that Malcolm Cameron had land to sell, and from him we bought 900 acres. We saw that Sarnia was going to be an important point on the Grand Trunk Railway, and we bought a very large tract there.[26]

In all, the four Gzowski & Co. partners and Macdonald, who also acted as their solicitor in this transaction, purchased a 1,084-acre tract, part of which they obtained from the Ordnance Department, for about £3,000. Later, in 1857, when they pulled out of the partnership, Holton and Galt each received £6,000 worth of bonds and other securities from the firm for their interest in this land. Then, in 1858, Macpherson, Gzowski, and Macdonald sold the property to the state-aided Grand Trunk for £30,000.[27]

The profits Holton, Galt, Macpherson, Gzowski, and Macdonald made were excessive, even by the standards of their time. At a meeting of Liverpool stockholders in the Grand Trunk in 1860, Henry C. Chapman, a large stockholder, accused E. T. Blackwell, the railway's managing director, of purchasing the land at an exorbitant price. He revealed that originally the property had been acquired "for a trifling sum."[28] As news of Chapman's revelations spread through Canadian newspapers, the heat and pressure of critical comment focussed on Macdonald, Holton, and Galt. The press reported the land scandal with rumour and innuendo, leaving a great deal to be sorted out by later researchers. Journalists were able to make Holton, Galt, and Macdonald angry, but they could not wring out of them any confessions of wrongdoing. The notoriety nevertheless cost them considerable prestige.

The railway industry in Canada developed haphazardly in the mid-nineteenth century, since it was largely free from regulation. The Sarnia land scandal revealed a major weakness: the existing provincial institutions' inability to regulate such a critical business event as the building of Canada's first trans-provincial railway. In the absence of a tradition of strong government empowering independent experts to define and safeguard the public interest, injustices occurred in the railway industry. Holton and his associates did not have much compunction about making extravagant profits in the Sarnia land deal, thereby helping to give the railway age its aura of speculation and chicanery.

* * *

Holton, however, did not speculate in land on the Toronto-Sarnia line in any sustained way. He concentrated his efforts, not on plundering Grand Trunk stockholders and Canadian taxpayers, but on building a fine road. The scar on Holton's reputation eventually went away, even though Liberal-Conservatives did their best to keep the Sarnia land deal alive in the newspapers. Gzowski & Co.'s great success – constructing an excellent road – crowded out the bad news. In the summer and autumn of 1853, Holton faced the problem of financing the fifty miles of difficult construction between Toronto and Guelph. From the outset, he handled substantial sums. He paid out a great deal of money for rapid construction, pushing the sub-contractors as hard as Gzowski & Co.'s resources would permit. He regularly took money in from the Grand Trunk as Alexander M. Ross, the chief engineer, provided the Canadian board with certified statements showing Gzowski & Co.'s monthly expenditures on the project. For example, in August 1853, Holton received £78,764 in cash for the work that had been done.[29] The cash was of crucial importance to Gzowski & Co.'s strategic plans. Earlier, the firm had been building the Toronto and Guelph in exchange for its stock, but no significant funds could be realized from the sale of the stock. With cash payments from the Grand Trunk, Holton was now furnished with enough capital to meet some of Gzowski & Co.'s obligations.

The next few years were, however, not kind to Gzowski & Co. Almost every problem that could beset a firm plagued the railway builders. Inflation was a constant threat, railway construction materials were in short supply, and new tools were expensive. The firm's costs did not end there – the cost of sub-contractors' services was high. Holton honed his skills in his struggle to survive these difficulties. In August 1853, he obtained a £7,348 loan from the Commercial Bank of the Midland District; a month later he secured £806.[30] Paying out only small dividends to himself and his partners, Holton retained most of Gzowski & Co.'s earnings for development. Even so, the firm remained hard pressed for working capital.

Gzowski & Co. needed money, lots of it, and that is exactly what the firm did not have. Railway building was a lot harder than Holton had ever imagined. As the firm's treasurer, he was in the same straits as other railway builders – he was stymied by a shortage of capital. The chilling knowledge that the Grand Trunk was sliding downhill in the overseas money market first penetrated Gzowski & Co.'s Montreal and Toronto offices in the fall of 1853. No longer was it possible for the railway to raise sufficient funds in London, England, to continue the rapid construction of the road. The contraction of the money market forced down the Grand Trunk's stock and bond prices and reduced sharply the line's earnings. War in the Crimea contributed significantly to disturbing British politics and making investors cautious. Grand Trunk offerings, which back in April had commanded confidence in Britain, now sold poorly.

Thomas Baring and Glyn, Mills were both at once sellers and holders of the railway's securities. Although these two houses continued to serve as the road's London bankers, they complained that the Grand Trunk's 872-mile system from Portland, Maine, to Sarnia had overextended itself and that Canadians had failed to take up the stock allotted to them.[31] Baring was particularly concerned, for he was not only the head of Baring Brothers but also the chairman of the Grand Trunk's London board. Bad planning and inadequate management were partly responsible for the Grand Trunk's financial difficulties. Baring and Glyn, Mills decided to intervene aggressively in the line's affairs to protect their interest in it. In November 1853, the Canadian Grand Trunk board in Quebec City accepted their advice: that Gzowski & Co. limit its expenditure on the Toronto-Sarnia section to £10,000 per month until the following spring.[32] Holton and his partners reluctantly agreed to the restriction. This interim measure was designed to prevent the further weakening of the Grand Trunk and provide the London bankers with enough time to search for a more permanent remedy for the road's lack of capital.

Gzowski & Co.'s goal of completing the Toronto-Sarnia road by mid-1857 slipped away. Holton discovered that the shortage of funds threatened to close the firm down. For him and his partners, the construction slow-down meant larger interest payments to the Grand Trunk. An important term of their contract was that they had to pay interest at the rate of six percent per annum on the capital their firm had actually expended until the works were completed and opened for business. Holton had only to look at the higher interest payments in the future to become alarmed.

But he responded predictably to this new threat. Hoping to realize cost benefits, he and his partners proposed confining construction largely to the line between Toronto and Guelph and deferring a good deal of the work west of Guelph. They knew that once the road would be opened to Guelph, there would be a considerable reduction in interest payments. One of Holton's strengths was his readiness to change, and Gzowski & Co. was centralized enough to respond to alterations with a minimum of effort.

Fortunately for Holton and his partners, the Canadian Grand Trunk board sometimes allowed their firm's monthly expenditures and receipts to exceed the £10,000 limit. The board remained convinced of the tremendous existing demand for the railway, especially at a time when the Canadian economy was booming. Canada still celebrated the good times – the growing import-export trade, the development of agriculture, and the rise of towns and cities – and confidently faced the future.

In early 1854, Holton and his partners vigorously pushed construction between Toronto and Guelph. They made arrangements to provide the line with the necessary bridges, iron rails, steam locomotives, and cars. Upon the opening of navigation, the iron tubular bridging, locomotives, and cars they imported from the Peto firm's Canada Works in Birkenhead near Liverpool, England, began arriving in Toronto on steamboats owned by Holton and Macpherson's former partners, as did the iron rails they imported from the Ebbw Vale Co. in South Wales through an arrangement with the Peto firm.[33] This buyer-supplier, debtor-creditor system interlocked Gzowski & Co. and the Peto firm into a web of mutual interests. At this time, neither the Grand Trunk shops in Toronto and Montreal nor any other shops in Canada were producing sufficient equipment to satisfy Gzowski & Co.'s needs.

Holton and his partners operated effectively in the spring of 1854, the results being enough to show a modest profit. The return on their investment came mainly in one basic form: profits realized on construction. The partners calculated net earnings by subtracting from the contract price of £8,000 per mile recurrent charges incurred by them such as construction materials and equipment, payments to the sub-contractors, and the salaries of the engineering corps.[34]

The building of the railway between Toronto and Guelph and its successful financial management might have come to nothing had Gzowski & Co.'s efforts to work together with both the Canadian and London Grand Trunk boards not also succeeded. There were discordant threads in the firm's relationships with these boards, but its competent performance inspired confidence. Holton and his partners wanted to have the £10,000 monthly expenditure restriction lifted so that they could increase significantly the pace of construction, and in March 1854, Galt crossed the Atlantic to discuss the matter with the London board.[35] From Chairman

Thomas Baring, he learned that the sales of the Grand Trunk's bonds and stocks had continued to prove disappointing. The lack of demand for the road's securities owed much to its low credit rating among British investors. Concerned about the Grand Trunk's large debt and its poor credit standing, Baring insisted that it was essential to cut costs by deferring construction west of Stratford. But he was also open to suggestions for pushing ahead more rapidly with the work between Stratford and Toronto.

Persuaded that the opening of the Toronto-Stratford section at an early date would be in the best interests of both the contractors and the railway, Galt, with the London and Canadian boards' concurrence as well as with the approval of Francis Hincks, devised a plan intended to reduce Gzowski & Co.'s risks and, at the same time, improve the Grand Trunk's credit. The proposal, put into effect in June 1854 by the action of the two boards and an amendment to the Grand Trunk charter in the Canadian legislature, dropped the £10,000 monthly expenditure restriction, postponed the building of the line between Stratford and Sarnia, and allowed Gzowski & Co. to tackle aggressively the eighty-eight miles of construction between Toronto and Stratford, not at the original price of £8,000 per mile but at the new price of £10,192 per mile to bolster the firm's receipts on the most difficult part of the Toronto-Sarnia line.[36] In the same month, under Gzowski & Co.'s sub-contractors, an army of 1,930 workers and 240 horses forged ahead on the Toronto-Stratford section of the road.[37]

As a railway builder, Holton had a trait that was found in many successful entrepreneurs. Although he was a tough businessman, he willingly recognized the achievements of his associates. More than satisfied with the way that Galt had handled the arrangements with the London board, already in April 1854 Holton had nothing but praise for his partner. "You have opened your negotiation or rather prepared the ground for it with consummate address," he told Galt, "guarding every point and leaving nothing to suggest or comment upon." Of the Canadian premier, who had indicated that he favoured Galt's plan, Holton wrote: "I am very glad that Hincks seized your idea so readily." Holton, a tireless letter writer, was also happy to see that Galt while in London was keeping up a detailed correspondence with him about the construction project. "If your present letter may be taken as a specimen," Holton added, "you need not apprehend any complaining of not being posted up this year, nor indeed in any case, for I think we know each other better now."[38]

* * *

Whatever Holton's faults, niggardliness in expressing affection was not one of them. Alexander Galt's children found in Holton great warmth.

When Galt went to London, he took his wife with him, leaving their children with relatives in Montreal. Holton often asked how the children were doing and sometimes dropped by to see them. "I saw your children this morning," Holton wrote Galt. "They are both perfectly well. Elliott desired me to tell you he was well, had been a good boy, and had got a carriage in which he draws baby. Master Alexander is a brave boy, the fattest, chubbiest little fellow I have seen for many a day. He promises to be a perfect *counterfeit presentment* of his illustrious sire."[39]

Holton helped run Gzowski & Co. with a sense of vitality and dynamism that infected the entire company. As a way of maintaining morale and keeping the lines of communication open within the firm, he invariably wrote informative letters to all his partners, creating a smooth-running organization. For instance, having exchanged views with Gzowski as well as with Robert Stephenson, chief engineer of the Victoria Bridge, on importing construction materials, Holton provided Galt with precise information on shipping iron tubular bridge parts from the Peto firm's Canada Works in Birkenhead to the Toronto-Stratford line.[40]

Luther Holton was not one to minimize the significance of the iron tubular bridges required for the road between Toronto and Stratford. Before the Grand Trunk amalgamation, Walter and Francis Shanly had begun building the bridges from stone and timber. But with the encouragement and financial support of the Peto firm, Holton and his partners instructed the Shanly brothers to replace the unfinished wooden structures with the iron tubular bridges produced at the Canada Works in Birkenhead.[41] The new design called for a bridge of stone or brick piers capped by an iron tubular superstructure anchored at each end with a stone abutment. Despite the Shanlys' initial opposition to the new design, Holton and his partners proceeded with the construction of the tubular bridges.

Quick to recognize the value of innovative technology, Holton and his associates seized upon the iron tubular bridge invented by Robert Stephenson to build high-quality tubular bridges across streams on the Toronto-Stratford line such as the Credit, Humber, Grand, and Speed rivers. The Gzowski & Co. partners, together with the Shanly brothers, applied this new technology to the road as rapidly and innovatively as possible. Holton's vision of innovation was certainly reinforced by that of his associates and the principal salaried engineers. While the builders of the Great Western Railway stuck to a suspension bridge over the Niagara gorge, Gzowski & Co. challenged them with the tubular system, which proved more substantial, safer, less expensive, and more permanent.[42] While Holton and his partners were preoccupied with the construction of the tubular bridges on the Toronto-Stratford line, as a citizen of Montreal, he also carefully watched Stephenson's own successful work on the tubular Victoria Bridge. This undoubtedly helped persuade Holton of the rightness of the tubular system.

But in helping to manage this innovative technological experiment, Holton encountered difficulties. In early 1854, for instance, to his dismay he discovered that John Worthington & Co., the sub-contractor for the Humber Bridge, had failed to make a good job of the masonry on the piers. The piers cried out for extensive changes. Holton and his associates concluded that the piers would have to be rebuilt if the bridge was to become functional.[43] John Worthington & Co. complied – the changes were not long in coming. While Holton sometimes had to remind the sub-contractors about the need for excellent workmanship, his instincts were conciliatory toward them, trying to motivate them in constructive ways.

* * *

Their methods of ensuring quality construction involved an almost perfect blending of the skills and personalities of Holton and his partners. Together, they created and maintained a management system that combined a strong personal touch with a set of precise guidelines. From time to time, the Gzowski & Co. associates involved themselves personally in virtually every aspect of their firm's management. Like his partners, Holton often travelled to the construction site to inspect the railway and judge whether it was up to the firm's standards. By July 1854, the masonry on the Humber Bridge was in good shape if still incomplete. But the adoption of the iron tubular system, which required long months and years of careful work, had contributed to slowing down construction on the Toronto-Stratford line.[44] As yet only thirty-five percent of the permanent materials such as cross-ties, iron rails, and fencing that were required had reached the construction site.[45] Additional money was needed to purchase these materials, and this was again in short supply.

As Gzowski & Co.'s treasurer, Holton was confronted by pressing needs for working capital to cover the costs of the large railway construction job. While he sought funding for building and equipping the Toronto-Stratford line, the sub-contractors continued to work on the road. Holton's main concern at this time was that funds for Grand Trunk construction were becoming very difficult to obtain, both in Canada and abroad. The Grand Trunk continued to rely on stock and bond financing, but the railway's weakness was reflected in the low prices of its stocks and bonds. In the London money market, the long decline in the Grand Trunk's securities from the summer of 1853 to the fall of 1854 gradually undermined the confidence of the investing public. As the year 1854 drew to its end, the railway's supply of capital became extremely scarce. The Grand Trunk leaders were unprepared for the financial difficulties that arose from the increasing scarcity of capital. With its finances so strained, the railway's credit was not good enough to sustain the sale of new securities at reasonable prices. The London and Canadian boards of the railway, together with the Peto firm, which had purchased large lots of the road's securities, decided not to sell additional Grand Trunk stocks and bonds before 1856-57.[46] Temporarily, the Grand Trunk sought to finance construction with capital that might come from further instalments on stocks and bonds that it had earlier allotted for public subscription, and on the bond subsidy from the province of Canada. But low investor interest in these offerings provided the Grand Trunk with only relatively small amounts of capital.

It was therefore necessary for Holton and his partners to slow construction on the Toronto-Stratford line, reduce expenses, and use earnings to pay interest and bills that could not be put off. Holton, no less than his associates, suffered repeated disappointments in the railway-building business. This period of stress in his business career coincided with an opportunity to go into politics. The highly political nature of the railway business helped increase Holton's willingness to seek a seat in the Canadian legislative assembly in Quebec City. Like some other entrepreneurs of the day, he stood ready to combine personal business with the public's.

* * *

The general election in July 1854 meant politics for him, preferably on the side of the Liberals, who, however, had not been notably successful provincially. Holton watched with some anxiety the political manoeuvrings in Montreal, a riding with three seats in the assembly. The Francis Hincks–A. N. Morin Reform government promised to promote railway development. This placed Holton, at least nominally, in the Reform camp. But although he had previously supported Louis LaFontaine, founder of the Reform party in Lower Canada, he could not identify with the present Lower Canadian Reformers' reluctance to develop the vital and abiding tradition and practice of self-government to embrace popular sovereignty. For a while, the situation in Montreal encouraged Holton to think that he could play both sides of the political street, remaining a Reformer while endearing himself to the Liberals. This earned him the reputation of an unsavory political manipulator prepared to trample on principle. He disappointed his friends, especially John Young, a Montreal merchant and Liberal who had earlier been one of his major customers in the forwarding trade. Young now reminded Holton about something he was well aware of: the year before, Francis Hincks as premier and finance minister had brought himself into disrepute with corruption, improperly using his influence to turn a handsome profit for himself through the purchase of Ontario, Simcoe and Huron Railway bonds.[47] When Young threatened to withdraw his important support from Holton unless he broke with Hincks, he agreed to stand as a Liberal and fight the government, but he did not attack Hincks for corruption in his campaign.[48] Behind Holton's silence on the issue of corruption lay political calculation. He took pains to keep his arguments positive, an approach he felt would secure for him many votes.

John Young. Courtesy of the National Archives of Canada.

Holton now committed himself fully to the new Liberal party in Lower Canada led by Antoine A. Dorion, a Montreal lawyer, often labelled a *rouge*, as were his French-Canadian followers. Like Holton, Dorion was fluent in English and in French. As in business, in politics Holton's bilingualism was a significant asset. He was playing a critically important part as a link between the English and French interests in the Montreal business community. He published his first election address to the Montreal electors in the *Montreal Herald*, *Le Pays*, the *Montreal Gazette*, and *La Minerve*. In doing so, he offered himself to them as a Liberal in opposition to the government. He stressed among other things the importance of "the early completion of the projected lines of railway centring" in Montreal.[49] He also emphasized the need for the Canadian legislature to ratify the recently negotiated Reciprocity Treaty, which provided for the reciprocal free admission of natural products of the United States and British North America, such as grain, lumber, livestock, and fish. On these issues, Holton spoke for the Montreal business community. Forward- and outward-looking, its businessmen eagerly sought rail connections and trade with the interior and the United States. Holton as well pledged to support any move to replace the existing narrow provincial franchise with a broader one and, in doing so, expressed his idea of how a free people should govern themselves.

Catapulting himself deeper into politics, Holton conducted a handshaking campaign, pausing to greet and talk with voters in many parts of Montreal, his sense of humour helping him to get through some situations in which the atmosphere became hostile. Young and Dorion, the other two Liberal candidates whose views were similar to Holton's, vigorously campaigned for him, as did the *rouge Le Pays* and the influential Liberal *Montreal Herald* and its Scottish-born editor David Kinnear, who was well connected to the business community.[50] J. L. Beaudry and

W. Bristow emerged as the two government candidates, and W. Badgley as the Conservative candidate. The campaign was a long and strenuous one, made all the more exhausting by the extreme summer heat and the worry about cholera, which claimed the lives of over one thousand people in the city during the election.

The political meetings at which Holton addressed his audiences were rough-and-tumble forums, rowdy and exciting. A favourite urban entertainment, they attracted hundreds of local people. This was Canadian democracy, Montreal democracy, at its basic level, the electors seeing and

Antoine A. Dorion. Courtesy of the National Archives of Canada.

hearing the candidates and their advocates face to face. On the hustings in the Haymarket Square, Holton boldly stated his views, answered his opponents, and depended on what he considered a careful examination of the issues. For instance, railway expansion, particularly that west of Montreal, still had his ardent support. When an opponent asked him "whether he had not after the dissolution [of parliament] offered his services to the government and canvassed some part of the city in their interest," Holton emphatically replied, "no!"[51] No one challenged his answer. But earlier, an observer had reported that "no person has any faith in Holton's sudden conversion."[52] There was, however, no ambiguity about his position now. He had gained personal satisfaction in being among other Liberals, noting their respect for his ideas and taking pride in being chosen by them as a candidate.

But Luther Holton and several other candidates, Liberal and Conservative, were troubled by the ever-present threat of violence. Montrealers were not known for their commitment to changing politicians and governments quietly and peacefully. Representing Holton, David Kinnear joined the representatives of other candidates at O'Neill's Metropolitan Saloon to promise that he would work to secure "free and uninterrupted voting during the present election" and that he would "not sanction the opening of houses of entertainment for voters, nor the hiring of men ... to intimidate or coerce voters, or influence the election by any species of violence."[53] To help keep the peace, sheriff John Boston immediately recruited 200 special constables for the election.

This was the era of open voting, when every vote was known and cheered or jeered, and when the electoral process itself was often put at risk by men who were hired to intimidate voters with the politics of fear. But at the end of the campaign, the *Globe's* Montreal correspondent reported that Montreal "witnessed the close of the most peaceably contested election that can be remembered in this city by its oldest inhabitant."[54] The election returns were announced on 28 July by the sheriff in the Haymarket Square. Holton received 1,571 votes – the second-highest number of any candidate – and was elected.[55] So were Dorion and Young, both of whom easily edged out the government and Conservative contenders. Holton and the other Liberals began their celebrations.

But across Canada, the election results confirmed deep divisions among the electors. Hincks and Morin were the constitutionally elected premiers, but they were not indisputably in control of things – the Reform victory was largely sectional. Morin carried a comfortable majority of the ridings in Canada East. By contrast, Hincks won considerably less than half the ridings in Canada West. Further clouding the mandate was the new strength of the Liberals in the eastern section.

* * *

In this uncertain political climate, Holton began to prepare for his first appearance at the Canadian parliament in Quebec City. Montrealers had deprived themselves of the capital in 1849 by burning the parliament buildings. Thereafter, to satisfy both Upper and Lower Canadians, the capital alternated between Toronto and Quebec City. Toronto served as the seat of government from the spring of 1850 to the summer of 1852, at which time Quebec City became its home.

As Holton readied himself for his new job in Canada's capital, he received what appeared on the surface to be welcome news from the Canadian board of the Grand Trunk in Quebec City. Within himself, his political career and his business life were already intertwined. The board informed him that it would soon pay Gzowski & Co. for its work on the Toronto-Stratford line for the month of July 1854. But there was cause for real concern, because it was not yet clear when the money would come. Holton immediately gathered more information from Benjamin Holmes, a Montrealer who was vice-president of the Grand Trunk and, at the same time, passed on what he knew about the railway's finances to his partner Alexander Galt, who had been re-elected as a Liberal in Sherbrooke.[56] Holton and Holmes had been friends from back in the 1840s, when Holton's steamboat enterprise had valued Holmes's produce firm as one of its most important customers. Now as treasurer of Gzowski & Co. and as an assemblyman, Holton looked forward to his term in parliament, partly because it would allow him quickly to see Holmes and the other Grand Trunk directors in their Quebec City office whenever he had to discuss an urgent matter about railway construction.

But first, Luther Holton needed to confer with his partners Gzowski and Macpherson in Toronto and see for himself the progress they were making at the works on the Toronto-Stratford line. Holton accordingly made arrangements for a steamboat trip to Toronto in mid-August 1854. But he did not go alone. Instead, he took his wife Eliza with him. While they were gone, Eliza's sister Sophronia, who was living with them in Montreal, looked after their children: Mary, Edward, and Amelia. On their way, Luther and Eliza got off the boat at Brockville and travelled by wagon to Soperton to visit his mother Anner Stafford, a widow whose second husband Cleveland Stafford had died four years earlier. A general merchant, he had left her in comfortable circumstances.[57] Eliza and Luther shared an affectionate reunion with his mother in her home.

The next stop on Luther and Eliza's journey by steamboat was Kingston, where Luther discussed construction on the Toronto-Stratford line with John Ross, the Grand Trunk's president and now also attorney-general for Canada West in the Hincks-Morin government. Holton predicted that the government would soon fall and be replaced by a Reform-Conservative coalition – he felt that the new cabinet would include Ross and John A. Macdonald. So Holton also took the occasion to visit Macdonald in Kingston in order "to ascertain something of" his "views."[58]

Finally, Luther and Eliza boarded a steamboat in Kingston and travelled to the Toronto harbour, before taking a carriage to ride to Gzowski & Co.'s office on Church Street and to the welcoming hands of David Macpherson and Casimir Gzowski. There was an anxious discussion about financing construction on the Toronto-Stratford line, and Holton seized the opportunity to visit the construction site. The future looked grim in part because the Grand Trunk was hobbled by its lack of financial power. Holton, Gzowski, and Macpherson nevertheless tried to put the best possible face on things, their worry mixed with hopes that the future would bring their firm a less bleak outlook than the one it now faced.

* * *

Shortly after Luther and Eliza returned to Montreal, Luther left for Quebec City. Holton's first session as a Canadian provincial legislator (5 September 1854 to 30 May 1855) was a memorable one. He was faithful in his attendance, participated in the debates on the floor of the house, and served on several committees, including the influential public accounts committee. Like most of the 129 other assemblymen, Holton stayed at one of the hotels in Quebec City, which bore names like "Russell's."[59] The legislative assemblyhouse, where the assemblymen met, was the public music hall, hastily altered after fire had destroyed an earlier capital in the city.[60] The assembly met in an attractive room, well ventilated, but the inadequate acoustics made it difficult for most members to make themselves distinctly heard.[61]

Holton had skills that might serve Canada and the Liberal party well. Even in fighting against the government, he worked with political factions in the assembly. He was certainly prepared for such co-operation. He showed leadership qualities at a time when parties provided little unity and direction for government action. Partly as a result of Holton's efforts, L. V. Sicotte was the successful candidate for speaker of the assembly.[62] Lacking the necessary support to carry on, the Hincks-Morin Reform government resigned. Along with the other Lower Canadian Liberals, including Antoine Dorion and Galt, and some influential Upper Canadian Liberals such as George Brown, editor of the powerful Toronto *Globe*, Holton opposed the new government formed by Allan MacNab and A. N. Morin, who had the backing of a large, new Liberal-Conservative coalition made up of Reformers and Conservatives from Upper and Lower Canada.

But there was a deeper level to Holton's political skills than his ability to manoeuvre and to balance factions – he had other qualities as well. He had an ego, a sense of self and security that permitted him to converse and negotiate with friends and political enemies. Holton's ego arose from self-knowledge and self-confidence. Unlike some of his Liberal friends, he openly defended the new government's pro-Grand Trunk policy, for it benefited Gzowski & Co. and Montreal. In choosing John Ross and John A. Macdonald as members of the new cabinet, MacNab and Morin recognized among other things the importance of the Grand Trunk. Macdonald became attorney-general of Upper Canada, and Ross entered the cabinet as speaker of the legislative council. Holton could also discuss with George Brown, whom he had known since the mid-1840s, the possibility of an alliance between the Lower and Upper Canadian Liberals in the future, but at this time there was no widespread interest in such an idea.[63] Holton's temperament and frame of mind nevertheless had immediate practical results: it helped keep party clashes within bounds, shaping common purpose and unity. Free trade with the United States was a source of intense interest throughout Canada, and on 19 September 1854 Holton joined the majority of the assemblymen in approving the Reciprocity Treaty.

Membership in the Lower Canadian Liberal party meant more than sectional issues to Holton. He felt that the party was founded on principles in which he firmly believed. To him, it reflected the promise of Canadian life in the united province in which Lower and Upper Canadians could work together to build a strong union. "A friend of the union," is the way in which Holton described himself.[64] Economically, the party stood for growth, for progress, for development. Its economic policy aimed at linking the trade of Lower Canada with the commerce of Upper Canada, so that the province's economy would become a large interconnected web of advance. This was a vision that appealed to young men who wanted to make something of themselves.

In return for his loyalty to the Lower Canadian Liberal party, Holton expected recognition, and he received this from Antoine Dorion, leader of the Lower Canadian Liberal Opposition in the assembly. For instance, Dorion recognized Holton as the party's financial expert in this first session of the fifth parliament of the Canadian union.[65] Holton hoped to offer constructive criticism of government finance. Enthusiastically, he threw himself into the work of examining the financial business in the assembly, establishing a conspicuous record for thoughtful comment. If he was new to Quebec City, so were many other elected representatives. Like any other freshman assemblyman, Holton was fairly brief when he first gained the floor to make some remarks.

In delivering his maiden speech in the house on 20 October 1854, Holton proved impressive – no destructive critic, but well-spoken, firm, and informed. He moved "that it is inexpedient to continue the present system of depositing all public money as received in one bank." He declared that "the inconvenience which merchants are exposed to at this time by the plan of the government depositing all the public money in the Bank of Upper Canada" was obvious.[66] Holton's goal was to correct a situation in which import merchants were at a disadvantage. Under the existing system, they usually borrowed the large amounts of money needed to pay customs duties from their local commercial banks, especially when payments on the huge spring importations were due, and then paid the duties in bank notes to the government's fiscal agent, the Bank of Upper Canada. The banks that issued these notes were immediately required to redeem them in specie, and the greater the volume of imports the greater the flow of specie from these banks to the Bank of Upper Canada. The resulting shortage of specie in the other banks led to a severe contraction of credit, making it extremely difficult for them to supply the importers with funds. All this was part and parcel of the Canadian past. To reform the system, Holton urged the MacNab–Morin government to allow the other banks, along with the Bank of Upper Canada, to receive for deposit a portion of the customs duties to make it easier for them to extend credit to the importers. Because the floating deposits of the government in the Bank of Upper Canada, which included the customs money, bore no interest under the existing system, Holton also proposed that any bank that held floating public deposits should pay interest at a rate of three percent on such funds to the government, so as to augment its income, most of which came from customs duties.

An important feature of Holton's speech was that it cut across all political lines, so that Liberals and Conservatives alike paid tribute to the assemblyman. "This gentleman," observed the Conservative *Montreal Gazette*, "did very well. Without any verbiage or waste of time, he clearly and succinctly explained to the house the grounds on which he acted; and he was listened to with attention."[67]

But Holton was hardly praised for his effort by Francis Hincks, who was still frustrated by memories of the recent defeat of his ministry. Before the house had a chance to debate Holton's motion, Hincks moved in amendment to it that a select committee be created to examine the impact of the government's bank policy on the commercial interests of Canada. Pleased with Holton's call for reform, Dorion defended him during the debate on the amendment. When the amendment passed without a division, Holton withdrew his motion. The committee consisted of three government supporters and two Opposition Liberals from Lower Canada, one of whom was Holton. He was acutely conscious that the Liberals were in a minority position in the committee, but he worked intently on shaping policy in the assembly. From witnesses – from the Commercial Bank of the Midland District, the Bank of Upper Canada, the Bank of British North America, and the Canadian receiver-general's office – came evidence that threw light on the subject. But the committee was so divided that it simply submitted the information to the house without comment.[68] In the MacNab–Morin government nobody at first paid much attention to the evidence that suggested that, while the continuation of a single government banker was best for the public service, a provincial multi-banking agency might benefit the mercantile community. Consequently, the Bank of Upper Canada remained the sole government bank. In the end, however, the ministry responded to Holton's original proposal by requiring all customs officials to accept in payment of duties from importers bonds issued by the government through the various commercial banks.[69] For the use of these bonds, which were payable at thirty or sixty days, the banks were required to pay the government three percent interest. This new approach not only produced additional revenue for the province, but also gave the banks a reasonable amount of time to meet the bonds and increased their capacity to lend money to importers faced with duty payments.

As the session progressed, Holton grew more at home in the assembly. His skill in debating steadily improved, and his colleagues, impressed by his mastery of parliamentary procedure and the technical language of legislation, started asking him to draft bills for the business community. He became more active in the debates, often using material drawn from his wide reading in British history and appealing to the sympathies of those who like himself admired figures such as Sir Robert Peel.[70] Capital expansion in banks, Holton told himself, would help satisfy the needs of businessmen. He introduced bills to increase the capital stock of the Bank of Montreal, the Commercial Bank of the Midland District, the City Bank in Montreal, and the Bank of Upper Canada. Recognizing that Holton had based himself on the broadest common denominator and had steered clear of partisanship, parliament co-operated by authorizing these capital stock expansions, thereby spurring the growth of the Canadian economy.

* * *

Holton needed the success in parliament to balance the trouble in his business life. On the surface, there were few signs of problems at Gzowski & Co. – construction on the Toronto-Stratford line continued. But behind the railway construction activity stirred the turbulence of a company short of working capital. Holton and his partners agonized over the worsening state of affairs. Once again, as had happened often before in his life, Holton stood to lose everything. Hoping to secure additional funds at this anxious time, in September 1854, he visited Grand Trunk president John Ross in his Quebec City office. For the work Gzowski & Co. had completed in August, it was entitled to receive a payment of £59,884 in cash. But Ross could come up with only £20,000 in cash, and the remainder he promised to pay over a specified period. But the Grand Trunk continued to weaken financially. When Holton went to see Ross in January 1855, the Grand Trunk president could not produce any cash. All he could do was to offer to make a mix of payments to Holton and his partners in the future: 40 percent in cash and 60 percent in Grand Trunk notes payable in six months.[71] But the depreciation of these notes added to the contractors' complications. Holton was resourceful, however. He arranged for loans from the Commercial Bank of the Midland District. Despite the frustrations of this winter season, Holton and his associates made slow but certain progress towards the completion of the Toronto-Stratford line.

The Toronto-Stratford line remained at the heart of their operations, but back in November 1853, Holton and his partners had diversified by entering into a contract with the City of Toronto to build the esplanade along the city's harbourfront for £140,000. This, however, was another financial headache. On this job, an unexpected event helped to produce disaster. There was a dispute between the contractors and the city over the terms of the contract and, in the spring of 1855, after they had completed a substantial part of the project, the city dismissed them and cancelled the contract. Allegations that the contractors had profited at the expense of the city, published in local newspapers, provoked an outcry from a shocked public. But by 1856, Holton and his partners and the Grand Trunk had assumed the entire burden of completing the Toronto esplanade.[72] People in the city were by no means unanimously happy, but the majority accepted the promise of an improved harbourfront.

By May 1855, the financial affairs of Holton and his partners had reached a critical stage. The high noon of investor optimism was over and railway stock prices in North America had declined – those of the Port Huron & Lake Michigan Railroad, the Montreal & Vermont Junction Railway, and the Woodstock & Lake Erie Railway and Harbour Company even more than some others. It also was an era when railways became favourite whipping boys for politicians, and the general public came to see the industry as a greedy monopolistic titan. All this affected Luther Holton's business life. In 1853, in Michigan, Holton and his partners had secured the contract to build the Port Huron & Lake Michigan Railroad, a line that was to link Port Huron at the foot of Lake Huron with Grand Haven on Lake Michigan.[73] All building on this road was, however, now suspended. Gzowski & Co. had contracted with the Montreal & Vermont Junction Railway, linking Montreal and Highgate, Vermont, to build that 41-mile road, but construction there now stopped as well.[74] Finally, all building ceased at this time on the Woodstock & Lake Erie Railway and Harbour Company road in Upper Canada, a line that Luther Holton and his partner Samuel Zimmerman of Niagara Falls had started to construct.[75]

So the Toronto-Stratford line continued to have the biggest place in Holton's career – it also remained at the centre of Gzowski & Co.'s operations. In June 1855, the needs of the firm were met by another bond subsidy from the Canadian legislature for the Grand Trunk, which Luther Holton, Alexander Galt, and John Ross helped secure in the face of a great deal of opposition.[76] The legislature permitted the Grand Trunk to issue £900,000 of six percent sterling bonds guaranteed by the province of Canada. From the outset, Holton and Galt saw the subsidy as a key to their firm's success. They wanted to complete the construction of the Toronto-Stratford line quickly, and they could not do so without additional support from the province. They dealt with the matter of the subsidy openly. If it meant the prospect of personal gain, it also promised to allow them to build a road that would open a large part of Upper Canada to settlement. The subsidy was, in fact, of province-wide importance. Ross turned to Thomas Baring and George Glyn in London, England, to raise the funds.[77]

Baring and Glyn at once offered the new provincially guaranteed Grand Trunk bonds in the London money market. The market at last accelerated, and the sales went well. At the time that these London bankers began offering this loan, the Grand Trunk had received a total of £2,898,427 from the sale of its stocks and bonds and had paid the Peto firm and Gzowski & Co. £2,888,218, leaving only £10,209 in its treasury.[78] The railway obviously very much needed the proceeds from the new bond sale to continue construction. Despite the new inflow of cash, the Grand Trunk's finances remained tight. But the railway was now in a somewhat better position to pay Holton and his partners.

The twelve months after the Grand Trunk's receipt of the June 1855 bond subsidy were hectic ones for Holton and his associates. But reflecting the railway's difficult financial position, they were required to accept payment for their work on the Toronto-Stratford line one-half in cash, and one-half in the railway's bonds and stocks. To ease the cash shortage still further, Holton and his partners agreed to accept sixty-day notes. In the autumn of 1855, they energetically pushed construction, spending about £30,000 per month.[79]

In the legislative assembly, as in Gzowski & Co., Holton was extremely active. He was determined that the government should be run effectively, even if he had to tear the old system apart and then put it back together in a new, hopefully more efficient form. In the second session of parliament, which lasted from 15 February to 1 July 1856, Holton was the proverbial man in a hurry, bursting with ideas, eager to plunge into important work. With the provincial capital now in Toronto, the city to which it had returned during the fall of 1855, he found himself in recently renovated parliament buildings and fairly close to the railway construction site. The assembly met in a well-furnished but poorly ventilated room, where members sat one or two to a desk.[80]

The impact of Luther Holton's work in the assembly extended far beyond this session. As a principal member of the public accounts committee, he sounded a theme that would influence public finance for a long time. He urged the reorganization of the handling of public funds throughout all government departments, with a view to controlling and reducing the expenditures of the provincial government. As an expression of a single compelling logic, his idea of reforming public accounts left responsible assemblymen fairly breathless with the thrill of a new day dawning. Holton was not alone in advocating reform; so did John Young, and especially John Langton, the auditor-general, whom Holton referred to "as one of the ablest and most efficient officers in the public service."[81] But to the problem of sloppy bookkeeping that prevailed in virtually every government department, Holton brought a strategy, a readiness to employ better methods to make public finance more efficient. Although his call for changes in the management of public money met with considerable resistance in 1856, eventually the Canadian parliament grew interested in his ideas and tried to apply them.

Through improvements in efficiency in their railway building firm, Holton and his partners had sought to reduce costs in construction. They succeeded, but they recognized that the Grand Trunk needed more public funds to pay their enterprise for its work on the Toronto-Stratford line. Holton clearly was still enthusiastic about the project, but he was quick to appreciate that legislators controlled the purse strings for subsidies to railways. He faced the formidable problem of strong opposition to further government financing of the Grand Trunk. But he worked in harness with Galt, publicly lobbying Lower Canadian Liberals and especially the Liberal-Conservative majority to back the railway. Holton and Galt relied on John A. Macdonald for support, and they left their mark on the law the Canadian legislature passed in June 1856 authorizing a bond subsidy of £2,000,000 for the huge corporation.[82]

With payments for construction on the way, Holton and his associates drove ahead the rails on the Toronto-Stratford line. The long-awaited opening of the first fifty miles to Guelph took place on Saturday, 14 June 1856. A special train, with five cars carrying railway officials, politicians, and important women and men from urban centres served by the line, left the Grand Trunk station at the Queen's Wharf in Toronto at one P.M. to inspect the fruits of the labours of Gzowski & Co. "On reaching the magnificent bridge which spans the Credit," wrote the reporter for the *Toronto Leader*, "the train stopped, and nearly the whole party walked down a very long flight of stairs to the bank of the river, to make a closer inspection of this piece of workmanship."[83] Even experienced railway men were awed at the human engineering that it symbolized. The reporter noted that "nothing particular occurred on the homeward trip" from Guelph, except that "in some cars singing was kept up all the way."[84] Grand Trunk officers toiled incessantly to attract business, and three days later the train

C. S. Gzowski & Co. completed the Grand Trunk Railway of Canada iron tubular bridge over the Credit River in 1856, shown here in a mid-twentieth century photograph. Courtesy of the Canadian National Railways Archives and the Engineering Institute of Canada.

carried nearly 150 passengers from Guelph to Toronto. With conveniently scheduled Grand Trunk trains on the Toronto-Guelph run, patrons were quick to appreciate the advantages of railway travel. All along the route, transportation sped up. Mails that had spent about two days in transit by stagecoach now arrived overnight.

The opening stimulated Holton and his partners to redouble their efforts to finish the road to Stratford. Tracks were pushed ahead rapidly and less than three months later, on 3 September 1856, they opened the Grand Trunk to Stratford, thirty-eight miles west of Guelph.[85] Thus, after working

Grand Trunk Railway of Canada. From the *Canadian Illustrated News*, 1871. The Grand Trunk's capacity to haul freight rapidly was extremely important, but it was especially the railway's passenger service that captured the Canadian public's imagination in the mid-1850s.

tirelessly for almost four years, they had opened eighty-eight miles for business. In the same year, the British firm Peto, Brassey, Jackson, and Betts finally completed the construction work on the 333-mile Grand Trunk line between Montreal and Toronto.

* * *

Technology had spoken: the sheer physical presence of hundreds of miles of railway. There was no need now to discuss, negotiate, or argue. Like many other Canadians, Holton saw the Grand Trunk as a rational railway network operating for the benefit of Upper and Lower Canada, Toronto, Montreal, and numerous other communities. In Montreal, where he had earned much respect as builder of the Toronto-Stratford line and member of parliament for Montreal as well as a reputation for doing excellent work as president of the Montreal Board of Trade since his election to that position in April 1856, the railway provided superb publicity for him. On 12 and 13 November of that year, Holton played a leading part in Montreal's celebration of the completion of the Grand Trunk between Montreal and Toronto. It was a grand affair and, besides serving on the committee that for this memorable occasion prepared and published *Montreal in 1856* (a 51-page pamphlet that described the rise of the city as an industrial centre in the railway age), Holton helped organize the event.[86]

There was much organization work, setting up the needed special facilities so that participants from Montreal and from outside the city could enjoy the celebration. The key, Holton knew, was co-ordination, for the event involved several phases. The preparations got off to a good start in September, as Holton as president of the Montreal Board of Trade helped arrange a public meeting at the Merchants Exchange to appeal to citizens for their support.[87] The outpouring of private funds to finance the

View of the Grand Trunk Railway of Canada at Point St. Charles, Montreal. From the *Canadian Illustrated News*, 1869-1870. In the mid-1850s Montreal, Canada's largest city, thundered on towards becoming the province's biggest railway centre.

celebration was impressive. In mid-October, Holton became a member of the executive committee charged with the responsibility of overseeing the event and inviting important people to participate. Trains filled to capacity brought thousands of guests from Lower and Upper Canada, Maine, Massachusetts, New York, and other states in the American Republic to the city.[88]

Part of Holton's job was to meet many of these guests and to assist them, most importantly to welcome Edward Kent, Harvard College graduate, lawyer, and ex-governor of Maine, who stayed in his home.[89] On 12 November, Holton joined the colourful procession that began in the Commissioners Square and moved along Great St. James Street through the city, finally ending where it started. Reflecting the growing importance of the industrial sector of Montreal's economy, the procession included individual horse-drawn cars carrying the products of manufacturers such as Redpath's Canada Sugar Refinery, the India Rubber Company, the St. Lawrence Cotton Mills, and the Montreal Nail Works.[90] In the late afternoon, at the specially prepared banquet hall in the Grand Trunk buildings at Point St. Charles, to which 4,000 guests came, Holton took a seat at the head table for a splendid dinner. But this was just the beginning. The next day, Holton worked at a furious pace to help organize an immense excursion to visit the piers of the unfinished Victoria Bridge and the wheelhouse for the opening of the city's new water works.[91]

* * *

Luther Holton also poured prodigious effort into his tasks in parliament, which continued to meet in Toronto. In the session that began on 26 February and ended on 10 June 1857, he again served on the public accounts committee, addressed the problems and needs of merchants and other people in trouble, and backed Antoine Dorion fully in his attempt to build up the fledgling Lower Canadian Liberal party.

On the floor of the assembly, Holton participated in the debates freely. By now one of the more experienced members, he sought among other things to impose rationality on business life. His involvements in issues of Canadian society were positive – he did a great deal for civil rights and liberty. For instance, in March, he supported a bill introduced by Dorion to improve the law pertaining to insolvent debtors in Upper Canada.[92] Providing for the repeal of the old Insolvent Debtor's Act of Upper Canada, the bill was designed to give adequate protection to both debtors and creditors in the Upper Canadian section of the union. Holton considered one aspect of the old regime an outrage; recently, under the old law, some women in Hamilton had been imprisoned for debt, and this was enough for him to cry out for its abolition. The measure was passed without a division. At the same time, Holton, along with Dorion and John A. Macdonald, was assigned to a select committee to consider the state of the law of bankruptcy and insolvency for the province as a whole.[93] Today's idea of bankruptcy protection had not entered Canadian consciousness in the 1850s, but Holton wanted debtors to have a better chance to obtain a new lease on life.

One of Holton's tasks in the assembly was to keep government funding flowing into the Grand Trunk. Financing for the railway, however, remained problematic. Holton's cordial relationships with members of the government such as John A. Macdonald would ultimately bring direct benefits to the Grand Trunk and indirect benefits to Gzowski & Co. In May 1856, a reorganization of the ministry had occurred, so that the Liberal-Conservative government was now led by E. P. Taché and John A. Macdonald. But railway funding created an issue that sometimes brought unintended consequences. Support for the Grand Trunk cut party lines, threatening to derange party allegiances. Holton's life in the assembly had rough spots, and he occasionally irritated Upper Canadian Liberal leader George Brown, who made negative assessments of Holton and his railway-building partners.

But Holton, with Galt's assistance, continued to help manoeuvre the Grand Trunk into position to win government financing. Holton's liaison activities, Gzowski & Co.'s reputation for fast and effective work, and shifting alliances in the assembly helped the railway gain an image as the province's most glamorous project. Ever since March 1857, John Ross, the Grand Trunk's president, had dreamed of once more harnessing the support of the Canadian legislature. In May, the legislators approved a subsidy of £2,200,000 for the Grand Trunk.[94]

* * *

Even as the Grand Trunk received additional assistance from the Taché-Macdonald government, Holton and his partners pushed forward their construction work on the railway. By June 1857, they had completed and opened the twelve-mile line from Stratford to St. Mary's.[95] In St. Mary's and Stratford, local residents expected that the coming of the Grand Trunk would speed the growth and development of their communities. The advent of the railway improved their connections to the outside world and helped introduce them to new trades and new industries, allowing them to provide employment for their rising populations.

Through vivid description, evoking several remarkable images, the editor of the *London Atlas* suggested a way in which construction on the line between Toronto and Stratford might best be understood. In April 1857, this journalist of London, Upper Canada, wrote:

> We had, a few days ago, an opportunity of passing over this line for the first time since it was opened. We were glad to find all we had heard in its praise so fully verified by our own experience. It requires one to make a trip or two on the Grand Trunk before a person can form a just opinion of its superior qualities. The solid, durable manner in which the road is built, its careful ballasting, the smooth, easy motion of the cars, furnish ample evidence of engineering skill, and liberal expenditure of money....The bridges over the different rivers, which this part of the line crosses, form the most striking contrast with those to which we are accustomed in this Province and the neighbouring Republic. The piers of these magnificent structures are principally of white brick finished with huge blocks of cut stone, which give them a grand and solid appearance; and the buildings at each station along the line are of the same costly style and highly convenient."[96]

In the comments of George Brown, however, the Toronto-Stratford line became the focus of criticism of Luther Holton and Alexander Galt. This criticism was not new, but during the past two years, few Upper Canadian Liberals had been closer to Holton than Toronto journalist George Brown. It is not difficult to understand why Brown and Holton were close, for they shared a great deal in common. Each had an amiable disposition, a knack for friendship, and a fondness for literature. The two men saw eye to eye on Anglo-Canadian relations and on international questions in general; both had a deep-seated aversion to slavery. In a letter to Brown,

C. S. Gzowski & Co. built the Grand Trunk Railway of Canada station at St. Mary's Junction c. 1857. Shown here in 1933. Courtesy of *The Journal-Argus*.

Holton had openly discussed his genial relationship with John A. Macdonald. But now, the issue of the Grand Trunk produced temporary discord between Brown and Holton. In the assembly, Brown had enough influence to secure a committee to investigate the finances of the railway in May 1857. Brown condemned the Grand Trunk and the Taché-Macdonald government for keeping him "in the dark," for following a course that was "most improper and injudicious," and for asking the Canadian public to support a road that "was clearly bankrupt." Brown charged that Holton had voted for the aid "bill, with one hundred thousand pounds at stake upon its fate." Holton protested that Brown's assertion was a huge exaggeration and denounced him for attempting "to read me out of the Liberal party."[97]

Alexander Galt, with Luther Holton at his side, spent weeks testifying before the committee, but he did not convince politicians and government officials that the record of the Grand Trunk and Gzowski & Co. was clean.[98] The investigation yielded enough evidence to suggest that Gzowski & Co.'s reputation was tainted by its involvement in land speculation at Sarnia.

But the Sarnia land speculation scandal did not undo Luther Holton. However grave his misdeeds, observers focussed more attention on his achievements as a railway builder.[99] The persistence of Holton and his partners had resulted in the completion of a long stretch of quality road west of Toronto. Holton's ability to persevere in difficult situations, his intimate control over Gzowski & Co.'s financial affairs, and his capacity to take command by employing candour and realism conveyed confidence and determination. His public image was not as negative as some contemporary critics seemed to think. Before long, Holton and Brown were able to put their quarrel behind them and concentrate on co-ordinating the efforts of the Lower and Upper Canadian Liberals.

Around this time, Holton faced a turning point in his business career. He could continue building the Grand Trunk in Upper Canada, but he preferred to draw back from railway construction. Like Galt, Holton retired from Gzowski & Co. in June 1857, leaving Gzowski and Macpherson to finish the line to Sarnia in 1859 and then go on to build other railways.[100] By this time, Holton had become disillusioned with the management of the Grand Trunk; more important, the depression had become so pervasive that he wanted out of the railway-building business. "That the money market of the Upper Province is much depressed; that the wild speculations in real estate, which have marked the few last years, have caused much loss and mischief; that traders and capitalists, as well as mere adventurers, have entered into this wild chase after fortune cannot be denied," observed the Montreal *Pilot* in May 1857.[101] With the onset of the depression, the climate for railways and railway builders changed. All railway building was not suspended, but construction slowed considerably. Their work on the Grand Trunk from 1852 to 1857 nevertheless proved profitable for Holton and his partners. "It is said that each of the partners cleared from 40 to 50M ($40,000 to $50,000) by the contract," noted the R. G. Dun & Co. credit correspondent for Toronto.[102]

For Luther Holton, work on the Grand Trunk was finished, but it was a good thing that he was still full of enthusiasm. He had no time to ruminate over mistakes in railway construction. Building railways helped turn Holton into a public personage – he was no longer an obscure man. By late 1857, the general election was on his mind; he was preparing once more to seek a parliamentary seat. His great interest in public affairs would continue to run through the rest of his life.

Chapter 5

Keeping Up an Active Interest
in Public Affairs

Public affairs claimed more and more of Luther Holton's attention after his return from Toronto to Montreal in the summer of 1857. Rubbing shoulders with other Lower and Upper Canadian politicians, participating in the debates in the legislative assembly, and observing where issues that affected the entire Canadian union were argued and decided had awakened in him a desire to continue in politics. Holton now balanced his interests between public and business affairs. For some time, he had been investing in Montreal real estate, mortgages, and bank stock, and these investments continued to be important sources of income, sufficient to support himself and his family. From his office at 5 Union Buildings, St. François Xavier Street, in downtown Montreal, he thus maintained significant aspects of his business career.

* * *

In addition to Holton's business dealings, he took an avid interest in provincial politics. Pondering his political future in the fall of 1857, he first considered leaving the Liberal party and supporting the Liberal-Conservative government led by É. P. Taché and John A. Macdonald. Holton's thoughts were still about the angry personal exchange between himself and George Brown in the assembly a few months earlier. The lingering effects of that exchange caused Holton to shrink from continuing to seek an alliance with the Upper Canadian Liberal Opposition. In a letter to Alexander Galt of 2 September, Holton let his friend know exactly how he felt: "Have you and I any particular inducement to assist in playing the Opposition game after the treatment we received last session?"[1] But after passion had done its worst, Holton and Brown worked out their differences and once more sought to unite the Lower and Upper Canadian Liberals.

Before the problem of uniting the Liberals could be tackled, the general election of December 1857 had to be won. For the second time in his life, Luther Holton really wanted to be elected in Montreal as a Liberal and was willing to put a great deal of effort into a campaign. He also sought to foil any attempt by John A. Macdonald to lure Liberals from the city into the Liberal-Conservative camp. "My aim is to prevent any new men passing to the government," Holton told Galt, his long-time political ally.[2] When Antoine Dorion refused to accept a cabinet post, Holton was immensely relieved and wrote Galt that Dorion's decision "was right."[3] Dorion was still prepared to lead the Lower Canadian Liberal Opposition. Holton, however, could not prevent the influential Galt from bolting the Lower Canadian Liberal Opposition to become an independent, an indication that the eastern Liberals were in turmoil.

But the traditions that had built the eastern Liberal party abided, and none was so potent as the ideal of popular government. Like his Liberal friends, Holton wanted to win, not just glory in the game of politics, but he also continued to stress that votes would determine who governed. Although he did not expect the Liberals to achieve power immediately, Holton made this a long-term goal. He also felt that he had enough support among the voters in Montreal to be re-elected. "There is little chance, I imagine, of ousting either Messrs. Holton or Dorion, the present deservedly popular representatives," observed the editor of the *Canadian News*.[4]

Feeling again the excitement of political combat, Holton, at forty, launched a vigorous campaign, announcing himself a candidate for the legislative assembly on 4 December. His political assets were clear. He was from Montreal, whose three ridings were important in the 1857 election. Holton was known as an effective debater who had held his own with leading Liberal-Conservatives in the assembly. He had solidly founded Liberal credentials, staked out in the assembly debates. But he also had a long-standing record of supporting transportation improvements in Canada. In his announcement, Holton spoke especially for the Montreal business community, while at the same time showing an interest in the broader needs of Canada as a whole. "Nothing will contribute more to the future greatness and prosperity of this city," he said, "than the development of the vast region drained by the Ottawa and its tributaries."[5] Holton drove and walked about the city, talking with numerous electors in English or in French and soliciting votes. As he made a speech on the Champs de Mars, emphasizing his commitment to the idea of making Montreal the provincial capital, his friends showed their support for him by cheering heartily.[6] Many Liberal supporters, such as David Kinnear of the *Montreal Herald*, favoured Holton on business and personal grounds.[7] The city's French-Canadian *rouge* newspaper, *Le Pays* also backed the bilingual Holton enthusiastically.[8]

But factionalism worked to the disadvantage of Luther Holton. After the nomination of Thomas D'Arcy McGee, an Irish Roman Catholic immigrant and editor of the *New Era*, as a Liberal, Holton and Dorion joined in the support of the editor. In religious matters, Holton was known as a tolerant man; certainly, in becoming McGee's political ally he revealed no bias against his religious affiliation. But the Irish Roman Catholic McGee faction and the Protestant faction in Montreal hurt Holton's campaign. "There seems to be a break up of the Montreal *Rouge* party, on account of the McGee coalition, which is very repugnant to Holton's Protestant supporters," wrote George E. Clerk in his diary.[9] Many of these Protestant voters, a number of whom were businessmen, switched their support to John Rose, the Liberal-Conservative Montreal lawyer who had recently become solicitor general in the reorganized Taché-Macdonald government.

The results of the election, not surprisingly, proved to be disastrous to Luther Holton. When the votes were counted in Montreal, he ran fifth in a field of six candidates; the top three were elected: Dorion, Rose, and McGee.[10] The *Montreal Herald* saw Holton's defeat "as a great loss to the province and the city."[11] Describing him as a highly intelligent person with an impressive grasp of commercial affairs, *Le Pays* very much regretted that Holton had been beaten.[12] Speaking on the Champs de Mars, McGee observed that "the city and the country would miss Mr. Holton's presence in parliament. No labour of the student could make up for the practical knowledge of the commerce of the country and the port of Montreal."[13] "The defeat of Mr. Holton," lamented the *Montreal Argus*, has "caused a vacuum in the legislature."[14] Holton interpreted his defeat in part as a sign that the Montreal business community had repudiated him, and so he resigned as president of the Board of Trade. But when the board gave him a vote of confidence by inviting him to stay on as president, he accepted and continued to provide solid leadership.

Across Lower Canada, the campaign of the Liberal-Conservatives proved overpowering as they swept the eastern section with a decisive majority. The election results dismayed the eastern Liberals; they suffered a terrible whipping, losing ground to the government. But in Upper Canada, the election of 1857 was a major and crucial victory for the Liberals, marking a political watershed. It provided a powerful public endorsement of George Brown and his party. John A. Macdonald and Taché nonetheless maintained control of the assembly, given the Liberal-Conservative majority in the Canadian union as a whole.

* * *

Although the Lower Canadian Liberals lost seats in the assembly, they remained a viable party. They were a minority but, as Holton believed, a respectable minority. He was convinced that they were well positioned to offer an alternative to the Liberal-Conservatives in future elections. For all his remoteness from parliament in Toronto, Holton was neither removed from the making of political decisions nor isolated from the planning of strategy in the Liberal party. Brown and Dorion, the makers of strategy, took

George Brown. Courtesy of the Metropolitan Toronto Library Board.

Holton into their confidence, giving him the information that allowed him to comprehend the plans and difficulties of the party leaders. He was consulted on all major decisions and, if he did not always agree with the leaders' actions, he understood their problems. Holton revealed his political ideas, as well as his impressions of the Lower Canadian Liberals, in his letters to Brown.

Holton hoped to formulate a new set of principles for the Liberal party in place of the old beliefs that were divisive. Without some new beliefs, there was a real danger that the Liberals in Lower and Upper Canada might continue to follow interests that were mostly local and sectional. Over everything else loomed one subject: there was a need to encourage the Liberal party to adopt a program relevant to the times. It was imperative, Holton thought, to develop a new Liberal ideology. He felt that he might be able to influence Brown to pursue a diplomatic solution to the problem of sectional strife between Upper and Lower Canada. Brown defended the principle of representation by population as a self-evident truth, but any politician who hoped for success in the mid-nineteenth-century Canadian union could not embrace this principle as the only truth. Everyone knew that, by 1851, Upper Canada's population stood at 952,000 as compared to 890,000 people in Lower Canada; thereafter the western section had certainly increased its lead through the coming of a larger proportion of immigrants to western lands that were fertile and empty.[15] Brown argued that it was necessary to replace equal representation of Upper and Lower Canada in parliament with representation by population in order to give Upper Canadians a larger voice in the Canadian union's affairs. But in both Upper and Lower Canada, some Liberals spoke in favour of the dissolution of the union. These arguments effectively polarized the political discussion and threatened to keep the Liberal party in Canada disastrously split and to erect an iron curtain dividing the union in two. Devoted as he was to Lower Canada, Holton wanted to meet the powerful sectional prejudices of the day with a new vision for realizing his goal of holding the union together.

So in mid-January 1858, it fell to Luther Holton to bring forward, during his visit to Brown in Toronto, the idea that a framework was needed for a totally new constitution for the Canadian union. At this point, Holton was still groping his way toward a workable concept of a federal union of Upper and Lower Canada. He was not ready yet to write a tract aimed at winning the support of Lower and Upper Canadian Liberals. But he urged Brown to allow reason to replace passion in facing the changes of the mid-nineteenth century. Holton harped on his pet theory, one he had articulated in the assembly back in 1856, that a remedy for the chief flaws in the existing constitution was "something like a federal union, in which the great interests of the country might be attended to by a federate parliament, and the parish business by the local legislatures."[16] The visit also served the additional purpose of helping to re-establish the relationship between Holton and Brown on a footing of affection and intimacy.

The timing of their rapprochement was significant: during the crucial weeks before parliament opened in Toronto on 25 February, Brown relied on Holton for advice on the possibility of co-operation between the eastern and western Liberals. Finding it difficult to communicate freely with Antoine Dorion, Brown did not contact the *rouge* leader. After his return to Montreal in the third week of January, Holton immediately met with Dorion and a few other Liberal friends to discuss the federal union idea. Holton emerged from the discussion as one willing to act as a go-between for the Lower and Upper Canadian Liberal leaders.

Holton's reputation as a political broker spread quickly by word of mouth. Before long, Liberals in both sections of Canada knew that he was serving as a channel of communication between Dorion and Brown. In late January and early February, Holton and Brown exchanged very important and highly revealing letters. They revealed both that the idea of a Canadian federation was being dealt with as a significant political question and that Holton was heavily involved in the decision-making process. Holton, functioning as Dorion's trusted personal emissary, reported from Montreal to Brown: "I have had a good deal of conversation with our French-Canadian friends on the points we discussed in Toronto. I find they are disposed to cling to the federation scheme as the true solution of the representation and other sectional questions now pressing for settlement. They say that any French Canadian who should favour representation by population *pur et simple* would be not merely ruined temporarily as a public man, but ostracized as a traitor to his race." Holton wanted Brown to know, however, that the French-Canadian Liberals understood his advocacy of representation by population. Holton added:

> Of course no intelligent man can suppose that two or three thousand Englishmen (and the number rapidly increasing) will consent to remain disfranchised (for that is what it amounts to) much longer. Our friends see this as clearly as we do. Altogether, it must be confessed their position is a difficult one. They ought certainly to be better judges of the state of feeling among their countrymen than I am but I incline to the belief that they overrate the strength of that feeling. If they are right there would seem to be but the alternative of dissolution or federation. The latter as you know is my favourite idea not merely as a means of evading present difficulties, but as the best and most statesmanlike scheme that can be devised for the government of the country.[17]

Then Holton injected an important concern into the debate. Continued apprehension about Upper Canada's intentions – separation if the rep by pop movement did not succeed – moved him toward his point: he feared that Canada's break-up would heighten the impact of the economic depression on Lower Canada. "I wish you and your friends," Holton emphasized, "could be brought to consider it seriously – a simple dissolution of the existing union is out of the question."[18] Canada and businessmen like Holton faced an economic crisis and needed political stability, which in his opinion could be provided by the transformation of the existing legislative Canadian union into a federal union. In Montreal and many other parts of the province, the economic depression sparked a rash of business failures and led to a marked rise in unemployment and much social unrest.[19]

Less than a week later, Holton added: "If the Union on its present basis is to be maintained, your views on the Representation Question must unquestionably prevail, and if the federation scheme which I prefer, can not be made acceptable I am persuaded men can be found in L. C. to assist in giving effect to them, whenever a decided and *persevering* majority in U. C. shall take their stand upon them."[20] Moved by Holton's conciliatory language, Brown replied:

> I am sure that a dissolution cry would be as ruinous to any party as (in my opinion) it would be wrong. A Federal Union, it appears to me, can not be entertained for Canada alone, but when agitated must include all British America … if you can suggest a Federal or any other scheme that could be worked, it will have our most anxious examination. Can you sketch a plan for Federation

such as our friends below would agree to & could carry? If so, pray let us have it as soon as conveniently possible.[21]

Holton sensed a softening and responded:

You demand of me the heads of such a scheme of federative union as our friends here would be disposed to support. A most reasonable request I grant, but one with which I am hardly prepared to comply, *impromptu*. I could very easily sketch *my own views*, and I may take an early opportunity of doing so in order to ascertain how far they are in harmony with those of my friends. I admit, however, the extreme difficulty of moving public opinion in our country on any theoretical question, and am therefore very much of your opinion that we must limit ourselves for the present to the practical question presented by U.C. liberals.[22]

Later, in 1859, Holton did contribute significantly to the making of a new constitution by writing what became an eastern Liberal comment upon a Canadian federal system. At the moment, Holton found reassuring his certainty that Brown would not push for dissolution of the Canadian union. Brown was seeking to conduct Liberal party business through Holton as an intermediary, and Holton was still willing to serve in that capacity. After writing to Brown, Holton immediately visited Dorion in his law office for a chat about the Liberal party, giving him a full account of his communication with Brown. No one did more to lay a foundation for co-operation between the Upper and Lower Canadian Liberals in parliament than Holton himself.

As the elements of Luther Holton's efforts in the Liberal party were beginning to move into place, sadness came into his private life. His mother, Anner Stafford, died on 12 July 1858 in Soperton at the age of sixty-seven. Characteristically, Anner had thought about her children's future. For instance, half a year earlier, she had transferred forty-seven acres of land in the township of Lansdowne to her son Cleveland Phillips Stafford, Luther's half-brother.[23] Luther had always been devoted to his mother; now he travelled to Soperton to pay his respects.

* * *

The next four months were turbulent in Holton's political career. A political crisis was looming in parliament. The issue on which the reorganized Liberal-Conservative government of John A. Macdonald and George-Étienne Cartier appeared to be most vulnerable was the seat of government. This was a subject to which Holton had given considerable attention.[24]

Like every other Lower Canadian Liberal, he wanted Montreal to become the capital on a permanent basis. Dorion continued to serve as the leader of the Lower Canadian Liberals in Toronto, still the seat of government, and in late July 1858, he introduced resolutions in the assembly declaring that the Queen's choice of Ottawa as the capital of the province was unacceptable. Treating this as a want-of-confidence motion, the government survived with a few votes. But several days later, on 28 July, the vote went against the government on a motion opposing Ottawa made by Joseph Piché, a Lower Canadian Liberal. Appearing to lack the support it needed to carry on, the government submitted its resignation to Governor General Edmund Head the following day.

Assemblymen feverishly discussed who might be asked to serve as premier to start building a new administration. Some names, undoubtedly including George Brown's, were whispered in the hallways of the legislature. Head did look to Brown, the Upper Canadian Liberal leader with the largest following in the opposition, inviting him to form a new ministry.[25] Brown agreed to try to construct a new administration, but he faced formidable problems. There was no accurate way of measuring Liberal support among the assemblymen until a vote was taken in the assembly. If the Liberals did not gain control of the assembly, there was no guarantee from Head that he would grant a dissolution of parliament should they ask him to do so. But when Brown considered the possibility of forming a government, the chances for securing the cooperation of Liberals from Upper and Lower Canada seemed good. Having made up his mind to serve as premier of Upper Canada and inspector general, Brown approached Dorion with a positive offer of a cabinet post as premier of Lower Canada and commissioner of crown lands. As head of the Lower Canadian Liberals in the assembly, Dorion accepted.

Now the main item on the agenda for Brown and Dorion was the selection of the rest of the cabinet. The best they could hope to do was to find men of ability to match the present political realities. They readily agreed that the office of public works must be offered to Luther Holton, in recognition of his services to the Liberal party and his position in the business community. They accordingly called him from Montreal to the capital, probably by telegram.[26] By Friday, 30 July, both George E. Clerk, editor of the Montreal *True Witness*, and the Toronto correspondent of the *Montreal Gazette* knew that Holton had been sent for.[27] It only remained for Holton to pack a few things, bid farewell to Eliza and his children, and board the Grand Trunk train and leave for Toronto. Passengers on the train no doubt found him genial and in good spirits, though the conversation always turned to the crisis in parliament. Self-confident, while at the same time acutely aware that the Liberals might lack enough support in the assembly to govern and that Head might then refuse to dissolve parliament and thus deny them the opportunity to go to the people, Holton accepted the challenge of the public works office when he arrived at the capital.

As the remaining members of the cabinet emerged, the balance of the Lower Canadian section consisted of J. É. Thibaudeau, president of the council; François Lemieux, receiver general; L.T. Drummond, attorney general East; and Charles Laberge, solicitor general East. The rest of the Upper Canadian part of the cabinet was made up of Sandfield Macdonald of Cornwall, a lawyer who became attorney general West; Oliver Mowat, provincial secretary; Michael Foley, postmaster general; and James Morris, speaker of the legislative council. In addition, Skeffington Connor, though not in the cabinet, agreed to serve as solicitor general West.[28] In many ways, under-less-than-favourable circumstances, it was one of the most promising cabinets in the history of the Canadian union, balanced and well formed to address the concerns of both sections of the province.

But a tense scene in the cabinet room, with most ministers worried about what might happen in the assembly, gave Holton a foretaste of the problems the Brown-Dorion government might face. The cabinet policy represented the kind of compromises and settlements necessary to keep the two sections of the union placated: it combined Brown's demand for representation by population with Dorion's insistence that to protect his French-Canadian, Roman Catholic "people in Lower Canada, constitutional checks, constitutional protections, must be granted for our local institutions."[29] For his part, Holton placed special emphasis on a point in the cabinet's policy that was stressed in its communication with Head: "His Excellency's present advisers have entered the Government with the fixed determination to propose constitutional measures for the establishment of that harmony between Upper and Lower Canada which is essential to the prosperity of the Province."[30] From this communication, Holton could not be quite sure what the new cabinet's policy on the constitution would be. There was no pledge to transform the present legislative union of Canada into a federal union, but at least he had the assurance that the cabinet's objective was to preserve the union and to deal with the sectional difficulties through constitutional change.

On Monday, 2 August, at noon, Luther Holton, along with the other ministers in the Brown-Dorion cabinet, took his oath of office and waited for the situation to unfold. The time came for a test of strength with the Liberal-Conservatives at three in the afternoon, when parliament met, but the ministers' role was severely limited by the rules of the day under which they had resigned their seats until by-elections might allow them to be returned.[31] Although Holton had no seat to resign, he too, like his colleagues, was forced to observe the proceedings in silence as he took his place beside them on a bench to the right of the speaker in the assembly. The new government thus had no opportunity to make a public announcement of its policy. Immediately, without notice, the Liberal-Conservatives moved a motion of want of confidence. In the heated atmosphere, this action kept the crisis boiling.

By this time, Holton and his colleagues were almost reconciled to the inevitable, but they were building a historical record to prove their worthy intent throughout the political crisis. After being decisively defeated in the assembly around midnight despite McGee's spirited defence of their position, they gave their policy a last chance on 3 August by asking Head to dissolve parliament. In the afternoon of the next day, they received Head's refusal. Head tried to defend his decision by arguing that

> ... an election took place last winter. This fact is not conclusive against a second election now; but the cost and inconvenience of such a proceeding are so great that they ought not to be incurred a second time without very strong grounds. The business before Parliament is not yet finished. The time of year and the state of affairs would make a general election at this moment peculiarly inconvenient and burdensome, inasmuch as the harvest is now going on in a large part of the country and the pressure of the late money crisis has not passed away.[32]

By four o'clock on 4 August, after holding office for only two days, the Brown-Dorion government had resigned.

The next few days saw a great infringement on the spirit of acceptable parliamentary practice. Promptly Head asked Alexander Galt, now a Liberal-Conservative, to form a government. Galt's attempt to do so ended in failure. At this point, Head approached Cartier, whose efforts to construct a ministry met with success. Cartier needed John A. Macdonald in the cabinet, who came in as attorney general West. The new Cartier-Macdonald government included Galt as minister of finance and John Ross as president of the legislative council. In Lower Canada the Liberal-Conservatives were in the majority, while in Upper Canada they were in the minority. The Cartier-Macdonald ministers, anxious to get around the law that required them to seek re-election, had themselves sworn into one set of portfolios which they had no intention of keeping and then, after relinquishing them within two days, had themselves sworn into those which they had held in the previous Liberal-Conservative government. In doing so they, like Head who participated in the proceedings, claimed that their actions were in accordance with the Independence of Parliament Act of 1857. They had indeed followed the letter of this law, but not its spirit, for it was intended to permit a minister to move from one portfolio to another within a month without going to his constituents again and thus reduce the number of ministerial by-elections. Propriety dictated that a minister should not use the law in any other way. It was easy for the *Globe* to denounce the actions of the Cartier-Macdonald ministers as the "double shuffle."[33]

* * *

Among Upper and Lower Canadian Liberals, there was a firestorm of criticism of the double shuffle and of the ministers and Head who were involved in it. Though he was out of office, Holton had no desire to be out of the public eye. In Montreal, he found in the double shuffle episode enough to warn electors against supporting the Liberal-Conservatives and to urge them to back Antoine Dorion in his bid to be re-elected. On Tuesday evening, 10 August, in front of the Richelieu Hotel in the Jacques Cartier Square, Holton entered the campaign wholeheartedly, making a speech in behalf of Dorion. "Mr. Dorion, at this moment," observed Holton, "occupies the most prominent position in Lower Canada, perhaps more than any man since the days of the old Reform party led by LaFontaine in the glorious struggle for constitutional liberty. It will, then, be the duty of Montreal to stand by Mr. Dorion to show that he merits the confidence of the Liberal party who won for it and the rest of the country that constitutional freedom we now enjoy." On this occasion, Holton also made an effort to excite his audience with praise for McGee: "I think it is due to you that I should say a word of commendation about … my friend Thomas D'Arcy McGee…. I have watched with special interest the public conduct of Mr. McGee … and I am bound to say no man has ever won his way so rapidly in the public confidence…. I have seen the conduct of Mr. McGee during the recent trying crisis, and I feel bound to say … it has left nothing to desire."[34]

Holton continued to work hard in an effort to persuade Montreal electors to vote for his close friend Dorion. In a letter to Brown on 2 September, Holton was optimistic about Dorion's chances for re-election. "The opposition to Dorion," he wrote, "has proved much less formidable than any of us ventured to hope. The complete rout of the ministerial forces here will have a most favorable effect throughout Lower Canada. It is now manifest that if we had got our dissolution we would have swept this part of the country."[35] Dorion was re-elected in Montreal by an overwhelming majority of 2,072 over J. L. Beaudry one day later.[36] The other ex-ministers in Lower Canada who had held seats in the assembly prior to the formation of the Brown-Dorion government – Lemieux,

Thibaudeau, Laberge, and Drummond – were also re-elected, although Drummond was defeated in Shefford before he triumphed in Lotbinière.[37]

Some of Holton's Liberal friends wanted him back in parliament and, therefore, tried to find a seat for him. In Brockville in mid-August, James Morris, a prominent lawyer, briefly thought that the St. Lawrence seat in the legislative council might appeal to him. St. Lawrence encompassed Soperton, Holton's birthplace. "I invited Holton up who spent a day with us and our friends were greatly pleased with him," wrote Morris to Brown, "but we have not put him in nomination as the chances are against us and his defeat would not only damage him but it would add to the triumph of our enemies."[38] Shortly thereafter, Dorion asked Holton "to stand for the Montarville division" near Montreal in the legislative council, "but he declined on the ground that he would be more useful in the Assembly and that he preferred to wait for a vacancy in the general election." Dorion then "had hopes that" Holton "would be supported in Lotbinière" for an assembly seat for that riding "and went to Quebec about it," but gave up the idea when the friends of Drummond, a Montreal lawyer, put his name in nomination in Lotbinière after his defeat in the Shefford riding. "It is a pity that" Holton "cannot be in the house for the next session," Dorion concluded in his letter to Brown.[39]

Acting in his role as ex-minister, Holton nonetheless made special trips to Upper Canada to promote the Liberal cause. The double-shuffle brought a new and unprecedented importance to his speeches, partly because he could show that the questionable double shuffle itself was unprecedented, unparalleled in Canadian history. His speeches not only intensified political discussion, but also energized partisanship, giving to politics the passion of a crusade. On 23 September, Holton joined hundreds of Upper and some Lower Canadian Liberals assembled at a banquet in the Mechanics Hall in Hamilton to honour the Brown-Dorion ministers. Holton dazzled the banquet guests with an oration based upon a broad knowledge of history and political philosophy. He began by observing that the sentiment expressed in the toast was "perpetual union between Upper and Lower Canada, having a proper regard for the rights, interests, and feelings of the people of both sections of the Province. That, gentlemen, is a sentiment to which I can heartily respond, as a Unionist from the start, and as having acted from my first advent into public life with that party whose policy it was to render that Union acceptable to both sections of the country." He went on to say:

> What is the feature most noticeable in this magnificent demonstration? Is it not
> that of seeing for the first time for, I think, some five or six years public men
> from both sections of the Province met together on a common platform discussing

questions of common interest to our common country? This is to me, at all
events, a most agreeable feature in our assembling here tonight.... Strange, is it
not, that such a party should have been foiled in their attempts to settle these
questions, and to consolidate the Union – and foiled, too, by the representative
in this country of Imperial interests, which, more closely than any other question
of provincial politics, are bound up in the Union of Upper and Lower Canada.[40]

Holton's speech did have an impact, for it brought loud and repeated cheers
from the many Liberals present. By following the technique of carrying
the attack on Governor General Edmund Head on his own terms, he helped
popularize the Liberal interpretation of the double shuffle. In Holton's
speeches at subsequent Liberal banquets at the Commercial Hotel in Elora
on 24 September, at the Kerby House in Brantford on 27 September, and
in Alexandria, County of Glengarry, on 21 October, the message was
always the same: he argued that it was his duty, as a Lower Canadian
Liberal and an ex-minister, to seek to maintain the Canadian union and to
chastise Head for denying the Brown-Dorion administration's request for
a dissolution of parliament.[41] Holton threw into his speeches every
argument he could muster. He insisted that Head had violated the
constitution by refusing to act on the advice of his ministers. Holton's
considerable experience with the theory and practice of responsible
government allowed him to offer a ringing endorsement of self-government
within the British Empire. Working within the established constitutional
system, he moved boldly against sectionalism, asking the eastern and
western sections of the province to pull together. Holton hoped that the
new sense of cooperation between the Upper and Lower Canadian Liberals
would strengthen his party's position in Montreal and Lower Canada.

At the same time, Holton recognized that the Liberal party in the
Canadian union faced formidable problems in fall of 1858. It was not
only a relatively new and imperfectly articulated political organization,
but it also had strong competition. Shrewdly, Galt proposed the federal
union of Canada and the other British North American colonies as a
solution to Canada's sectional difficulties. Early in October 1858, three
Liberal-Conservative ministers – Cartier, Galt, and John Ross – left Canada
for London, England, to discuss with the British government the proposal
for a federal union of all British North America and to seek imperial
assistance to finance Canada's railway and canal projects and the
construction of the Intercolonial Railway.[42]

To counter the appeal of the Liberal-Conservatives' proposal for a British
American federation, Holton thought it important for the Liberal party to
send a representative to London to "put our case on the record."[43] But

Brown doubted the wisdom of taking such a step. The reaction of Sir Edward Bulwer Lytton, the colonial secretary, to the Liberal-Conservatives' proposal for a federal union of British America was negative. "The question of the Federation of the Colonies," Bulwer Lytton told Head, "is necessarily one of Imperial Character, involving the future government of other North American Colonies, equally bound with Canada by the common tie which unites all members of that Empire. It is therefore one which properly belongs to the Executive authority of the Empire, and not that of any separate province, to initiate."[44]

In Montreal, Holton continued to call for the creation of a Canadian federation. Encouraged by Dorion, he wanted to take Brown in the same direction. The idea of a federal union of Upper and Lower Canada was very much on Holton's mind when he and Dorion spoke with Lord Bury, a rising English Whig, in Montreal on 23 November. That same day, after seeing Bury, Holton wrote to Brown, urging him to draft a statement on a Canadian federation for submission to the colonial office in London:

> Dorion and I called on Lord Bury today. In discussing with him the best mode of getting our case before the House of Commons I mentioned our idea of sending a statement of facts bearing our own signatures to the Colonial Office, which would serve as a sort of *brief* to our friends in Parliament. He thought that decidedly the best plan that had been suggested, and I hope you will devote a few hours *some day soon* to the preparation of a draft. Having more leisure than you, I would willingly do it, but not being a practiced writer I could not do it well, it ought to be *very* well done.[45]

Although Brown did not follow his advice, Holton stayed in close touch with him to help strengthen the ties between the Lower and Upper Canadian Liberals.

* * *

During the first half of 1859, Holton continued to associate himself with the vision of a new constitution and a new Canada – a federal union of Upper and Lower Canada. Constitutional issues were the basic diet of democratic politics, and politics was one of Holton's passions. His many years of doing business in Upper Canada, combined with his recent participation in Liberal rallies in the western section, had a great impact on him. It made him see himself as more than a Lower Canadian; it convinced him that he was a Canadian businessman and politician. But Holton found his efforts to woo Upper Canadian Liberal support frustrating. It was a warning of their disaffection that some Upper Canadian Liberals, especially Brown and his *Globe*, began calling for the dissolution of the Canadian union in May.[46] Brown was nonetheless just the kind of contact Holton needed – a prosperous journalist with powerful connections. As both a journalist and politician Brown had a lot to offer Holton. If anyone could help promote the idea of a Canadian federation, it was going to be Brown himself.

When a letter came from Brown in early July indicating that he was trying to work things out with Lower Canada through constitutional change, Holton was quick to respond positively.[47] "I am very glad indeed to learn from your letter," replied Holton, "that the question of constitutional changes is taking hold of the popular mind in Upper Canada. You do not require to be told that on *that* subject I am entirely with you. I was at one time, however, afraid that the *Globe* was going a little too far in the advocacy of a dissolution *pur et simple*. It may be necessary to advance that idea as an *alternative* and it would be difficult to deny the justice of a demand for it on the part of Upper Canada if Lower Canada should doggedly persist in opposing any change in the existing unjust, corrupt, and ruinous system. But it is only as a *dernier resort* that I am disposed to contemplate the question of a simple dissolution of the union."[48]

Besides trying to keep the fragile coalition of Upper and Lower Canadian Liberals together and to further the Canadian federation cause through his contact with Brown, Holton evoked friendship in Montreal and called on David Kinnear and Edward Goff Penny, editors of the *Montreal Herald*, to support the "constitutional changes which our party in L. C. have always favoured."[49] To Holton's delight, Brown thought that it would be possible to find a place for him in parliament by having him seek the York North assembly seat in a by-election. "I am gratified by your reference," he told Brown, "to a desire to bring me into Parliament if a vacancy should occur. Personally I had no desire to anticipate the period of a general election. The question is one for the consideration of the party, at whose service I shall hold myself. There would perhaps be less embarrassment in my sitting for an U. C. constituency now than at any time during the last four or five years."[50] As it turned out, however, the majority of the Toronto Liberals had other ideas and persuaded Adam Wilson, a lawyer and mayor of the city, to run for the York North seat, and he won it. Being passed over for the York North seat was not unbearable for Holton, for he was too familiar with political disappointments to be very much discouraged.

In a positive sense, Holton offered constitutional change as a means for Upper and Lower Canadians to embrace both their concept of equality and their commitment to their social institutions. He also continued to think of Canada as a land of opportunity where businessmen like himself could get ahead. The economy was moving toward larger units of production, marketing, and finance. Holton had no doubt that the rich resources of the province could be better developed in an atmosphere of political stability, which he was still confident could be achieved through a Canadian federation. He offered an escape from the blind alley in which politicians had to pander to the prejudices of their sections. In mid-September 1859, Holton tried to build support for a federal union of Lower and Upper Canada by encouraging Brown in his plan to hold a Liberal convention in Upper Canada to discuss the question and by taking an active role in Liberal meetings in Montreal to address the same issue. After participating in a meeting with other Lower Canadian Liberals in the home of Antoine Dorion, Holton wrote to Brown:

> [W]e are most anxious that you should adopt the federation scheme, believing it to be the best *per se* and the one on which we could best make a stand in L. C. Besides, and this is a point of much practical importance with reference to ultimate success, the agitation of this scheme would not prevent the formation of an administration by the present opposition if the occasion should arise, for I take it that we have to seek reorganization of a better constitutional system through the instrumentality of the existing machinery.

At the same time, Holton recognized that the Lower Canadian Liberals faced a problem:

> The misfortune is that the *Rouge* party though embracing the best intellect of the Franco-Canadian race does not command the requisite material resources for sustaining a vigorous agitation throughout the country. They can at best, therefore, only wage a species of guerrilla warfare but should circumstances arise to give them the *prestige* of success they would carry the country with a rush.[51]

Holton was clearly again trying to keep a discussion going in the hope that reason would prevail even while appeasing popular opinion in the eastern and western sections of the province. He shared Brown's new enthusiasm for a Canadian federation when he learned that his friend had succeeded in persuading the Upper Canadian Liberal parliamentary Opposition to accept his resolutions for the federal union of the two sections of the province at a meeting in the Rossin House in Toronto on 23 September. Promptly, Holton sent Brown an encouraging letter: "I was delighted to hear of the success of your meeting, and of the conclusion come to after full discussion. It establishes a basis on which we can all stand."[52] Eager to coordinate the efforts of the western and eastern Liberals,

Holton asked Brown to send him a copy of the resolutions to allow the Lower Canadian Liberals to consider them at a meeting they hoped to hold in Montreal in mid-October.[53]

Ready to commit himself to a firm pledge to seek a Canadian federation, Holton went to work on his home ground. He spent long hours at a meeting of the Lower Canadian Liberals – eleven parliamentary Opposition Liberals and twelve to fifteen Liberals outside parliament – in Montreal on 13 October, where the debate centred on Brown's resolutions. Thinking about the situation overnight, the next day Holton sent Brown his analysis of the meeting:

> The Federation scheme formed the chief topic of discussion and was generally accepted as the best if not the only practicable solution of existing difficulties though some to whom it was comparatively new desired further time for consideration before pronouncing themselves definitively.... Some of our more advanced *Rouges* while giving in their adhesion to the proposed movement avowed their individual preference for a continuance of the Legislative Union with Representation by Population. They fear the ascendancy of retrogressive ideas and especially the effects of clerical domination in Lower Canada if separated from Upper Canada.

Antoine Dorion, Louis-Antoine Dessaules, St. Hyacinthe author and member of the legislative council, Thomas D'Arcy McGee, L. T. Drummond, Charles Laberge, and D. E. Papineau, brother of Louis Joseph Papineau, "pronounced themselves emphatically and unreservedly in favor of Federation, and I need not add that I took the same side," wrote Holton. He argued that "our aim should be to familiarize men's minds with the necessity for fundamental changes and with the advantages of the particular change we propose and leave the difficulties attending it to develop themselves at a more advanced stage of the movement." The Liberal meeting in Montreal appointed a committee, consisting of Dorion, Holton, Drummond, Dessaules, and McGee, "to prepare a basis of future action for" the Lower Canadian parliamentary Opposition.[54]

Holton was assigned the task of writing a report, and in doing this job he kept three goals in mind: "It appeared to me," he wrote Brown, "that our objects should be first to impart some vigor to our own party in L.C. by initiating an earnest discussion of the present condition of affairs and the remedies proposed. Second to find some common ground of action between Liberals East and West, and third to give what moral aid we can to the movement in Upper Canada." The report Holton wrote met with the hearty approval of all the members of the committee. But about one thing he was certain: a convention of Lower Canadian Liberals could not be assembled. "We are not in a position to enter upon a general agitation, or to call a convention, matters not being yet sufficiently advanced with us," explained Holton.[55]

Instead of trying to organize a convention, in the evening of 25 October, Holton, Dorion, and a number of other Lower Canadian Liberals met at Compain's Cosmopolitan Saloon in Montreal to discuss the report.[56] The fright engendered by the *Globe*'s recent agitation for the dissolution of the Canadian union had brought on a sense of urgency. Holton needed no pressing to stamp the whole thing as a crisis. He had developed an extraordinary sense of how the provincial government worked, and in his spare time he had delved into the histories of Great Britain, Canada, and the United States, wondering what had gone wrong with the Canadian union. His own experience in the Canadian legislature was a better guide than books, however, for he had seen a great deal of bickering over sectional interests and local prejudices. Now he had impressed his colleagues on the Liberal committee in Montreal with a mature judgement, an ability to dig into the heart of a problem.

All this was reflected in Holton's report, in which he set "forth the gravity of the existing crisis, attacking the present system and the present administration, as vehemently as could with propriety be done in such a paper, and treating argumentatively the questions of dissolution, Representation by Population, and Federation concluding by strongly urging the adoption of the latter as a basis of future party action." As he told Brown, "I had necessarily to treat the whole subject somewhat from a L. C. and French-Canadian standpoint, but not, I flatter myself, so much so as to embarrass you."[57] He had worked on the report with the same diligence he gave to any assignment in public life. While the words were mostly his, they had been edited by the other members of the committee. "Although the original draft has been pretty closely followed, it has shared the fate of all such documents in being mutilated here, amplified there, and modified not everywhere but in many points. One is not prone to fancy his work improved by such a process, but possibly he is not the best judge, and we all know the thing is unavoidable whenever several minds have to be satisfied," Holton said to Brown.[58] Despite the changes that had been made in Holton's report with respect to a Canadian federation at the meeting, it was favourably received as a manifesto.

Although the manifesto was not formally adopted by the meeting, Dorion, Drummond, Dessaules, and McGee, as members of the Lower Canadian Liberal parliamentary Opposition, signed it and arranged to have it published in the *Montreal Herald*, *Le Pays* (Montreal), the *Montreal Gazette*, the Montreal *Pilot*, the *Montreal Transcript*, the Quebec *Morning*

Chronicle, and the *Globe* at the end of October and the beginning of November.[59] "Whether we consider the present needs or the probable future condition of the country," the manifesto read, "the true, the statesmanlike solution is to be sought in the substitution of a purely federative for the present so-called legislative union." The manifesto emphasized that "by restricting the functions of the federal government to the few easily defined subjects of common or national concern, and leaving supreme jurisdiction in all matters to the several provinces, the people of each subdivision would possess every guarantee for the integrity of their respective institutions." Going on to discuss the provincial boundaries and the distribution of powers in the new regime, the manifesto stressed that

> ... the old division line between Upper and Lower Canada must be preserved. In the distribution of powers between the local, or state, and the federal governments, the controlling and pervading idea should be to delegate to the federal government such authority only as would be essential to the objects of the federation; and by necessary consequence to reserve to the subdivisions powers as ample and varied as possible. The Customs, the Post Office, the laws concerning Patents and Copyrights, the Currency, and such of the Public Works as are of general interest to the whole province would form the chief if not the only subjects with which the general government should be charged; while everything relating to purely local improvements, to Education, to the Administration of Justice, to the Militia, to laws relating to property, and generally all questions of local concern – in fine, the power to legislate on all matters not specifically devolving on the federal government would be lodged in the government of the separate provinces.[60]

This was Holton's Lower Canadian Liberal report – the embodiment of considerable research and almost half a decade of experience in public life. He doubtless urged these ideas before the Montreal Liberal meetings because they seemed to remedy the major weaknesses in the legislative union of Canada. They provided a constitutional option that might be called upon, a response promising flexibility in making the constitution fit changing political and social needs. Holton believed that Canada's salvation lay in a fairly strong central government empowered to impose customs duties and raise revenues in order to pay its bills, establish a postal system and thus provide all citizens with a reliable means of communication, issue currency and coin money thereby creating a national medium of exchange, authorize patent and copyright laws to protect the rights of pioneers of new technologies, and use federal government resources for improving harbours, rivers, canals, roads, and railways. Holton's report stated that any power not specifically granted to the federal government was reserved to the provinces. He probably interpreted this point as restricting the power of the central government, believing it gave more power to the provinces to safeguard the institutions within their boundaries. Later, once he accepted confederation, Holton would favour the creation of a much more energetic national government.

In 1859, Holton's plan for a new governmental structure still left many questions unanswered. For instance, there were differences of opinion concerning federal economic policy, differences rooted in varying business interests. He was nevertheless the master behind the proposal that recognized the flaws of the legislative union by explicit provision for a federal union of Canada. The orderliness of his mind was amazing. Without intending to do so, Holton carved out a special niche for himself in Canadian history by deciding to record the deliberations of the Montreal Liberal meetings in his letters to Brown. Although the general public remained in the dark as to the authorship of the report, the message Liberals received was clear enough. Holton, Dorion, and some of their eastern Liberal friends wanted a Canadian federation.

Despite the appearance of the manifesto in a number of Lower Canadian and especially Montreal newspapers, the absence of strong, effective Liberal press support in Montreal proved to be a serious handicap. "I am afraid," Holton wrote Brown, "the *Herald* may be against us. I should regret this exceedingly and have done all in my power to avert it, but we can't afford to *stand still* at a time like this to suit the purposes of a newspaper however highly we may prize its support and esteem its conductors. I still hope they may be with us."[61] But Holton's hopes were dashed. "We have an instinctive ... feeling against cutting up political bodies into small states," wrote the *Montreal Herald*.[62]

It was an era when newspapers played a major role in public affairs. The press could organize and lead public opinion in the direction of its thinking. Fortunately for Holton and the Lower Canadian Liberals, the *rouge Le Pays* and the Liberal *Montreal Transcript* were more positive in their response to the Liberal manifesto's advocacy of a Canadian federation. *Le Pays* acknowledged "the absolute and immediate necessity of constitutional change ... along the lines of the report adopted by the" Lower Canadian Liberal parliamentary "Opposition."[63] The *Montreal Transcript* wrote: "The whole subject is argued in a calm, able, and statesmanlike manner, and the views and arguments presented will well repay careful perusal and study on the part of all who are interested in the future of our country."[64] Despite the support they provided, *Le Pays* and the *Montreal Transcript* were relatively small newspapers and had limited impact on the general public. The main problem was that, although Holton could influence the views of the *Montreal Herald*, the city's most powerful Liberal paper, on the economic development of Montreal and Canada, it remained sceptical about the Canadian federation scheme.

But at a time when the political system in Canada was beginning to unravel and east-west polarization was reaching new dimensions, Holton was striking a new theme in response to the province's sectional difficulties. When he visited the Upper Canadian Liberal convention on constitutional reform at the St. Lawrence Hall in Toronto on 9 November as an observer, he had a wonderful opportunity to extend good will to Upper Canada and encourage the convention led by George Brown as it proceeded to adopt the principle of Canadian federation.[65] A week later, following his return to Montreal, Holton was still filled with a sense of achievement. "The Toronto Convention," he wrote Alexander Galt, the Liberal-Conservative finance minister with whom he was still in contact, "was the most imposing gathering I have ever seen in this country. No one could look on the six hundred men there assembled without being satisfied that there was the *power* if there was also the purpose of moving the country. It must be peculiarly gratifying to you to find the policy of a *Canadian Federation* adopted by the whole Liberal Party East and West."[66] Despite the failure of the Lower Canadian Liberal parliamentary Opposition to meet in Montreal on 22 November to adopt the eastern Liberal manifesto as it had planned to do, Dorion, Holton, and other prominent eastern Liberals continued to embrace the idea of a federal union of Upper and Lower Canada.[67]

Out of the letters and resolutions that moved back and forth between Montreal and Toronto between September and November 1859, several distinctive Liberal party principles emerged: no dissolution of the Canadian union, a pledge to protect Upper and Lower Canadian institutions, and a commitment to a Canadian federation. Much as he recognized the relative weakness of the eastern Liberal parliamentary Opposition, Holton made it clear to Brown that he remained optimistic about the future of the Liberal party as a whole and interested in the long-term viability of Canada.[68] He sought to keep the Canadian union together at all costs. The Canadian federation policy, which Holton had helped shape, was an important step in the long process by which Canadians and other British North Americans ultimately created the federal union of British North America.

One key to Holton's success was George Brown. The relationship between the two men was complex. In the years 1858-60 Holton came to be known as one of Brown's most loyal friends. This led some Lower Canadians to believe that Holton lived too much to serve the Toronto journalist. But this was not the case, for Holton did not always support Brown's policies. But as he grew close enough to Brown to become one his most trusted advisers, Holton made it his job to assist Brown financially, for example helping him secure a $20,000 loan from the Montreal mercantile firm Edmonstone, Allan & Co. in December 1859 to develop his lumber interests at Bothwell, Kent County.[69] This larger friendship made Holton more valuable to Brown than if he had been only a political adviser.

In later years, Brown came to see other personal qualities in Holton. He appreciated his straightforwardness, humour, and sensitivity. When Brown became seriously ill in March 1861, Holton wrote to him:

> It is a poor consolation to be told by your friends, especially by your political friends, in whose behalf you have spent so much of your apparently exhaustless energy that you have over-wrought the machine and are paying the penalty of violated natural law. But such is undoubtedly the fact and I venture to hope that the lesson will not be thrown away ... when the recuperative powers of your system have done their work and restored, as they soon will, your strength.

Holton went on to encourage Brown to "husband that strength and not again attempt to perform the labor of at least three men with unimpaired constitutions."[70]

* * *

All the while, Holton was enmeshed in Montreal and Lower Canadian politics: endless discussions, letters, and decisions. During the general election in June 1861, attention focussed on Holton as a possible Liberal candidate in Montreal Centre, one of the three newly created ridings in the city and the traditional heart of the Montreal business community. But he said that he was disinclined to seek the Montreal Centre seat in the assembly because he felt there was not enough support among businessmen for him. John Young and over 400 other electors signed a requisition inviting Holton to stand against the Liberal-Conservative candidate John Rose in this riding, but the list of names showed that Holton could not count on the majority in the business community to vote for him. This was Holton's major handicap, and so he decided not to make a bid for Montreal Centre. Holton, however, remained in the fight for Liberalism, becoming personally involved in Liberal party organizational activity. Besides working for Dorion in Montreal East, he nominated McGee in Montreal West and made a speech in his behalf. After the nomination of Benjamin Holmes in Montreal Centre at the Haymarket Square, Holton took the lead in backing the former vice-president of the Grand Trunk. When the show of hands first for John Rose and then for Holmes was not too clear, Holton cried out, "Let the crowd divide – the Holmes men to the right!" The bewildered sheriff was still uncertain about who had the most support; he hesitatingly declared: "my impression is the majority is on the side of Holmes." In the end, while McGee triumphed, Holmes and Dorion were defeated.[71]

Across Canada, the election of 1861 produced mixed results. In Lower Canada, the election proved a setback for the Cartier-Macdonald government as the eastern Opposition picked up twenty-six assembly seats. But in Upper Canada the government increased its strength, for its candidates survived a majority of the Liberal challenges. Liberal casualties included George Brown. The Cartier-Macdonald regime was back in power, but only with a slim majority. Holton told Brown that "it is obvious that we are going to have a very mean House and *personally* I have no regrets at not being of it."[72]

But Holton did not drop out of sight. His interest in provincial politics continued unabated in the early 1860s. He and a few others, including Dorion and Brown, tried to prevent the Upper and Lower Canadian Liberals from returning to their favourite sport: cutting each other to ribbons in sectional fights. As an important confidant of both Dorion and Brown, Holton's influence in both the eastern and western sections of the province was of inestimable value in the efforts to unite the Liberals. Dorion very much regretted that Holton was not in the assembly. "His usefulness," Dorion wrote Brown, "in the present house would be very great, there being such a total absence of men understanding anything in the finances of the country."[73]

Holton bided his time outside parliament. But when the Cartier-John A. Macdonald government was defeated in the legislative assembly in May 1862, Holton threw his support behind the newly formed Liberal ministry of Sandfield Macdonald and L. V. Sicotte. Cornwall lawyer Sandfield Macdonald was premier of Upper Canada and attorney general West, while Sicotte, a St.-Hyacinthe lawyer, served as premier of Lower Canada and attorney general East.[74] After resigning their seats in accordance with the rules of the day, all the new ministers faced the challenge of recapturing them in by-elections. In Montreal, it did not take Holton long to show his colours. On 5 June at the Haymarket Square, he nominated McGee, president of the council in the new ministry, urging the electors in Montreal West to back him. At the same time, Holton paid a warm tribute to Dorion, who had become the new provincial secretary, "as a high-minded man, a single-hearted patriot," adding that he hoped "that those who had votes in the County of Hochelaga would give him their cordial support." The next day Holton wrote Brown: "I have I need not say unabated confidence in the integrity and singleness of purpose of Dorion. I hope the result will show that he has done wisely in taking office, for his influence will always be exerted in the right direction."[75]

The election returns brought no surprise. McGee was re-elected by acclamation and Dorion was elected without opposition.

* * *

There were other events that claimed Luther Holton's attention, including President Abraham Lincoln's decision to issue the preliminary Emancipation Proclamation in September 1862, thereby freeing all slaves in the Confederate states on the first day of the following year. Emancipation was not something that could be easily defined; Holton understood the bitter struggle over the meaning of freedom, even after the final abolition of slavery in 1865. He had long ago acknowledged that slavery was a moral evil. But while some Canadians remained silent on the passions, divisions, and unrest slavery brought about, Holton spoke out against it. He was acutely conscious of the increasing number of black people who came to Montreal from the United States after Congress passed the Fugitive Slave Act in 1850, which was designed to facilitate the capture in the Northern free states of runaway African-American slaves by their Southern masters. Worrying about slavery south of the border, Holton favoured freedom for blacks in American society. As always, he took a strong interest in affairs in the United States, where his Northern business friends such as S. Lester Taylor of Cincinnati were working for emancipation in the South.[76] At the Bonaventure Hall in the Victoria Square on 4 December 1859, Holton revealed his attitude toward slavery by playing a prominent role in organizing Montreal's Anti-Slavery Society.[77] On the same occasion, he joined nearly one thousand other citizens, one-third of whom were black people, in extending his sympathy to the family of John Brown, the abolitionist who had been executed after leading a raid on Harper's Ferry, Virginia.[78]

Perhaps Holton's ideas were not fully developed on the difficult question of making black people the political and social equals of white people, but for him the matter became a particularly important issue on the eve of the American Civil War. For some time, he had been closely following the case of John Anderson, a fugitive slave from Missouri who in 1853 had killed a white man in his home community during his escape to Upper Canada. Free until the fall of 1860, when he was arrested and charged with murder, Anderson was tried in December of that year before chief justice John Beverley Robinson in the Court of Queen's Bench in Toronto. The decision was for extradition to the United States.[79] In Montreal, Holton sought a rational way to deal with this problem caused by the existence of slavery in America, and on 10 January 1861, he was named a member of a committee assigned the task of arranging for a public meeting on behalf of Anderson. At an overflow gathering in the Mechanics Hall a week later, Holton seconded a resolution urging that if the court's decision was not reversed in Canada, an appeal should be made to the Judicial Committee of the Privy Council in London, England, the highest tribunal of the British Empire.[80] Holton had special sympathy for blacks, as did Anderson's counsel Samuel B. Freeman, who appealed to the Court of Common Pleas in Toronto, the result being a ruling on 16 February 1861 that permitted Anderson to walk away a free man.

In April, Holton was heartened by the news that Lincoln had appointed Joshua R. Giddings of Ohio as Consul General of British North America at Montreal. Like Holton, Giddings, who arrived in the city at the end of May, was an ardent abolitionist. As time passed, Holton helped make Giddings feel at home in the city while simultaneously finding him a good source of information on developments in the United States.[81]

Even before the arrival of Giddings in Montreal, Holton wanted to know more about what was happening south of the border. On 23 April, eleven days after the Southern attack on Fort Sumter marked the start of the Civil War, Holton wrote to Galt that "it is difficult to foresee how the Southern War (if it develops into a regular and protracted war) will affect our material interests. *Not* favorably I think, for in the order of providence no people can in the long run benefit by their neighbours' misfortunes."[82] The Civil War reverberated throughout Canadian society in many ways, some more obvious than others. The conflict had a profound impact on the lives of Canadian businessmen. As a businessman who understood the importance of a stable environment for Canada's growing trade with the United States, Holton feared that a long, drawn-out war would threaten the orderly operations of business in Montreal and Canada and perhaps even result in an enormous reversal of fortune for the province.

Ten months later, in February 1862, as the Civil War continued, Holton was surely among those Canadians who assumed the best-case scenario. Holton wrote Brown:

> I cannot attempt in a brief note to answer your pregnant queries about the effect on my views of recent events in the U.S. I must reserve that for a *long talk*, the opportunity for which will I trust soon arise. I will merely say now that though my faith has been at times sorely tried it has never for a moment been shaken. I have believed that *somehow* twenty millions of Englishmen would fight their way through any difficulty without endangering either the liberty or the order that have always and everywhere characterised this *master race* of ours. I believed that if old leaders were found unequal to the crisis new leaders would be produced by it. To this faith I cling and shall cling until driven from it by the logic of facts. Thus far the facts

have, to my poor apprehension, been more favorable to the views of the friends of liberal institutions than to those of Conservatives and reactionists. But the end is not yet. This American Civil War is (to use a favorite phrase of the day) the crucial test of free institutions, not only in America but throughout the world. And I confess I look to its issues, as bearing on the theories of Gov't and human progress, which I have cherished all my life with intense concern."[83]

The words that resonated most memorably with Brown were "free institutions." Holton was indeed encouraging his political colleague to seize the high ground of the conflict south of the border and maintain it.

* * *

Around this time, wealth allowed Luther Holton to plan to make travel to Great Britain and continental Europe part of his lifestyle. For wealthy Canadians, such a trip was the ultimate educational experience, a way to give themselves and their children something that books could not do. British and European travel was the thing to do, and Holton wanted to do it. As he told Brown in February 1862, "I have always had a vague purpose of going abroad whenever circumstances should admit of my prolonged absence, and quite lately I have begun to specify a time. I feel that if I am ever to derive pleasure or instruction from foreign travel, I must not wait much longer. My children, moreover, have reached the age when the tour would be of incalculable advantage to them." Mary was twenty-one, Edward nineteen, and Amelia thirteen. Luther and his wife, Eliza, were both forty-five. "I am therefore striving to snug up my affairs," Holton continued, "so as to get away early in the summer and be gone at least six months."[84]

It appeared, however, that the need to look after his business interests – especially his real estate operations – might get in the way of Holton's dream of a trip abroad. "My business, of course, is not very complex just now," he told Brown. "Still, I have a good many matters at rather loose ends and I hold that no man should voluntarily encounter the perils of six months travel without bringing his affairs in such a state as would, in the event of any thing befalling him, entail as few sacrifices on his family as possible. My being able to go, therefore, as early as I hope is still surrounded with some uncertainty."[85]

Holton nevertheless made detailed plans. He wrote Galt:

My idea is to make England the central point, the main object of the tour – and London in my view is a large part of England. I have thought, therefore, that my plan would be to take lodgings in London, make that my Head Quarters, my home so to speak, and start thence on brief excursions to other parts of the Kingdom, and the same with reference to the continent unless I should conclude to spend a winter there. It is the first time in my life I have seriously set about preparing for a long holiday, and I am very full of it. But I am too well schooled in disappointment not to contemplate the possibility of it in this as in any other project. One good result is likely to flow from the mere conception of it. It affords a potent motive for doing what might otherwise be neglected – getting my affairs into compact form.[86]

* * *

Unfortunately, Holton did not get his business affairs into the kind of compact form that he desired, and so he decided to drop his idea of a vacation with Eliza and their children in Great Britain and continental Europe. A contributing factor to the collapse of his plans for a grand tour abroad was his return to parliament. At his Montreal friends' urging, Holton seriously considered becoming a candidate for the Victoria division seat in the legislative council. Victoria, a division composed of west and central Montreal, was to choose its representative in September 1862. This time Holton could count on the support of not only his Liberal friends but the English-speaking and French-speaking business establishment as well. Besides the strong backing he received from the *Montreal Herald*, more than fourteen-hundred electors signed a requisition inviting him to seek the Victoria seat.[87] Having paid his political dues, Holton ran for this seat in the legislative council. He promised "to promote the welfare of my native country and to advance the prosperity of the city which has been my home from early childhood, and with which all my interests no less than my affections are identified."[88] The Montreal business community wanted to secure stronger representation for itself in parliament and it was pleased to see Holton elected without opposition on 11 September.[89]

Holton showed a keen interest in strengthening the Montreal and Canadian economies throughout his short career as a legislative councilman in the second session of the seventh parliament in Quebec City, which lasted from 12 February to 12 May 1863. For instance, from the beginning, he played an active role in the immigration committee, which provided Great Britain with information on economic opportunities for immigrants to Canada.[90] British migrants could immensely improve their condition if they were willing to make the transatlantic crossing. Holton also participated in the committee's work of sending circulars to leading merchants, manufacturers, and farmers across Canada to obtain their support in efforts to expand the opportunities for manufacturing in the province.[91] While agriculture remained the dominant element in the

Canadian economy, important manufacturing advances were occurring at this time.

Much as he was involved in the work of the session, Holton shared John A. Macdonald's belief that the Liberal government of Sandfield Macdonald and Sicotte did not possess enough strength to last very long. As early as 19 February, Holton wrote George Brown that "John A. says that the Gov't can't live through the session, and I confess to great fears that they cannot."[92] Enlisting all the help he could, John A. Macdonald moved non-confidence in the government on 1 May. Despite George Brown's powerful speech in support of the ministry, it was defeated by the vote on Friday morning, 8 May, 59 to 64. Firmly wedded to the principle of responsible government, Governor General Lord Monck then granted Sandfield Macdonald's request for dissolution of parliament and a general election.[93] Monck prorogued parliament on 12 May and immediately afterward dissolved it.[94] Even before prorogation occurred, leading Liberals tested the waters and found that Holton was willing to become the finance minister of Canada in a reconstructed Liberal government.[95]

Chapter 6

Minister of Finance

Luther Holton's appointment as finance minister was a complicated event and the demand for his talents played a part. Fundamental to what happened was that Antoine Dorion and George Brown advanced Holton because they believed that he had the ability to handle the finance office. With such help, and with his own considerable ambition, he was ready to move upward in provincial politics.

Holton's opportunity came after the defeat of the Sandfield Macdonald-Sicotte government on Friday morning, 8 May 1863. For a while, confusion reigned. There was a serious erosion of support in the Lower Canadian section of the Liberal party as Sicotte lost the backing of a number of his followers.[1] Sandfield Macdonald, premier of Upper Canada and attorney general West, immediately appealed to George Brown for help in reconstructing the government. If his ministry was to be successful, he needed the support of Brown, who was the best-known and most powerful Liberal. Brown himself declined to go in, but he promised to assist as an outsider, advising Sandfield to make Dorion leader of the Lower Canadian section of the cabinet. Sandfield approached both Dorion and Holton, asking them to enter the government. They proceeded cautiously, agreeing to think about the offer and letting Sandfield know that their response would depend on what he could do to reconstruct the Upper Canadian section of the cabinet.[2] More communication took place between Sandfield, Dorion, Holton and Brown, and the door to the finance portfolio opened to Holton.

That afternoon, the situation became more complicated as Sicotte, still premier of Lower Canada and attorney general East, invited Holton to join the Lower Canadian section of the ministry under his leadership. Hoping to serve under Dorion rather than under Sicotte, Holton declined the offer.[3] The next day, Saturday, Luther Holton left Quebec City for Montreal to spend the weekend with Eliza and their children. There is no

Luther Holton as Finance Minister of Canada in 1864.
Courtesy of the Ontario Archives.

evidence to show that Eliza begged Luther not to accept the finance portfolio; she was willing to share him with Quebec City. Returning to the capital on Tuesday, Holton discovered that Sicotte and the rest of the Lower Canadian section had resigned. Sicotte, who had tried to continue working together with Sandfield, was resentful at what he considered betrayal by the Upper Canadian premier. On Wednesday, Dorion, upon agreeing to become premier of Lower Canada and attorney-general East, offered the finance office to Holton. Although Holton felt a growing compulsion, he persuaded Dorion to first accompany him to Montreal and talk with their friends about the subject.[4] They assured Holton of their support. In the end, Dorion had his way, and on 16 May, Monck made the appointment and Holton took his oath of office.[5]

Holton took his oath within the abiding traditions of responsible government. Devoted to democracy and the order of law, he was committed

John Sandfield Macdonald.
Courtesy of the Ontario Archives.

to a political system that he hoped would move Canada toward its highest ambitions. He believed in orderly change, wanted economic growth, and sought to preserve a government that provided both.

The salient feature of the Sandfield Macdonald-Dorion cabinet was the pre-eminent standing of Holton and Oliver Mowat, the postmaster general. A Toronto lawyer and a forceful man in public life, Mowat enjoyed a rising provincial reputation. The presence of Holton, who had a good understanding not only of Lower Canada but also of Upper Canada, indicated that Sandfield Macdonald and Dorion were trying to overcome the image of their party as a collection of rival interest groups and to head a unified, coherent organization – a truly provincial administration. These two men – Holton and Mowat, in that order – would be the prime influences acting on the premiers.

* * *

Even as the news of his appointment became official, Holton had to prepare for the general election. The Liberals, led by grain merchant John Young, Alexander F. Cockburn of the Montreal Brass Foundry, import merchant David Torrance, and lawyer Rodolphe Laflamme, and supported by the *Montreal Herald* and *Le Pays*, carefully organized the candidacy of Luther Holton for Montreal Centre. The program Holton offered the electors contained spending cuts, an increase in taxes, a relatively high tariff to protect manufacturers and raise revenues, a low level of import duties on raw materials required by industry, and the improvement of the Canadian militia. In his speech at Nordheimer's Hall on 20 May, Holton emphasized that "the connexion between Canada and the great Empire of which we form a part must be maintained at all hazards. Whatever sacrifices the maintenance of that connexion involves, whether in the form of privation or even of actual war, we must meet them like men."[6] In the context of Canadian politics in the mid-1860s and of the American Civil War, Holton's program was dramatic.

The Liberal-Conservative party countered with John Rose, the popular Montreal lawyer. Holton and Rose fought a bitter battle, complete with mudslinging on both sides. Rose attacked the personal integrity of his opponent by charging that Holton was "playing fast and loose to both sections of the province." Holton shot back "that is the policy of your leader, John A. Macdonald."[7] *La Minerve*, which was contemptuous of George Brown, sniped at Luther Holton as Brown's "alter ego," not a strong independent voice in Lower Canada's affairs.[8] Holton was no choirboy, but he shied away from brazen skulduggery in his political quarrel with *La Minerve*. The quarrel did not destroy Holton's deep-rooted French-Canadian sympathies. Seeing himself not only as a friend of but also as an adviser to Brown, Holton's hope was that the *Globe* editor would show more affection for the French-Canadian culture. "The chances of success between Rose & Holton seems pretty even," noted a Liberal-Conservative observer.[9] But when McGee, a Sicotte follower and an influential politician, bolted the Liberal party and fiercely attacked Holton, the defeat of Holton was almost certain. Holton lost to Rose by eighty-eight votes on 9 June.

Later, on 23 June, the candidacy of Luther Holton proved overpowering in Chateauguay, a rural riding just south of Montreal, as he swept to victory. When officials counted the votes, Holton won the Chateauguay seat, outpolling both of the other two candidates, Liberal-Conservative H. J. Clarke and Independent J. Taillefer.[10]

Liberals carried the elections in Upper Canada fairly impressively: about 40 seats fell to the party. In Lower Canada, however, Liberals lost ground; they had taken only about 24 seats. When observers explained the losses, the opposition of Sicotte and his followers was listed first. In an important sense, Sandfield Macdonald and Dorion understood that, in winning about 64 seats, they might have a slender majority in the assembly for a while when the new parliament met later, in mid-August.

* * *

In his very first days in his office in Quebec City, in mid-May, Luther Holton had to reacquaint himself with the finance department. As often as he had dealt with it as a member of the public accounts committee in 1854-57, now he saw it from the inside. Standing in some ways first in seniority, the finance department consisted of several bureaus, each headed by a chief to administer separate functions of the public purse. The deputy inspector general was responsible for the collection of canal tolls, the commissioner of customs handled customs duties and excise taxes, and the auditor general audited the accounts of the various departments. John Langton had held the post of auditor general since 1855, and he had won Holton's esteem at that time. Now they forged an even closer union as Langton impressed the finance minister with his ability and fairness. In the past, the management of public funds had been far from efficient. Canada's accounts were somewhat confused, and delays in collecting and organizing financial information had long plagued the finance department. In many ways, Holton found Canada's system of accounting and statistics lamentably inadequate to the task of coordinating and assessing the province's financial operations. Sensitive to the need to address these concerns, Holton enlisted the auditor general's aid to lay the foundation for an improved system of accounting and audit.[11] Eventually, this led to the development of new techniques of political accountability and to budget reform that helped move fiscal administration closer to the ideal of responsible representative government.

Managing the finance department could be a thankless task, made easier only by the fact that Holton enjoyed cordial relations with most of the top civil servants under him. Besides himself and the senior people, the finance office contained many clerks, some messengers, and a few watchmen. With this staff, Holton had to manage all the affairs, paperwork, and maintenance of the public purse. A key to his success was his capacity to master detail, run his eye over columns of figures, and draw useful conclusions or detect problems. Like all successful administrators, he could see the forest as well as the trees.

During his time in his office, Holton soon discovered that patronage was one of the facts of life in a cabinet post. With a new government in the provincial capital, a number of Liberals wanted a piece of the spoils.

But Holton made it a matter of policy that there would be no spoils system. Regardless of their politics, clerks who performed satisfactorily kept their jobs. Competent political friends, however, did get jobs if there was a vacancy. For example, Holton appointed Benjamin Holmes collector of customs in Montreal. In this case, even the Liberal-Conservative *Montreal Gazette* approved of Holton's decision: "Holmes is likely to perform the duties of his new office in a manner to give satisfaction to the business community, with whom, we believe, his appointment will be generally regarded with favour. The party owe him this much for his services, for the manner in which he has repeatedly rushed into the breach in times of difficulty."[12]

Holton ran the finance department with a decisive and brisk energy. He quickly understood that he needed co-operation from the bureau chiefs in the department, and he began to identify with their concerns. They appreciated his warm sympathy and support. Willing to hear their ideas, he often must have lightened the atmosphere of an argumentative session with a smile, or a laugh, or a story. They knew that he could be impatient and short-tempered, but this was not the Luther Holton of their everyday experience. Organizing them into an informal group, he gathered their advice and then issued orders about canal tolls, customs duties, and excise taxes. He took his responsibilities seriously, but he did not assume the attitude that he was literally responsible for everything that occurred in his department. He was a delegator, ready to entrust authority to the bureau chiefs. Dorion and Sandfield Macdonald admired Holton's administrative skills. They also knew the value of being able to rely on a subordinate who could take the heat for actions the premiers did not wish to be blamed for.

* * *

Holton's communications with Grand Trunk officials revealed a man expecting trouble, hoping for peaceful dealings but ready to face conflict to maintain the government and the principles it stood for. In the finance office, he provided bold initiatives for the provincial political economy, initiatives that sparked a swirl of political controversy in 1863-64. He was deeply disturbed by Cartier and John A. Macdonald's policy of linking the politics of the Grand Trunk, the Bank of Upper Canada, and Canada's financial agents in London (Baring Brothers and Glyn, Mills & Co.) to the fortunes of the Canadian government.[13] Holton believed that the success of the Sandfield Macdonald-Dorion government and the province depended, not on Canada's identification with the political ties of the Bank of Upper Canada, the Grand Trunk, and the London agents, but on a new political economy that promoted sound finance in the provincial government. Holton's policy became a point of bitter dispute between him and the Grand Trunk.

Holton focussed the lines of power on his office, winning authority over things such as government contracts with railways for the carriage of the mail. At the same time, he worked in harness with Oliver Mowat, the postmaster general, and conferred with Dorion and Sandfield to address the problem of paying the Grand Trunk for the postal services it was supplying. Devoting considerable thought to the problem that he had inherited from the Cartier-John A. Macdonald regime and the Sandfield Macdonald-Sicotte government, Holton also discussed the matter with C. J. Brydges, the railway's managing director. Holton then helped prepare an order-in-council that authorized Mowat to increase the payment to the Grand Trunk for an improved scale of postal services from $70 to $100 per mile per annum.[14] But Brydges, who distrusted the Liberal government as did the other Grand Trunk executives, complained that the new sum was not high enough. Backed publicly by engineer Walter Shanly, a Liberal-Conservative, Holton argued that the amount was adequate and fair. When the Liberal-Conservatives later again achieved power, they left the sum unchanged.

An equal or greater challenge for Holton was Grand Trunk president Edward W. Watkin's allegation that the finance minister was wrongfully refusing to return £42, 500 of the railway's bonds. Earlier, the Cartier-John A. Macdonald government had accepted these bonds as security for a large loan it had made to the Grand Trunk; the bonds were in the safe vaults of Baring Brothers and Glyn, Mills & Co. Again, Holton had inherited a problem from a previous regime. To complicate matters, Brydges charged that first the Cartier-Macdonald government and then the Sandfield Macdonald-Sicotte ministry had illegally applied the railway's postal earnings to the repayment of the loan. The confused affair did not end there. Watkin wrote Holton lengthy vituperative lectures. In his letters to the Grand Trunk president, Holton called Watkin to account for his statements of complaint and reproach, reminding him that as finance minister he was doing his utmost to protect the public purse and satisfy the needs of the railway. In the end, after Holton had secured evidence of the full repayment of the loan and had arranged for the return of the bonds to the Grand Trunk, Watkin withdrew his "charge of willful wrong" and the finance minister accepted "your unreserved withdrawal."[15]

In many ways, the clash between Holton and Watkin reflected political conflict. Holton was appalled by what he saw as Watkin's favouring of the Liberal-Conservatives in towns and cities across Canada during the recent general election. More significant, Watkin's close ties with the Liberal-Conservative party seemed to result in a provincial fiscal program that was on the verge of collapse. The same Luther Holton who in the years 1853-57 had paid little attention to the impact of the Grand Trunk on the public purse now came down forcefully on the side of reforming Canada's fiscal policy. Liberally using his political power, Holton bucked Watkin whenever he thought it necessary, advancing thereby fiscal reform at the expense of corporate privilege and corruption.

Holton's approach did not mean that he believed railways to have no stake in public well-being. Rather, he envisioned Canada as an arena in which all important railways, including the Grand Trunk, the Great Western, and the Northern, would be free to provide transportation services and meet the needs of Canadians. His predecessors in the finance office had committed the province to using its capital resources to establish long-term funding for these railways; Holton honoured this commitment by continuing to assist in financing them.[16] He was interested in creating a political economy based on sound public finance and favourable to commerce and manufacturing as well as to railways.

Later generations of historians have not all seen the same picture that Luther Holton saw. But Douglas McCalla has emphasized the role of railways in nation-building, saying that "in mid-nineteenth-century Canada, railways were the major collective economic project of leading elements in the provincial business community and of the provincial government, and they were thus a central element in the state-making process."[17]

* * *

No one ever argued that Holton did not attend to his duties. Even when he wanted a few moments of peace and quiet, one of his bureau chiefs would appear with government business that he could not put off. In mid-May 1863, in his early days in his office, the merchants of Port Dalhousie on Lake Ontario and of Port Maitland on Lake Erie asked him to lower the wharfage dues at the harbours of these port towns. These towns had long been lake-shipping points, but the local merchants now found the wharfage dues to be particularly burdensome. Responding to their request, Holton persuaded the cabinet to reduce the wharfage dues on goods shipped at these harbours from five to two cents per ton.[18]

From the outset, Holton looked out for manufacturers, seeing them as a vital part of the Canadian economy. For example, he assisted the Canadian Rubber Company in Montreal, which was in difficulty because the India rubber belting it had exported to England in 1858 had attracted no buyers. By allowing the rubber belting to re-enter the province without requiring the company to pay customs duties, Holton ensured that it could minimize costs as it sought a local market for its product. The law provided that such goods could be re-imported duty free only within three years from the date of exportation. But because there had been a change in ownership of the Canadian Rubber Company since 1858, there was agreement in the cabinet that Holton's action followed the spirit of the law. Holton found, not for the last time, that he could stimulate output by working with manufacturers in Montreal and elsewhere in Canada.[19]

More importantly, Holton indirectly aided manufacturers tremendously by maintaining the relatively high tariff on manufactured goods that Alexander Galt as finance minister had introduced in 1859.[20] Facing stiff competition from firms abroad, both in Great Britain and the United States, these producers needed a protective tariff to survive and develop within Canada. While Holton planned to revise the tariff with a promise of lower customs duties on some items, he decided to keep the tariff high enough to protect the market for Canadian manufacturers' products.[21] Across the province manufacturers of everything from shoes to brass instruments to carriages benefited immensely from Holton's tariff policy.[22]

But throughout his months as finance minister, Luther Holton endured a frustrating life, touched by the Liberal party's uncertain support in the assembly. It began with the battle to have the party's choice of speaker accepted. On 13 August 1863, the Liberals won the first division in the new parliament on the appointment of the speaker, Lewis Wallbridge, 63 to 58, but their control of the assembly remained in doubt.[23]

But the welfare of Canada demanded legislation, meaning that the Liberals would have to organize and discipline themselves. The first session of the eighth parliament, meeting from mid-August to 15 October 1863, produced a number of important provincial laws. Holton publicly advocated most of the legislation the Canadian legislature passed, and he lobbied Liberals to remember the program that together they had supported during the general election.

* * *

It was time to address the problems and needs of a society whose neighbour to the south was involved in a civil war. There had also been several snags in Anglo-American relations. For instance, in November 1861, Jefferson Davis, president of the Confederacy, sent James M. Mason and John Slidell to serve as commissioners in Great Britain and France, respectively. As they were travelling aboard the British mail steamer *Trent*, a U.S. Navy vessel stopped and boarded the ship to seize the Confederate diplomats. The *Trent* affair caused an international crisis and pushed Britain to the brink of war against the United States. Thousands of imperial troops sped across the Atlantic to protect Canada. But, like most Canadians, Holton was trying to calm the waters. He did not wish to provoke the Americans. Always an acute observer of affairs in the United States, he sensed that President Abraham Lincoln wanted not war against Canada, but peaceful adjustments in Anglo-American relations. Given this political reality, Holton adopted a strategy designed to promote peace between Canada and the United States.

Ties of kinship and commerce linked Canada to the Northern free states. Like many other Canadians whose parents came from the United States, Holton saw it as a great example of a progressive, dynamic society. He firmly believed that the old American virtues of liberty, freedom, and order would prevail.[24]

Holton wanted the North to succeed, for he thought that it embodied a sense of order, a devotion to freedom, a commitment to liberty, and a nationalism that under Lincoln did not require the invasion of Canada. Holton felt that the values of the North were the values of Canada and Great Britain. He had often visited the United States, particularly New York City, and his knowledge of things American was extensive.[25] Though unhappy about anti-British tendencies in America, especially those of William H. Seward, Lincoln's secretary of state, who was interested in the annexation of British North America, Holton shrewdly avoided a direct challenge to him. Usually generous to those with whom he disagreed, he had no desire to provoke American annexationists.

Holton's efforts to avoid collision did not mean that he refused to consider measures to defend Canada. He was just as interested in enhancing Canada's security as he was in promoting the province's economic interests. As minister of finance, he rallied behind the Sandfield Macdonald-Dorion government's decision to improve and expand the Canadian militia. At the end of August, Holton, backed by all the other cabinet members, made clear in the assembly that he was prepared to support militia reform along these lines.[26] In the second week of September, the ministry won parliamentary approval for its two bills that significantly enhanced the militia.[27] The first bill provided for a service militia composed of men on the volunteer rolls who could be made available quickly in response to an emergency. Henceforth, militia officers had to have attended a school of military instruction, and men under them could be ordered out for six days of drill per year. On the strength of the second bill, the volunteer force could be increased to thirty-five thousand. As it happened, the Canadian authorities did not call out the new militia because Lincoln remained totally opposed to an invasion of Canada.

But Canada could never rule out the possibility of an American attack, and Holton helped Canadians toughen up their defences. In 1863, militia expenditures grew with his support to $481,116, as compared to $98,444 spent on this item in 1862.[28] The improvements that came with this increased defence expenditure included the opening of two new military schools in Canada in 1864, as well as the distribution of new uniforms and equipment to militiamen.[29] It was Holton's role to deal with the financial side of strengthening Canada's defences and he obviously had a clear idea of what strategy should be followed. Although he knew that an invasion of the province would require large operations far beyond the competence of the Canadian militia, his policy to build up this force had merit.

* * *

The first need now was money: not only to pay the militia but also to conduct the rest of Canada's business. After the passage of the militia bills, Holton prepared to put his budget before the assembly, but he faced serious political problems. In the lower chamber, the Liberals were never really a cohesive political force. They were certainly not strong enough for any major financial legislative initiative. The main measure that Holton planned to introduce at this time was his supply bill. Even this might run into difficulty, given the Sandfield Macdonald-Dorion government's precarious parliamentary majority. There was still open division in the Lower Canadian Liberal party. The rebels, who followed Sicotte, remained dissatisfied with Dorion's leadership. To win back the rebels, Dorion worked for reconciliation with Sicotte by offering him a judgeship. Within a few days, Sicotte accepted the offer.[30] Several of the Sicotte Liberals now committed themselves on Dorion's side. The parliamentary basis of the Sandfield Macdonald-Dorion government remained uncertain, however.

To give the government more time to improve its position, Holton used delaying tactics; he planned to present only an interim budget with a supply bill as its centrepiece now and a full budget including new taxes later, in the spring of 1864. This in a nutshell was Holton's conception of how the government was going to survive, at least for a while.

Even so, the lack of adequate Liberal support remained a burning issue. This placed a heavy responsibility on Holton when he opened his interim budget in the assembly on 15 September 1863. His budget represented a new sense of accountability and a new sense of who in the Canadian government was responsible for the province's finances. He articulated a model of the finance minister as a citizen who favoured "the restoration of our public credit to a sound basis."[31] The Upper and Lower Canadian Liberal-Conservatives were bound together in their opposition to the budget. But Holton's budget speech, according to John A. Macdonald, the acknowledged leader of the Upper Canadian Liberal-Conservatives, was "a calm statement, in very temperate language."[32] More than anything else, his speech placed Holton in the public eye. Holton's "exposition of the state of our finances," wrote the *Montreal Herald*, "was frank and sufficiently lucid to be understood by any person giving ordinary attention, and possessed of ordinary capacity."[33] The budget speech also helped Holton's standing in the public press in London, England. The *Economist* referred to it as "the progress of sound financial views in Canada," and the *Times* was pleased "to find a Minister of Finance who can look affairs boldly in the face and tell the representatives of the people what it behooves them to do."[34]

Faced with the problem of a budget deficit accumulated largely by the Liberal-Conservatives and to some extent by the Liberals over several years, Holton had to make some difficult economic policy decisions.[35] Although the Canadian people generally appreciated the economic and social benefits that came from government spending, the public also wanted to retire the huge provincial debt of $70 million. There was a strong sense that so much debt was a serious danger, an obstacle in the path of economic recovery and long-term prosperity.

The condition of Canada's finances thus demanded action from Holton. Energetic and self-assured, he was eager to put his financial expertise at the service of the province in these difficult times. Holton's budget speech contained his three-pronged plan of action: the cutting of public expenditures, the reduction of the canal tolls, and the appointment of a new government banker. Parliament, Holton added, could look forward in the next regular session, in the spring of 1864, to the introduction of his new system of taxation.[36] That was his long-term strategy.

In the assembly, there were over three weeks of debate on Holton's supply bill; it did not have an easy passage. Holton had the duty, among other things, to raise revenue and control expenditure. As the principal force behind the government's supply bill, he was responsible for arguing its case at second reading and for seeing it through the committee stage, and this involved daily and lengthy attendance in the assembly. Holton tried to get the assemblymen to think about what the budget was and what the taxpayers' money went for.

Throughout this period, the supply bill suffered slings and arrows from the Liberal-Conservatives. Galt criticized the finance minister for failing to introduce new taxes in order to provide additional revenue. This was an important issue, and Galt argued his point well. The prospect of the government's defeat loomed. But Holton was one of the few men in Canada capable of going toe-to-toe with Galt in debate over financial policy and holding his own as he drew from deep personal resources. Holton also worked frequently behind the scenes with Dorion, wooing wavering votes in the assembly. The issue there was close, coming down in the end to a matter of three crucial votes. On 8 October 1863, in the waning days of the short session, the house rejected Galt's no-confidence motion by 64 to 61 votes.[37] As the fateful vote was tallied, twenty-three Lower Canadian and forty-one Upper Canadian Liberals voted in the majority. So finally the supply bill went through, and Holton gained a reputation as an astute public financier. Then, on 15 October, at a moment of the Sandfield Macdonald-Dorion ministry's own choice, Monck prorogued parliament.

* * *

In the following weeks, Holton did all he could to implement his policies. On the first of his financial changes, the cutbacks in government spending, he was indefatigable, working long hours and taking pride in his drive for fiscal economy. In his time, there was no thought of the intricate calculation that about seven decades later began to characterize government account keeping, whereby government debt was managed and considered a positive good, essential to the well-being of the nation's economy. Holton happily recalled the reforming British government of Sir Robert Peel, whose budget surplus in the mid-1840s had ended the long history of budget deficits in Britain, and he looked to the tradition of Peelite finance for inspiration.[38] Holton's job was to identify potential spending cuts and then seek to achieve them. He found effective allies in the provincial capital, especially Auditor General John Langton, as well as his colleagues in the cabinet, in his drive to effect economy in public expenditure.[39] Nobody argued with Holton's decision to reduce provincial spending by about $500,000.[40] There were deep cuts in the crown lands department, in the finance department, and also in the roads and bridges area of the public works department.

At the same time, Holton took a leading hand in securing a substantial increase in defence expenditures. He never veered off his charted course to seek to prepare for a possible attack from the United States. Holton's budget for the fiscal year 1863 as proposed to parliament, called for estimated expenditures of $13,639,223 against expected revenues of $12,191,713, creating a deficit of $1,447,510 – a huge amount at the time.[41]

On the canal tolls, Holton accepted that, in a moderate form, they were essential to produce revenue to help bring down the deficit. He did not, however, support the less flexible position that his predecessor in the finance office, W. P. Howland, had taken. Back in 1860, the Cartier-John A. Macdonald government, in addition to abolishing the tolls on the St. Lawrence canals, had provided for refunding ninety percent of the tolls collected on the Welland Canal from forwarders whose vessels also used the St. Lawrence canals. This major toll change was a decisive step in increasing the St. Lawrence trade. But in April 1863, Howland and his colleagues in the Sandfield Macdonald-Sicotte government, in an attempt to produce more revenue, had suddenly reimposed the tolls in full without notifying forwarders in good time. The government's action obviously posed problems for the forwarders. At that time, Holton had unsuccessfully tried to talk Howland out of reimposing the tolls for the year 1863.[42] It was evident to Holton that the abrupt revival of the tolls involved severe risk for the forwarders, who had already entered into contracts with flour millers and other shippers on the assumption that there was no need to build toll charges into their freight rates.

Fears among Montreal forwarders and other local businessmen pushed them to organize a deputation that approached Holton in his office at Quebec City shortly after he became finance minister in mid-May 1863.[43] He listened sympathetically to their concerns. He was aware that a number of them, including forwarder George E. Jaques, shipbuilder Augustin Cantin, and flour miller James McDougall, had recently met in Montreal to protest the re-imposition of canal tolls.[44] They argued that Howland's toll policy threw their plans to expand their businesses into limbo, for the St. Lawrence trade was bound to decline with the revival of the tolls.

Flexible and more than ready to make a reduction, Holton advocated what he called moderate, rather than excessive, tolls. The Sandfield Macdonald-Dorion cabinet, including Receiver-general Howland, now agreed with Holton's moderate position. Consequently, Holton pushed ahead with the second main change in his budget for 1863. Instead of maintaining the existing high tolls, he lowered them, so that they amounted to only five cents on a barrel of flour and only one cent on a bushel of wheat through the whole chain of canals between Lake Erie and tidewater.[45] His principal objective clearly was to bring down the provincial deficit by creating additional revenue, while simultaneously encouraging forwarders, flour millers, and other business concerns interested in water-borne commerce to develop their businesses.

Accounts kept at the capital in the year ending 31 December 1863 do not offer a clear picture of the revenue produced by the revised toll system on the Welland Canal and the St. Lawrence canals alone, but the available evidence shows that the receipts from all the provincial canals grew from $213,487 to $385,220 between 1862 and 1863. This made a positive if relatively small impression on the Canadian government's financial plight.[46] In the same period, however, traffic on the Welland Canal fell by eight percent and on the St. Lawrence canals by seven percent. There was nevertheless agreement among some of the Montreal forwarders that the decline in traffic arose less from the revised tolls than from the short crop in the American midwest and the low wheat prices in Europe in 1863.[47] By contrast, when compared to the traffic in 1860, the first year of free canals, the traffic in 1863 increased by twenty-one percent on the Welland Canal and by twenty-two percent on the St. Lawrence canals.[48] Although Holton's approach to the canal toll issue thus did not remove every problem from the system, it was better than the old approach.

On the third of Holton's major financial changes, the appointment of a new government banker, his most important objectives were the prudent management of the public debt and the improvement of Canada's credit. In the past, parliament had failed to exert proper control over the provincial debt. By the time Canada had absorbed the cost of improving the militia in 1863, the provincial debt exceeded $70 million and one third of the public revenue was going to meet the interest payments on the debt.[49] The bulk of the provincial government's revenue came from customs duties, consisting of about $5 million in 1863.[50] But this was not nearly enough to cover the debt charges and the cost of the government's normal administrative functions. In late 1863, Holton felt obliged to deal with the immediate problem arising from the lack of funds; he had to enlist those men who had wealth and who managed strong financial institutions. So he took the initiative in borrowing $1.5 million from the Bank of Montreal.[51] Even though this loan by itself was a welcome success, it increased the provincial debt. This difficulty was superimposed on a problem of longer standing: the precarious state of Canada's credit in London, England.

Another disturbing aspect of the Canada's financial condition was that the government was unable to borrow from the Bank of Upper Canada, the provincial banker since 1850. Before he had secured the $1.5 million loan from the Bank of Montreal, Holton knew that the Bank of Upper Canada could deliver no such sum.[52] The extremely weak position of the Bank of Upper Canada made financing the public debt through this Toronto-based institution a hopeless proposition. Lamed by the financial crisis in 1857-58, the important Bank of Upper Canada had never really recovered from the loan losses of those years. In addition, it continued to have problem loans in real estate and railways, especially the Grand Trunk, and remained heavily dependent upon the major provincial deposit.

Holton had a good knowledge of the Bank of Upper Canada in particular and the nature of the banking industry in the province in general. He had served as a director first of the City Bank in Montreal and then of the Commercial Bank of the Midland District. In 1854, as a member of an assembly committee on the subject of the government deposit account, he took the lead in closely examining the Bank of Upper Canada on its handling of this account.[53]

Now, in 1863, Holton, as finance minister, undertook to reform the government account and the provincial debt. He prepared a supply bill designed, among other things, to give him authority to borrow the money he needed at present from one or more of Canada's commercial banks. It was because the Bank of Upper Canada as a source of such a borrowing was out of the question that Holton approached the Bank of Montreal for a loan. He also tried to borrow from the Commercial Bank of the Midland District.[54] At the time, he was a shareholder in both of these banks and a major customer of the Commercial Bank. While the Bank of Montreal immediately declared itself willing to meet the Sandfield Macdonald-Dorion ministry's requirements, the Commercial Bank expressed regret that it was not in a position to lend the government any money. Holton and the Bank of Montreal were in close touch from the moment its loan offer was on the table. For its part, parliament gave the green light to the Bank of Montreal to proceed with its loan proposal by passing the supply bill.

As the Bank of Montreal was a highly respectable and conservative institution, one which he knew and trusted, Holton now offered to put into its hands all of the Canadian government's business in the province. Lending to the government and holding the provincial account together formed a valuable business; consequently, the Bank of Montreal was delighted to enter into negotiations with Holton to take the account. He saw his role in these successful negotiations as a creator of a new government–bank relationship, and his high hopes of moving into a new era were embodied in an order-in-council by which on 1 January 1864 the Bank of Montreal became the sole banker and fiscal agent for the Canadian government in the province.[55] Under it, Holton transferred the provincial account from the Bank of Upper Canada to the Bank of Montreal. In the process, the Bank of Upper Canada lost its status as government banker. The Canadian government received from the Bank of Montreal the $1.5 million loan, payable in three years at an interest rate of five percent per annum and secured by provincial debentures. The Bank of Montreal supplied Holton with these funds at once and this allowed him to bridge over the longer period required to secure revenue from his promised new taxes. He was truly exuberant about the outcome of these complex negotiations.

* * *

Holton was confident that he had reached a satisfactory solution and had successfully defended the interest of the public purse committed to his care. Imaginative and constructive, his reforms brought some order into financial administration and made it possible for him to obtain larger domestic distribution of the provincial debt. Holton certainly regarded borrowing from the Bank of Montreal as preferable to borrowing on the London money market at this juncture. Political instability in Canada and the province's precarious finances, as he well knew, had made British investors skeptical about Canada bonds. Growing domestic participation in Canadian government loan operations, however, helped drive some of their doubts away.[56] Holton's reforms in their entirety thus contributed to a modest improvement in the government's credit in London. The promise for the future rested upon Canada's ability to raise capital in the London money market. Holton recognized that Canada, saddled with an unbalanced budget, a large debt, and a rather disappointing economy, would again need British capital to keep the government functioning.

London was indeed still by far the most important source of money for the Canadian government, and Baring Brothers and Glyn, Mills & Co., the province's agents in the city since 1837, raised all the capital that came from there. But even though the London market, in the light of Holton's financial reforms, now took a slightly more favourable view on lending to Canada than it had a year or so earlier, the attempts by these two banking houses to raise funds for the government met with relatively little success.[57] For a finance minister who needed to fill an empty purse, the condition of the money market was still far from ideal. The Canadian government's difficult position, combined with continuing political instability in the province and the possibility of war between Britain and America, dampened British investors' enthusiasm.

As a result, in June 1863, when Holton asked Barings and Glyn, Mills to bring out a £250,000 issue of Canada bonds to aid him in meeting the interest payments on the provincial debt, they agreed to do so but not until the time was right.[58] They knew that they could place these bonds, not at par, but only at prices between 97 and 98, the same prices that the Canada bonds already on the market commanded. Then in July, the prices continued to slide to between 95.5 and 96.5.[59] Fearing that British investors might lose what confidence they had in Canada's ultimate ability to redeem its pledges, Holton now approved the delay in offering the issue to them. By the end of 1863, Barings and Glyn, Mills had placed only a small loan for the financially pressed Canadian government. No member of the assembly was more aware than Holton that Canada's shaky credit made it impossible for the financial agents to raise any more capital in the London market.

The money British investors had loaned to the young province was almost an embarrassment – not only were the securities discounted but the interest was in arrears. Barings and Glyn, Mills, anxious to maintain their firms' own prestige and to serve the best interests of the province, advanced some funds to the Canadian government to help it pay the interest on the provincial debt. By September 1863, the government's total indebtedness to Glyn, Mills had reached $1,755,179, while that to Barings had grown to $1,587,991.[60] For his part, Holton, though unable to reduce Canada's debt to these houses, made a determined effort to meet its interest payments. Although some Canadians went about their business without any concern about what happened to Canada's credit in London, Holton worked hard at the problem. Fortunately, the unexpected increase in customs receipts helped him to make some headway in servicing the debt. Despite the difficulties that remained, Holton thus played an important role in putting the province's finances on a firmer basis.

* * *

Over the short run, however, Holton faced serious opposition from within the Liberal party. Criticism suddenly came especially from George Brown, who detected a problem in Holton's motivations. Financial and political motives were intermingled in Holton's attempt to put provincial finance on a firmer footing. Upper and Lower Canada fiercely competed for government favour, and the appointment of the provincial banker presented an opportunity for patronage that no finance minister could ignore. But Holton's scheme to transfer the government account from the Bank of Upper Canada in Toronto to the Bank of Montreal in Montreal had a negative side. From Brown's viewpoint, it was an obvious example of showing special favour to Lower Canada.[61] It is not surprising that Holton's transfer scheme also drew immediate opposition from the Bank of Upper Canada that was anxious to keep the government account. Defending the Bank of Upper Canada, Brown protested the transfer. The effect of this was to divide the slender Liberal majority in the assembly. Holton's basic instincts led him to try to win Brown to his side. The finance minister was obviously not prepared to write off Upper Canada to secure political support in Montreal and Lower Canada.

There were things to do, and quickly. Perhaps it was not yet too late for Holton to repair his relations with the Toronto journalist. He entered into active correspondence with Brown about the government account matter, reminding him that he was helping the Bank of Upper Canada work through its difficulties.[62] The finance minister found himself in the position of a man fighting on two fronts, battling to put Canada's finances on a sounder footing and struggling to retain the support of the Upper Canadian Liberals.

If the ardour of making his case and corresponding with his old friend strained Holton, his writing did not show it. His logic gained momentum, his style appeared more lively, as he dashed off letters to meet the mail. Holton tried to persuade Brown to view the appointment of the Bank of Montreal as the new government banker, not as a strike against Upper Canada, but as a means of obtaining the money required to meet the financial needs of the province. "The truth is," Holton wrote Brown, "Montreal is as much the commercial and monetary capital of Canada as New York of the U.S. or London of Great Britain, and when people want to borrow large sums of money they must go to the great money centres."[63] In a sense, Holton saw himself as a finance minister in the mold of Britain's chancellor of the exchequer, William E. Gladstone, and America's secretary of the treasury, Salmon P. Chase. "Is Mr. Gladstone," Holton asked Brown, "accused of local partiality because he addresses himself to the capitalists of London instead of Glasgow or Mr. Chase for negotiating his loans in New York instead of Cincinnati? What London is to Britain and New York to U.S. Montreal is by the operation of irresistible laws to *Canada*, Upper and Lower."[64] Brown disagreed. All he could think of was that Holton's plan was an injustice that shortchanged Upper Canada.[65]

The plan was too lopsided for Brown, even though Holton told the Toronto journalist that pragmatic political considerations had also motivated him to remove the government account from the Bank of Upper Canada. The bank seemed to Holton to serve especially the interests of the Liberal-Conservatives and the Grand Trunk, not the department of finance.[66] Holton was dismayed by what he saw as the bank's lack of concern about general prosperity in the province. He wanted to use the removal of the government account from the bank to diminish the political influence of the Grand Trunk. This may have been to Brown's liking, but it was not enough to convince him that Holton's action was necessary.

Holton designed his bank policy mainly to increase the Canadian government's financial resources, but this concern did not conceal from Brown his Montreal and Lower Canadian bias. Holton nevertheless tried to help the troubled bank. By arranging to convert the large government deposit in the bank into a long-term loan bearing a low rate of interest, he gave the institution substantial assistance.[67] But Brown still felt that the Montrealer's sectionalism was hurting the bank. Despite their disagreement over the bank problem, this issue had no discernible effect on Holton's personal friendship with Brown. The two continued to respect each other, and Brown remained Holton's single most intimate correspondent. The special friendship that reverberated throughout the Holton–Brown correspondence surrounding government matters was completely genuine.

Holton thought of his bank policy primarily as an instrument for initiating the improvement of Canada's credit, a process that had a high and immediate priority for him. He believed that it was the supreme responsibility of the finance minister to stabilize the province's credit rating through the appointment of the Bank of Montreal as Canada's banker; Holton never wavered from this theory. Wedded to a concept of a political economy that envisioned Canada as a province of merchants, manufacturers, and farmers, he found it easy to adjust his thinking to the coming of a new era. In his mind, the new provincial banker was capable of helping the finance department cope with Canada's multimillion-dollar debt and promote economic growth. Holton had reported this huge debt in the assembly – it was a painful fact to him. But for the first time, the province and its leaders knew the truth. Far from simply telling the truth and then standing back, Holton had offered a plan that promised to bring some order out of the existing chaos in public finance.

* * *

Bank of Montreal credit provided Holton as finance minister with the money he needed to fund the government's program of internal improvements such as the work of the Geological Survey of Canada and its director, Sir William Logan, as well the recent publication of his book, *Geology of Canada*. In 1863, Geological Survey of Canada expenditures grew with Holton's strong backing to $23,600, as compared to $17,400 spent on this project in 1862.[68] But within the cabinet, support for the Geological Survey of Canada was not universal, as revealed by Sandfield Macdonald's opposition to public funding for the publication of *Geology of Canada*. Quick to disagree with Sandfield, Luther Holton told the assembly that "he felt that money could not be better laid out than in procuring this information and having it published."[69] In June 1864, after he was out of office, Holton continued to support the Geological Survey of Canada and its director, Sir William Logan. The survey, Holton argued in the assembly, "had been of immense value to the country" and "had contributed to the development of mineral resources." He thought the survey was "something to be proud of" and that native-born Sir William Logan had added much "to the body of scientific knowledge."[70]

Holton was caught up in the enthusiasm for science and technology. As a director of the Montreal Mining Company in the early 1850s, which was interested in the development of the mineral lands around Lakes Superior and Huron, and as a member of the Montreal committee of the American Association for the Advancement of Science in the late 1850s, he regarded Logan's work as an integral part of the whole process of launching the new Canada.[71] As Suzanne Zeller noted in 1987, the Geological Survey of Canada "served the interests of an incipient industrial community."[72] Few people sought to encourage science and technology as a means of Canadian improvement more than Holton. Toward this end, he remained firm in his support of the Geological Survey of Canada.

The credit available to Holton as finance minister at the Bank of Montreal also made it possible for him to finance the survey of the projected Intercolonial Railway, to be built from Halifax, Nova Scotia, and St. John, New Brunswick, west to Rivière du Loup, Lower Canada, connecting with the Grand Trunk and, thus, with Upper Canada. A stumbling block came in the government, where some members were still not sure if they favoured a survey. Holton himself wanted more information, and soon he was evaluating public opinion, collecting financial data, and soliciting gossip in the assembly. Generally the evaluation unearthed good news. So in the supply bill debate on 23 September 1863, Holton asked permission from the assembly to use $10,000 to cover the cost for the survey of the Intercolonial route. Seeing an immediate need for this survey, the assembly granted Holton's request.

The Sandfield Macdonald-Dorion government at once appointed the civil engineer, Sandford Fleming, to proceed with the survey as soon as the necessary arrangements with New Brunswick and Nova Scotia had been completed. Speaking for the survey, Holton declared that "the government was in earnest about" it, "that the Intercolonial Railway was a desirable thing *per se*," and that "the survey was intended to show whether the work could be undertaken consistently with the resources of the province."[73] There were many reasons for supporting the Intercolonial project, including the stimulus it would give to trade between Canada and the maritime provinces, but the most obvious one was that the railway would be needed for defence if there was an American attack.

Holton's grasp of the Intercolonial situation was matched by his practical understanding of the Reciprocity Treaty of 1854. Under this treaty, which established free trade in natural products between the British North American colonies and the United States, the American market had been important to Canada from the start. Canadian manufacturers, merchants, and forwarders benefited from the opening of the American market to Canadian goods. Selling their products in markets south of the border, many of Canada's businesses prospered. The essential strength of Canada sprang, Holton believed, from the power of her economy, and, given his American roots through his parents and his long record of successful, personal business dealings south of the border, he naturally felt that the continuation of free trade with the United States would contribute significantly to the province's economic development. But Holton was now convinced that the tide of public opinion in the Northern states was moving against the treaty, reflecting the view that reciprocal trade was much less advantageous to them than to the British North American colonies.[74]

* * *

Businesses in Canada, as Holton well knew, were beginning to brace themselves for what they expected would be unwelcome change if Congress decided to abrogate the Reciprocity Treaty. Many Canadian firms in towns and cities in the St. Lawrence-Ottawa-Great Lakes region had invested a great deal of capital in the trans-border trade. They were involved in the export of timber, wheat, barley, oats, hops, flax, horses, cattle, sheep, and wool to the United States, and in the import of goods from south of the border such as pork, tallow, lard, coal, pitch, tar, turpentine, ashes, rice, hides, furs, and unmanufactured tobacco. More than fifty percent of this commerce was handled by firms in Montreal.[75] No one was more aware than Holton that not all Canadian businesses benefited from reciprocity, but he also knew that among those that gained from the trans-border trade were a new sawmill firm on Lake Simcoe and twenty new tobacco manufactories, most of which were located in Toronto and Montreal.[76]

In the interest of these and many other Canadian firms, Holton and Sandfield Macdonald turned to George Brown for help in January 1864, asking him to go down to Washington, D.C., to enlist the support of Congressmen for the renewal of the Reciprocity Treaty.[77] Brown was not in a position to undertake the task, but he urged Sandfield Macdonald to send Holton. "It appears to me," wrote Brown, "that Mr. Holton is the man best fitted to do this. From his commercial training, and his knowledge of the subject and the men he would have to deal with, Mr. Holton would be of the greatest service in the negotiations, and his official position as Minister of Finance would give him a standing at Washington that no unofficial person could possibly have ... if Mr. Holton goes to Washington, I will most gladly & heartily lend him all the aid personally or otherwise that I possibly can."[78]

Brown accepted that Holton, who enjoyed the friendship of Governor-general Monck, possessed a keen understanding of the complex network of relationships upon which the survival of the Reciprocity Treaty largely depended. Considering the centrality of the United States in Holton's worldview, it is not surprising that Brown believed he would serve Canada well in its diplomacy toward its neighbour to the south. Much as he wanted to go to Washington, Holton could not spare the time, because he was in the final stages of preparing his budget for the approaching parliamentary session. He now decided to ask his Montreal friend John Young, whose instincts and judgement he trusted and whose ideas about relations with the United States largely coincided with his own, to travel to the American capital to serve as a conduit between the Sandfield Macdonald-Dorion ministry and Congress. "We are very anxious about the doings in Washington respecting Reciprocity," Holton telegraphed Young from Quebec City on 3 February. "Could you run down there for ten days before Parliament meets to survey the ground and report confidentially to this Government? If so, desirable you should come down here first to see Governor [Monck] and confer with us. See Dorion in Montreal."[79] Young immediately accepted the assignment. After talking with Dorion about the government's policy on reciprocity, Young went down to Quebec City to get briefings from Holton, Sandfield Macdonald, and Monck.

Holton obviously liked to move quietly in his effort to shape events, letting only a few friends know the picture. Following his trip to Washington, Young formally reported to Holton on 8 March that his impression was "that the notice to repeal" the Reciprocity Treaty "will be carried" in Congress.[80] Earlier, in mid-February, Holton had received from Young in Washington a communication to the same effect. Much concerned about the possible consequences, Holton on 19 February, the day the 1864 session of parliament began, persuaded the Sandfield Macdonald-Dorion government to act.[81] According to Monck's letter to Lord Lyons, British minister at Washington, the cabinet meeting decided to agree to "Holton's proposal ... to institute at once negotiations for a modified treaty."[82] Holton put the case for reciprocal trade with the United States as a first priority. Monck himself faced the reciprocity question boldly and fully supported the cabinet's decision. He, therefore, urged the imperial government to take the initiative in opening negotiations with Abraham Lincoln and his administration for a modified commercial treaty based on free-trade principles between the United States and the British North American colonies.[83]

Holton brought up the subject again in his assembly speech on 25 February, saying that he hoped Cartier and John A. Macdonald would support the government in its efforts to obtain "such a renewal of the treaty as would benefit the trade of the province."[84] Even after he was out of office, in 1865, Holton maintained a prominent international dimension by serving as one of the judges in an essay contest on the subject of reciprocity with the United States. He was proud of the winning essay, *The Reciprocity Treaty: Its Advantages to the United States and to Canada*, for it was written by Arthur Harvey, fellow of the Statistical Society of London, England, who had served under him as the statistical clerk in the department of finance.[85] But by this time, there was little Holton could have done to modify, much less to change, the anti-reciprocity thrust of the United States. Congress was increasing pressure for the abrogation of the Reciprocity Treaty, which finally took effect in March of 1866.

* * *

The Reciprocity Treaty with the United States nevertheless became a vital part of Holton's budget plans in March 1864. But with a diverse population to satisfy, Holton had to avoid extreme measures that might alienate Canadian groups. An extremely adept politician, he moved with the growing protectionist tide but still reassured free traders. In defence of reciprocity, he argued that an increase in trade with the United States would further economic growth and trigger prosperity across the province. At the same time, he did not plan to reduce tariff duties, for he believed that they were needed both to promote and protect domestic industry and to provide revenues to balance the budget and to retire the provincial debt. Another argument that Holton used against a reduction in tariff duties was that such action would "raise a storm of enraged special interests about our heads," especially the manufacturing interests that he actually supported.[86] This balanced and careful strategy illustrated the many economic and political imperatives that shaped Holton's decisions on reciprocity and the tariff.

Holton planned to make use of other sources of revenue as well. There was now a deficit of $982,491, and he promised to meet this in part by increases in a variety of stamp duties and property taxes.[87] Another essential part of Holton's budget scheme was the establishment for the first time of parliamentary control over annual expenditures through accounting and audit reform.[88] In planning to publicize accurate financial reports, he hoped not only to promote financial stability and enhance the credit of the province but also to allow the general public to make informed decisions about its political representatives. Holton was concerned about providing an image of improved provincial administration to potential investors in Canada's securities. He saw in his plan for a reformed budget a means to revitalize representative democracy and to enable it to satisfy the demands of the industrializing Canadian society. His ambitions thus ranged far beyond the idea of simply restructuring fiscal administration.

It proved impossible, however, for Holton to introduce his budget in the session of 1864 – the government was not strong enough to allow him to proceed. The besetting nightmare of the Sandfield Macdonald-Dorion ministry was that it had no stable parliamentary majority. Other problems erupted to aggravate the situation. The Liberals' dream of electing Albert N. Richards, the new solicitor general West, in the South Leeds by-election in January 1864 was never realized, leaving the government with one less

Upper Canadian supporter in the assembly.[89] In Lower Canada, Dorion and Holton failed to secure additional support despite their considerable influence. That Holton's own frustrations rose with the events surrounding him was evident in his complaint to Brown that the eastern Liberals' "weakness arises wholly from our persistently striving to stand on ground that would enable us to act with the U. C. majority."[90] In a less nerve-racking time, Holton might have thought better of making such an exaggerated statement, but now he turned his ire on Upper Canadian Liberals. Then, too, for the finance minister, Brown's pro-confederation leaning by mid-March was disconcerting. Through it all, however, the depth of the Holton–Brown friendship could still be found in the two men's correspondence. Holton's thoughtful mention of Brown's wife Anne and his ailing brother Gordon reflected favourably on Holton's personality.

* * *

Luther Holton also responded to his own family's need for affectionate attention. A few days before Christmas 1863, he found pleasure in seeing his daughter Mary married in Montreal to Byron M. Britton, a Kingston lawyer. Mary brought into her marriage the intellectual and cultural heritage of her Montreal upbringing. Four years earlier, when she wanted to enter the highly regarded Agassiz School (forerunner of Radcliffe College) in Cambridge, Massachusetts, Luther and Eliza made it possible for her to go. Mary was joined by her cousin Eliza Jane Holton of Belleville at Agassiz, where for the most part the two young women were taught by Harvard University professors.[91] In sending Mary to Agassiz, Luther and Eliza were clearly at the forefront of a lifestyle in Montreal in which families were willing and able to give their daughters a university education. Such personal preparation for whatever might lie ahead was uncommon for women in mid-nineteenth-century Montreal.

Holton's crowded, unpredictable schedule in the finance office and preoccupation with the public purse limited his capacity for involved fatherhood in 1863. But being a parent was never a burden. Despite his longer or shorter absences from home, he gave Mary the affection a daughter needed. When she left the family home in Montreal to live with her husband Byron Britton in Kingston, Holton naturally missed her very much. "My own household," Holton wrote Brown, "is made desolate by Mary's departure even under circumstances that give promise of as much future happiness as parents can reasonably expect of their children. I feel it very acutely myself but my wife is so forlorn that I can hardly find heart to return to my work."[92]

* * *

Holton nevertheless soon returned to the work in his office in Quebec City, but the weight of those responsibilities was extremely heavy, partly because the Liberals' support in the assembly was insufficient to resolve the problem of Canada's outstanding debt through the passage of legislation to increase taxes. The details of the problem kept running through his mind. Over the years, Canada had issued a great number of securities, most of which were held by British investors. The payment of the province's debt, Holton believed, would cause the price of securities to rise and to enhance its credit. If Canada would pay its debt and go into the black, he thought, British capitalists would invest in its securities and contribute to the province's economic recovery. But because the Sandfield Macdonald-Dorion government was almost politically impotent, little progress could be made in paying off Canada's obligations. As finance minister, Holton chafed at the government's impotence and felt frustrated by his inability to implement his long-term fiscal program. "God knows I have no love for the ceaseless drudgery of my present position unrelieved by the higher aspirations which a more comprehensive policy would engender," Holton had told Brown earlier.[93] Holton, however, continued to work within the limitations imposed by democratic government. When new problems arose, he toiled on, determined to see the task through.

The Sandfield Macdonald-Dorion ministry could, however, not win any more support in the assembly. The virtual deadlock in the house exposed the raw sectional biases and the tenuous ties of the Canadian union Luther Holton wanted so much to bind more closely. Writing to Thomas Baring of Baring Brothers on 20 March, John Rose said:

> ... we have another crisis on hand.... The present Ministry see they cannot go on & have made up their minds to resign. It will probably be announced tomorrow....
> A coalition will be tried in which perhaps some 4 or 5 of the present men will figure & the rest will I think be mostly new men.... Mr. Holton will of course retire, but it is impossible to say whether *we* may find it politic to include him in the new arrangements or not. If we do we will make our own terms.[94]

The next day, on 21 March 1864, the Sandfield Macdonald-Dorion ministry resigned.

News of the ministry's resignation quickly reached Montreal. "The ministry," wrote the *Montreal Herald*, "has still found itself too weak to undertake to carry any important measures, especially that one most important and most difficult of all, the increase of taxation."[95] In the next few days, Holton spent most of his time in the assembly urging Liberals to rise above sectional compulsions and trying to forestall the breakup of the Liberal party, "striving quietly among our friends to prevent mischief," as he told Brown.[96] Holton thought that Monck would likely ask the Liberals to form a new government. But Holton was wrong. As it turned out, on 22 March, Monck invited Fergusson Blair, the Upper Canadian Liberal and former provincial secretary, who was "personally popular with men of all parties," to form "a new administration on a broader basis."[97] Fergusson Blair immediately approached Étienne P. Taché, the veteran Quebec City Liberal-Conservative. As Taché explained to the assembly on 31 March, Fergusson Blair made it clear to him that he "desired to retain Dorion and Holton in the cabinet as most likely to inspire confidence in Upper Canada."[98] Taché was not willing to serve with Dorion, arguing that he would "mutilate some of the institutions of the country," especially the French-Canadian, Roman Catholic institutions.[99] Monck, as Taché put it, nevertheless wanted "to retain Holton ... to give him an opportunity of putting his financial scheme into operation."[100] Taché, however, indicated that Holton might not have the backing of enough Lower Canadians in the assembly to allow Fergusson Blair to construct a strong ministry. Fergusson Blair then turned to Antoine Dorion, but he also was unable to create a Lower Canadian section for a new cabinet. With that Fergusson Blair's attempt to form a coalition government died. What emerged in the end was the Liberal-Conservative ministry of Taché and John A. Macdonald.

Holton was now out of the government but not out of the scene of political action, parliament in Quebec City. Having recently turned forty-seven, he was still a robust man. There was work to done in the assembly on constitutional matters, and Holton was ready to become involved in this effort.

Chapter 7

Continuing Challenge of Politics

Parliament adjourned on 31 March 1864. Luther Holton had a week to relax at home in Montreal before he and Eliza boarded the Grand Trunk train for a vacation at family and relatives in Upper Canada. The train chugged into Kingston, where they visited their daughter Mary and her husband Byron Britton. Even on his holiday, politics continued to offer Holton challenge. In Kingston, he was "sorry" to see his Liberal son-in-law Byron Britton "dragged out" to oppose Alexander Campbell, the new commissioner of crown lands in the Liberal-Conservative government led by Taché and John A. Macdonald, in the Cataraqui division by-election on 11 April. "He is too young" wrote Holton, "and can't afford it." But before going down to defeat, Britton was popular enough to give Campbell "some trouble not to say anxiety," added Holton.[1] Luther and Eliza went on to Belleville to visit his brother Ezra, who was still active as a merchant, before returning to Montreal during the third week of April.

* * *

On 13 May, Holton stepped into the public spotlight in the assembly in Quebec City as an old friend of Governor-general Monck. "While this country is governed by a British statesman [Monck] who has learned his duty at the feet of the giants who wield the destiny of this empire, there need be no fear that the prerogative of the Crown will be debauched and debased for partisan purposes as it has been before," Holton told the assemblymen.[2] Holton was quick to appreciate that Monck was pivotal to Canada as it faced political deadlock, a situation in which the Liberal-Conservatives and Liberals were so evenly balanced in the assembly that neither party could govern for long. Far from solving the political crisis, the new Taché-Macdonald government precipitated a new one – a momentous struggle over the terms of the constitution in a province supposedly dedicated to the equality of Upper and Lower Canada. The

155

province, Holton was convinced, could not shed sectionalism like a suit of clothes; it had to find a new identity through reconstruction of the constitution. Change of this kind could not be realized without profound political transformation. Reconstruction demanded nothing less than that the Liberals and Liberal-Conservatives co-operate in search of a new route under a non-partisan governor-general. With this in mind, a week later Holton joined Brown, leader of the western Liberals and member for South Oxford, Dorion, Galt, Cartier, John A. Macdonald, and others in creating a parliamentary committee to discuss constitutional change. A singular figure in the story of constitutional reform, Brown was the initiator and chairman of the committee.

Holton was a skilful and tough-minded debater. He made friends easily and quickly and was equally at home with leading provincial politicians and ranking businessmen. It was this warm, affable man whom Brown had persuaded to enter the committee. Holton met with members when they wished and listened to their suggestions. He was politically savvy enough to know that he needed to be sensitive to them in order to find a solution to the constitutional problem. He certainly recognized the seriousness of the crisis. Brown conducted the committee meetings ably and was still politically and personally important to Holton. On 14 June, Brown asked the members to support his report of the constitutional committee. Holton remained so committed to preserving an abiding constitutional process that he voted for the report, but he was the only Lower Canadian Liberal to do so. Dorion did not support it. At the moment, however, Holton, most of the other members, and Canada turned toward a transforming future. Brown read the report in the assembly: "the committee," he said, "have held eight meetings and have endeavoured to find some solution for existing difficulties likely to receive the assent of both sections of the province. A strong feeling was found to exist among the members of the committee in favour of changes in the direction of a federative system, applied either to Canada alone, or to the whole British North American provinces."[3]

It was obvious to Holton that his support of the report might affect the Lower Canadian Liberal party, but there was little time to think about that now as events rushed forward. That same day the Taché-Macdonald ministry was defeated, Brown approached some leading Liberal-Conservatives about establishing a coalition to deal with the constitutional question, and Monck not surprisingly encouraged his ministers to co-operate in this move. On 17 June, Brown invited Dorion and Holton to join him, Taché, Cartier, and John A. Macdonald in forming a coalition government.[4] When Dorion declined, so did Holton, reluctantly but nevertheless firmly, because he decided to remain at Dorion's side and aid him in trying to keep the eastern Liberal party together in opposition to confederation. By his own admission, Dorion "always had been, and was now, a determined opponent of a federal union of the provinces."[5]

The consequences of Holton's decision were not yet fully clear; at this stage, it meant that he was withdrawing from the process of constitutional reform and becoming an opponent. Surely this was difficult for him to do after spending so many years in providing leadership for the Canadian federation plan, one of the options that the Taché-Macdonald-Brown coalition had incorporated into its constitutional policy. The coalition's top priority was, of course, to seek to establish a federal union of British North America. Holton found no fault with Brown and Monck for their role in the formation of the coalition. Chaotic as it might seem, all this activity was taking place in a fairly well-defined context. Holton spent hours preparing his response, seeing it largely as public persuasion, not only communication or argument with Brown. On 22 June, Holton rose in debate in the assembly:

> ... although the political relations between the member for South Oxford and himself must necessarily be changed by the step that hon. gentleman had taken, he trusted that those feelings of personal friendship which had so long existed between them would remain undisturbed. He had long been of the opinion that the federal system would be desirable for the government of the British North American provinces; but he did not believe the time had yet come to carry it into effect. He did not think the feeling of the people ripe for such a change.[6]

Holton's response to Brown was reassuring and worrisome at the same time. It demonstrated his close bond with the Toronto journalist – there was no flash of temper. It was also an argument to let the coalition know that Holton's arsenal was not empty. He could find ways to oppose supporters of British North American union. Holton knew that he was fighting for the minds and hearts of Lower Canadians, and he likely also knew that some of them would read his speech published in the newspapers for signs of his ability and his determination to build eastern Liberal resolve. Despite his refusal to admit it, he probably was haunted by the thought that he and his fellow Lower Canadian Liberals might be beaten in the end.

* * *

By the beginning of July, Holton was back at home in Montreal, quite pleased to be out of Quebec City for a number of months, though he was hardly out of the maelstrom of politics. In Chateauguay, Holton's riding,

Canadian Gleaner editor Robert Sellar complained about "the leaving
out of all representatives of the *Rouge* party" from the coalition cabinet.
Sellar also chastized Holton for not going into the coalition to back Brown
in what it saw as his attempt to overcome French domination of Canada
through representation by population.[7] The English-speaking population
in Lower Canada and its Protestant separate schools, the editor believed,
were deeply in danger. Holton was sympathetic to the needs of these
schools, but he maintained his independence of action. He was in touch
with the sentiments of both English and French Canadians in Chateauguay.
In his speech at Durham, he avoided the topic of English-Canadian
Protestant interests. He was influenced by other imperatives that counselled
caution. In his own way, he was trying to shape a strategy for the province
that would satisfy the needs of both the French and English cultures. He
wanted to keep the forces of local intolerance at bay and co-operate with
both cultures to redress their problems. But at this time he did not wish to
speak to the people of Chateauguay to explain his actions as an opponent
of confederation. It was a defensive posture, one symbolic of the eastern
Liberal party itself. No wonder Holton sought comfort in promoting
agricultural development in Chateauguay by throwing his support behind
the local agricultural association. There he was quite comfortable,
unchallenged, and could feel not completely powerless.[8]

Holton was more successful in maintaining his friendship with Brown.
The coalition minister was returning to Toronto from the Charlottetown
Conference, and awaiting him in Quebec City was a telegram from Luther
Holton asking him to come at once to his house. When Brown got off the
Grand Trunk train in Montreal, Holton was there to meet him. Brown was
happy to see not only Luther but also Eliza and their children in their
home.[9] The topic of the conference on British North American union
undoubtedly came up in Brown's conversation with Holton. A month later,
as Brown was returning from the Quebec Conference, Holton again greeted
him at the Grand Trunk station in Montreal. "Stayed the day with the
Holtons &" other friends, Brown wrote his wife.[10] Once more the
conversation between Brown and Holton must have turned to
confederation. Both conferences had been closed, but during his stopovers
in Montreal the coalition minister became a valuable source of information
on the proposed union for Holton.

Before long, Holton hurried down to Quebec City to learn more about
the coalition government's confederation policy and to place his own ideas
before the people of Canada. He listened intently as John A. Macdonald
told the assembly that he would introduce the seventy-two Quebec
Resolutions on confederation as a whole, as an act of parliament. On 3

February 1865, he rose to declare his support for Antoine Dorion. Holton expressed the eastern Liberals' viewpoint when he stated that the Quebec Resolutions "had been prepared and passed by a self-constituted body, without the House or the people ever having been consulted on the subject."[11] This comment, like so many he had made in the past, associated Luther Holton with the most democratic version of the Canadian dream. He denounced the coalition's unwillingness to move each resolution separately and saw hints of a design to prevent a detailed and thorough examination of the Quebec confederation scheme. He could not understand what Canadians had done to deserve this. Holton had done his homework; he offered the assembly an alternative, a plan identical to the proposal for the federal union of Upper and Lower Canada, which he had written and which a number of eastern Liberals had approved in 1859. Not a few of Holton's associates looked upon the proposal as a remedy to Canada's sectional problems. At the heart of the distinction between friends and opponents of Holton's plan was a basic difference of opinion on the role of a central government. Holton and his friends believed that Canada's future lay with a fairly strong national government empowered to do things such as collect customs duties and raise revenues, establish a stable and uniform currency, and create a postal system. They wanted to leave all authority not specifically granted to the national government in the hands of separate provinces, in addition to giving them control over matters such as education, the administration of justice, property, and the militia. To the opponents, especially John A. Macdonald who was responsible for incorporating the concept of a strong central government into the Quebec scheme, resistance to powerful provincial governments was a natural outgrowth of their knowledge of the American federal system and civil war. Holton's way took more of a middle road between the Quebec scheme of those who sought a strong central government and his own impulse to balance federal and provincial powers. Skirmish lines formed in the assembly. But the debate became something like an unequal chess game. The large coalition majority out-manoeuvred Holton until it finally rejected his plan.

Personally, Holton still stood high with his Lower Canadian Liberal colleagues in the assembly. They supported him as he tried to throw a roadblock in the path of the Quebec scheme. His opportunity came when news reached Quebec City that Leonard Tilley's unionist government had been defeated in the general election in New Brunswick. On 7 March, Holton rose to say that the confederation "scheme had received its first check. I may add that a majority of the present parliament of Nova Scotia is averse to it. In Prince Edward Island there is no probability of the scheme being accepted."[12] Holton thus placed his finger on the crucial problem in the Maritime provinces. The situation in the Maritimes seemed to put the whole confederation movement in jeopardy.

Holton now led the eastern Liberals' attack on the financial aspects of the Quebec scheme. He portrayed the proposed strong national government and the future national debt as threatening to the very spirit of business adventure that was at the heart of Canadian enterprise. He felt that the heavy hand of the national government would impose excessive burdens upon the Canadian taxpayer and businessman. But without specific facts and figures, he could not make a forceful argument for contracting the scope of federal government intervention in the private sphere in the provinces. But his economic expertise and grasp of financial and monetary questions commanded his fellow Lower Canadian Liberals' respect. As it turned out, the Anglo-Canadian links forged during Holton's tenure as finance minister between the Bank of Montreal and Baring Brothers and Glyn, Mills & Co. were essential in arranging the loans and credits that underpinned the confederation fathers' efforts to stabilize the Canadian currency, solve the public debt imbroglio, and regenerate the economy of the Dominion of Canada. But even Holton could not have imagined just how significant the economic strength of the old united province of Canada and the Bank of Montreal would quickly become.

The confederation debate in Quebec City exposed the raw sectional feelings in the Liberal party. Holton and Brown wanted to bind the flimsy ties of the party more closely, but such a desire had its limits. Inevitably, tensions came to the boil. Before long, the Montrealer and the coalition minister were making slighting remarks about each other's impact on Liberalism. Eventually, however, the two men would display a similar dedication to the ideal of establishing a strong Liberal party.

But in February and March 1865, the two friends' sympathies were diametrically opposite. Holton's sympathy was with the old Canadian union. By contrast, Brown shared the pro-confederation sympathies of his Liberal-Conservative associates in the coalition government. He helped formulate the government's policies on the constitution for the union of British North America. Brown experienced success on 11 March, when the Quebec Resolutions were adopted, 91 to 33. However, the Lower Canadian vote on them was 37 for, and 25 against, thus showing that Dorion and Holton had a substantial anti-union following.[13]

In 1865 and 1866, Holton's predilections led him into repeated clashes with Brown. During this time, the personal relationship between the two men remained almost unaffected by their sharp constitutional policy disagreements.[14] Holton even felt some sympathy for the dilemma in which Brown's position in the coalition government placed him. Although their attitudes toward confederation diverged, both believed that British and American decisions could vitally affect the economic fortunes of Canada. Even while Canada remained officially neutral during the American Civil War, both Holton and Brown expected their province to assume a far greater role than previously in the organization and maintenance of the future international order. Part of this expanded Canadian international economic role, they hoped, would be the development of a larger market for Canadian products.

Holton's thoughts were often about the uncertainty of events in the Maritime provinces. After Leonard Tilley's pro-confederate forces achieved power in a general election in New Brunswick in June 1866, Charles Tupper manipulated the Nova Scotia legislature's approval of confederation despite overwhelming opposition to union in that province. Once colonial secretary Lord Carnarvon had rejected Holton and Dorion's petition for a general election on the Quebec scheme and had incorporated the London Conference resolutions adopted by the Canadian, Nova Scotia, and New Brunswick union delegations into the British North America bill, Holton was eager to join the confederation movement and help make possible the emergence of a new constitution despite his regret that the Canadian people would not have a chance to express their views on union in an election.

* * *

As he wrote Brown in January 1867, "if confederation does come I shall soon be reconciled to it. Of one thing I am quite satisfied, any thing is better for us than the prolongation of this *Interregnum*."[15] Within a short time, Holton rapidly changed from an anti-unionist to become one of the boldest advocates of the new constitution. His change of mind highlighted a basic trait of character evident throughout Holton's life: the essential flexibility of his nature. Making clear his first priority, Holton now called for meaningful authority to be vested in a strong federal government – a government that could exercise real power and, if necessary, override divisive provincial interests but still be acceptable to the provinces. Without such federal government leadership, he thought, the new Canada would shatter into a series of interest groups and factions. A coherent Canadian nation, in short, was impossible without a strong central government.

Holton took the lead in trying to persuade his Lower Canadian Liberal friends to back confederation. At the end of March, after the British North America bill had received royal assent, he published his pro-union article in the *Montreal Herald*.[16] It was, Holton argued, "the duty of all to give the new system a fair trial, and to endeavour to secure to the country, through its instrumentality, the blessings of a stable and efficient and economical government."[17] Holton, Dorion, and other eastern Liberals talked long and earnestly about the new constitution, the British North America Act. Coming to the nub of his argument, Holton said that "*It is our constitution. We must therefore live under it, work it, and if we can improve it.*"[18] He did it all with the typical Holton touch – open, reassuring, helpful. Holton and Dorion needed to share their thoughts as some Lower Canadian Liberals began to talk about mounting an agitation for the repeal of confederation. Such an agitation, Holton stressed, would be nothing less than a blunder, and Dorion seemed to agree. "Dorion is about two thirds with me and has said nothing publicly in a contrary sense. If he refrains from doing so a little while longer I am sure his good judgement and his strong liberal instincts will ultimately put him wholly right," reported Holton to Brown.[19] Holton correctly calculated the mood of Dorion on this occasion. Holton's dream of winning the Lower Canadian Liberals over to a federal union of British North America certainly had a chance, and as he worked to make the idea a reality, he grew more confident. He was also an important figure behind the careful scenario that recognized the need for "the formation of a Liberal party for the whole Dominion" in order to put the Liberals in a position to seek power in the new nation.[20] In the emerging pattern of party politics, the Liberal party leaders would eventually make an effort to achieve this goal.

Like many other people in Montreal, Holton found that the birth of his new country generated much excitement. Throngs attended the Dominion Day celebration in the city on Monday, 1 July 1867. First, as the midnight hour struck, the Montreal Field Battery appeared on the balcony of the Crystal Palace, singing God Save the Queen, and giving cheers to Queen Victoria and to the new Dominion of Canada. Then, as the sun rose at four o'clock, twenty-one guns boomed a royal salute from the reservoir on the southern slope of Mount Royal. The day "broke cloudless and beautifully cool, auguring very favourably for the enjoyment of the crowds of citizens who had determined to keep the holiday."[21] In the evening, businessmen lighted up their business establishments in support of confederation. For instance, James Crathern, senior partner in the wholesale hardware firm Crathern & Caverhill on St. Paul Street, had a handsome display of transparencies.[22]

On that same day, Luther Holton set out on a tour by horse and carriage to see the electors in his Chateauguay riding.[23] At the Mechanics Hall in Durham, he freely entered into genial conversation with the people who had come to hear him, showing his warmth and openness to them. The manifestations of good feeling buoyed his spirits, and he became especially animated when he spoke of confederation and his intention to promote it in the new parliament if he was elected.[24] At the end of the meeting, his friends promised to give him their hearty support.

For some time, Ottawa, the nation's capital, and possible leading members of the new federal government had been on Holton's mind. He expected that Monck would "be more than ever sensitive to public opinion in this country." "I suppose J. A. [Macdonald] is to be the new premier. Galt's friends talk as if he were certain to be Minister of Finance. *I hope he will be*," wrote Holton.[25] On the morning of 1 July, things unfolded in Ottawa much as Holton had anticipated. Monck was sworn in as the governor-general of Canada. Then the first ministry of the new Dominion was installed, with John A. Macdonald as prime minister. The new federal government of Canada was the old coalition government of the united province of Canada, including Cartier as minister of militia and defence, Galt as minister of finance, and three Ontario Liberals (but George Brown was not among them), plus a Conservative and a Liberal from Nova Scotia and two New Brunswick Liberals including Leonard Tilley as minister of customs.

* * *

Holton's basic strategy for the upcoming summer general election – which would choose 181 members of the new nation's House of Commons: 82 from Ontario, 65 from Quebec, 15 from New Brunswick, and 19 from Nova Scotia – was to work for "the early ascendancy" of a national Liberal party. This, as he told Brown, was the "only chance of a fair trial for" the "great experiment" of building a new nation.[26] Holton made a number of speeches, supporting Liberals against Liberal-Conservatives in the Montreal area, but he played an especially important role in the election of hardware merchant Thomas Workman, his old school mate, in Montreal Centre.

In planning his own campaign in Chateauguay, Holton gathered around him a group of hardworking and dedicated advisers. A number of them were familiar faces from previous campaigns. Antoine Dorion was, as always, loyal, valuable because of his contacts among French Canadians in Chateauguay. Alfred Goff Penny, editor of the *Montreal Herald*, was an old and close political friend in Montreal. In Chateauguay, Holton counted especially on Dr. A. Dugas and James McGowan.[27] Robert Sellar, editor of the *Canadian Gleaner* in Huntingdon, now trusted Holton to support Protestant Lower Canada's separate schools and was one of his most staunch backers.[28]

Holton moved into his campaign in Chateauguay with the knowledge that he faced the well-tuned Liberal-Conservative machine of T. K. Ramsay, a Montreal lawyer. Considering his own chances for victory,

Holton was painfully aware that he had lost strength by his opposition to confederation until January 1867 and that his association with anti-clerical *rouges* had cost him more. When his friends put Holton's name in nomination at St. Martine on 26 August, he responded by speaking first in French and then in English. He outlined the vital issue of the day as he saw it. "When a great change had come," he observed, "when a new constitution had been adopted, it was our duty to forget the past and to give it a fair trial, and not to engage in old party quarrels and keep alive old animosities."[29] What effect Holton's speech had on the outcome of the 1867 election in Chateauguay was hard for him to tell. Many farmers in the countryside were Liberals, ardent supporters of Luther Holton. But it proved to be a tough campaign. "My own contest," he wrote Brown, "is a *very severe one*. I expect to win but with the whole influence of Gov't and (with one or two exceptions) of the R.C. clergy against me it would be folly not to admit that the result is doubtful."[30] But on 3 September, he won decisively, receiving 1,013 of the 1,599 votes cast. Little could the voters of Chateauguay know that in sending Luther Holton to the House of Commons in this election, they were beginning to bind their fortunes to his own in the Dominion parliament for more than a decade.

Across the new Dominion the summer election, however, proved a serious setback for the Liberals as John A. Macdonald's government picked up a working majority of thirty-five House of Commons seats. Even before it was official, the government's election was expected. But while Macdonald celebrated, the Liberals possessed only eighteen of the sixty-five Quebec seats, thirty out of eighty-two Ontario seats, and eight of the fifteen New Brunswick seats. The anti-confederate Liberals, who took eighteen out of nineteen Nova Scotia seats, claimed that they did not want to be part of Canada. But the government comfortably dominated the House. Far from forming a cohesive group, the Opposition Liberals had no common purpose and lacked a national leader.

* * *

As the victorious candidate of the Chateauguay election and respected politician, Luther Holton felt a strong responsibility for the future of the nation that he had helped to create. Being a public-spirited citizen, his foremost concern was the establishment of a secure and permanent union of the three former provinces. Anyone looking for a particularly progressive feature in Holton's thinking could have found it in his effort at a positive and practical vision of democratic government. All this led him to play a prominent role in shaping the development of the new Dominion. When Holton arrived in Ottawa on 5 November, he took lodgings at the Russell

House, where he could enjoy the company of other members of parliament.[31] His first session as a House of Commons member (6 November 1867 to 22 May 1868) was an important one. He was an active participant in the proceedings, exceptionally faithful in his attendance, and generally worked closely with Quebec Liberal leader Antoine Dorion, beside whom he sat in the front Opposition row.[32] Immediately on Holton's left were L. S. Huntington, member for Shefford; Alexander Mackenzie, stonemason of Sarnia, member for Lambton, and leader of the Ontario Liberals; Stewart Campbell, member for Guysborough, Nova Scotia, who soon became a unionist; and Joseph Howe, member for Hants and leader of the Nova Scotia anti-confederates, in that order. Behind Mackenzie, in the second row, sat Edward Blake, member for Durham West, a bright Toronto lawyer. Much to Holton's regret, George Brown was not there, because he had been defeated in South Ontario.

Several weeks after the opening of the session, Hansard reported that Holton rose in the House to say that

> ... he felt it his duty to aid the government as far as he could in carrying out in a proper way all the incidents of confederation.... Confederation having been accomplished and acquiesced in by a majority of his own province, and perhaps all of them, he came to this legislature not to obstruct its fair working, but to aid as far as he could the object of all our politics, the good government of our country.[33]

Holton had political skills that might serve the nation well. An open-minded politician, he knew how to organize political strength, how to persuade and encourage friends and foes, and how to foster unity. At the same time, it was clear that he was ready to fight the government when he disagreed with its policies, to advance the Liberal cause, and to seek to shape the legislative agenda.

Holton united with the government in December 1867 in supporting its resolutions to acquire Rupert's Land and the Northwest Territories, for which Canada paid the Hudson's Bay Company £300,000 a few years later when the transfer took place. "A natural consequence of this confederation," Holton emphasized in his speech, "was undoubtedly the annexation of this territory to the country, and he had been and was now prepared to support the government in aiding that object."[34] As a result of this acquisition, by the early 1870s hundreds of new farms were settled, thus expanding the numbers of independent farmers and validating further the government and Holton's vision of the nation. But soon there were additional costs in opening up the West: to Native Canadians whose lands were taken and to those Metis and white farmers whose property fell into speculators' hands. But for better or for worse, parliament had fulfilled the confederation fathers' pledge that expanded the promise and wealth of the nation in the midst of western unrest.

Holton also tried to subsume railways and other internal improvements into his vision. In the struggle to build a stronger union, it was expedient to bind central Canada and the Maritimes. Holton thus supported the

government's bill providing for the construction of the Intercolonial Railway. Although he did not fully appreciate the railway's commercial and military importance, he regarded it as "a political necessity."[35] Long a supporter of advances in river, lake, canal, and railway transportation, all of which formed part of his vision of a flourishing Canadian society, Holton was now convinced that unless the new Dominion was to fall far behind other countries, it must back internal improvements such as the Intercolonial Railway with the nation's credit.

While Luther Holton celebrated the development of the nation, the Nova Scotia anti-confederates in the House wanted to

Luther Holton, c. late 1860s.
Courtesy of Thomas L. Brock.

march to secession. On 29 April 1868, E. M. McDonald, member for Lunenburg, introduced resolutions condemning confederation and calling for a repeal of the union. Holton responded by declaring that "he was not disposed now at this stage to vote that it should be repealed." But he found no purpose in embittering anti-confederate feelings. Seeing the need to calm the waters and reassure the anti-confederates that the solution to their problems lay in the preservation of the union, Holton said that he "desired to make the Union acceptable to the people of Nova Scotia, and he thought it would be the part of wisdom and statesmanship for this House … to admit they had grievances … and to endeavour by every legitimate means to satisfy them through the operation of this constitution."[36] These sentiments revealed the maturity of Holton's outlook to let reason and good will shape politics. Practical matters continued to inform his argument against the repeal movement. Relations between Canada and Nova Scotia would continue, Holton believed, and peaceful dealings between friends were far better than difficult negotiations between alien countries. In this way, he tried to strengthen feelings of national community.

Holton was determined, above all else, to develop a powerful and lasting federal union, and to achieve this end he was prepared to work hard to keep the new Dominion in the British Empire. As one who had grown to manhood in the British Empire, he consistently voiced his belief that the maintenance of Canada's political and economic ties with Great Britain was desirable, even necessary, for the survival of the young nation and the general welfare of its citizens. By contrast, his fellow Quebec Liberals Antoine Dorion, John Young, and L. S. Huntington were beginning to advocate Canadian independence. But Holton was unwilling to jeopardize the federal union within the British Empire for the nebulous vision of a new order. Friendly newspaper editors and publishers helped give his ideas wide circulation in July 1870. Calling himself Anglo-Canadian, Holton published his article on the imperial connection in the *Montreal Herald* and the *Montreal Gazette*. In part it read: "the main difficulty with the advocates of immediate independence is that they have wholly misjudged the depth of British feeling and the strength of the attachment to the British *name* which pervade the country." Following this up with a letter to the editor of the *Montreal Herald* signed in his own name, Holton emphasized that "in the present circumstances of the country I do not regard Independence as either desirable or attainable. No adequate cause of Revolution exists among us, and in the absence of any such cause I do not believe our people can be induced to demand a Revolution."[37] It was a unique opportunity for Holton to use his considerable powers of persuasion to try to influence public opinion in Quebec. The simple logic and appealing sentiment of his remarks helped rally the pro-British element. Ultimately, his arguments would prevail in Quebec's federal Liberal party.

* * *

Nowadays it is difficult to think of a politician serving in two legislatures, but in Holton's time the system of dual representation allowed him to simultaneously hold seats in the House of Commons and the provincial assembly in Quebec City, two law-making bodies that met at different times, the latter usually for one or two months in the winter. Perhaps some arm-twisting was needed, but in the provincial election in June 1871 the Liberals in Montreal Centre persuaded Holton to run against Conservative Edward Carter, a local lawyer; they elected Holton, and he held the seat until January 1874, when he resigned presumably to spend more time with his family.[38] As a representative of the Montreal business community, he focussed on economic matters. Assigned to the railway committee, Holton supported the Conservative government of P.J.O. Chauveau in securing approval for the City of Montreal's $1 million subsidy to the Montreal Colonization Railway that was projected to run from Hochelaga to Ottawa. In his speech, Holton said that the best argument for acting now was that "Montreal wanted an independent railway into the interior of the country."[39] Turning his energies in another direction, he backed a measure providing for the building of the St. Francis and Megantic Railroad south of the St. Lawrence.[40] In an effort to facilitate trading in securities in Montreal, Holton introduced and shepherded through the assembly a bill to incorporate the Montreal Stock Exchange.[41]

* * *

All the while, Holton remained active in Ottawa. Already, there was public recognition that Holton was a leading member of the House of Commons, with his speeches reported in the Ottawa and Montreal newspapers and then reprinted in other parts of the Dominion with increasing frequency. Alongside John A. Macdonald, Antoine Dorion, and Alexander Mackenzie, he was emerging as one of the authentic public figures whose views were sought out and known to carry influence with thinking Canadians who had learned to respect his judgement. In international affairs, Holton made it clear that he favoured the Washington Treaty of 1871, which was designed to bring about a settlement between Great Britain and the United States. As one who was asked to help shape the treaty in a small way, John A. Macdonald tried to defend Canadian interests but was only partially successful. The arrangements made in Washington provided that Americans could fish in Canada's rich inshore fisheries; the price the United States had to pay for this privilege was the remission of duties on Canadian fish imports plus an unspecified cash sum. In addition, the Americans could navigate the entire St. Lawrence in perpetuity in exchange for the same Canadian privilege on three Alaskan rivers. Ratification of the treaty carried by 121 votes to fifty-five in the Canadian House of Commons at midnight on 15 May 1872.[42] During the debate on it, Holton was still not feeling well after having been ill for some days, but as usual he was in his place and remained in good spirits.[43]

The argument that Holton advanced in support of the treaty at three o'clock on that day, while at the same time admitting that Canadian interests had been sacrificed, was that "he regarded the measure as altogether an imperial one. Canada as part of the Empire was more interested than any other portion of it in ratification.... We needed capital to develop our resources, and capital was regardless of politics or national sentiment or anything of that kind. All it asked was security, and this could not be guaranteed in this country unless the difficulties between the United States and Great Britain were satisfactorily settled." He added that "it would

Luther Holton, c. early 1870s. Courtesy of Thomas L. Brock.

have been" an "honourable course on the part of the government frankly to avow that they were called upon to make sacrifices and were willing to make them in view of what the Empire had done for us."[44] Holton clearly recognized that the achievement of an entente between Great Britain and the United States through the treaty was essential to Canada's economic development. The treaty was a divisive issue, however, for Alexander Mackenzie, Antoine Dorion, and Edward Blake voted against it.[45] It was an indication that the federal Liberal party was still in a disorganized state.

* * *

In the 1872 general election, Luther Holton was trying to gather Canadian Liberals around a particular theory of economic development. It was economically desirable, he believed, for Canada to maintain good relations with Great Britain and the United States. Substantial trade with these two nations, he argued, was necessary for Canada's economic growth. Fortunately for Holton, most of the Quebec and Ontario Liberals bought his theory. Now, as the Conservatives flexed their muscles, he became increasingly determined to advance the Liberal cause. He found the chance to fight for the unity of Liberalism at a dinner in honour of Dorion and himself in the St. Lawrence Hall in Montreal on 3 July 1872, which was attended by over 170 Liberals including his son Edward. In his speech, Luther Holton declared that "the presence of Alexander Mackenzie was evidence that the Liberal party was spreading over the Dominion. At Confederation that party was dislocated, but the presence of Mr. Mackenzie was a sign and seal of the union of the Liberals."[46] Two weeks later, in the Chaboillez Square, Holton paid tribute to his old friend and prominent local businessman John Young, Liberal candidate for the Montreal West seat in the House of Commons, stressing that he desired Montreal to be well represented. He unhesitatingly stated that "Mr. Young possessed the necessary qualifications in a degree possessed by few."[47] Holton's labours thus continued unabated.

Then, Holton drove by carriage to Chateauguay, where local storekeeper and farmer Robert Stewart was his Conservative opponent. As the campaign progressed, Holton raised the Treaty of Washington question. In his speech at Ste. Martine on 24 August, he referred to his own vote for the treaty in the House of Commons, noting "that bad as that Treaty was in many respects ... it was better for the interests of Canada and Great Britain, better in the interests of peace, that it be ratified."[48] Holton managed to carry off the victory against his challenger in Chateauguay, by a majority of 238 votes.[49]

Holton continued to take part in the campaigning for Young, who was elected in Montreal West. Antoine Dorion carried Napierville.[50] When the election returns came in across Quebec, it was clear that the Liberals had won twenty-seven seats in the House of Commons, an increase of seven. In the rest of the nation, the result was generally the same. The Liberals were strongest in Ontario, where they captured fifty seats. Altogether, the Liberals took ninety-seven seats, leaving the Conservatives with a diminished majority of six. Despite some observations to the contrary, the many Liberal victories were seen as a prelude to the organization of a national Liberal party.

* * *

On 4 March 1873, after bidding goodbye to his family, Holton left Montreal for Ottawa. He already had some idea of what the temper of affairs there would be like from letters he had received from fellow Liberals. There was a general feeling that the time had come for action on the question of party leadership. For all his importance in the party, Holton himself had no leadership aspirations. Two days later, at a meeting of the Quebec and Ontario Liberals in a House of Commons room, he nominated Alexander Mackenzie as leader of the Liberal party.[51] Mackenzie was troubled by the absence of Liberals from Nova Scotia, New Brunswick, and Manitoba, but the meeting chose him as leader. Like any new party chief, Mackenzie was a bit nervous. "It would be impossible," he wrote Brown, "to make handsomer speeches than those made by Holton, Dorion and Blake."[52] From the beginning, the new leader looked especially to Holton for advice. Holton advised Mackenzie to encourage the party to stand united in order to be in the best position to achieve his larger goal eventually, power.

If Holton needed anything to show him how fast men and events were moving, it soon came in the House of Commons. The Conservative administration of John A. Macdonald had been successful in the general election of 1872. But the issue on which the Conservatives appeared to be vulnerable was the prime minister's role in the Pacific Scandal. Within a month of the opening of the session, Huntington rose in the House and charged that Hugh Allan, the Montreal steamship entrepreneur, had received the charter to build the Canadian Pacific Railway for supplying campaign funds to principal Conservative ministers during the 1872 general election. Doubtless his conviction of the inevitably of a crisis impelled Holton to pay close attention to this question. Like every other Liberal, he wanted to see the evidence on which the explosive charges were based.

Many Liberals looked to Holton in the following months, all expecting that he would be an important figure in the debate on the Pacific Scandal. During the parliamentary recess, on 4 and 18 July 1873, there appeared in the *Montreal Herald* stunning documents: a letter from Allan revealing that he had the government's backing for his presidency of the Canadian Pacific Railway, as well as telegrams from Macdonald and Cartier asking Allan for huge sums of money for the 1872 election campaign.[53] Macdonald's proposal to appoint a royal commission to inquire into Huntington's grave charges was insufficient for Liberal leaders. In Montreal, they were rounding up support for a parliamentary committee to investigate the charges. Holton was the first speaker at a rally of over 5,000 people on the Champs de Mars in the evening of 5 August 1873. Frankly, he declared, a "Royal Commission for inquiry into charges against Ministers of the Crown is an outrage on the privileges of Parliament."[54] To him, a royal commission was unacceptable, for it could be controlled by its creator: Macdonald's Conservative administration. Holton succinctly expressed his view of the situation: "I say parliament is alone competent under the British system of Parliamentary Government to deal with such charges as those which have been laid against Ministers."[55] The huge meeting quickly acted to stand behind Holton, adopting his resolution demanding a thorough parliamentary investigation.

Holton thought that the continuation of the present session of parliament would checkmate Conservative strength; his fellow Liberal Richard J. Cartwright, a Kingston businessman, agreed. On 13 August, after members of parliament had reassembled, a delegation led by Cartwright approached the new governor-general, Lord Dufferin, with a petition signed by many Liberals, including Holton, Mackenzie, Dorion, and Blake, asking him to refrain from proroguing parliament.[56] But Dufferin, who had already approved the establishment of a royal commission, rejected their petition. Shortly after three o'clock that afternoon, Holton at his seat nevertheless seconded Mackenzie's motion calling for an inquiry by a House of Commons committee into Huntington's serious charges.[57] At John A. Macdonald's request, however, Dufferin immediately prorogued parliament before the motion could be considered by the House. Minutes later, in the railway committee room, where the Liberals had gathered to protest the prorogation, Holton mounted a chair and made the first speech, denouncing Dufferin for preventing "the House of Commons from inquiring into the most stupendous political and electoral frauds which had ever hitherto been heard of."[58] He reached for the loyalty of the Liberals with a promise to continue the fight against the government; all of them were inspired.

The attention of the nation was riveted on events in Ottawa, on the debates in parliament when it met again on 23 October. The damaging findings of the royal commission, which had carried out its investigations during the recess, made it impossible for John A. Macdonald to continue in office much longer. On the morning of 5 November, Macdonald's administration resigned. Within hours, Alexander Mackenzie accepted Dufferin's invitation to form a government and by the evening was making his cabinet; the governor-general had also granted a dissolution of parliament. Speculations about cabinet appointments covered a number of leading Liberals. Some thought Luther Holton would be minister of finance. But two days later, at 3 o'clock in the afternoon, just before parliament was prorogued, Holton rose in his place in the House to announce the names of the new Liberal ministers. Alexander Mackenzie, Antoine Dorion, and Richard Cartwright all had commanding positions, as ministers of public works, justice, and finance, respectively.[59] Then Holton left Ottawa for his home in Montreal feeling that he had done his part in bringing a Liberal government.

A cartoonist's view of the political situation in Canada at the time of the Pacific Scandal. "House of Commons in Full Session. Sir John announces the resignation of the Ministry. Grits surround Alexander clamouring noisily for places." Luther Holton third from right. From the *Canadian Illustrated News*, January 1874.

As fall faded into winter, Luther Holton was mulling over all the discussions about the cabinet a month and a half earlier, during the evening of 5 November. He was beginning to realize that he should explain to the general public why he had declined Mackenzie's invitation to enter the cabinet as finance minister. The opportunity came two days before Christmas, on 23 December, at a dinner in honour of Huntington in the St. Lawrence Hall. The *Montreal Herald* reported that, in his brief speech, Holton said that "he had been himself requested to take office in the new government, but time would hardly permit him now to enter into the causes and motives which led him to decline it.... He owed it, however, to them to say that his motives were merely personal. He had no want of confidence or agreement with the government."[60] Privately, Holton had earlier told Mackenzie that "his duty to his family" had also prevented him from accepting office.[61] Holton certainly had not jumped at the invitation. But guessing games still filled political circles over his decision to decline a cabinet appointment. No one suggested that he did not wish to serve under Mackenzie as prime minister. Perhaps Holton preferred the seniority and security of his House of Commons seat to a cabinet post, and in some ways he could help the government more by staying where he was and serving in the role of elder statesman. There were also pressures of time, for his business responsibilities in Montreal still often required him to be at home to attend to them.

* * *

As Canadians went to the polls in the general election at the beginning of 1874, Holton was again up for re-election to his seat in the House of Commons. In preparation for the campaign, he got in touch with many of his supporters in Chateauguay, took assertive action aimed at securing the nomination, and carried off the Liberal prize.[62] Holton had already made his position clear by hitting hard at the Conservatives involved in the Pacific Scandal. As usual, however, there was a fight. His Conservative rival, Joseph Santoire, ran a store and tavern in St. Jean Chrysotome. He was a formidable opponent. But clearly something in the fifty-seven-year-old Luther Holton spoke to the voters in Chateauguay in a voice and manner that they liked. He not only won on 29 January, but succeeded in rolling up an increased majority, 381 as compared with his more modest victory over Robert Stewart two years earlier.[63]

In addition, there was plenty to do in Montreal. Holton enthusiastically supported his friends in the city: lawyers Bernard Devlin and Louis-Amable Jetté in Montreal Centre and Montreal East, respectively; and businessman Frederick Mackenzie in Montreal West, making speeches to expose the "corruption" of the Conservatives and confirm the soundness of the Liberal candidates' position on responsible government.[64] Holton's optimism did not diminish throughout the campaign. He believed that Liberal victories in Montreal would help keep the ball rolling. Although Devlin could not carry his riding, Jetté and Mackenzie won in theirs. In Quebec, the Liberals took thirty-five of sixty-five seats, an increase of eight from their count in 1872. Elsewhere in Canada, apart from British Columbia – Ontario, Nova Scotia, New Brunswick, Prince Edward Island, and Manitoba – the Liberals had also done well. Altogether, they won 138 of the 206 seats in the House of Commons. The party, greatly increased in numbers and spirits, thus stood confident and strong in Ottawa.

* * *

Soon Luther Holton became a prime ministerial intimate and policy adviser. The most important use to which he put his time was to acquaint himself with the federal government's problems. For four years, Luther Holton was at the side of Prime Minister Mackenzie, helping to shape the government's public relations efforts. As Mackenzie's most highly placed and trusted confidant with wide-ranging and critical contacts, Holton wrote to him often from Montreal when parliament was not in session. The candid, fresh, disarming approach of the Montrealer was a distinct asset to the prime minister, because his remarkable personal magnetism was constantly evident, whether in charming Liberal friends or warring on Conservatives. Critics accused Mackenzie of neglecting the West. The prime minister, in fact, aligned himself with western development, partly by promoting the railway to the Pacific. At the same time, he was determined to hold down spending. These issues were particularly vital because in 1873 the economy had plunged downward, wiping out many Canadian businesses. It was virtually impossible to find entrepreneurs with sufficient capital to undertake the Pacific railway project as a private venture. Investors were timid and private funds were hard to raise. But British Columbia, clinging to John A. Macdonald's earlier promise, expected to see the road by 1881.

Alexander Mackenzie.
Courtesy of the Ontario Archives.

If the time was ever ripe for Holton to apply his analysis to the situation, it was now. He believed that the federal government had no option but to assume the responsibility for building the railway as a public work. In years when the state of the national economy handicapped financing and government costs had to be held down, it made good sense for Holton to suggest that the construction of the road should be undertaken in piecemeal fashion – section by section – rather than push forward rapidly and see the rails outrun the line's resources and drift to ruin. Holton wrote Mackenzie in February 1874:

> The Pacific Railway is our Elephant. It would be easy to devise a scheme for constructing it or sections of it if we had any faith in its merits as a commercial enterprise either now or within a moderately distant future; but in the absence of such a faith any scheme which does not contemplate the provision of the entire cost by our government in money or lands must be a mere speculation on the credulity of foreign capitalists.[65]

Holton thus proposed a constructive alternative to the Conservatives' previous disastrous attempt to have the Pacific railway built as a private enterprise. Prudent Liberal government spending would allow work on the federal government road from Lake Nipissing to British Columbia to begin and then gradually proceed. Holton wanted the government to step in, not to compete with private enterprise in railway construction but to spur economic development.

Mackenzie followed this course and, after parliament convened on 26 March, pushed the Pacific railway bill through the House of Commons and Senate.[66] By supporting Mackenzie's move, Holton confirmed his place in the prime minister's inner circle. Eventually, Holton's efforts would help bring tremendous economic advantages to Montreal and Quebec, for the railway would run eastward through the Ottawa Valley. "We in Montreal, we in the province of Quebec," Holton soon predicted, "will secure at the earliest possible moment the benefit of a great arterial line of railway from tide water to the upper lakes."[67] Holton's aim was to convince the general public that an efficient national rail transportation system was essential to the well-being of the Dominion.

During Mackenzie's regime, Holton voted repeatedly for money bills to finance the building of the Canadian Pacific Railway. With many millions involved, he took a lively interest in the project. The government's capital expenditures on the construction of the railway amounted to $1.5 million in 1874-75; $3.3 million in 1875-76; $1.7 million in 1876-77; and $2.2 million in 1877-78.[68] By the end of 1878, there had emerged several sections: tracks had been laid on the eighty-four-mile Pembina branch between Selkirk and Emerson on the Canada-United States border to connect with the St. Paul, Minneapolis and Manitoba Railway; tracks had moved forward for a total of 188 miles on sections of the 410-mile line from Selkirk to Fort William; of the 120-mile Canada Central branch from Pembroke to Lake Nipissing, twenty-five miles were under construction; supplies had been delivered for the fifty-mile Georgian Bay branch between Lake Nipissing and Cantin's Bay, French River; and in British Columbia, the 125-mile line from Kamloops to Emory's Bar near Yale had been surveyed.[69] Progress on the construction of the Canadian Pacific Railway was obviously slow. During the depression of the mid-1870s, the federal government project nevertheless overcame limitations and quandaries that would have baffled many business executives. In the midst of the economic crisis, Holton showed himself willing to encourage the government to do whatever work was possible on the railway and thereby provide a positive stimulus to economic recovery.

In his fight against the economic depression, Holton also supported Mackenzie's efforts to secure a Reciprocity Treaty with the United States. In January 1874, Mackenzie assigned the task of negotiating the treaty with the American government in Washington to George Brown, whom he had recently appointed to the Canadian Senate.[70] Besides including everything of the 1854 treaty, the new draft treaty added a broad range of manufactured goods, especially farm implements, wood, iron and steel products, boots and shoes, paper, cotton, rubber, and leather goods. Like Mackenzie and Brown, Holton viewed such a reciprocal trade agreement with the United States as a recovery measure for Canada. Once reciprocity was achieved, he reasoned, the path would be clear for the federal government to develop a fiscal system that would rely less on customs duties and more on direct taxation for revenue.

Mackenzie called Holton to Ottawa in mid-June to discuss the draft Reciprocity Treaty. In the excitement of backing Mackenzie and Brown, Holton wrote to Blake: "The Washington business looks very hopeful ... a treaty of the character of the one which seems to be approaching completion will metamorphose things in our country and involve a recast of our whole fiscal system."[71] Speaking at a by-election in Montreal West on 4 December 1874, Holton observed that the treaty "would be eminently advantageous to every interest of Canada, and especially advantageous to the industrial interests of Canada."[72] Some Canadian manufacturers shared Holton's view.[73] In reality, the treaty divided manufacturers, for some stood to gain from the removal of restrictions and the expansion of trade abroad, while many others might well be hurt. By the end of June, however, it was clear to numerous observers in Washington that the American Senate had no intention of carrying the draft treaty. It got no further than the Senate's Foreign Relations Committee, where it quietly slipped into oblivion. In these circumstances, Canada could not actually write off the draft treaty as a failure until around mid-December.[74]

But long before the collapse of the draft Reciprocity Treaty, Holton, fearing the worst, had begun to fight against the economic depression through another approach: by advocating an increase in the Canadian tariff. Seeing the tariff as essential for the growth of manufacturing within Canada and especially in Montreal, Holton supported Cartwright's budget, particularly the provision for raising the duty on certain imports from 15 to 17 ½ percent *ad valorem*, in the spring of 1874. On 30 April, Holton rose in the House, declaring that "the Finance Minister deserved the highest praise of the country."[75] The Montrealer clearly hoped to shape the Liberal party along progressive lines.

By 1875, Holton was determined to provide even more protection for Canadian manufacturers in the face of the deepening depression. He wanted the Mackenzie government to include in its budget, among other things, an increase in the duties on refined sugar and tea imports. But the Liberals were divided, and the proposed changes were not incorporated into the budget for it was impossible to secure a majority for higher sugar and tea duties. Holton nevertheless "advised Cartwright to take parliamentary authority to deal with both the sugar and tea questions and to take time to obtain information." As Holton argued, "this would have given all parties interested an opportunity of making their views known."[76] But Cartwright did not accept this advice. Instead, in response to a demand in April for more protection by the Redpath sugar refinery in Montreal, the government passed an order-in-council to lower the tariff on raw sugar imports. The order-in-council, coming as it did right on the heels of Cartwright's rejection of his advice, offended Holton, the spokesman for the Montreal business community. "No one can appreciate," he told Mackenzie, "the humiliation it has inflicted on me who does not understand the extent to which I am held responsible by the English speaking people, especially the mercantile portion of this community, for the acts of the present administration and the sting of the humiliation is in the fact that I can not frame even a plausible defence for the action of my friends without abandoning first those constitutional views which as a public man I have always insisted upon and secondly the free trade principles on which I have had to vindicate some exceedingly unpopular acts of the administration. It is doubtful whether the order in council is legal."[77] As it turned out, the order-in-council was not legal, and so the government was forced to revoke it.

Despite his humiliation, Holton continued to promote increased protection for Canadian manufacturers. In a by-election in Montreal West on 13 October, he spoke in Perry's Hall, backing Liberal candidate Thomas Workman, who noted that "if he were fortunate enough to have the honour of representing this great division, he should advocate a certain protection to our manufacturing industries and the adoption of every means to foster their progress and development. Our industries" are "now suffering from depression, due in some measure to competition of the manufacturers of the United States."[78] Workman won Montreal West by a very small majority.[79]

By this time, the Mackenzie government's tariff policy was coming under increasing criticism from Montreal Liberals like Holton and Workman as the problems of Montreal manufacturers began to call the policy into question. Holton's goal was to construct a more popular Liberalism, which could secure the support of a wide range of groups including manufacturers and help create a broad-based prosperity. In Ottawa, early in 1876, Holton discussed the situation with Liberal James Young of Galt, Ontario, and the two men urged Mackenzie to raise the tariff to 22 ½ percent.[80] Holton was soon disappointed, however, for on 25 February, Cartwright's budget showed that the Mackenzie government preferred to avoid a change to the tax system that would alienate especially free trade Nova Scotia Liberals.[81] Trying not to accentuate any differences that existed between Liberals, Holton took no part in the repeated and acrimonious debates over the tariff in the House of Commons during the next two years, except on 8 March 1878 when he briefly acknowledged that he still favoured additional protection for manufacturers.[82] In the end, he was only partially successful in his drive for the adoption of higher duties on foreign-made manufactured goods.

* * *

As in his struggle against the economic depression, Holton had only limited success in his fight for an improvement in English-French relations. His most notable service to the nation in this field was his willingness to urge equal opportunity for English-speaking and French-speaking Canadians. He was liked in many French and English homes as a politician with the conviction that no form of racial prejudice was acceptable. Holton wanted to avoid collision between the two cultures and develop a peaceful Canadian society. On 30 March 1874, English-Canadian feeling against French Canadians rose dramatically as Louis Riel, after being elected in Provencher, Manitoba, entered the House of Commons, took the oath of office and signed the members' register, and then fled to Hull for fear of being arrested on the charge that Thomas Scott had been shot for insubordination as a prisoner in the Northwest. On 15 April, Mackenzie Bowell, member for North Hastings and Grand Master of the Orange Order, made a motion for the expulsion of Riel. Emotions ran high as some members screamed "carried" and others yelled "lost, lost."

Holton immediately moved in amendment that Bowell's motion should be postponed until the select committee of the House had a chance to report on the question of amnesty. In his short speech, Holton declared that "the business of the House was to do what it could to allay the unfortunate feelings which existed in respect to the subject matter of the motion."[83] After the amendment had been defeated by 117 to seventy-six votes, the motion carried largely on racial lines.

Even in such circumstances, Holton kept up his spirits, continuing in his effort to nourish good will between English and French Canadians. He joined French-Canadian Liberals in Quebec in demanding amnesty for Riel. In English Canada, Holton placed himself at the head of the amnesty movement. Ever since 1870, he had favoured amnesty legislation.[84] Now, in January 1875, he put forward a bold proposal for unconditional amnesty for Riel in his correspondence with Mackenzie. "Every consideration of statesmanship," Holton told the prime minister, "points to unconditional amnesty."[85] But Mackenzie thought that no legislation to this effect could pass and, on 11 February in the House of Commons, moved an address granting a general amnesty to all persons involved in the Northwest troubles five years before, which included Riel, but on condition of five years' banishment from Canada.[86] The address carried the next day, by 126 to fifty, with Holton voting for the amnesty. Public pressure for him to redefine his position had grown so great that he had agreed to the condition for Riel. Holton was named to a select committee responsible for preparing the address to Governor-general Dufferin.[87] The dispute over Riel had, of course, not been settled. Despite the persistence of racial animosity, Anglo-French unity remained a central focus of Holton's hopes.

Holton was always searching for avenues to make the French and the English more fully aware of each other's needs. His own personal friendship with Antoine Dorion provided irrefutable proof of the unique bond that could be formed between two men of different cultural backgrounds. Holton had no patience with English Canadians who criticized French Canadians, or who attempted to elevate English Canada's image at French Canada's expense. He was upset with postmaster general Huntington for a speech he made in Argenteuil on 30 December 1875 condemning the French-Canadian Roman Catholic clergy for taking sides against English-Canadian, Protestant Liberals in elections.[88] "I first read that speech in New York," Holton wrote Mackenzie in January 1876, "and I immediately said to myself (I had no one to communicate with on Canadian politics) here is the deadliest blow at the Liberal party of Lower Canada delivered these twenty years."[89] Initially, Holton said little publicly, because he was seeking the least divisive solution to the problem. But on 14 February 1876, he rose in the House of Commons, denouncing Huntington's

> ... attempt to import a new element into our midst which, if successful, would render all legitimate politics in Quebec and throughout the Dominion impossible, and transform that which, I may say, is the pleasantest society in the Dominion if not in America, to wit, the society of Quebec, into a pandemonium.[90]

Like Wilfrid Laurier, who became minister of inland revenue the following year, Holton was totally opposed to the intervention of the clergy of any denomination in politics. What Holton found objectionable in Huntington's behaviour in Argenteuil was racism. Despite his affable manner, Holton could be a firm, resolute politician. The path to Anglo-French co-operation was certainly strewn with obstacles, but many of his contemporaries viewed Holton as a positive force, important to the advancement of cultural harmony.

* * *

Holton, however, had his moments of uncertainty and self-pity. As early as October 1875, he whined to Mackenzie, "the feelings of the Gov't or certain members of it towards me have undergone a decided change during the past few months."[91] But from the prime minister came reassuring words: "No member not in the government could have more influence.... I have on all occasions frankly acknowledged the benefit of your advice and assistance."[92] Contrary to Mackenzie's belief that Holton "lately has been pressing for the fulfilment of an office," Holton was not seeking a cabinet post.[93] "Office has no attractions for me,"

Wilfrid Laurier. Courtesy of the McCord Museum of Canadian History, Montreal.

he told the prime minister.[94] At the same time, Holton did not want to be separated from Mackenzie. The two men had forged a close personal as well as official relationship over the years, and this special connection remained intact. Mackenzie certainly continued to consult Holton on all major questions relating to government policy. For his part, Holton kept up his familiar, incessant, wide-ranging correspondence with the prime minister during parliamentary recesses.

Before long, Holton was also gaining the trust and confidence of Wilfrid Laurier, and this made a favourable impression upon Mackenzie.[95] In Montreal, Holton arranged a dinner in honour of Laurier in the St. Lawrence Hall for 4 December 1877. Laurier quickly relaxed as Holton established informal rapport with him. "Here we are gentlemen," Laurier told the dinner guests,

[M]y next neighbour (Mr. Devlin) is an Irish Catholic, his neighbour (Mr. Holton) is an English Protestant; I am a French Canadian. This is the circle of our society. There is the link. What is the link and what are the principles which bind Mr. Holton, Mr. Devlin and myself? Gentlemen, the principles of the Liberal party.... I want the Irish to remain Irish, the Scotch, Scotch, the English, English, the

French, French; but I want all, Scotch, French, Irish and English, to be, above all, British subjects and Canadians.... From the very days when I was a boy, the name of Hon. Mr. Holton has been prominent as a leader of the Liberal party in the Province of Quebec. We that are French Canadians – and there are many here today – we always took special interest in him, always had special regard and affection for him.[96]

Laurier admired Holton's sharp wit, warmth, and sense of realism.

* * *

Holton tried hard to keep his own role in perspective. During the weeks before the federal election on 17 September 1878, he knew that his job in Montreal was to establish a positive link between the Mackenzie government and the people of Canada, not to put himself forward. In this spirit, he sought to provide damage control of rumours about the government's record. Conservative opponents predicted that it would lose all three Montreal seats to John A. Macdonald men because of its neglect of the city's manufacturing interests.[97] A report circulated that Holton's friends wanted him to run in Montreal West.[98] Stories of the government's stand on the tariff were resurrected, with charges that it had failed to give adequate protection to the growing industrial sector of Canada's economy.[99] All these rumours and charges Holton did not attempt to refute, but he gave his full support to the three Liberal candidates: William Darling, a hardware merchant, in Montreal West; Bernard Devlin in Montreal Centre; and F. X. Archambault, a lawyer, in Montreal East.[100] Reporters covering Holton during the campaign soon noticed that in his speeches he avoided the key issues – tariff, industrial protection, and jobs – and concentrated on the personal strengths of the candidates and their faith in the Mackenzie government. For instance, he described Darling "as one of the ablest merchants of the city."[101] Darling himself advocated a high revenue tariff, "a high tariff in order to obtain sufficient money for the prosecution of the public works," while Devlin "was determined to support the highest protection schemes ... to build up manufacturing."[102] Archambault "was in favour of protection to our industries."[103] The Liberals were obviously not entirely united on the tariff issue.

Holton recognized that the disorganized state of the Liberal party in Montreal could have far-reaching consequences. "Unless something can be done to rescue the party from the chaotic condition into which it has fallen in the city," he wrote Mackenzie, "there is imminent danger of our losing the three divisions, and worse perhaps than even that such is the influence of the city over the country that a want of vigour and confidence here may cost us several county seats, enough possibly to imperil the whole position."[104] By contrast, the Conservative campaign in Montreal was well co-ordinated, with all three candidates – M. H. Gault, M. P. Ryan, and C. J. Coursol – asking voters to support John A. Macdonald's national policy, a high protective tariff.

In Chateauguay, Holton did not become involved in the religious issue, the Protestant-Catholic conflict.[105] Rather, he devoted all his time and energy there to public appearances designed to promote agriculture. In his speech at the show of the Chateauguay Agricultural Society, he demonstrated genuine interest in local farming.[106] Holton's quiet, self-effacing charm added strength to his words of encouragement. The strong campaign of Conservative Louis A. Seers, a Beauharnois lawyer and editor of *L'Avenir de Beauharnois*, failed to prevent a Liberal victory. Holton triumphed at the polls in Chateauguay on 17 September, though with a diminished majority of 180 votes.[107]

But the Conservatives swept the Liberals from power in Canada with the aid of John A. Macdonald's national policy. The Liberals went down to defeat in all three Montreal ridings, and took only eighteen of Quebec's sixty-five seats in the House of Commons.[108] John A. Macdonald the Opposition leader became John A. Macdonald the prime minister. With the election out of the way, Holton soon began preparations to take up his duties in the new parliament. Holton wrote Alexander Mackenzie, now Liberal Opposition leader again, on 1 February 1879:

When we reach Ottawa, (I propose going up on the 12th) we must consider whether we can advantageously submit any proposition respecting Bank Management and the Law concerning Brokers. I have long held very definite views on these points, well calculated in my judgement to prevent some of the evils we now complain of. But I could never elicit that degree of approval of them in the class principally affected which would have justified me in formulating them. *Now* I find lots of backers.[109]

Observers might have thought that the important events in parliament occupied all of Holton's time, but his business at home in Montreal also demanded his attention. During most of his long political life, he was active as an entrepreneur as well, continuing to respond to business opportunities. He constantly moved between his business and political worlds, juggling different roles, different entrepreneurial undertakings, and different political concerns. In business, the co-ordination of his varied activities was one of his main challenges and it also helped him emerge as one the most successful businessmen in Montreal. To thousands of Canadians, he was as much an entrepreneur as a politician.

Chapter 8

Financing the Canada Engine Works

When his cousin Ebenezer E. Gilbert founded the Canada Engine Works in Montreal in October 1849, Luther Holton provided the business with significant financial backing and an important steadying influence. Originally established as Gilbert, Milln & Bartley, the fledgling firm's other two partners were William W. Milln and William P. Bartley. From the start, Holton assumed the role of creditor and displayed an understanding of finance that was just what the tottering partnership needed. With his assistance, the firm manufactured marine engines and other iron products and sold them in Montreal and the surrounding area. Canada Engine Works turned out to be a success story, but it was considered a risky move at the time he decided to back it. To skeptics who wondered if the firm would ever amount to anything, Holton responded by confidently continuing to put his money into it, thus helping it survive its infancy, mature, and produce and repair marine engines for decades. Although he knew relatively little about manufacturing engines, he educated himself in the main aspects of the business and helped plan future directions for the firm.

During Holton's life, Canadian society passed from merchant capitalism to the beginnings of industrial capitalism. Through a look at his role in financing the Canada Engine Works, one may gain insight into the workings of industrial capitalism in a strident but also successful phase in Montreal. The founding of the Canada Engine Works and the activities of its forerunners occurred as a part of the city's industrial development. Canada's most dynamic inland river port since the French regime, Montreal grew up as a centre for trade in furs, timber, and wheat. After the mid-1830s, however, the city also developed an industrial economy. In the mid-nineteenth century, Montreal businessmen searched for and found solutions to numerous problems hindering the growth of their industrial concerns. Between 1851 and 1871, Montreal's population increased from

57,715 to 107,225, providing an expanding local market for goods produced in the city. The completion of the railway network centred in Montreal made it possible for manufacturers to distribute their products provincially more economically than ever before. New manufacturing technology and some tariff protection allowed local industrial enterprises to grow and mature.

Canada Engine Works' early growth also took place against a background of important developments in the foundry and engine industries. In Montreal, the value of foundry output grew dramatically in the 1860s and 1870s, rising from $263,500 to $681,900 ten years later. Associated with this significant growth in the value of foundry output was the marked increase during the same period in the number of foundry employees, from 427 to 724. Between 1852 and 1871, the total number of all foundries in the city grew from seven to sixteen, and the number of engine foundries increased from one to five. In 1871, Montreal's five engine foundries turned out products valued at $519,175, while the nation's total of twelve foundries together produced goods valued at $1,004,525.[1] Mid-nineteenth century industrialization in Canada concentrated especially on developing the technology for the production of machines. It was in these exciting times that the Canada Engine Works came into being. Within this vibrant firm, there was plenty of scope for the exercise of individual talent, initiative, and responsibility. The interplay of external circumstances and the personal talents of Luther Holton and Ebenezer Gilbert played a significant part in Montreal's industrial processes and growth.

* * *

The early and mid-1850s were expansionist in Montreal, and Holton's personality suited this ethos very well. Not only did his forwarding business grow, but his enthusiasms carried him into several other businesses. Besides building railways, he mustered the resources and the will to help make Gilbert, Milln & Bartley competitive. As would be true of those involved with Canada Engine Works at a later time, the partners in Gilbert, Milln & Bartley had close personal and business connections with the Montreal business community. These ties were particularly strong in the case of Ebenezer Gilbert, one of the remarkable figures in nineteenth-century Canadian business, whose family was long established in the city. Born in Montreal in 1823, Ebenezer was the son of Moses Haskell Gilbert, a lumber and provisions merchant. Moses Gilbert died in 1843, at the age of fifty-three, leaving his wife, Cynthia, and two children, Ebenezer and Cynthia, both minors.

As a result of the untimely death of his uncle Moses, Luther Holton became guardian of his two cousins, Ebenezer and Cynthia, who were close friends of his from the days of their childhood.[2] The consequent responsibilities gave Holton, who by this time was manager of the forwarding firm Henderson, Hooker & Co., additional training in finance. Holton assisted aunt Cynthia in managing the inheritance the family received from Moses Gilbert's estate.

As a boy, Ebenezer attended a local school and helped his father in the family business. He inherited his father's business talents and had a strong mechanical bent as well.

In Ebenezer Gilbert, Holton saw potential for a business career and, in 1840, was instrumental in hiring him as a clerk at Henderson, Hooker & Co. Ebenezer tackled his new job with enthusiasm and curiosity. Human muscle was amply available to load and unload the steamboats' cargoes, but Ebenezer thought about how to make the task easier. A hoisting apparatus existed first as one of his ideas, then as a sketch, and finally in 1845 it became an iron contrivance that could load

Ebenezer Edwin Gilbert (1823-1889) in 1871, Luther Holton's cousin. Courtesy of the McCord Museum of Canadian History, Montreal.

steamboats with goods.[3] As a clerk, Ebenezer found the creative work he did perfecting the device a welcome way of using up surplus time and energy. In the office, his aptitude for penmanship allowed him to keep beautiful ledgers. His prospects were encouraging, for in 1847 he married Emma Boys, who had been born in England.

* * *

Holton had the resources to take the stage as financier when Ebenezer Gilbert stepped into the world of industrial creation, as part owner of Gilbert, Milln & Bartley. While his cousin was the technical genius, Holton had a natural affinity for figures and money. With Holton's backing, the firm built a foundry on the Lachine Canal next to Augustin Cantin's shipyard, in the heart of Montreal's industrial district. A modest but ambitious industrial city, Montreal boasted a number of factories. The manufacturing area was crowded and alive with noise and bustle, its air filled with smoke and fog. In 1850, when the city was starting to recover from the economic depression of the late 1840s, Gilbert, Milln & Bartley began operations and produced its first marine engine. The engine was technically unremarkable, but it performed well enough that Ebenezer Gilbert decided to manufacture more for forwarders and shipbuilders. From the beginning, the growth of the foundry was closely linked to the development of allied industries, especially forwarding and shipbuilding. A self-taught engineer without the benefit of formal training, Gilbert relied on his own inventive abilities to improve the efficiency of his processes and the quality of his products. He learned and refined his skills through experience at the foundry. Gilbert needed water to power his machinery and to cool his furnace. Fortunately for him, the Lachine Canal supplied plenty of water for the foundry, the site of which consisted of three lots that he had leased from the Canadian government.[4]

Holton's outgoing personality helped him build good relations with Gilbert and his partners. As one of the firm's major creditors, Holton had a personal stake in the foundry's future. Holton and Gilbert worked out financial arrangements to enable the foundry to increase and diversify its production, manufacturing not only marine engines, but also stationary engines, boilers, and other iron products. Their way of doing business was creative and flexible. Attuned to Holton's own business principles, Gilbert followed a policy of retaining most of the earnings and allowing capital to grow.

All signs indicate that Holton understood at least some of the consequences of his actions. He believed that if he could guide the firm past the early financial shoals into good markets, the foundry would survive and grow. The main problem at the start was the large debt Gilbert, Milln & Bartley contracted in its efforts to construct the foundry. This amounted to £13,450, a sum that represented a heavy capital expenditure for the firm.[5] Engine making was a highly capital-intensive industry. To make matters worse, Milln withdrew from the enterprise in 1850 and took his capital with him. Gilbert now had a sixty-three percent interest in the foundry, while Bartley's share was thirty-seven percent.

* * *

Like most fledgling marine engine builders at this time, Gilbert & Bartley seemed to have none too bright a future. Financially, the firm stood on the brink, but Holton's backing enabled it to continue production. His forwarding career was prospering, and this permitted him to use some of his profits to support the foundry.

Convinced that constant improvement in the foundry's products would help keep it afloat, Holton encouraged Gilbert to acquire the most up-to-date machinery and move toward production of high-quality goods. His cousin had the intelligence, strength, and stamina to make progress in his work. By consistently making good metal, Gilbert built a reputation that brought him business and earned him a respected place in Montreal as well as outside the city. Soon the manufactured items embodied the foundry's attention to fine detail, smoothness, and durability. Gilbert was far from having the field of iron products to himself in the early 1850s. A number of competitors surfaced in Montreal, including especially the St. Lawrence Engine Works. While eventually Gilbert would outstrip some Montreal competitors in diversification and attention to markets, at the start he had to toil diligently to get a foothold in the local iron industry. Gilbert & Bartley's foundry was a hot, dangerous, dirty place where they prepared moulds, poured iron, and allowed metal products to take shape. Fresh from the foundry, a steam engine and a boiler were sold to George Smith, a Montreal forwarder.[6] Like many of Gilbert & Bartley's other sales, this one was based on a contract between the foundry and the buyer that called for customized products, though the firm manufactured a number of standard items as well. The foundry also repaired steam engines and other machines and tools. In an effort to further diversify, Gilbert & Bartley produced and sold several iron buckets to the Montreal Harbour Commissioners for the harbour dredge.[7]

But Holton's job of financing the foundry was made difficult by the withdrawal of Bartley from the partnership in the summer of 1851. Bartley also withdrew his capital and then started his own foundry business. He was now Gilbert's rival and soon expanded by admitting a partner, James Dunbar, an engineer. Before long, Bartley & Dunbar acquired the St. Lawrence Engine Works. Holton was nevertheless able to take in stride the problem arising from the shrinkage of capital at Gilbert's foundry.

* * *

Although he nervously eyed the competition, Holton continued to help Gilbert stay in production. Gilbert's foundry was not isolated from mainstream developments in Montreal's economy. His products were not simply passive items; rather, they interacted directly with other industries, providing goods not only for forwarders but also for factories and government agencies. Among other things, Gilbert built a steam engine and boiler for the Montreal Harbour Commissioners' tugboat on Lake St. Peter. With solid financial backing and top-quality products flowing from his foundry, Gilbert garnered a priceless reputation for integrity and close attention to his business. Ebenezer Gilbert is "a man of good character and habits, and doing good business. Aided by Holton of Hooker & Holton," reported the R. G. Dun & Co. credit correspondent in the fall of 1852.[8]

One of Holton's strengths was his capacity to size up other people. He had the uncanny ability to extend credit to reliable and talented men, such as his cousin, who had always liked him. Holton allowed Gilbert enough freedom to exercise his own creative talents. This blend of business purpose and freedom helped Gilbert's foundry grow. The foundry's rising sales included marine engines and boilers for H. Jones & Co.'s new steamboat, as well as for the Montreal and New York Railroad Company's new steamboat that was to ply on the ferry between Lachine and Caughnawaga.[9] Together, an engine and a boiler were priced at between £1,250 and £2,100, and over the next few years the foundry sold a number of units.

Despite the respectable sales record, trouble assaulted Gilbert at every turn. Short of money, H. Jones & Co. failed to pay Gilbert.[10] Under ideal circumstances, steamboats came to the foundry from shipyards such as Cantin's all ready to have machinery installed. Otherwise, Gilbert could not meet contract deadlines. But he discovered that the Montreal and New York Railroad Company's steamboat needed more work at the shipyard.[11] Later, Gilbert landed a marine engine contract from Louis A. Sénécal. Sénécal's old steamboat was, however, hardly in a condition to have an engine installed.[12] All these problems caused delays in Gilbert's operations and slowed down the cash flow.

But Gilbert went to work and toiled at a steady, hard pace all day in the foundry, accomplishing as much as he could. He was the kind of man production workers liked. Gilbert was often lifting unwieldy, grey iron castings, getting his hands black, and gasping for air as his nostrils filled with soot. His employees, including the apprentices such as eighteen-year-old William Inglis, who later went on to a brilliant engineering career in Montreal and Great Britain, had little difficulty understanding their boss. Gilbert was articulate and had insight into their world. Initially, the apprentice engineers were paid one shilling per day; it was one of the terms of the apprenticeship contracts their fathers had signed. Once they gained more experience, their pay increased. The pay was about average for apprentices in Montreal's manufacturing establishments at mid-century.[13]

* * *

Gilbert, however, knew that his working capital position was not adequate to continue operations much longer. He needed money quickly to stay in the foundry business. To solve this problem, Gilbert began to seek a partner possessing some capital as well as the technical expertise required in the foundry. In David J. Macfarlane, an engineer and draftsman of Montreal, he found such a partner and, on 4 October 1853, the new partnership of Gilbert & Macfarlane began its existence.[14] Gilbert had a two-thirds interest in the new firm's stock-in-trade, while Macfarlane's share was one-third; the two partners shared the profits and losses in the same proportions. Macfarlane, however, contributed only £500 to the business. Gilbert remained in sole possession of all the immovable property, including the foundry buildings. The partnership paid Gilbert £100 plus 10 percent per annum on the cost of the buildings and the other improvements for the use of the foundry and its grounds. Each partner was entitled to an annual salary, Gilbert's being set at £400 and Macfarlane's at £200.

The new business was modestly successful, but it was cash poor. While financing its operations internally through retained earnings, Gilbert & Macfarlane required additional capital from outside sources. The partners tried to raise the necessary funds through loans from family or friends and credit from enterprises that provided them with goods and services. Gilbert was the driving force behind the partnership, and he handled its finances. After others declined his request for a loan, he approached Holton.

The challenge was exactly the kind of adventure that excited Luther Holton. In August 1854, he lent Gilbert £300.[15] A month later, Gilbert borrowed £409 from Holton, thereby further strengthening his firm's financial position.[16] The relationship between the two men was characterized by good humour and affection. Ebenezer Gilbert "is backed by Holton," the R. G. Dun & Co. credit reporter noted. Gilbert is "attentive & industrious, honest, but not worth much. Doing pretty well."[17]

Holton's policy by this time was to function simultaneously as a railway builder and as a supplier of funds to cousin Gilbert and thus to receive the profits or sustain the losses of both roles. Holton continued to favour only a few close friends and business acquaintances as stewards for his outside investments. His reputation was that of a highly successful railway contractor on the Grand Trunk, but he also benefited from his investment in Gilbert's foundry. Interest on the capital Holton put into this manufacturing business amounted to six percent per annum.[18]

But as it grew, Gilbert's foundry needed more money than what Holton could supply. Another significant outside source of funding was Frothingham & Workman. This well-established local hardware firm, owned and managed by John Frothingham and Thomas and William Workman, served as Gilbert & Macfarlane's principal supplier, providing it with imported raw materials, especially pig iron from Scotland. At the same time, Frothingham & Workman became Gilbert & Macfarlane's main creditor, assisting the foundry to keep functioning by the provision of substantial credit.[19]

The funds from Luther Holton, Frothingham & Workman, as well as other suppliers such as the general wholesale house of I. Buchanan, Harris & Co., in addition to the foundry's earnings, enabled Gilbert & Macfarlane to finance its development.[20] With the foundry's growth came sales to new customers. For example, in November 1853, the firm sold a stationary steam engine to Brown, Hibbard, Bourne & Co., a Montreal rubber manufacturer.[21] While Gilbert & Macfarlane's primary focus was still the local market, its linkages were beginning to spread far and wide in Canada. The partners were keen to sell their products across the province. In 1854 and early 1855, the firm's marine engine customers included G. & A. Davie, a Quebec City shipbuilding firm, and George Bryson, who operated a steamboat in connection with his lumber trade on the Ottawa River, above Ottawa in Mansfield Township, Pontiac County, Lower Canada.[22]

But as early as November 1854, Gilbert & Macfarlane found its financial resources severely stretched, so much so that it could not meet its obligations. The fundamental problem was that Gilbert, the firm's manager, had to contend with many customers who were falling behind in their payments for the products he had sold them. Bad debts complicated the situation and resulted in heavy losses. Gilbert's efforts to tighten control on the collection of debts proved abortive. Red ink flooded Gilbert & Macfarlane's financial ledgers, and the search for new capital became more difficult. At the foundry feelings of panic and hopelessness took hold of the partners. The partnership nevertheless limped along, but in May 1855, it dissolved and at the same time Gilbert became the sole owner of the foundry and made an assignment for the benefit of his creditors.[23]

* * *

Gilbert had experienced a drastic reversal of fortunes – he had become bankrupt. A quick settlement was precluded by the diversity of interests and of potential solutions involved. Among the possibilities were foreclosure and liquidation as well as renegotiation with terms more favourable to Gilbert. Holton and Gilbert's other creditors rejected foreclosure as a penalty too harsh for him and his family. Instead, they allowed him to stay in business to enable him to pay off his debts. There were no formal court proceedings. Rather, the creditors decided to appoint Luther Holton, Alexander Campbell of I. Buchanan, Harris & Co., and Thomas Workman of Frothingham & Workman as trustees for the bankrupt estate of Ebenezer Gilbert. Holton's previous experience at Hooker, Holton & Co. with customers' debt and bankruptcy problems clearly demonstrated that a feasible plan could be drawn up in this situation. It was Holton who played the most important part in renegotiating terms and in steering cousin

Gilbert through the crisis. Holton, Campbell, and Workman, after long discussions with Gilbert, worked out a plan whereby he could gradually pay off the £10,780 he owed thirty-three creditors over a three-year period. Gilbert promised to make payments in quarterly instalments to the creditors until they were paid in full. The creditors secured their loans by taking and recording a mortgage on Gilbert's cottage and its seven-acre lot on St. Joseph Street adjacent to his foundry, as well as on his foundry with its stock and machinery.[24]

As a creditor, Holton's problem of trying to make his investment in the foundry productive once more was not outside his control. Because Gilbert had up-to-date books, he could provide trustees Holton, Campbell, and Workman with a precise picture of his financial situation. Gilbert's initial review of his books made plain what Holton had suspected all along: unable to collect debts, Gilbert had failed but with assets significantly exceeding liabilities.[25] Holton was not eager to throw everything to the winds because Gilbert's foundry still showed considerable promise of survival. Thanks to Gilbert's technical expertise and persistence, the foundry was now producing some of the best marine engines in Canada.

This was not total calamity. Despite all the major challenges at the foundry, Gilbert had kept track of details. So when he opened his books, he could explain to Holton and the other trustees all notes on outstanding loans. Frothingham & Workman, Bartley & Dunbar's foundry, and Holton were the three largest creditors, and Gilbert owed them £2,301, £1,087, and £929, respectively.[26] Other major creditors included W.D.B. Janes, a commission agent; the house of I. Buchanan, Harris & Co.; John M. Gilbert, a coal and commission merchant and Ebenezer Gilbert's relative; the forwarding firm Hooker, Jaques & Co.; Charles Garth, a plumber and brass founder; and David J. Macfarlane, Ebenezer Gilbert's former partner. Among the medium-sized and smaller creditors were the City Bank and Molson's Bank.

Holton's unswerving belief in his cousin, coupled with his ability to work well with him, helped make the new start a smooth one. Ebenezer Gilbert could repay his debts because money from the sale of products was now coming in at a steady clip. His principal source of repayment was income from the sale of marine engines and boilers, followed by earnings from the sale of forges and brass and iron castings. After meeting the payments on the outstanding loans, he ploughed most of the balance back into the business. Holton was constantly amazed at how well the foundry was doing. He did not live in a fairyland, but he could see that cousin Gilbert was rigorously abiding by his agreement with the trustees.

* * *

So impressed were Holton and his fellow trustees with Gilbert's success in reducing the debt that they cancelled the deed of assignment in October 1855.[27] Around this time, Gilbert began operating under the name of the Beaver Foundry. There was plenty of space on its site for the works. The Beaver Foundry, a wooden, brick and iron structure, was 100 feet long and fifty feet wide.[28] It housed, among other things, lathes, drills, and shaping and cutting machines. The finishing shop, 125 feet long and fifty feet wide, was partly of one storey and partly of two storeys. There was a brick engine house containing a large steam engine. By 1856, Gilbert's Beaver Foundry employed from sixty to eighty men and boys, and it turned out products valued at £7,300 during the six months ending on 1 October of that year.[29]

BEAVER FOUNDRY, E. E. GILBERT.

FIRST GATE PAST TOLL GATE

ST. JOSEPH STREET,

MONTREAL.

Is now prepared to execute orders for Steam Engines, Boilers, Mill Work, Heavy Forges, Brass and Iron Castings of every descripton.

The Beaver Foundry in Montreal advertised the variety of its products. From *The Montreal Directory for 1855.*

There was, however, still a difficulty: the Beaver Foundry produced a variety of iron goods for local and provincial markets, but it lacked a specialty product to provide it with an advantage over its competitors. Ideally, Gilbert should have been running his foundry at full capacity. In fact, he was operating it at only half capacity because of stiff competition and falling demand.[30] Profits dropped sharply. Gilbert did not hunker down to await better days. Instead, he did all he could to hustle new business. But with his cash resources severely strained, Gilbert was forced to borrow money to pay for the foundry's raw materials and to meet the payroll. Desperate for capital, he again approached Holton.

Luther Holton was ready to help people who he believed would help themselves. He remained a key behind-the-scenes player at the Beaver Foundry. Most important was his continued willingness to finance the operations with his resources. In November 1855, he lent cousin Gilbert at least £800. The loan, coupled with the marine engine sales it was able to make, allowed the Beaver Foundry's cash position to stabilize. Gilbert repaid the loan by assigning to Holton a judgment of £800 in Gilbert's favour that had resulted from a court case over a dispute between the Beaver Foundry and the Montreal and New York Railroad Company.[31] The money, however, was slow in coming in, so in May 1856 Gilbert put pressure on the railroad through Holton to hand over the £800 plus the interest charges.[32] Ebenezer Gilbert "is getting through difficulties, supported by L. H. Holton ... who is wealthy," noted the R. G. Dun & Co. credit reporter.[33]

Luther Holton continued to have great regard for and pride in Gilbert's work. The reliable marine engines produced at the Beaver Foundry reflected his cousin's fierce belief in quality. Committed to craftsmanship, Gilbert wanted no dissatisfied customers growling for better products. Because the quality of products remained paramount, Gilbert was able to sell more marine engines, show profits, and thus meet nearly all his obligations to his creditors. In March 1857, the R. G. Dun & Co. correspondent reported that Gilbert "has paid up most of his installments promptly thus far & probably gets along, has had some good contracts lately & made something."[34] By the autumn of 1857, the Beaver Foundry's marine engines provided power for thirteen well-known steamboats plying Canadian waters, including *Castor*, *Ranger*, *Voyageur*, *Rambler*, *Champlain*, *St. Peter*, *Iroquois*, *Verchères*, and *Salaberry*.[35] Marine engines continued to be important in the foundry's production; one, for example, was produced for the steamboat of Henry B. Wales, a farmer of Pointe Fortune, Lower Canada.[36] Around this time, the Beaver Foundry seized the opportunity to diversify into the production of sawmill engines with alacrity, selling them to customers such as Gilmour & Co. of Trenton, Joseph Aumond of Ottawa, and William Price of Quebec City.[37]

Gilbert had obviously taken advantage of golden sales opportunities, and Holton was pleased with his cousin's performance. In September 1857, Holton and Gilbert basked in the aura of the foundry's ongoing success. But even in that bright moment, Holton, who always had his ear close to ground, could sense the rumblings that portended stormy times. In October, a continent-wide financial crisis struck and threatened to plunge the Beaver Foundry into ruin.[38] Traditional market patterns fell apart. As the market malaise spread across Canada, the financial community became nervous and began to tighten up. When many of Gilbert's customers stopped paying their bills, he found it extremely difficult to meet his commitments to his suppliers, especially Frothingham & Workman, still his chief supplier and creditor. Frothingham & Workman and the banks became wary of extending more credit to the foundry, and its problems grew worse.

Facing up to the seriousness of the situation, Gilbert ruefully reported to Holton that the till at the Beaver Foundry was growing progressively emptier. Cousin Gilbert was no doomsayer, and Holton listened to him. He knew that Gilbert needed money quickly and, on 15 October 1857, he lent him £2,015 to carry the foundry until the market returned to normal.[39] Holton fixed the interest rate on the loan at six percent per annum and took as security a mortgage on Gilbert's St. Joseph Street house and its seven-acre lot. Then, in a particularly important step, Holton made additional funds available to Gilbert by purchasing the Beaver Foundry's machinery, tools, implements, and engine for £2,000.[40] At the same time, Holton leased all this equipment to his cousin for two years at the rate of £200 per annum.

* * *

Besides being a creditor, Holton was thus now also a major part owner of the Beaver Foundry. The pulse of the foundry quickened. Gilbert and Holton were still certain that they had splendid marine engines to offer the public, but the depression hindered them. They managed through herculean efforts to squeeze a number of engines from their foundry – and still lost money because customers did not pay their bills. Conditions were rapidly moving from bad to worse. No matter what Holton and Gilbert tried, it did not bring the desired results. Talk in the foundry of survival, cash depletion, catastrophe, and bankruptcy frightened them. Finally, they gave up on the Beaver Foundry's chances of going it alone in the savage marine engine marketplace and seriously considered a merger. The path Gilbert and Holton trod was hardly straightforward, but in February 1858, they merged with William Bartley who had gone bankrupt the previous year. The new partnership, Bartley & Gilbert, opened for business at the Beaver Foundry and at Bartley's old works.

But the merger scenario did not play out the way Holton and Gilbert had envisioned. For a while, the new partnership made progress. In August 1859, the R. G. Dun & Co. credit correspondent reported that Bartley & Gilbert "are pretty full of orders just now, and have over 100 men employed. Both partners are practical men & although 'under the weather' they are thought to be improving their condition slowly."[41] But by April 1860, the firm owed Frothingham & Workman $60,000. The foundry's losses depleted its cash reserves. Red ink was seeping across Bartley & Gilbert's ledgers, and by the middle of the following year, the firm's deficit was more than $100,000. To make the situation worse, the growing needs of his family, which by now included his two sons, moved Gilbert to pay himself a large dividend – a step that violated the partnership agreement. The dividend drained the foundry of precious funds. Bartley and Gilbert desperately struggled to remain in marine engine production, but they disagreed sharply about the production schedule, and this bred a lack of confidence in the future of the foundry. In December 1861, Bartley & Gilbert made an assignment for the benefit of their creditors. Quickly, news of the firm's bankruptcy spread throughout Montreal and beyond. According to the R. G. Dun & Co. credit reporter, "the cause of the failure was partly on account of Gilbert drawing more than double the amount agreed upon for private expenses ... debts & want of confidence & disagreement between him and Bartley, one pulling against the other to the injury of the business."[42] The creditors nevertheless allowed the firm to stay in business.

But without additional outside help, the foundry had no future. Holton groused about his cousin's large dividend, but he did not blame all the foundry's woes on him. When Gilbert and Bartley dissolved their partnership in mid-1862, Holton propped up Gilbert's morale by promising to help him continue in business. Nothing could daunt Gilbert for long. Having earlier gone through a financial crisis that would have licked most businessmen, and having recovered with Holton's assistance, he quickly pulled himself together. Now somewhat chastened but still optimistic, Gilbert plunged into the foundry business with typical energy.

E. E. GILBERT,
Canada Engine Works,
MONTREAL, P. Q.

View of E. E. Gilbert's Canada Engine Works in Montreal in 1871. From *Lovell's Province of Ontario Directory for 1871.*

* * *

Holton identified with his cousin's new start by readily accepting his decision to rename the foundry the Canada Engine Works. Gilbert, of course, was happy to keep Holton as a major part owner of the foundry. Holton's lasting contribution to the Canada Engine Works was his constant willingness to provide substantial financial backing and to support the production of reliable, mechanically sophisticated marine engines. By December 1862, Holton and Gilbert had charted a course that enhanced the firm's reputation for making high-quality products. The two men, concluded the R. G. Dun & Co. credit reporter, worked well together: "at present Holton is his principal creditor & as he is easy with him he [Gilbert] gets along in a comfortable way though his capital is small … [Gilbert] is a steady, hard-working man & a good mechanic."[43]

In Holton's eyes, his cousin was the epitome of the man of self-education, taste, and imagination. Almost forty years old, Gilbert could look at the career he had chosen and feel justified. His marine engine business was evolving and, although shaken at times by economic troubles, was proving stable. And he had the Canada Engine Works as an outward sign of success. Holton appreciated Gilbert's fertile and inventive mind. The time seemed ripe for providing his cousin with funds to enable him to develop and promote an engine he had designed earlier. Back in 1859, Gilbert had carried out a dramatic change in his approach; he had developed a specialty product for a niche market, a Corliss marine engine.[44]

At the Canada Engine Works, Holton and Gilbert now based their plans for the foundry's future on the revenues they expected to receive from the production and sale of the Corliss steam engine for steamboats, a machine that George H. Corliss of Rhode Island began developing in the mid-1840s.[45] Until the early 1860s, most steamboats in Canada used steam engines in which the valves were inadequate. The problems of such valves lay in the difficulty of manufacturing them, maintaining them, keeping steam tight, and regulating the speed of the engine. The Corliss engine, possessing valves and a governor that could better control steam and better regulate engine speed, offered a solution to these problems.

Gilbert was among those to see the potential of the Corliss steam engine. Exemplifying the innovative engineer in mid-nineteenth-century Canada and personifying the adaptation of American technology to the needs of Montreal industry, Gilbert had built an engine to George Corliss's design for a paddle-wheel steamer.[46] If he was not the original source of this innovation, Gilbert had the ability to develop and apply Corliss's ideas. But it did not happen overnight. It took some time for the concept to go from Gilbert's head to a working model and drawings that could be submitted to the Canadian Patent Office. In the end, his wonderful idea was vindicated. Patent number 910 for "an improved steam boiler," filed on 20 January 1859, clearly was a representation of his vision of a better boiler and marine engine.[47] Another important inventor quickly learned of Gilbert's breakthrough and collaborated with him in development work. In 1860, Gilbert, with the help of his former apprentice William Inglis, manufactured a Corliss marine engine for use in the paddle-wheel steamer, *Montreal*.[48]

In a further creative move, Gilbert introduced the forced blast for the boiler in this steamer.[49] This invention made the process of combustion more efficient. Although he had perfected his Corliss marine engine to the point of marketability, Gilbert continued his experiments, trying to refine his technology. He did actually improve his engine, but more than technological advance was needed for long-term economic success. The experiments were expensive, and Gilbert required additional money to proceed with them.

Luther Holton was ecstatic about his cousin's proposal to make further improvements on his Corliss marine engine. Gilbert the practical and innovative manufacturer and Holton the financier viewed research on the Corliss engine from the same perspective. Both men wanted the research to lead to an improved product of commercial value to the Canada Engine Works. Most important, they expected something of considerable commercial value to come out of the creative work at the foundry in the very near future. Holton lent Gilbert $8,061 to perfect his Corliss marine engine and to continue production of his conventional marine engines at the same time. In May 1863, the R. G. Dun & Co. credit correspondent reported that Gilbert is "doing a fair business, is in a better position than he has been for some time, capital small, has a credit for a small amount."[50] Gilbert was a good manager of time, resources, and employees, but he was not earning enough from the production and sale of conventional marine engines to repay Holton. But Holton could not simply demand payment on overdue notes. The total sum was so large, and the firm's resources so small, that such a move would bankrupt the Canada Engine Works. So in December, Holton gave his cousin an extension on the $8,061 loan.[51]

The year 1864 found Holton and Gilbert in the full flush of their powers and virtually unstoppable in attaining their industrial goals. Their genius at co-operation at the Canada Engine Works put a relentless pressure on their competitors and their ongoing emphasis was on innovation, high-quality products, and vigorous marketing. They worked hard to create and sustain customer loyalty. In all this activity, Holton was content to allow the general public to focus their attention on Gilbert the successful manufacturer, while he himself remained behind the scenes as financier and major part owner of the foundry. The author of *Montreal Business Sketches*, published in 1864, wrote: "Mr. Gilbert has peculiar facilities for engine building; the engines in some of the best steamers on the St. Lawrence and the Ottawa are of his manufacture. His engines are to be found in operation in every part of Canada.... He is the only person in the province who makes what is known as the Corliss engine."[52] Holton could take satisfaction from important statistics: by this time, Gilbert had produced about ninety steam engines, a number of which were Corliss marine engines.

Luther Holton's instincts for the value of promotion and publicity were sharply honed, and he recognized that his cousin's positive image spoke directly and effectively to many potential customers. Holton agreed with Gilbert on the foundry's advertising efforts. Gilbert helped popularize his engines and other iron products through advertisements of the Canada Engine Works in the annual *Montreal Directory*. Holton continued to fund the production of Gilbert's new specialty product, the Corliss marine engine, which found a profitable niche in the market. At the same time, Holton had the financial resources that allowed Gilbert to design and build other steam engines with a high degree of finish and better than average reliability. In 1864, the market for Gilbert's engines widened geographically, with sales going to customers such as the General Cuban Steam Navigation Company of Havana, Cuba.[53]

But the year 1865 was a critical period for the Canada Engine Works. The firm had to have more capital. Luther Holton came through just in time with a loan of $5,000 that made it possible for the production of marine engines and other iron products to continue.[54] Under the terms of the loan, Gilbert was to repay his debt to Holton over four years. The two men stayed alert to sales opportunities and, between 1865 and the early 1870s, found a number of marine engine customers, including Hugh Allan's Canadian Navigation Company.[55] Advertisements suggested that the Canada Engine Works was expanding. By 1871, the firm stood as an important, diversified manufacturing concern employing 145 workers and achieving thousands of dollars in annual sales. The firm's workers used complex machinery and advanced technology to accomplish their tasks, turning out especially marine engines and boilers but also forgings, castings, and machinery for sawmills, gristmills, sugar factories, and tanneries. Its facilities – two machine shops, a blacksmith shop, a boiler shop, a moulding shop, a foundry, a fitting shop, and a pattern shop, with several smokestacks belching black smoke into the sky – were still at the Lachine Canal site, and it sold goods and services to customers across central Canada.[56]

In retrospect, the Holton-Gilbert duo proved a durable partnership, with Holton remaining in the Canada Engine Works until he retired in the early 1870s. He was ready to let a new generation take his place. By this time, Gilbert's sons Frank and Walter were apparently working for the firm; a few years later, they would join it, signalling the start of a new stage in its evolution. For more than two decades, Holton had devoted part of his attention and tremendous energies to developing and maintaining the firm, twice helping to save it from liquidation. The time and money he had invested in it had brought him financial gain. During this period, he had also been prominent in the development of the Montreal City and District Savings Bank. The business genius that had helped lead the Canada Engine Works into the future played with full force over this new field.

Chapter 9

Savings Banker

In April 1846, Luther Holton turned to a new challenge: he became a founding and managing director of the Montreal City and District Savings Bank, whose geographical area of operation was the city of Montreal and its suburbs.[1] His timing was propitious, because the port city was ready for this kind of institution. Initially, it was essentially a traditional trustee savings bank – a benevolent institution sponsored by Roman Catholic Bishop Ignace Bourget and numerous merchants, politicians, and lawyers to encourage thrift among the working classes. As such, it had no public stockholders, but it still had an obligation to report annually on its operations to the public it served and to the Canadian parliament. Holton threw himself into part-time work in the bank's business with great energy and passion. He liked to submerge himself in the bank's clientele, rubbing shoulders with factory workers, stevedores, and teamsters. Here was a microcosm of humanity, including Irish, French Canadians, Scots, English, and American Canadians. Holton loved to talk with these people, enjoying the familiar faces he saw frequently. This became an important part of his life.

Holton was able, by reason of his business sense and his humanitarian instinct, to visualize the bank as one of promotion of business as well as stimulus to thrift. In 1871, as the bank's president, he completed the transformation of the institution from a concern designed to cater to the labouring classes into a limited liability joint stock corporation capable of providing a wide range of banking services and promoting the social welfare of its community. As a leading figure in the enterprise from the beginning, Holton thus took a central place in the early development of a bank that survived and prospered for 141 years and then, in 1987, became the Laurentian Bank of Canada, distinguished by its full range of banking services and its national orientation.[2]

* * *

In the mid-1840s, Holton's business genius was to grasp the idea of a true market for savings bank services. As he saw it, working people would deposit their savings in the bank and improve their economic situation through interest paid on the sums. Detractors scoffed at the idea. Conventional wisdom held that such people were not interested in a savings bank. A preposterous scheme, some businessmen told each other and anyone who would listen.

Luther Holton as president of the Montreal City and District Savings Bank, c. 1871. Courtesy of the Laurentian Bank of Canada.

Like a few of his friends, however, Holton was prepared to challenge the status quo. William Workman, the bank's first president and an Irish immigrant, helped him make his vision of a savings bank a commercial and social reality at mid-century. Workman in fact invited him to serve as a member of the bank's founding group early in 1846 when he was "a very young businessman," recalled Holton many years later.[3] Though a man without banking experience, Holton's background made him a reasonable choice. He was well known not only for his entrepreneurial zest, but also for his humanitarian and philanthropic efforts. For example, in 1841 he became personally involved in providing poor people in Griffintown in the St. Ann's Ward, many of whom were Irish, with food, clothing, fuel, and other things they needed.[4] Holton's business career suggested that he would help bring financial respectability to the bank. He evidently impressed Workman both with his ability to run the forwarding firm Hooker, Holton & Co. and with his understanding of mercantile finance. Around this time, Holton and Workman were also prominent members of the building committee for the newly organized Unitarian Church in Montreal, where they co-operated in working out a financially feasible plan for the construction of the church's building.[5] Soon, the two men found themselves drawn together in another project: in 1847, Holton became a director of the City Bank and, two years later, Workman joined him on the City Bank's board as president.

Henry H. Judah, another founding director of the Montreal City and District Savings Bank and a Montreal lawyer, once said that Holton "had been the originator and master spirit of the bank ... he had brought the bank through its infancy."[6] To which Holton responded: "with the help of Mr. Workman," whom he called "the father of this organisation."[7] Holton appreciated the business acumen and wisdom of Workman, the hardware merchant who was ten years his senior and had helped make the firm Frothingham & Workman one of the

William Workman. Courtesy of the Laurentian Bank of Canada.

most progressive concerns in the local hardware industry.

By dint of personality and energy, Luther Holton was probably the bank's most visible managing director, apart from the president. He was a tireless motivator, with the indomitable urge to spread the message of the savings bank to every corner of Montreal and its region. Workman's presidency of the Montreal City and District Savings Bank lasted for six years, from 1846 to 1852, and during this period Holton shared with him the task of trying to build a solid foundation for the bank. When Holton attended the first meeting of the board of directors in early April 1846, not much more than the general framework for the bank had been determined and several problems needed to be resolved before the institution could open for business.[8] The most immediate problems were drawing up the rules of conduct for the bank, finding premises, and recruiting staff.

Workman, Holton, and the other directors wasted little time in establishing the rules of business for their bank. Besides meeting the requirements of Canada's Savings Bank Act of 1841, they looked to Great Britain for an example, finding in British savings banks their model.[9] The bank, in their plan, also closely paralleled the savings banks that appeared in the United States.[10] Private citizens would hold all the fifteen managing directorships.

At the managing directors' meetings, Holton spoke enthusiastically about the advantages the Montreal City and District Bank offered. With mounds of facts at his fingertips, he emphasized that the deposits would be limited to £500. In effect, the bank would be an institution especially for the "industrious classes," holding their "small surplus earnings" on deposit and paying them interest at the rate of five percent per annum. The managing directors, who were properly and annually elected by sixty honorary directors, including Bishop Bourget, would donate their time and experience, receive no salary, and be forbidden to profit from their position. Their reports, providing detailed information about the operations of the bank, would appear in Montreal newspapers in the spring of every year. All profits, Holton stressed, would be distributed among depositors and charitable institutions. The bank's funds would be invested in debt issued by the Canadian government or other public authorities and in chartered bank stock. Lending on the security of real estate would be strictly prohibited.[11]

First premises of the Montreal City and District Savings Bank in 1846, shown here in a pen drawing. Courtesy of the Laurentian Bank of Canada.

Holton and his fellow directors at the Montreal City and District Savings Bank could look upon their accomplishments with satisfaction by the early 1850s. They had inspired habits of thrift among the working classes in the city and its suburbs. In the spring of 1847, after the bank's first ten months of operations, the number of persons who had deposits in it was 500. By the end of 1851, this figure had risen to 1,313. In the first ten months, the average account in the bank was £59; in the year 1851, it was £66.[12] Many Montreal workers had obviously caught the saving habit. Holton's original notion that there was a market in Montreal for savings bank services was coming true.

As early as 14 April 1846, Holton and the other directors had found temporary quarters for their bank at 46 Great St. James Street, in downtown Montreal. The rent they agreed to pay for these premises was £40 per year.[13] The directors, however, soon had to make new arrangements. Their preference was to remain in the main business section, and by 1849, the bank had re-housed itself in an office at 29 St. François Xavier Street. To handle the growth of its operations, in 1852, the bank moved into new and larger rooms at 4 Great St. James Street – a three-storey building that it rented from the Sulpician Seminary of Montreal, one of its depositors and borrowers, for £150 a year – in the heart of the financial district.[14]

One of Holton's goals was to provide a safe depository for the depositors' funds through the appointment of a reliable and competent manager. He felt a deep personal responsibility for the safety of the depositors' savings. The directors chose to hire John Collins, a Montreal dry goods merchant, at an annual salary of £150.[15] In addition to serving as the bank's manager, Collins immediately became its secretary, and he performed well in both roles until his retirement from the bank in 1855.

* * *

On 20 May 1846, six days before the Montreal City and District Bank opened for business, its relationship with the larger commercial banks and the other savings banks in the city was the principal topic of discussion at the directors' meeting. At the start of that year, there was, in addition to two other savings banks – the Montreal Savings Bank and the Provident Savings Bank of Montreal – a relatively small group of chartered banks active in the business community: the Bank of Montreal, the City Bank, the Banque du Peuple, the Bank of British North America, the Commercial Bank of the Midland District, and the Bank of Upper Canada. The principal business of the chartered banks, which did not have savings departments at this time, was to lend money to major enterprises. Besides discussing the matter of competition with the other savings banks, Holton and his colleagues talked about how best to establish a connection with a commercial bank so as to secure additional funds to meet the financial needs of their clients. They decided to keep money on deposit in the City Bank, thus ensuring their access to the funds of this larger bank when they needed them.[16]

In those early months, everything was new for Luther Holton: attending weekly directors' meetings, serving in the bank about two days each month, doing various jobs such as accepting deposits, and coming home exhausted but content. Although he was new to savings banking, he was confident, bubbling over with ideas and plans. Holton wanted to run the bank efficiently in order to provide the depositors with a good return on a safe investment. All day long, he did business with Montreal's working people, who were largely Irish immigrants and native-born French, with whom he often spoke French. He possessed the personal skills and charm to attract clients, no matter what their ethnic background. Like the other directors, Holton was not compensated for his services before 1862.

The Montreal City and District Savings Bank benefited from Holton's personal attention to its operations. His style was to cooperate with his colleagues, to listen, and to focus on basics; when it was appropriate, he would express his own views and move toward a consensus. The directors' strategy of encouraging workers to provide for themselves by leaving their small deposits in the bank proved a success. Their 1847 annual report noted optimistically that:

if any thing were wanting to convince the most sceptical of the great utility of such institution, it could be furnished from the daily experience of the board. It has been found that by placing the minimum amount of a deposit so low as one shilling the advantages of the bank are made available to the humblest class of society, and hence numerous instances could be adduced where small sums which under ordinary circumstances might have been spent foolishly, or to a bad purpose, have been placed in the bank and have formed a nucleus to a larger amount, and produced an incentive to habits of increased industry and economy.[17]

The wisdom of the directors' move to establish the minimum of a deposit at one shilling became ever more obvious as the number of small depositors grew. By the spring of 1848, ten percent of the depositors had an account of £1 or less; forty-four percent £20 or less; and sixty-seven percent £50 or less.[18] Holton and his fellow directors frequently declined the "large deposits from the mercantile and wealthier portions of the community."[19]

* * *

The late 1840s were difficult for the Montreal City and District Savings Bank, as they were for most businesses and citizens. Mass unemployment resulted from the severe economic depression in this period, which began at the start of 1848 and deepened over the next two years. Total deposits at the bank peaked at £62,675 in January 1848, and then fell sharply to £44,560 by December.[20] As unemployment worsened in the city, an increasing number of depositors sent shock waves through the bank by withdrawing their deposits, many of whom joined the mass departure of 14,000 Montrealers for the United States.[21] Holton and the other directors eased these shock waves by mounting a successful campaign to attract new depositors. The bank, however, was hurt even further as many citizens hoarded money to deal with the depressed conditions in the city. Strapped for cash, Holton and his colleagues succeeded in securing financial aid from the Commercial Bank of the Midland District. Holton and Workman's close ties to that bank were a crucial factor in the discussions with its board that led to assistance.[22] This infusion of cash helped the Montreal City and District Savings Bank to meet all its depositors' demands promptly and to maintain the public's confidence in the institution.

But Holton and his colleagues now faced another problem: the trauma of the depression hit the City Bank hard and put at risk the Montreal City and District Savings Bank's funds, which they had invested in the City Bank's stock.[23] Their bank, in fact, suffered a loss of £1,900 because of the depreciation of the City Bank stock. In mid-March 1849, the directors met to work out the details of a plan to save the Montreal City and District Savings Bank. Workman proposed that all the directors contribute to a fund to wipe out the large deficit.[24] Everyone at the meeting knew something had to be done quickly if the bank was to be prevented from running out of cash and being forced to close its doors. By the end of March, the directors had agreed to make individual loans to the institution. Workman himself set a good example by offering a £425 loan. Five directors each provided an advance of £225, while two, including Holton, each responded by lending £125 to the Montreal City and District Savings Bank.[25] One director came forward with a £100 loan, bringing the total to £1,900.

In rescuing the Montreal City and District Savings Bank, Holton and his colleagues were following the principles of self-help and voluntary cooperation touted by some contemporaries as remedies for the depression. Some even hoped that voluntary contributions would spur economic recovery. At the Montreal City and District Savings Bank, voluntary action had succeeded because everyone had pulled his fair share. Coming to the conclusion that he must chip in to save the weak bank was not easy for Luther Holton. But he was an intelligent man and understood the validity of the argument in favour of a co-operative rescue, especially the point that the reputation and image of all banks would suffer if any bank collapsed in the city. Calls from others to abandon weak banks in Montreal were heard. Holton, however, tried to avoid such problems by fostering a consensus that in the long run the interests of all people in the city would be served by collective actions that encouraged the return of economic growth and development.

But the ink was hardly dry on the March agreement before funds were again needed to save the Montreal City and District Savings Bank. Holton and his colleagues had made an arrangement by which the bank held the bulk of its cash not as vault money, but as a deposit with the Commercial Bank of the Midland District, where it earned interest at the rate of four percent per annum, which was passed on to the depositors. By July 1849, however, the bank had overdrawn its account at the Commercial Bank by £3,000 in order to satisfy the depositors' demands for funds.[26] Fearing a huge loss on the account, the Commercial Bank demanded payment.

The struggling Montreal City and District Savings Bank was on the brink of failure. When the directors asked Workman and Holton to devise and execute a plan to rescue the bank, they agreed to do so. After lengthy discussions, they approached Workman's firm, Frothingham & Workman, for a £4,500 loan to enable the bank to meet its obligations to the Commercial Bank and other creditors.[27] Frothingham & Workman responded positively, making the requested loan. Although Holton did not dip into his own pockets this time, he co-operated in the bailout of the Montreal City and District Savings Bank by giving a great deal of his time and energy to working out a solution.[28] In doing so, he helped reassure customers of the safety of their deposits.

* * *

Luther Holton continued to play an essential role in the strategic decisions made at the Montreal City and District Savings Bank. As the economy improved in 1850, he strongly supported the directors' decision to encourage small customers, including not only labourers but also businessmen, to put their savings in the institution. He enjoyed the confidence and friendship of scores of customers around the city and its region. Deposits grew significantly, and at the end of December 1850, the funds the bank kept as deposits at the Commercial Bank stood at £7,000.[29] With the continuing growth of deposits, Holton and his fellow directors searched for another outlet. In March 1851, they placed £5,000 of the funds deposited with them in the City Bank, which paid interest at the rate of five percent.[30] Typical depositors included Antoine Masta, a voyageur whose deposit in the bank amounted to £46, and William Robert Orr, a hotelkeeper, who had £150 in his deposit account.[31]

Holton was eager to seize the investment opportunities available to the Montreal City and District Savings Bank. Despite the limited number of markets open to the bank, he and his colleagues were aggressive and far-sighted in their portfolio management. They invested unused funds in the stock of the Banque du Peuple, the City Bank, the Commercial Bank, the Bank of Montreal, and the Bank of Upper Canada.[32] Their idea was to conduct investment on a safe basis, as well as to move into both French-Canadian and English-Canadian markets. The largest investment during the presidencies of William Workman, Alfred LaRoque (1852-55), and Joseph Bourret (1855-59) was in the Banque du Peuple, a chartered bank dominated by French-Canadian directors. With his wide-ranging contacts in the French-Canadian community, Luther Holton knew that the Banque du Peuple was a stable institution.[33] He also understood that it took co-operation between English-speaking and French-speaking people to make the Montreal City and District Savings Bank function effectively. He not surprisingly worked closely with LaRocque, a well-known philanthropist, and Bourret, a respected lawyer. Holton also became a trusted adviser of Edmond J. Barbeau, who succeeded John Collins as manager around 1855. As Barbeau said years later, Holton proved to be his "wise counselor."[34]

Holton and his colleagues proceeded to capitalize on the goodwill the bank enjoyed across Montreal and its suburbs, concentrating on appealing to labourers for deposits when they had accumulated the minimum sum of one shilling. Like the other directors, Holton tried to communicate the bank's goal of helping workers to help themselves. Many lodged their small sums in the bank, taking in return a deposit receipt, and coming back from time to time for a new receipt with the interest added on. In this way, numerous citizens with a small income discovered, through the Montreal City and District Savings Bank, the reward of compound interest over the years. With the expansion of business, the bank needed larger quarters. As a member of the Canadian assembly in 1856, Holton played an important role in preparing and pushing through parliament a bill that authorized the bank to acquire and hold land for the purpose of conducting its operations.[35] In early 1859, around the time when Bourret died and local businessman and long-time director Edwin Atwater became the president of the bank, the

Edmond J. Barbeau. Courtesy of the Laurentian Bank of Canada.

institution started to erect a building at 6 Great St. James Street on its own land.[36] It was a structure of three stories, with housing accommodation for the cashier above the bank office on the main floor, costing $20,000.[37] The move to the handsome new premises in 1860 provided Atwater, Holton, and their colleagues with a sense of accomplishment and strengthened the Montreal City and District Savings Bank's identity in the community.

In early 1862, Alfred LaRocque, who had become president the previous year, Holton, and the other directors thought that the time had arrived to incorporate their bank and, in June, they transformed their institution into a Canada-chartered corporation. It still had no public stockholders, and it still had to report annually on its operations to the public through Montreal newspapers as well as to the Canadian parliament.[38] It still could not make real estate loans, and it still imposed a strict limit on the size of deposits – $2,000, which left the traditional limit unchanged. Certainly one reason for incorporation was to extend the lending powers of the bank. From the beginning, commercial enterprises had been the backbone of the loan business at the bank, but it now began to play a larger role in financing these enterprises and also diversified into industrial and marine transportation lending.[39] In January 1865, for instance, the bank renewed shipping magnate Hugh Allan's note of $20,000 for three months.[40] Holton and his colleagues personally approved this and other loans. The interest on the large loans provided the bank with significantly more capital to do business. The bank thus offered essential borrowing facilities to a broader segment of society and did more to aid economic development by increasing credit.

Holton and the rest of the directors knew, however, that deposits continued to make up a high percentage of the bank's total capital. The bank still held deposits from many customers, especially small ones but also those with larger accounts, and used those deposits to help finance trade and industry. Few Montrealers expected that the Montreal City and District Savings Bank would soon be in trouble. But on 7 March 1866, the Canadian government called out the militia in response to the threat of an invasion by the Fenians, Irish-Americans who were organizing on American soil to attack Canada. Fearing that their money was in danger, many depositors panicked and demanded their money. Under the new president, Henry Mulholland, a major local hardware merchant who had succeeded LaRocque in the previous year, the directors immediately appointed Mulholland, Luther Holton, and Atwater as a committee to find ways to meet the depositors' demands. With a substantial portion of the bank's funds not tied up in business, the committee quickly set aside enough cash to meet the withdrawals of the depositors.[41] By the end of the summer, the bank began to recover from the March panic.

The important role Luther Holton played in the bank was even more obvious when Alexandre M. Delisle, a member of the Montreal harbour commission, was president from 1867 to 1869. In October 1867, the bank was placed in some danger by the failure of the Commercial Bank. With a deposit of $20,000 in the Commercial Bank, the Montreal City and District Savings Bank feared the loss of this money. Holton, a major stockholder in the Commercial Bank, was asked by his fellow directors in the Montreal City and District Savings Bank to take the lead in trying to protect it against loss.[42] With his numerous personal connections in the banking world, Holton was ready to assume this responsibility. This vigorous man, having shown his ability in his long tenure as director, proceeded with remarkable skill. In early March 1868, he was instrumental in persuading the Merchants Bank in Montreal to acquire the Commercial Bank and become the Merchants Bank of Canada in the process. Holton also figured prominently in the complex negotiations that led to the transfer of the Montreal City and District Savings Bank's entire deposit at the Commercial Bank to the newly organized Merchants Bank of Canada.[43]

Like the other chartered banks, the Merchants Bank of Canada paid five percent interest on bank's deposit. Thus, the bank, rather than sustaining a loss on its deposit at the Commercial Bank, was able to lodge its funds profitably in the Merchants Bank of Canada.

Holton's significant action reinforced public confidence in the Montreal City and District Savings Bank and this, in turn, contributed to its growth in deposits. Holton now helped the bank to resume the aggressiveness of its youth. There were new bursts of activity in gathering deposits. In December 1867, the bank's deposits totalled $1,532,495.[44] This figure rose to $1,861,574 a year later.[45] During this same period, the number of depositors increased from 5,039 to 5,714.

Luther Holton, however, recognized that the growing bank was not free from problems of space. During his tenure as vice-president from 1869 to 1871, under the presidency of Henry Starnes, a Montreal businessman, Holton felt that the bank's premises needed improvement. A scheme was decided upon and carried out by Holton and his colleagues between April 1870 and the spring of 1871. The fine lines of the exterior of the new building at 176 St. James Street demonstrated a confident institution.[46] Inside was a spacious telling room, setting a high standard in Montreal for the reception of the public.

* * *

The affairs of the Montreal City and District Savings Bank rested on the shoulders of Luther Holton from 4 April 1871 to October 1872. At the start of this period, shortly before the new bank building opened, the board elected Holton as the bank's ninth president and Henry Judah as vice-president.[47] Holton was the kind of man who made friends, both among his managing director colleagues and among the bank staff. Besides enjoying a warm relationship with Judah, with whom he had served on the board for twenty-five years, he got on well with the manager, Edmond Barbeau. In carrying out his presidential responsibilities, Holton regularly examined the books, kept his colleagues on the board informed of new developments, and offered helpful advice to the manager. Holton often stopped by to see Barbeau, and the two men had "long conversations," as Barbeau recalled. During these conversations, Holton was tactful, and it was appropriate that Barbeau referred to him as "a sincere friend."[48]

A man of broad culture, Holton was a leading Canadian banker in the early 1870s and one of the most active thinkers on banking theory and practice. As president of the Montreal City and District Savings Bank, he felt the weight of his position. He formulated a coherent philosophy of banking, so that his position would be firmly grounded. Once he had arrived

Montreal City and District Savings Bank in 1871, shown here in a late twentieth-century photograph. Courtesy of the Laurentian Bank of Canada.

at sound principles, he felt he had no alternative but to try to persuade his fellow directors to accept them and adopt a new approach. Holton recognized that the existing trustee savings bank was cash-poor – it was inadequate to meet the pressing needs to finance businesses in Montreal.[49] Although the managing directors or trustees had provided good administration up to this point, the bank lacked a business structure that would permit it to survive and grow into an effective financial intermediary between savers and borrowers. In place of this uncertain organization, Holton proposed an institution that would be organized along joint stock enterprise lines and operate under a federal charter. He wanted to develop a code of conduct for such a bank, so that there would be stability and orderly growth.

Public opinion in the Dominion of Canada had already become thoroughly convinced of the need for some change in the nature of savings banks, but the precise details still had to be worked out. The John A. Macdonald government introduced its legislation in this regard in March 1871, and it became law as "An Act respecting certain Savings Banks in the Provinces of Ontario and Quebec" on 14 April.[50] The act required the existing trustee savings banks to make a choice: they could transfer their assets to the federal government's new savings bank or to a chartered bank;[51] or they could seek a federal charter and operate as a joint stock corporation in which stockholders would have the advantage of limited liability. In looking at a savings bank that wanted a federal charter, the act declared that it had to have a minimum capital of $200,000 with shares of at least $400, of which each director had to hold at least twenty-five.

In keeping with his banking philosophy, Holton and his colleagues chose, not to transfer their assets to the federal government's savings bank, but to seek a federal charter. While Judah looked after the legal aspects of the proposed charter, Holton focussed on the financial side of it. Holton called a special board meeting for 15 April, at which the directors examined a draft of a petition containing the terms they wanted the Macdonald government to put into the charter for their proposed bank in Montreal.[52] Assured of the support of all the directors including Joseph A. Berthelot and William Workman in the boardroom two days later, Holton then forwarded the petition to Ottawa.[53] Satisfied that the petition met the requirements of the law, on 21 April, the government granted the old ten directors a charter, incorporating them as the new Montreal City and District Savings Bank and naming them as its provisional directors.

Observers took note of Luther Holton's success. They commented on his creativity and flexibility. Everyone realized that the charter brought the new Montreal City and District Savings Bank into legally recognized existence.[54] Capital stock in the new bank totalled $2 million, divided into 5,000 shares of $400 each, of which $20 per share had to be called up immediately. At the first meeting of the provisional directors on 24 April, the new joint stock bank took off. The directors approved Holton's motion to appoint William Workman as chairman of the meeting.[55] Then the ten provisional directors subscribed to all of the bank's capital stock of $2 million and paid in a capital of $100,000 for the new concern as required by the charter.[56]

An important reason for incorporation obviously was the chronic need for capital to carry on the bank's operations. As the bank grew, it needed more money. With its promise of limited liability to investors, the corporate form of organization offered a potential way to secure the necessary additional financial resources. Holton, by nature averse to boasting, was reluctant to make claims for the new bank. But he knew instinctively that it would be a winner. Like the other directors, he invested at least $10,000 in the institution. Over the next few years and, indeed, far beyond, it grew and prospered.

At their first meeting on 27 April, notice of which had appeared in the leading English-language and French-language newspapers in the city (*Montreal Herald*, *Montreal Gazette*, and *La Minerve*), the ten stockholders in the Montreal City and District Savings Bank elected themselves as the directors of the bank.[57] The new directors then chose Holton as president and Judah as vice-president. They also appointed Edmond Barbeau and his old staff of nine men as the staff of the new corporation.

* * *

Like its predecessor, the new Montreal City and District Savings Bank conducted business on a personal, face-to-face basis. Holton and his fellow directors, who also were its only stockholders at first, knew a great deal about each other's personalities and abilities. They also knew the bank's staff well. This close knowledge of his colleagues and the staff, in addition to his clear understanding of the overall banking situation in Montreal and in Canada, helped Holton in reorganizing and transforming the Montreal City and District Savings Bank into an important business enterprise.

Holton's grand strategy to reposition the bank's image for business was coming together even as it was launched. During his administration, the ideology as well as the practice of the corporation began to differ from those of its predecessor. Benevolence and philanthropy remained, but they yielded to business to a considerable extent. Changes also occurred in the relationship between the bank and its depositors. Although the traditional emphasis on service to small savers certainly did not disappear, there was a new focus on the importance of the return the bank provided on the stockholders' investments.[58] The directors' financial motives obviously became more and more significant in the bank's operations.

In reorganizing the Montreal City and District Savings Bank in the interest of business, Holton was responding to difficulties in the Montreal economy. The problem was that Montreal did not have enough chartered banks. As a result, there was insufficient capital in relation to the city's commercial and industrial needs. The rebirth of the old Montreal City and District Savings Bank as a chartered bank was thus a step in the direction of creating more capital. Holton certainly found that his scheme for the bank, with limited liability and substantial capital, was acceptable in the city and its suburbs.

Under Luther Holton's direction, the Montreal City and District Savings Bank proved that it could help meet the growing demand for banking services, but it still faced a problem. While it had become a chartered bank highly commercial by nature, it remained a savings bank in name and differed from regular chartered commercial banks in that the law forbade it from issuing bank notes of its own and required it to make donations to charitable institutions. Holton and his fellow directors were convinced of the long-term worthiness of continuing to donate sums to charitable organizations, but their inability to issue bank notes gave them less clout as a commercial bank – they could not generate profits on the circulation of notes. But they learned how to compete in the marketplace by using Dominion notes as money.

During Holton's presidency, the history of the Montreal City and District Savings Bank was a playing out of the need to balance public accessibility with the need for stability and size. His primary goal was to increase the bank's stability. In his view, the best guarantees of stability were prudent management and growth. Since the maximum limit on the amount anyone could deposit was still $2,000, he also was expected to continue to attract small depositors. It was still Holton's policy to aid the labourers who wished to save by offering them a stable rate of interest – about five percent – on their deposits. As the Montreal working class grew, the potential for small deposits increased. Working people continued to make up a significant portion of the bank's depositors. For the year ending 31 December 1871, thirty-two percent of the depositors had an account of $50 or less.[59] Personally involved in various Montreal philanthropies, Luther Holton as president of the bank was happy to maintain its practice of making annual donations to charitable societies, such as the Hospice de la Providence, the St. Patrick's Orphan Asylum, the Hospice St. Joseph, and the Montreal Lying-In Hospital.[60]

Holton wanted the bank to respond to the needs of the growing Montreal economy and to compete with at least one substantial Montreal bank, the City Bank. Under his direction, the Montreal City and District Savings Bank gained more commercial business and diversified further into industrial lending. Loans to the directors including Holton, all of whom repaid them promptly, helped to sustain loan quality and maintain high earnings. The bank grew to the size that inspired confidence and allowed stability. Between 1870 and 1872, total assets increased from $3,088,332 to $4,832,881. Deposits rose by $299,746 in the two years after 1870 to reach $3,180,515 in December 1872.[61] In the same period, the volume of loans made by the Montreal City and District Savings Bank grew from $1,457,247 to $2,060,255.[62] The largest part of this increase consisted of lending in the areas of commerce and manufacturing. Carrying an interest rate of five to eight percent per annum, the loans varied in size from $300 to $150,000. Collateral included stock in regular chartered banks and in corporate enterprises such as the Montreal Telegraph Company and the Montreal Permanent Building Society, as well as City of Montreal bonds and Montreal Harbour Commission bonds.

Catching up with the leading banks in the city such as the Bank of Montreal was not Luther Holton's aim, but he knew that he was gaining in the race for deposits and quality loans. When there was an unexpected run on the Montreal City and District Savings Bank in early October 1872, he demonstrated that he could cope with the situation. The bank's major customers and substantial earnings had allowed Holton to build up sufficient cash reserves to overcome the challenge. Before long, confidence in the bank's stability was restored.[63]

Having prepared the successful bank to function effectively without him and having groomed Henry Judah to succeed him, on 21 October Luther Holton resigned as president, because he wanted to reduce his work load and devote more time to his duties in the House of Commons as well as to his other business ventures in Montreal. In particular, he was eager to pursue his long-standing interest in real estate development.[64]

Chapter 10

Real Estate Entrepreneur

The real estate business in Montreal was particularly well suited to Luther Holton's personality, for the purchase and sale of property provided him with important challenges and possibilities. He approached this job with his customary enthusiasm. Using money generated by his forwarding trade, in 1847, he began by purchasing a little house at 17 King Street, in the St. Ann's Ward, and renting it to Patrick O'Brien, a labourer. This was Holton's first real estate deal, and it introduced him to the intricacies of property finance. By 1848, O'Brien had moved out, and Holton had rented the house to another labourer, his cousin James Wait.[1] The income from this rental property provided Holton with funds he could use to help keep himself and his family in plain rented quarters in the St. Antoine Ward: in one of John Young's houses at 12 Lagauchetière Street until 1848, and after that year in a house at 21 St. Monique Street owned by Hannah Lyman Mills, the widow of John E. Mills.[2] In January 1849, Holton added to the real estate he held by purchasing a lot on the corner of Côte des Neiges and Shakespeare roads from Donald Lorn MacDougall, a Montreal stock broker.[3] Over the next two years, Holton acquired two lots on Wellington Street, in the St. Ann's Ward.[4] Later, it would astound Luther's son, Edward, to see the records of his father's estate, consisting of several valuable city holdings. By 1857, Holton had sold his Wellington Street and King Street properties, likely for a fairly good price.

* * *

In a sense, Holton's interest in real estate reflected his attempt to unify his quest for a suburban home and his desire to make money on land. To achieve these goals, he scoured the southern slope of Mount Royal on the outskirts of Montreal in search of farmland that he hoped might be for sale. His efforts eventually bore fruit. In March 1853, his rising fortunes allowed him to buy a beautiful, well-maintained, five-acre farm for £8,000 on the corner of Sherbrooke Street and Ontario Avenue from Joseph

Savage, a local jeweller.[5] The farm was bounded along the front by Sherbrooke Street, along the rear by a large estate, on one side by the Seminary of Montreal, big estates and the Côte des Neiges Road, and on the other side by large estates. Well-heeled entrepreneurs, who had succeeded in their search for upward economic and social mobility, lived in this area. They were important figures in their community. The improvements on the farm included a house, a barn, and other buildings, as well as a garden and an orchard.

Holton naturally considered this farm on the southern slope of Mount Royal an excellent bargain. Savage had not been in a position to hold out for a higher price, because he needed the money fast to save his troubled jewellery business.[6] Holton put down £2,000 in cash and gave Savage a note for the balance of £6,000, on which he paid interest at the rate of six percent per annum. He was wildly optimistic about the farm. "I have long had an eye on the Savage farm as a very eligible speculation," Holton wrote Alexander Galt in early April.[7] One plan he certainly had was to sit tight and wait until the value of the farm increased, subdivide part of it into lots, and then speculate his way into modest wealth. Holton, however, did not want to sell all the land, for he also planned to build a fine home on part of it for himself and his family. But this required considerably more money than he could raise at the moment, and so the Holtons settled for continuing to live in rented quarters at 21 St. Monique Street as long as necessary.

At the moment, Holton's principal focus was to make the old Savage farm productive. He needed someone reliable to look after the place, and it made sense for him to turn to Savage, who wanted the farm products for another season. After discussing the matter with Savage, Holton leased the farm to him for £100 until November 1853. When the lease expired, Holton found a good tenant for the farm in Michael Corrigan, who agreed to maintain it for two years for £150 per annum.[8] Then, in January 1856, Holton leased the Savage farm to another responsible tenant, Lawrence Quinn, for a two-year period at the same rate.[9]

Attending to his duties on the farm was a full-time job for Quinn, as it had been for Corrigan, involving the proper care of the woodlot, the fruit trees, the ornamental trees, the vines, the shrubs, the garden, and the grounds. It also meant cultivating the fields and fertilizing them with manure, and keeping the buildings, fences, roads, bridges, ditches, and drains in good shape. In placing these responsibilities upon the shoulders of Quinn and those of Corrigan before him through a lease, Holton's concern was not only with maintaining and increasing the farm's market value but also with preserving its orderliness and picturesque beauty in which he took great pride and pleasure. Fortunately for Holton, under both Corrigan and Quinn, the farm flourished.

* * *

The Holton Sherbrooke Street home in Montreal, shown here in an 1899 painting by W. Baker. Courtesy of Thomas L. Brock.

No one understood better than Holton that developments in Montreal in the mid-1850s also boosted the value of the farm. Following the destruction caused by fires in Montreal in 1850, 1851, and 1852, which drew attention to the inadequate water works and accelerated suburban growth, civic leaders decided that a new water storage system was the answer to the city's water problem. Begun in June 1853 and completed in October 1856, the new water works included an aqueduct that brought water to two reservoirs on the southern slope of Mount Royal from the St. Lawrence River above the Lachine Rapids.[10] This endeavour provided a stable water supply, allowed pollution control, and assured housing growth near and on the side of the mountain above Sherbrooke Street. Holton personally gained much from the establishment of the system of sanitary water and sewerage, because it permitted him to use this service at his new house and helped raise the value of his property.

Few imagined the transformation Luther Holton's new home on the corner of Sherbrooke Street and Ontario Avenue would bring to the old Savage farm. But in 1856, when he and his family moved into it, it already provided the farm with a fashionable look.[11] Pictures of the house (at first numbered 315 and later 1043 Sherbrooke Street) show a spacious, two-storey, stone building with three chimneys, a balcony above the front

Eliza Forbes Holton (centre right), her eldest daughter Mary Eliza (far left), her youngest daughter Amelia Jane (far right), her son Edward (standing), her sister Sophronia Forbes (centre left), her niece Mary Julia Wood (seated on the floor), shown here c. 1860-1862. Courtesy of Thomas L. Brock.

portico in the fashion of the time, and the large windows opening onto a lush front lawn. Visitors were stunned by the graceful, dignified interior complete with several fireplaces. On the grounds behind the house, there were several buildings, including an icehouse, a stable for Holton's two horses, a driving shed to cover and protect his two carriages and his sleigh, and a stable for his cow. As was the case with other well-to-do suburban businessmen, a carriage or a sleigh, depending on the season, carried Holton from and to his splendid home. This middle-class home on the southern slope of Mount Royal, with a view across the Montreal harbour filled with the ships of all nations as well as across the St. Lawrence River, set the tone for the future Savage farm subdivision.

From the beginning, the new house was filled with warmth and humour. Affable and approachable, the gregarious Luther Holton was comfortable not only with his immediate family but also with relatives and servants. In 1861, when both Luther and his wife Eliza were forty-four, they lived their lives vigorously. In one way or another, the other people in their home thrived.[12] There were their three children – twenty-year-old Mary, eighteen-year-old Edward, and twelve-year-old Amelia – as well as Eliza's younger sister Sophronia and Luther and Eliza's niece Eliza Jane Holton of Belleville. In addition, there were three servants, all of whom had been born in Ireland: John Laughlin, a Roman Catholic, was thirty-eight and looked after the farm; Mary Gaskell, a Presbyterian, was twenty-five; and Maria Meany, a Roman Catholic, was twenty-one. The presence of these efficient servants added a satisfying dimension to the life of Luther and Eliza, enabling them to do more to establish order and comfort than would otherwise have been possible.

Sophronia Forbes, c. 1870. Courtesy of Thomas L. Brock.

Luther and Eliza's sense of responsibility, however, carried them beyond what servant help could do for them to their own deeds. They did all they could to help their children with their school plans; in the context of the day, they tried to instil in them progressive values. Like their parents, all the children found books exciting. They were spirited, intelligent, and attractive besides. The oldest, Mary, was doing well at Agassiz School in Cambridge, Massachusetts. She witnessed stirring and historic events on the eve of the Civil War. Eliza and Luther were thrilled by her newsy letters. The younger two, Edward in Arts at McGill University and Amelia at a local elementary school, were also succeeding in their studies. The children's happy state reflected years of loving care by their parents. Luther and Eliza hoped Edward might go on to study law, and they were clearly pleased in the spring of 1862 when he decided to enter McGill's law school.[13] They were obviously devoted to the promotion of Edward's career, and the Montreal law firm Torrance & Morris was prepared to take him on as an apprentice. Later that same year, in November, Luther paid the firm $400 to allow Edward to start his apprenticeship in its office.[14] In June 1867, after joining several other candidates in sitting the bar examinations, Edward was admitted to the bar of Lower Canada.[15] He then opened a general practice in the Mechanics Bank Chambers at 86 Great St. James Street with a growing number of clients, including his father's cousin Ebenezer Gilbert.[16]

Edward Holton in 1871. Courtesy of the McCord Museum of Canadian History, Montreal.

Despite his new independence as a lawyer, Edward continued to turn to his parents for a sense of security and companionship. Luther and Eliza's ways were familiar, warm; and they continued to welcome their son as a resident of the Sherbrooke Street home. They were proud of his success and determined to help him. Edward, of course, had grown up amid the exciting Liberal politics of his family and their circle of friends; it would have been odd had they not influenced him in any way. He was, in fact, to become an important Liberal in Montreal.

Much as Luther Holton himself enjoyed his hilltop home and the fresh air in its picturesque surroundings, he never lost contact with the common people in the city below Mount Royal, many of whom were poor. He continued, for instance, to treasure those hours he spent with such people in the office of the Montreal City and District Savings Bank, in downtown Montreal, where he assisted customers with modest incomes in their attempt to build up their savings.[17] The progress of the ordinary people, Holton believed, was very important in itself. In a sense, his response to their needs reflected, through the eyes of one man, part of the story of Montreal's social consciousness in the mid-nineteenth century. He also was aware that such progress would help create the necessary favourable social environment for his real estate operations.

Meanwhile, Holton had turned his attention to the problem of raising money from various sources to pay for his home and the five acres of land that belonged to it. The total cost of the house together with furnishings is unknown, but at the end of March 1853, after he had made the down payment on the Savage farm, Holton still owed Joseph Savage £6,000. To meet his obligations,

Holton obtained funds from the proceeds of the sale of his steamboat interests in early 1854, as well as from the income from the Grand Trunk Railway contract in the mid-1850s. Personal connections were also important in securing the needed financing for his home. As was typical of businessmen in nineteenth-century Canada, Holton called upon his friends, especially David L. Macpherson, for financial help. In return for a substantial sum of money from Macpherson, Holton gave him an interest in the Savage farm in March 1853. Five and a half years later, in October 1859, Holton was finally able to buy out Macpherson's interest.[18]

* * *

Even so, Holton's cash crunches, both immediate and long-term, were far from resolved. He did not have enough money to meet the payments on the Savage farm. Already a year earlier, his remarkable facility with numbers and his ability to grasp a situation quickly had told him he must find a new source of funds. There were several complicating external factors, including the economic depression in 1858, which made it extremely difficult to raise capital. So Holton took the initiative in creating a new financial institution. He and other local real estate entrepreneurs such as M. H. Gault, John Young, and George Frothingham founded the Montreal Permanent Building Society, a venture incorporated under Canada's general incorporation laws in 1858. As was the case with other building societies in Canada, the new corporation engaged in financing real estate transactions through mortgage debt.[19] The rise of Canadian building societies as mortgage lenders began in Montreal in 1845, when the Montreal Building Society was formed, but Holton's perception was that a new building society was needed in the city.[20] When the directors of the Montreal Permanent Building Society met for the first time in 1858, Holton was elected president of the board.[21] Like the other directors, he invested at least £250 in the society, as was required by law.[22]

Holton and his colleagues formed the Montreal Permanent Building Society at an inauspicious time. They felt hobbled by the depression in 1858, which hurt many new businesses in the city. But the society survived the depression and grew during the late 1850s, the 1860s, and the early 1870s to become a financial corporation of some repute.[23] As the society's first president from 1858 to 1859, Holton played a key role in the early days of the concern's evolution. By appointing Torrance & Morris, who had experience in the property business, as the new corporation's solicitors, he was able to obtain expert legal advice on real estate lending.[24] He chose a reliable notary, T. Doucet, to prepare the notarial documents for the real estate transactions. Holton picked the architectural and civil engineering firm Hopkins, Lawford & Nelson to survey the properties in which the society was interested. Finally, he pulled in L. B. Lawford as secretary and treasurer. In the society's office at 22 St. François Xavier Street, Holton, along with other directors, guided the corporation in arranging mortgage financing for real estate deals.[25] Providing the glue that held the various parts of the society together, they performed their tasks in finance within the general context of the overall business.

They needed to sort out winners from losers in the hodgepodge of firms that applied for loans. Presumably, although no lending records have survived to show it, Holton and his colleagues themselves borrowed from the Montreal Permanent Building Society on the security of their real estate.[26] At a time when entrepreneurs everywhere in the city were having trouble meeting their obligations, Holton and his fellow directors repaid their loans promptly, thus contributing to their society's growth. In this way, Holton was able to raise some capital to help pay off the Savage farm, as well as to fund his other real estate operations.

* * *

To survive in the competitive environment in Montreal, however, Holton needed more financial resources. His flexible approach to raising funds once again proved its value. In part, he met his needs by the resale of property. For instance, in March 1856, he purchased two lots, one of which had a house on it, on Sherbrooke Street from David L. Macpherson for £6,750.[27] Holton made a down payment of £700 and gave an eight-year mortgage on his property at 315 Sherbrooke Street for the balance of £6,050, on which he paid interest at the rate of six percent per annum. Almost two years later, in May 1858, Holton sold the Macpherson house and one lot to Charles A. Low, a Montreal architect, for £5,000 cash.[28]

The resale of more property was nourished by improving economic conditions. Holton had been holding his vacant lot on the corner of Côte des Neiges and Shakespeare roads for a decade in hopes that its value would increase; in June 1859, he sold it profitably for £250 to Sarah Coates Leeming, wife of Montreal merchant John Leeming.[29] Sarah Leeming paid £150 down, and gave Holton a one-year mortgage on the lot for the balance of £100, paying six percent interest on it. The final mortgage payment was due in June 1860, but in September 1859, Sarah Leeming elected to pay Holton in full.[30]

The time had come for Holton to respond forcefully to opportunities in the real estate market. In March 1862, he bought eight vacant lots fronting on Drummond Street between Drummond and Stanley streets from John Glass, a local stock broker, for $5,000. Three months later, the Victoria

Skating Club of which Holton was a founder offered him the same amount for these lots. He accepted the offer, knowing that he could make some interest money on mortgage arrangements.[31] The club made a down payment of $2,000 and gave a three-year mortgage on the lots for the balance of $3,000 on which it paid seven percent interest; but as early as the end of October 1862, it paid Holton all that was owing on the property, including the interest.[32]

But sometimes Holton suffered losses in his real estate business because he miscalculated the direction in which prices would go. For example, in July 1862, he paid Alexander Galt $16,000 for a vacant mountain lot on Redpath Street in Montreal.[33] This venture worked out rather poorly. In reality, no money changed hands because Holton took this lot as part of an exchange in which Galt received Holton's interest in some Toronto properties that supposedly had roughly the same value. At this point, Holton's existing investment in land was too great a burden for him to sink cash into another piece of real estate. As he had written Galt in January, "of course neither of us desires to increase his landed investments or to come under any considerable money engagements on account of land. Certainly *I* do not."[34] Instead, Holton was trying to save money for the six-month vacation he hoped to take together with Eliza and their children in Great Britain and continental Europe in the near future.[35] Apparently, the Holtons never went abroad. But they were not all serious business. They enjoyed their family and friends in Montreal, took trips into the surrounding countryside, travelled to the Eastern Townships in Lower Canada, holidayed at Saratoga Springs, New York, one of the principal resort communities of North America, and visited Luther's brother Ezra and his family in Belleville, among other things.

If Holton's grand plans for a trip abroad came to naught, his experience with the Redpath Street lot he obtained from Galt was also extremely disappointing. In May 1868, Holton sold this lot to sugar manufacturer John Redpath, not for $16,000 or more, but only for $8,697.[36] Even though Holton had the advantage of receiving the full amount in cash from Redpath right away, the lot in effect proved a money drain.

Luther Holton, however, did not disappear from the pages of history. A willingness to try new things, to admit mistakes, and to press on characterized his work in the real estate market. Near the beginning of his tenure as finance minister of Canada, in July 1863, there emerged a picture of his wealth. According to the report of the R. G. Dun & Co. credit correspondent resident in Montreal at this time, Holton "is now estimated worth in real estate & bank stock over 150M ($150,000) – many think him worth more." The correspondent added that Holton "is not likely to make engagements he cannot meet, holds a high position in this country, is honorable in his dealings &

Eliza Forbes Holton in 1870.
Courtesy of the McCord Museum of Canadian History, Montreal.

generally esteemed."[37] Staying alert to new opportunities in the real estate market, Holton remained strong financially over the next decade despite occasional losses in his deals. While others reeled in disappointment when the going got tough, Holton retained his aplomb.

* * *

Montreal's population growth and economic development created the need for real estate entrepreneurs like Luther Holton. Comfortable by Canadian standards, he was determined to endure despite setbacks. He certainly put his financial resources behind the Canadian dream: the desire to acquire land and own a home. During the period from the 1850s to the 1870s, the housing shortage in Montreal, triggered not only by the increase in people but also by the spread of commercial and industrial activity into the city's old residential communities, was severe enough to drive many growing

Luther Holton and his youngest daughter Amelia Jane in 1872.
Courtesy of the McCord Museum of Canadian History, Montreal.

working families into inadequate shelter. Hundreds of families lived in crowded conditions with relatives who owned small houses, while others fought to retain places in decrepit rented quarters.[38] Hard times robbed labourers of employment and decent wages, dulling the spirit of enterprise and hampering the elevation of the working classes. But many had incomes sufficiently large to permit them to move, often to the new suburbs such as St. Antoine. They wanted to invest their money in land and higher-status housing, and Holton was ready to assist them. He revelled in the growing arena now open to him.

Luther Holton the real estate entrepreneur was the man of action, sharp, decisive, and swift, who could produce land on demand. In June 1866, for example, he sold John Rankin, a Montreal merchant, a vacant lot for $8,000 above Sherbrooke Street in the St. Antoine suburb.[39] Rankin put down $2,000 in cash and gave a two-year, $6,000 mortgage on this lot, on which

Mary Holton Britton, c. 1880.
Courtesy of Thomas L. Brock.

Byron M. Britton, c. 1863.
Courtesy of Thomas L. Brock.

he paid interest at the rate of seven percent per annum. By 1867, Rankin had erected a house on the lot, and by January 1869, he had completely repaid the loan from Holton. Holton, who had helped Rankin finance his middle-class home, thus continued to live up to his reputation.

Holton himself was obviously a relatively new middle-class suburbanite, and as such he viewed his new, clean community as the best place to raise his children. They did not chafe at the bonds of family and home. Instead, they were comfortable, greatly enjoyed life, and generally conformed to the expectations of their friends and neighbours in the Sherbrooke Street community. Holton's home was filled not only with security, stability, and order, but also with freedom, laughter, and animated conversation. As one who frequently corresponded with out-of-town politicians and businessmen, Holton liked to include news about family members in his letters. His children, including Mary who now lived in Kingston with her own family, were often in his thoughts. He wanted to assure Mary's well-being so much that in July 1867 he gave her a valuable Sherbrooke Street villa lot, close to the family home.[40]

Holton moved easily between his business life and his family and social life with no apparent difficulties in adjusting to their different needs. Characteristically, he was cheerful on 27 February 1867 when, together with his wife Eliza, Edward, and Amelia, he attended the ball in the St. Lawrence Hotel given by the American consul general W. W. Averell in celebration of George Washington's birthday.[41] Close on the heels of this event, Holton relished the chance to discuss with his friends new business opportunities in the Montreal real estate market.

* * *

Luther Holton's spirits lifted as he mulled over the market possibilities of his land. By this time, he had fully paid for his Sherbrooke Street home, as well as for what had previously been the Savage farm. He also was keenly aware that the value of this land in the St. Antoine suburb had increased significantly. At last, Holton was ready to diversify by beginning the process of subdividing that portion of the five-acre farm that he did not need for his own family. But any attempt to subdivide his property, build homes on the lots, and develop a middle-class suburb would have required an enormous amount of capital, much more than he could have raised. Instead of trying to follow such a course of action, he decided to subdivide gradually and finance development internally through retained earnings. He wanted to start by selling a few vacant lots to friends and relatives, not by erecting and selling finished homes. The moment had arrived, and in August 1867, Holton sold a villa lot, not an ordinary house lot, on Côte des Neiges Road for $6,090 to his Montreal Liberal friend, Médéric Lanctot, lawyer, publisher of *L'Union Nationale and Irish Express*, and leader of working men.[42] Holton wanted to make more sales, however.

They came, in spades, a year later. Holton plunged ahead, selling a large villa lot on Sherbrooke Street for $50,000 to his brother-in-law, Orrin Squire Wood, former superintendent of the Montreal Telegraph Company.[43] Many years before, Holton had given his sister-in-law, Julia Forbes, Eliza's youngest sister, to whom he was devoted, in marriage to Wood.[44] From the beginning, Wood, who had been the first student of Samuel F. B. Morse, inventor of the telegraph and the Morse code, at New York University, enjoyed a good relationship with Holton.[45] They were bound not only by their kinship ties, but also by their interest in scientific and technological advances such as the telegraph.

Orrin and Julia Wood were frequent guests at the Holton home. They often came for dinner, when the Holton family gathered for food and conversation. Luther could be counted on to entertain his fellow diners with talk of his latest ideas about his property. He felt certain that the value of his Savage farmland in the St. Antoine suburb would rise over the next few years, and he favoured substantial civic improvements as likely to contribute to such a development. Central to his real estate efforts were advances in transportation, which spurred growth. Particularly important was the extension of the Montreal City Passenger Railway along St. Catherine Street from Mountain Street to Greene Avenue between 1864 and 1872.[46] The railway's horse-drawn streetcars facilitated the movement of people between Montreal's St. Antoine suburb and its downtown business district. Before long, St. Antoine became one of the city's most desirable suburbs.

Luther Holton demonstrated not only an acute sense of timing, but also an ability to discern the dynamics of the real estate industry. To take advantage of the great opportunities resulting from these transportation improvements, he engaged Joseph Rielle, Montreal architect and local provincial land surveyor, to survey his Savage farm property.[47] Initially, Holton had only a crude plan, but the architect was receptive to his ideas. During the spring of 1872, Holton, assisted by Rielle, put many hours of creative energy into drawing up a precise plan for the property's subdivision. In July, Holton completed the work of subdividing his land into seven blocks, the seventh block being the villa lot that he had earlier sold to Médéric Lanctot. Then, Holton carefully filed a copy of his Savage farm subdivision plan in the office of his notary, J. S. Hunter, who kept it among his notarial records for public use.

Holton made risk taking in real estate a tremendous adventure. His subdivision plan reflected his desire to create a beautifully laid-out middle-class community in which he and his family would want to live. His expectation was that from his nearby Sherbrooke Street home, it would be easy to keep a close eye on the details of the development of the small residential subdivision. Like other creators of suburban residential neighbourhoods in North America in the late nineteenth century, Holton sought a distinct market and hoped to attract especially businessmen and professionals through the use of deed restrictions.[48] Holton as well had an accurate understanding of the services required to develop such a market – services that included water, sewer, a street railway, and carriage roads. He also knew that the view from his Savage farm property on the southern slope of Mount Royal increased the incentive of the would-be resident to buy a lot and build a home on it. According to the *Montreal Gazette*, "the view from this property is probably the finest in the Dominion" of Canada.[49]

Along with his talent for planning, Holton's knack for attracting important clients – a skill no doubt reinforced by his genuine enthusiasm for his project – helped him flourish as a real estate entrepreneur. To implement his plan, in July 1872, he sold blocks one, two, three, four, five, and six in his Savage farm property, plus a house, stable, and lot on the Côte des Neiges Road, for $160,000 to Frank Bond of Bond Bros., Montreal stock brokers.[50] Bond put down $23,000 in cash, and gave Holton a seven percent, ten-year mortgage on these properties for the balance of $137,000. Holton's financial role in the project remained important, for in effect he provided Bond with a long-term loan.

Like all entrepreneurial ventures, launching the Savage farm property development entailed risks. In seeking to prevent the risks from growing too large, Holton kept three points in mind. One was that he wanted to provide an environment that would be attractive to prospective lot owners and contribute to the enhancement of real estate values in the community. Holton's second aim was to control the construction and style of the homes on these lots and ensure that they would be occupied by middle-class people. His third goal was to co-ordinate the development of the Savage farm property with public street improvements and with private land uses in the surrounding area. All these objectives, he believed, could be realized by writing restrictions into the deed of sale and by setting a high standard for quality lots.[51]

Holton obviously had a great personal stake in the business; he recognized that he could not succeed without Bond's co-operation. Bond's keen sense of obligation to Holton, combined with his confidence in the Sherbrooke Street entrepreneur's ability to oversee the project, prompted him to accept the restrictions. These restrictions explicitly limited the future use of the Savage farm property, the size and cost of the lots, and the pattern of streets and lanes. Bond also was required to apply the payments he received from individual lot purchasers to the amount he still owed Holton for the land. Most importantly, Bond could only proceed with the sale and development of the Savage farm property after he had submitted a detailed plan made by a licensed land surveyor to Holton for approval.[52] In sum, these deed restrictions ensured that the Savage farm subdivision would be developed under Holton's guiding hand.

Besides being comfortable in his dealings with Bond, Holton was skilled at identifying and meeting the needs of customers. For about three years, the relationship between the two men worked mostly as anticipated. Under Holton's direction, Bond hired architect and land surveyor Joseph Rielle to subdivide blocks one through six in the Savage farm property into villa lots in order to pave the way for the appearance of prestigious suburban residences set in extensive grounds.[53] Bond also engaged John J. Arnton, Montreal auctioneer, to dispose of the villa lots at auctions. Working with Rielle, who had produced lithographic plans of the villa lots and printed them in quantity, Arnton started by making these lithographs available to potential buyers in his office at 79 St. James Street.[54] By early 1875, a number of citizens had purchased villa lots and had erected handsome residences on them. Luther Holton revelled in the excitement and attention that came to the district around his own elegant home. His approach

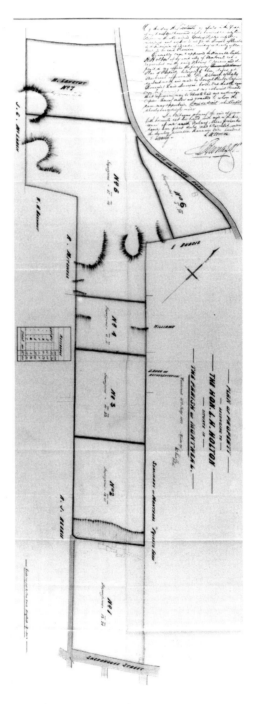

Luther Holton's plan of Savage Farm property in Montreal, shown here in an 1872 pen drawing by Joseph Rielle. Courtesy of the Archives nationales du Québec, Montréal.

Joseph B. Learmont in 1888.
Courtesy of the McCord Museum
of Canadian History, Montreal.

Amelia Holton Learmont in 1872. Courtesy
of Thomas L. Brock.

combined the traditional policy of providing high-quality service with an awareness of the need to control costs. The suburban community "on the most picturesque and pleasant slope of" Mount Royal had suffered setbacks caused by delinquent debtors and the presence of speculators.[55] It had not only survived these problems, but had also grown. In the process, the old Savage farm was gradually being transformed into a well-developed, middle-class neighbourhood.

* * *

As the elements of Luther Holton's suburban community were beginning to move into position, his family life was shattered by tragedy. In April 1875, Amelia, who two years before had married hardware clerk Joseph B. Learmont, was diagnosed as having pulmonary tuberculosis.[56] For a time, while she was being treated in Montreal, she and her baby son Holton Hamilton Learmont were staying in Luther and Eliza's home. But when the treatment did not work, Dr. George W. Campbell told her that her condition was incurable. Luther and Eliza spent a great deal of time with Amelia in their home over the next six months. In mid-September, Luther wrote Edward Blake that "My poor daughter continues to suffer intensely with steadily failing strength and no hope whatever of ultimate recovery. I have passed a sad summer."[57] To Alexander Mackenzie, Luther wrote: "My daughter's case has become so hopeless and she suffers so much that even the intense affection we have for her will hardly justify the wish that her suffering shall be long continued. I hope this terrible discipline of sorrow will not be lost upon me."[58] On 30 September, Amelia died with her husband and Eliza and Luther at her bedside.[59]

Luther and Eliza and Joseph Learmont were devastated by their profound grief. "My poor wife," Luther Holton told Mackenzie, "is terribly cast down by our great sorrow, but her health is I think improving. At one time I feared she would break down."[60] Establishing a trust fund of over $4,500 for his one-year-old grandson Holton Hamilton gave Luther quiet comfort amid his sorrow. The money came from the sale of one of his rental properties on St. Catherine Street, the same street on which lived his son Edward with his wife Helen, daughter of Robert M. Ford of Kingston.[61] Under Luther's guidance, a family gathering appointed Joseph Learmont as his son's guardian.[62] As Amelia's death had induced grief, Luther's grandson brought hope. More than ever, he treasured his warm, understanding friends and most of all his family. Rather than collapsing into self-pity, Luther strengthened himself with good memories.

* * *

By this time, the developments in Holton's Savage farm subdivision were overshadowed by the depression of the mid-1870s. In December 1876, the economy continued to plunge downward, wiping out Bond Bros. and sending shock waves through Holton's suburban community.[63] The failure of Bond Bros., happening as it did at the same time as a halt in real estate development, could have proved ruinous to Holton, but it did not, in large part because he had the financial resources to ride out the storm. These resources left him well positioned to benefit from distress buying at the bankruptcy sale of the Bond Bros.' real estate. In 1877, Holton stepped up with enough money to pay cash for fifteen villa lots in the Savage farm subdivision.[64] He thus acquired valuable properties at bargain prices and, in doing so, increased his investment in the St. Antoine suburb.

Holton was his usual optimistic self, saying that the Savage farm subdivision was here to stay because the need for middle-class housing would always exist. He did not think that he would get quick deals, but he could truly claim that the suburban community was still a profitable venture.[65] Running through it was a curving carriage road that bore Luther Holton's name: Holton Avenue. In 1880, it was one of the shortest avenues in Montreal, but it would persist for more than a century.

* * *

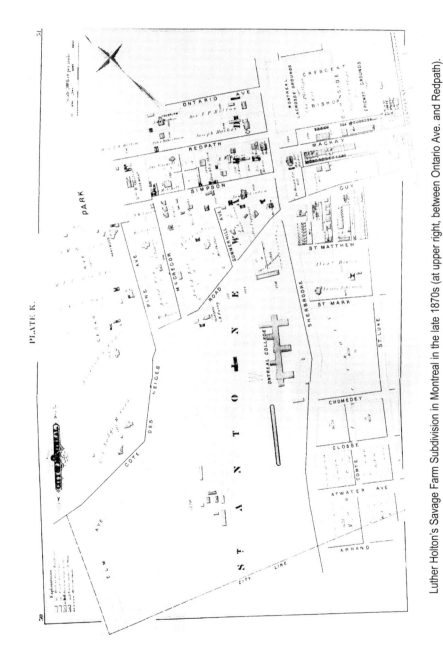

Luther Holton's Savage Farm Subdivision in Montreal in the late 1870s (at upper right, between Ontario Ave. and Redpath). From Henry W. Hopkins, *Atlas of the City and Island of Montreal 1879.*

In the late 1870s, his interest in federal politics and contemporary affairs, along with his service to McGill University as a member of its board of governors, crowded out any inclination toward devoting more than occasional attention to the development of the St. Antoine suburban community. Besides aiding McGill financially, Holton gave the board the benefit of his tremendous knowledge of educational developments in Montreal and elsewhere in Canada.[66]

Visitors to the House of Commons in Ottawa noted that Holton participated actively in the debates, kept his facts straight, and captured both the immediate and long-term meaning of events. On Saturday evening, 13 March 1880, after writing his customary daily letter to Eliza and his family, he attended a dinner in the Rideau Club given by Mackenzie Bowell, minister of customs. Full of his old vitality and wit, Holton entertained those around him with stories. "He joined in conversation with all his characteristic cheerfulness," reported the *Montreal Witness*.[67] The dinner party broke up about 11:30 P.M. Shortly thereafter, Holton followed his usual routine and headed past his friends in the lobby of the Russell House to bed.

Less than two hours later, Luther Holton died almost instantly from a massive heart attack.[68] The night porter, who was with him, left his side long enough to summon Dr. James A. Grant by telephone. Isaac Burpee, hardware merchant and member for Saint John, who was also at his bedside, tried to relieve his suffering. Dr. Grant soon arrived but could do nothing to revive him.[69]

Other members of the Commons later that same day commented on Holton's many achievements as a human being who cared about others, on his affection for his family and his country, and on his successes in business. Many singled out his singular contribution to the Commons, where he served for many years and came to be recognized as a great parliamentary authority. One member remarked that "to his equals in parliamentary experience he was a brother, to young members he was in truth a political father." John A. Macdonald said that "I feel that were any member to rise today and enter into any discussion of importance, he would see that empty chair; he would think of that kindly countenance, and he would feel with me that we ought to show respect to his memory by adjourning the business of this House today."[70]

A balanced summing up of what he meant to French Canadians and to Quebec as a whole came from Wilfrid Laurier, who had known him as well as anyone outside his family:

There is no one in this House who has more reason to lament the death of Mr. Holton than myself. It was my privilege when I was a very young man to become acquainted with him, and from that moment up to the moment of his untimely end, many have been the occasions when I have been enabled to appreciate the noble qualities which have endeared him to all with whom he came into contact.... You, Mr. Speaker, are aware that his loss will be keenly felt by his fellow countrymen of French origin. All French Canadians today feel that the man who has just departed from us was the connecting link between the many discordant elements of our province.[71]

Charles J. Coursol of Montreal noted that "his heart had always been with the people. French Canadians in particular would have cause to revere his memory. To the poor of Montreal, his charity was ever ready."[72]

In a letter to Eliza Holton, Agnes Macdonald, the prime minister's wife, caught the essence of Luther Holton's personality when she wrote:

I trust you will not consider this note an intrusion on your great sorrow. It is indeed many long years since you & I last met, but sympathy draws me near to you, today. And I feel impelled to send you a few lines expressive of Sir John's and my own sincere regret for the loss you, his friends & his country have sustained in the death of the late Mr. Holton. It was a great shock to my husband whose contemporary Mr. Holton was, & I who have for many years seen him so often in Ottawa & so constantly in his place in Parliament, feel that one of the first among our Canadians have passed away leaving after him only the memories of a kind, useful, and faithful life – only the echoes of a voice which while constantly speaking in opposition to my husband & his party always spoke fairly & honestly, and has left no sting to remember. Forgive me, if I do wrong in troubling you with these few lines. I believe they are well meant. My husband desires to join in expressions of sincere sympathy.[73]

These words recognized Holton's fair-mindedness, personal warmth, and his identity as a great Canadian. He was optimistic about the long-term viability of the Canadian nation he had helped create. His sense of humour and his awareness of the complexity of experience helped keep party divisions within bounds, shaping unity and keeping men's eyes on making the political system work. Holton shared with his fellow founders the realization that the Dominion of Canada had been established and that the political-constitutional process had endured. He understood that the nation would continue to debate issues at the polls, change governments, and settle problems in legislative halls and in courtrooms. Holton's mastery of and devotion to the political-constitutional institutions of his time helped focus Canada's will and its resources on maintaining the historic enterprise of a free people. His ideas of the right to get ahead based on a person's own labours and of expanding freedom within the context of existing traditions continued in subsequent generations.

Funeral services were held in Holton's home church, the Church of the Messiah (Unitarian) in Montreal. In the city's mercantile and professional circles, the businesses were closed for half the day. A special train came from Ottawa carrying about eighty members of the House of Commons and the Senate. The Reverend John Cordner said that

> ... the career of our departed friend shows the possibilities that lie within the reach of the young men of Canada. When I first knew him he was attending to his private business in a plain office down by the river side. Through industry and ability as a businessman he secured a competence in early middle age.... No husband and father ever had a deeper hold on the love of wife and children. And the usual daily letter written on Saturday last to his wife and family, on its arrival at its destination, found his wife a widow and his children fatherless.[74]

Mourners rising to over three thousand five hundred and marching four deep followed the cortege to Mount Royal Cemetery. There were "ministers and ex-ministers of state, merchants and clerks, stock brokers and stock owners, bench and bar, press and pulpit, tradesmen and others from more humble walks of life."[75]

At a meeting of the board of governors of McGill University, it was resolved:

> that the members of this board deeply regret the removal by death of the Honorable Luther Holton and to express their high estimation of his character and public services, as well as of the value of his aid and counsel as a member of the board of governors of McGill College and University.[76]

Holton was sixty-three years old when he died. During his life, he not only witnessed the birth of the steamboat era and the railway age, but also was one of the assiduous attendants at these events. While he helped make it possible for many men to accumulate vast fortunes, he was able to leave a substantial estate. The size of his personal estate of more than $70,000 – which he left to his wife and his children – was evidence of the extent to which he shared especially in the profits of railways.[77] Beyond this, he had a long and varied business life, ranging from financing marine engine manufacturing and managing a savings bank to involvement in real estate development. The *Ottawa Free Press* observed:

Throughout his active career he was identified with almost every movement that was started at Montreal for the development of the country, and his name gave character and stability to the commercial, banking, educational, and other institutions which have raised that city to a first position in the Dominion.[78]

The *Canadian Illustrated News* paid tribute to Luther Holton in language any man would savour:

His ample private means gave him leisure for reading and study. His mind, in truth, was so well filled with the facts and incidents which have led to what may be called the regime of parliamentary government, that conversation with him was always both pleasant and instructive, and this was one of the charms of his personal character.[79]

* * *

Thoughtful Canadians reading Luther Holton's obituary in mid-March 1880 realized that one of Canada's important entrepreneurs had passed from the scene. Because of his many contributions to economic development, he deserves high ranking on any list of Canadian business leaders in the nineteenth century. By the time he was forty, Holton's name was widely known in Canadian households. He was a risk-taking, visionary individual. His mind was sharp until his death. Some of the traditions that he embodied have endured, remaining vital and viable to the present time. As one who helped lead business organizations in forwarding, railway building, manufacturing, and banking, he recognized that they could not exist for long without providing high-quality service. Without top-quality service, businesspeople could not hope to remain competitive in a rapidly changing environment. Holton also helped to create diversified enterprises, so that he and his associates never had to rely too much on one product for their profits. True to their tradition of diversity, the businesses in which he provided leadership remained diversified. In pursuing a strategy of diversification, the businesses were to some degree similar to other Canadian enterprises in the mid-nineteenth century. Diversification was frequently the investment trend as Canadian entrepreneurs sought new outlets for their profits. Given the enormous personal risks involved in their enterprises, Holton and his colleagues were determined to maintain their independence from creditors as much as possible. Consequently, there developed a long tradition in these businesses: they were often self-financed, through reinvested profits and from the personal fortunes of the owners.

The enterprises also were transformed over the years. The forwarding firm Hooker, Holton & Co., starting as a relatively small partnership, became a major steamboat line in the Montreal forwarding industry. In Gzowski & Co., Holton and his partners began with a contract to build the fifty-mile road between Toronto and Guelph and then chose to become involved in the railway building industry in a big way by undertaking to construct the 172-mile Toronto-Sarnia line. Beginning with a small foundry in Montreal, Ebenezer Gilbert, aided financially by Luther Holton, transformed the enterprise into the impressive Canada Engine Works. At the Montreal City and District Savings Bank, Holton and his colleagues eventually transformed the trustee savings bank into a limited liability joint stock corporation committed to offer a broad range of banking services and to promote the social welfare of Montreal and the surrounding area. A compassionate man, Holton was sensitive to the cries of the poor and black people.

In his long political career, Luther Holton relied on certain traditions. As he established a place for himself in Canadian politics, he had to face an unresolved tension between English and French Canadians – a tension that was present in almost every development that touched the two cultures. Broad-minded and able to speak both English and French fluently, Holton developed a reputation as a man who identified with the tradition of co-operation between French and English Canadians. He was proud of the accomplishments of both cultures and exemplified the strategy of recognizing the contributions each was making to the development of Canadian society. As a politician, Holton also was well attuned to the tradition of promoting business enterprise in Canada. A great deal of his creative energy concerned not only his own businesses, but Canadian economic development as well. Holton's record for dependability, economy, and speed in carrying out his business responsibilities was very good. Before he and his partners in railway building obtained a Grand Trunk contract that carried Canadian government assistance, he had proved himself as an entrepreneur. What was needed to provide the public with a reliable system of long-distance transportation was capital, which was always short in youthful Canada at mid-century, and entrepreneurship, which Holton and his associates helped to supply. While Holton viewed the Grand Trunk contract as a means of achieving his own immediate, personal financial goals, he at the same time belonged to a group of farsighted men who saw the new technology as a force in the unification of what would become the central region of the Canadian nation.

In the 1850s and early 1860s, critics and opponents charged that Holton's work for the Grand Trunk was tainted with extravagant profits, and they made sure that his railway work was investigated. On balance, his critics were on target in accusing him of making excessive profits, but his reputation for helping to build an excellent road remained intact. By participating in the construction of the trunk line in Canada, Holton contributed to the state-making process.

In the mid-1860s, Holton as finance minister lent his influence to the struggle to reform the finance department in the Canadian union. He saw accounting and audit reform as a means to ensure that the Canadian government would become more accountable to the citizens of the province. In his hands, the budget became not only a tool of efficient administration, but also a way to maintain responsible democratic government in Canadian society. As a budget reformer, he sought to order relations between the provincial government and private enterprise. In doing so, he encouraged economic growth.

In reviewing Holton's career, one is struck by the great changes that occurred in his lifetime. In 1817, when he was born, the age of steam on water had just dawned and the fastest vehicle on land was the stagecoach. By 1880, the year of his death, the railway age was well under way. As one of the leading actors in the transportation revolution, Holton was associated with the contributions the steamboat made to shipping on the upper St. Lawrence and the Great Lakes. In those areas that were favoured with navigable waterways, it was the main instrument for the development of the Canadian interior between the 1820s and early 1850s. During the mid-1850s, Holton played a key role in the efforts that enabled trains to become the basic means of transportation in the province, regardless of the existence of water routes and the continuing significance of the steamboat. Creating the modern concept of travel, this pioneer railway was the dependable form of overland transportation for which Canadians longed. Railway building occurred on an unprecedented scale in the 1850s, and the impact of the Grand Trunk was felt quickly on patterns of interregional trade, urban growth, and social relations. Besides carrying people and their goods to many cities and towns, and stimulating the development of these urban places in the process, the Grand Trunk was a revolutionary force that changed Canadian society and drew many communities out of their isolation.

In the Canadian railway age, there were in reality two transformations going on: as railways converted the province's land from an obstacle to movement to highways of commerce, politicians transformed the British North American colonies into the Dominion of Canada. Luther Holton's contributions to constitutional change place him among Canada's outstanding political leaders. Though initially opposed to confederation, he became one of its most ardent supporters. Moving what he saw as a great society forward – bringing a new constitution, a strong central government, safeguards for the preservation of the French and English cultures, more British capital, and economic expansion to the Canadian nation – was to him a worthwhile endeavour.

Notes

Abbreviations in Notes

ANQM Archives nationales du Québec à Montréal
AO Archives of Ontario
JLA *Journals of the Legislative Assembly of the Province of Canada*
NAC National Archives of Canada
RGDC R.G. Dun & Company Collection

Chapter 1
Work on the Harbourfront

1 T. L. Brock Collection, Victoria, British Columbia, Athens, 18 January 1910, Saxon Washburne to Geoffrey Gilbert.

2 Geoffrey Gilbert, ed., "The Ancestry of Ezra Holton of Northfield, Mass. and Soperton, Ont., 1785-1824" (typescript copy, Victoria, British Columbia, 1953), 14, 34, 130; John Douglas Borthwick, *History and Biographical Gazetteer of Montreal to the Year 1892* (Montreal, 1892), 179.

3 Moses Whicher Mann, *Glimpses into the Holton Family History* (Mt. Hermon, Mass.: Holton Family Association, 1924), n. p.; Gilbert, "The Ancestry of Ezra Holton," 31, 35.

4 T. L. Brock Collection, Athens, 18 January 1910, Saxon Washburne to Geoffrey Gilbert.

5 Gilbert, "The Ancestry of Ezra Holton," 35,130.

6 Archives of Ontario (AO), Assessment Rolls for Rear of Leeds and Lansdowne, 1817-1819.

7 Radcliffe College Archives, *Seaview Gazette* (Belleville), May 1894.

8 National Archives of Canada (NAC), RG1, L3, vol. 230a, Canada Land Petitions, H. Bundle 13, no. 52, York, 9 January 1822, Ezra Holton to Sir Peregrine Maitland; MG24, G4, second regiment of the Leeds militia, annual return of the company commanded by captain Levi Soper, 5 June 1820.

9 NAC, RG8, British Military and Naval Records, C Series, vol. 121, Kingston, 2 October 1816, John Wilson to Lieutenant-colonel Addison, 293-296.

10 AO, Assessment Roll for Rear of Leeds and Lansdowne, 1821.

11 NAC, RG1, L3, Vol. 230a, Canada Land Petitions, H. Bundle 13, no. 52, York, 9 January 1822, Ezra Holton to Sir Peregrine Maitland.

12 *Seaview Gazette* (Belleville), May 1894.

13 T. L. Brock Collection, Victoria, British Columbia, letter: Athens, Ontario, 18 January 1910, Saxon Washburne to Geoffrey Gilbert; *Seaview Gazette* (Belleville), May 1894.

14 Information on Ezra Holton's age and the date of his death is taken from the Holton family gravestone in the old cemetery in Sheffield's Corners (now Soperton).

15 Hastings County Historical Society Archives, file 218, Business in the 1870s, newspaper clipping, obituary of Ezra William Holton, 27 June 1879; Henry J. Morgan, ed., *The Dominion Annual Register and Review 1879* (Montreal: John Lovell & Son, 1880), 405.

16 Geoffrey Gilbert and Eva L. Moffatt, eds., "The Ancestors of Moses Haskell Gilbert of Vermont and Montreal, 1790-1843" (typescript copy, Victoria, British Columbia, 1954), 60.

17 Thomas Doige, *An Alphabetical List of the Merchants, Traders, and Housekeepers Residing in Montreal* (Montreal: James Lane, 1819), 103.

18 *Montreal Herald*, 2 December 1826.

19 Geoffrey Gilbert, ed., "The Ancestry of William Forbes of Barre, Mass. and Montreal, Quebec, 1788-1833" (typescript copy, Victoria, British Columbia, 1953), 18; *Montreal Gazette*, 14 December 1833.

20 *Canadian Courant*, 6 January 1827; Mrs. A.N. St. John Collection, Toronto, Ontario, manuscript: Benjamin Workman's journal, 193-194, 214-215, 245.

21 *Montreal Herald*, 28 June 1864.

22 Ibid.

23 Ibid.

24 Montreal Unitarian Church Archives, Minute Book A, 6 June 1842.

25 Gilbert and Moffatt, "The Ancestors of Moses Haskell Gilbert," 60.

26 Henry J. Morgan, ed., *The Dominion Annual Register and Review 1880-1881* (Montreal: John Lovell & Son, 1882), 412-413.

27 *Canadian Courant*, 6 January 1827.

28 Archives nationales du Québec à Montréal (ANQM), H. Griffin, 7789, contract and agreement, between Moses Haskell Gilbert and John Cliff, 12 July 1828.

29 ANQM, I. J. Gibb, 6901, Inventory of the Estate of Moses Haskell Gilbert taken at the request of Cynthia Phillips Gilbert and Luther H. Holton, 9 August 1843.

30 NAC, Manuscript Census of 1842, City of Montreal, C-729, 52.

31 ANQM, I. J. Gibb, 6901, Inventory of the Estate of Moses Haskell Gilbert taken at the request of Cynthia Phillips Gilbert and Luther H. Holton, 9 August 1843.

32 Gerald J. J. Tulchinsky, *The River Barons Montreal Businessmen and the Growth of Industry and Transportation 1837-53* (Toronto: University of Toronto Press, 1977), 35-50.

33 Robert Sweeny, "Internal Dynamics and the International Cycle: Questions of the transition in Montreal, 1821-1828," Ph.D. thesis, McGill University, 1985, 259-260; James Croil, *Steam Navigation and Its Relation to the Commerce of Canada and the United States* (Montreal: Montreal News Company, 1898), 317-328; Henry Youle Hind, ed., *Eighty Years' Progress of British North America* (Toronto: L. Nicols, 1863), 133-141.

34 *Montreal in 1856: A Sketch Prepared for the Celebration of the Opening of the Grand Trunk Railway of Canada by a Subcommittee of the Celebration*

Committee (Montreal: John Lovell, 1856), 14.

35 Kingston *British Whig*, 29 March 1880; Neil F. Morrison, "John McEwan: First Sheriff," *Windsor Public Library Scrapbooks*, vol. 27b, 59.

36 For a description of the Montreal harbourfront in the 1830s, see Newton Bosworth, *Hochelaga Depicta: The Early History and Present State of the City and Island of Montreal* (Montreal: William Greig, 1839), 196. A comment on the condition of Montreal's streets in these years can be found in the *Canadian Courant*, 12 November 1831.

37 *Journals of the House of Assembly of Lower Canada*, 1835-1836, vol. 45, Appendix J, Banks, Abstract from the Books of the City Bank, Montreal, 7 November 1835; *Montreal Transcript*, 6 June 1837.

38 New York Public Library, Phelps Dodge & Co. Papers, invoices of goods consigned by Phelps Dodge & Co. to Henderson, Hooker & Co. for the account of Edward Jackson & Co. for 1836.

39 ANQM, N. B. Doucet, 23573, protest, William Bradbury against Henderson, Hooker & Co., 11 June 1836; N. B. Doucet, 24138, protest, William Bradbury against Henderson, Hooker & Co., 8 February 1837; receipt, Henderson, Hooker & Co. per L. H. Holton to William Bradbury, 8 February 1837.

40 *Montreal Transcript*, 28 November 1837.

41 *Montreal Gazette*, 14 March 1833, 14 December 1833.

42 ANQM, N. B. Doucet, 26949, inventory of the estate of William Forbes and Submit Phillips Forbes taken at the request of James Wait and Luther H. Holton, 2 September 1840.

43 ANQM, J. Blackwood, 778, contract of marriage, between James Wait and Emma Forbes, 14 April 1837.

44 *Montreal Gazette*, 7 May 1839; ANQM, Register of Baptisms, Marriages and Burials of Erskine Presbyterian Church, Montreal, marriage certificate of Luther H. Holton and Eliza Forbes, 27 April 1839; Robert Campbell, *A History of the Scotch Presbyterian Church, St. Gabriel Street, Montreal* (Montreal: W. Drysdale & Co., 1887), 523-524.

45 *Montreal Herald*, 24 November 1863.

46 ANQM, N. B. Doucet, 26819, compromise, between the estate of Andrew Yale and Henderson, Hooker & Co., 7 July 1840.

Chapter 2
In a Plain Office Down by the River Side

1 *Montreal World*, 18 March 1880.

2 ANQM, I. J. Gibb, 7808, sale and transfer, from John M. Tobin, Charles H. Castle, and Alfred Hooker, executors of the will of James Henderson, to Luther H. Holton, 29 March 1845.

3 ANQM, I. J. Gibb, 12102, power of attorney to prove claim in bankruptcy, from Hooker, Holton & Co. to George E. Jaques, 5 January 1849.

4 Neil F. Morrison, "John McEwan: First Sheriff," *Windsor Public Library Scrapbooks*, vol. 27b, 59.

5 *Montreal Gazette*, 8 June 1842, 21 February 1843; *Montreal Directory for 1844-1845*, 266.

6 *Montreal Gazette*, 19 May 1841.

7 ANQM, I. J. Gibb, 5569, declaration and protest, Joseph Laurent, captain of the *Highlander*, against

246 • LUTHER H. HOLTON

Henderson, Hooker & Co., 15
August 1842.

8 *Montreal Gazette*, 23 November
1843.

9 *Montreal Gazette*, May to November, 1841-1845, all issues.

10 NAC, RG16, A, 5-2, Montreal Port
Records, Customs, 1843-1845,
vols. 2-9.

11 Phelps Dodge & Co. Papers,
Montreal, 13 October 1841,
Henderson, Hooker & Co. to
Phelps Dodge & Co.

12 Richard Lowitt, *A Merchant Prince
of the Nineteenth Century: William
E. Dodge* (New York: Columbia
University Press, 1954), 28.

13 *Montreal Gazette*, 22 June 1841.

14 *Montreal Gazette*, 28 June 1844.

15 Bank of Montreal Archives,
Commercial Bank of the Midland
District, Directors' Records, vol. 4,
1 May 1845.

16 *Journals of the Legislative
Assembly of the Province of
Canada (JLA)*, 1842, vol. 1,
Appendix C, Abstract from the
Books of the City Bank, Montreal,
26 June 1841.

17 *Montreal Directory for 1842-1843*,
51; *Montreal Directory for 1844-
1845*, 270.

18 Bank of Montreal Archives,
Commercial Bank of the Midland
District, Directors' Records, vol. 4,
1 May 1845.

19 *Montreal Gazette*, 15 May 1841; 1
June 1841; 27 July 1841; 6 June
1842; 14 June 1842; 21 September
1842; 24 June 1843; 21 November
1843; 18 May 1844; 28 June 1844;
13 May 1845; 17 May 1845; 7
June 1845; 17 June 1845; 1 July
1845; 29 September 1845; 10
November 1845; 19 November
1845.

20 *Montreal Gazette*, 5 June 1841; 12
July 1841; 24 May 1842; 14 July
1842; 22 July 1843; 19 September

1843; 21 May 1844; 7 June 1844;
9 August 1844; 16 May 1845; 23
May 1845; 19 June 1845; 16 July
1845; 30 July 1845; 29 September
1845; 18 October 1845; 3 November 1845.

21 NAC, CO42, vol. 477, Montreal,
26 January 1841, Lord Sydenham
to Lord John Russell, 131-132;
Gerald J. J. Tulchinsky, *The River
Barons Montreal Businessmen and
the Growth of Industry and
Transportation 1837-53* (Toronto:
University of Toronto Press, 1977),
39-40.

22 *JLA*, 1841, vol. 1, Appendix EE.
Montreal, 14 July 1841, Sidney
Jones & Co. to H. H. Killaly.

23 NAC, MG24, I36, R. W. Shepherd
Papers, Personal History of Robert
Ward Shepherd, 11-12.

24 Personal History of Robert Ward
Shepherd, 12; H. R. Morgan,
"Steam Navigation on the Ottawa
River," *Ontario Historical Society,
Papers and Records,* 23 (Toronto,
1926), 373.

25 Personal History of Robert Ward
Shepherd, 13.

26 Personal History of Robert Ward
Shepherd, 15.

27 *JLA,* 1841, vol. 1, Appendix EE.
Evidence of Francis Henderson, 7
July 1841.

28 *Montreal Gazette*, 25 July 1842.

29 *JLA*, 1841, vol. 1, Appendix EE.
Montreal, 12 August 1841, Sidney
Jones to W. H. Merritt.

30 NAC, CO42, vol. 492, Kingston,
19 April 1842, Sir Charles Bagot
to Lord Stanley; J. M. S. Careless,
*The Union of the Canadas: The
Growth of Canadian Institutions,
1841-1857* (Toronto: McClelland
and Stewart, 1967), 58-74.

31 Douglas McCalla, *Planting the
Province:The Economic History of
Upper Canada, 1784-1870*
(Toronto: University of Toronto
Press, 1993), 50-56.

32 *Montreal Gazette*, 2 May 1844.
33 *Montreal Gazette*, 20 June 1844.
34 *Montreal Gazette*, 16 November 1844.
35 *Montreal Gazette*, 8 May 1845.
36 ANQM, Court of Queen's Bench, Montreal, judgements for the year 1843, no. 1403, *Macpherson, Crane & Co. vs. Henderson, Hooker & Co.*, 14 March 1843.
37 *Montreal Gazette,* 25 March 1845.
38 *Montreal Gazette*, 27 March 1845.
39 *Montreal Gazette*, 25 March 1845.

Chapter 3
Developing Steamboat Services

1 ANQM, I. J. Gibb, 15257, dissolution of co-partnership, between Alfred Hooker and Luther H. Holton, 12 January 1854.
2 ANQM, Register of Wills, vol. 7, no. 441, will of James Henderson, 2 April 1845.
3 ANQM, I. J. Gibb, 7808, sale and transfer, from John M. Tobin, Charles H. Castle, and Alfred Hooker, executors of the will of the late James Henderson, to Luther Holton, 29 March 1845.
4 Montreal *Pilot*, 29 March 1845.
5 *Kingston Chronicle and Gazette*, 30 April 1845.
6 Gilbert Norman Tucker, *The Canadian Commercial Revolution 1845-1851* (Hamden, Conn.: Yale University Press, 1936), 118.
7 Travis L. Crosby, *Sir Robert Peel's Administration 1841-1846* (Hamden, Conn.: Archon Books, 1976), 138-156.
8 *Canadian Economist*, 2 May 1846; 18 July 1846; 27 March 1847.
9 *Montreal Gazette*, 28 May 1845.
10 Kingston *Argus*, 29 May 1846, 12 June 1846.
11 Eric Ross, *The Canadas in 1841: Full of Hope and Promise*

(Montreal: McGill-Queen's University Press, 1991), 59-63.
12 *Montreal Herald*, 14 February 1889.
13 *List of Canadian Patents from the beginning of the Patent Office, June 1824, till the 1st of January 1869* (Ottawa, 1868), 12; Obituary: "E. E. Gilbert," *Transactions of the Canadian Society of Civil Engineers* 3 (1889), 364.
14 *Montreal Gazette*, 3 April 1846.
15 Ibid.
16 *Montreal Gazette*, 20 May 1845; 7 June 1845; 17 June 1845; 1 October 1845; 3 Noember 1845; 7 May 1846; 9 May 1846.
17 *Pilot*, 18 April 1848.
18 NAC, RG12, A1, vol. 175, shipping register, Montreal, 137.
19 *Pilot*, 16 June 1849.
20 *Montreal Herald*, 19 July 1848.
21 *Pilot*, 22 May 1849.
22 Kingston *Argus*, 1 April 1847.
23 *Montreal Transcript*, 6 June 1850.
24 *Montreal Gazette*, 18 June 1845.
25 R. G. Dun & Company Collection (RGDC), Baker Library, Graduate School of Business Administration, Harvard University, Canada West, vol. 13, Carleton County, 214; *Pilot*, 28 November 1848.
26 RGDC, Canada West, vol. 15, Grenville County, 205; *Republican* (Ogdensburg), 16 July 1861.
27 Bank of Montreal Archives, Commercial Bank of the Midland District, Records of the Board, vol. 4, 1 May 1845, 21-24.
28 *Montreal Gazette*, 9 June 1847.
29 Commercial Bank of the Midland District, Records of the Board, vol. 4, 29 September 1845, 64; 24 November 1845, 75; 30 March 1846, 107; 15 June 1846, 119; 18 June 1846, 119; 8 October 1846, 148; 15 February 1847, 182; 2 September 1847, 218; 7 August 1848, 297; 17 May 1849, 358.

30 Commercial Bank of the Midland District, Records of the Bank, vol. 4, 7 August 1845, 53.

31 Commercial Bank of the Midland District, Records of the Board, vol. 4, 30 November 1846, 158. Hastings County Historical Society Archives, Belleville, Ontario, newspaper clippings file.

32 *Montreal Transcript*, 24 September 1846; *Pilot*, 16 September 1847; Montreal *Pilot*, 21 August 1849.

33 Montreal Board of Trade Archives, Montreal Board of Trade, Minutes of the Board of Trade Council, 13 June 1854, 15-17.

34 RGDC, Canada West, vol. 15, Frontenac County, 127.

35 ANQM, I. J. Gibb, 12102, power of attorney to prove claim in bankruptcy, from Hooker, Holton & Co. to George E. Jaques, 5 January 1849; ANQM, W. M. Easton, 3697, protest, Hooker, Holton & Co. against W. Gamble & others, 4 July 1849; *Montreal Gazette*, 12 March 1849; NAC, RG16, A, 502, Montreal Port Records, Customs, 1845-49, vols. 7-13.

36 *Montreal Herald*, 13 October 1849; A. G. Doughty, ed., *The Elgin-Grey Papers 1846-1852* (Ottawa, 1937), vol. 2, 523-524, Niagara, 19 October 1849, Lord Elgin to Earl Grey.

37 *Montreal Gazette*, 16 November 1849.

38 *Globe*, 15 March 1880.

39 Toronto Public Library, Baldwin Papers, Montreal, 25 March 1847, F. Hincks to R. Baldwin.

40 *Pilot*, 10 May 1849.

41 AO, Edward Blake Papers, 2 February 1876, L. H. Holton to E. Blake.

42 *Montreal Herald*, 17 November 1849.

43 Baldwin Papers, Montreal, 26 October 1849, F. Hincks to R. Baldwin.

44 NAC, RG4, Series B29, vol. 5, militia records, Montreal, 31 January 1855, L. H. Holton to A. de Salaberry.

45 Montreal Registry Office Archives, partnership book, vol. 1, 126.

46 NAC, MG24, D84, H. C. Bayley Papers, Montreal, 31 May 1850, L. H. Holton to Bradley & Canfield.

47 *Globe*, 11 March 1851; *Pilot*, 14 April 1853.

48 NAC, MG24, D24, Donald Bethune Papers, Articles of Agreement, 25 April 1850.

49 *Montreal Herald*, 3 April 1871.

50 Ibid.

51 NAC, RG16, A-1, vol. 191, file Montreal 1852 part 3, Montreal 24 August 1852, L. H. Holton to R.S.M. Bouchette.

52 Queen's University Archives, John Macaulay Papers, vol. 2, Montreal, 28 April 1851, W. Murray to John Murray.

53 RGDC, Canada West, vol. 15, Frontenac County, 127.

54 *British Whig*, 12 April 1853.

55 ANQM, I. J. Gibb, 15257, dissolution of co-partnership between Alfred Hooker and Luther H. Holton, 12 January 1854.

Chapter 4
Railway Builder

1 *JLA*, 1852, Vol. XI, Appendix XX, Fourth Report of the Standing Committee on Railroads, Canals, and Telegraph Lines, Stock Book of the Montreal & Kingston Railway Company, Montreal, 23 August 1852; *Le Pays*, 10 September 1852.

2 *JLA*, 1852, Vol. XI, Appendix XX, Montreal, 1 September 1852, L. H.

Holton to A. N. MacNab; *La Minerve*, 7 October 1852.

3 *Montreal Gazette*, 5 November 1852.

4 RGDC, Canada West, vol. 26, York County, 252.

5 NAC, MG24, E9, Casimir S. Gzowski Papers, vol. 2, Agreement between C. S. Gzowski, D. L. Macpherson, L. H. Holton, A. T. Galt and the Toronto & Guelph Railway Company, 26 November 1852.

6 *Globe*, 11 November 1852.

7 Henry C. Klassen, "Luther Holton: Mid-Century Railwayman," *University of Ottawa Quarterly* 52 (July-September 1982), 327-328.

8 *Montreal Gazette*, 5 October 1852.

9 RGDC, Canada West, vol. 26, York County, 252.

10 Frank Walker, *Daylight Through The Mountain: The Life and Letters of Walter and Francis Shanly* (Montreal: The Engineering Institute of Canada, 1957), 260, 264, 293-295; Bank of Montreal Archives, Bank of Montreal, Records of the Board, vol. for the years 1850-67, 14 December 1852, 130.

11 *Guelph Advertiser*, 14 April, 1853; 23 March 1854.

12 NAC, Galt Papers, Ogdensburg, 15 February 1853, L. H. Holton to A. T. Galt.

13 Toronto & Guelph Railway Company, Second Annual Report of the Directors, 6 June 1853, 13.

14 Galt Papers, Ogdensburg, 15 February 1853, L. H. Holton to A. T. Galt.

15 Galt Papers, Hamilton, 26 March 1853, L. H. Holton to A. T. Galt.

16 Galt Papers, Montreal, 10 April 1853, L. H. Holton to A. T. Galt.

17 *Montreal Gazette*, 7 June 1853.

18 Galt Papers, Montreal, 10 April 1853, L. H. Holton to A. T. Galt.

19 Galt Papers, Toronto, 2 June 1867, C. S. Gzowski to A. T. Galt.

20 Walker, *Daylight Through the Mountain*, 265.

21 Galt Papers, Montreal, 10 April 1853, L. H. Holton and A. T. Galt.

22 Walker, *Daylight Through the Mountain*, 265.

23 Ibid., 268-273.

24 Ibid. 275-284.

25 Galt Papers, Montreal, 10 April 1853, L. H. Holton to A. T. Galt.

26 *Globe*, 30 November 1860.

27 AO, Francis Shanly Papers, box 81, Sarnia, 14 July 1853, James Stewart to F. Shanly; *Montreal Gazette*, 1861, Montreal, 25 January 1854, L. H. Holton to J. A. Macdonald; NAC, RG 30, vol. 2062, Grand Trunk Railway Agreements, no. 129, Sarnia Land Trust, pp. 1-7.

28 *Globe*, 24 November 1860.

29 RG30, vol. vol. 1000, 17 August 1853.

30 RG30, vol. 487, August and September 1853. See also Bank of Montreal Archives, Commercial Bank of the Midland District, Inspection Report 1857-1864, 14-15.

31 A. W. Currie, *The Grand Trunk Railway of Canada* (Toronto: University of Toronto Press, 1957), 31; D.C.M. Platt and Jeremy Adelman, "London Merchant Bankers in the First Phase of Heavy Borrowing: The Grand Trunk Railway of Canada," *Journal of Imperial and Common-wealth History* 18 (May 1990), 219-220.

32 *JLA*, 1857, vol. 15, Appendix VI, Report of the Special Committee of Inquiry on the Grand Trunk Railway, 1857.

33 *Guelph Advertiser*, 30 October 1854; Montreal *Pilot*, 26 May 1854.

34 Galt Papers, Toronto, 15 April 1854, C. S. Gzowski to A.T. Galt.
35 *JLA*, 1857, vol. 15, Appendix VI, Report of the Special Committee of Inquiry on the Grand Trunk Railway, 1857.
36 Ibid.
37 Toronto *Leader*, 4 August 1854.
38 Galt Papers, Montreal, 13 April 1854, L. H. Holton to A. T. Galt.
39 Ibid.
40 Ibid.
41 Walker, *Daylight Through the Mountain*, 264.
42 Stanley Triggs et al., *Victoria Bridge: The Vital Link* (Montreal: McCord Museum, 1992), 41-45; Walker, *Daylight Through the Mountain*, 264.
43 Walker, *Daylight Through the Mountain*, 264.
44 Toronto *Leader*, 14 June 1854.
45 Montreal *Pilot*, 2 August 1854.
46 Currie, *The Grand Trunk Railway of Canada*, 33.
47 Paul Romney, "The Ten Thousand Pound Job: Political Corruption, Equitable Jurisdiction, and the Public Interest in Upper Canada 1852-6," in David H. Flaherty, ed., *Essays in the History of Canadian Law, Volume II* (Toronto: University of Toronto Press, 1983), 143-199; George A. Davison, "The Hincks-Brown Rivalry and the Politics of Scandal," *Ontario History* 81 (June 1989), 129-151.
48 Mrs. H. M. Hague Collection, Montreal, 30 June 1854, John Young to L. H. Holton.
49 *Montreal Herald*, 8 July 1854; *Le Pays*, 8 July 1854; *Montreal Gazette*, 8 July 1854; *La Minerve*, 13 July 1854.
50 *Montreal Herald*, 17 July 1854; *Globe*, 31 July 1854.
51 *Montreal Gazette*, 15 July 1854.
52 NAC, George Brown Papers, Montreal, 1 July 1854, J. M. Ferres to G. Brown.
53 Ibid., 22 July 1854.
54 *Globe*, 31 July 1854.
55 *Montreal Gazette*, 29 July 1854; *La Minerve*, 29 July 1854.
56 Galt Papers, Montreal, 14 August 1854, L. H. Holton to A. T. Galt.
57 Brockville Registry Office, will of Cleveland Stafford, 28 August 1849.
58 Galt Papers, Montreal, 14 August 1854, L. H. Holton to A. T. Galt.
59 *Pilot*, 4 September 1854.
60 *Montreal Gazette*, 8 May 1854.
61 *Globe*, 22 June 1854.
62 Brown Papers, Montreal, 6 June 1862, L. H. Holton to G. Brown; *Pilot*, 6 September 1854.
63 Galt Papers, Montreal, 14 August 1854, L. H. Holton to A. T. Galt; J. M. S. Careless, *Brown of the Globe, Vol. One, The Voice of Upper Canada 1818-1859* (Toronto: Macmillan of Canada, 1959), 20.
64 *Globe*, 19 May 1856.
65 *Montreal Herald*, 4 July 1854.
66 *Montreal Gazette*, 24 October 1854.
67 Ibid.
68 *JLA*, 1854-55, vol. 13, no. 9, Appendix (E.E.), Report of Select Committee on the Subject of Public Deposits, 27 October 1854.
69 *Globe*, 14 November 1854.
70 *Montreal Gazette*, 4 December 1854.
71 RG30, vol. 1000, Grand Trunk, Board of Directors, Minutes, 20 September 1854; 17 January 1855.
72 Toronto City Hall Archives, City of Toronto Council Minutes, 1853-1856, n. p.; City of Toronto Council Journal, 1854-1855, n. p.; Toronto Public Library, *Minutes of Information Given Before the Select Committee of Council on the Esplanade Contract*, Toronto, 17 April 1855, C. S. Gzowski & Co. to the Citizens of Toronto; MG24, E9, vol. 2, C. S. Gzowski Papers,

agreement between the Grand Trunk and C. S. Gzowski, D. L. Macpherson, L. H. Holton, and A. T. Galt, 10 December 1856; Peter G. Goheen, "The Struggle for Urban Public Space: Disposing of the Toronto Waterfront in the Nineteenth Century," a paper presented at the 78th Annual Meeting of the Canadian Historical Association, 6-8 June 1999, Sherbrooke, Quebec.

73 Gzowski Papers, agreement between the Port Huron & Lake Michigan Railroad and C. S. Gzowski, D. L. Macpherson, L. H. Holton, and A. T. Galt, 1853; *Sarnia Observer*, 31 August 1854; Galt Papers, Toronto, 20 February 1860, C. S. Gzowski to L. H. Holton; Montreal, 21 February 1860, L. H. Holton to A. T. Galt.

74 ANQM, J.C. Griffin, 10793, contract and agreement between C. S. Gzowski & Co. and the Montreal & Vermont Junction Railway Company, 24 February 1854; *Statutes of the Province of Canada*, 24 Victoria, Cap. 81 (1861).

75 NAC, MG24, D16, Isaac Buchanan Papers, vol. 100, Report of the President and Directors of the Woodstock & Lake Erie Railway and Harbour Company, 10 July 1855; vol. 101, Woodstock & Lake Erie Railway and Harbour Company contract, 30 March 1854.

76 *Montreal Gazette*, 12 May 1855.

77 Currie, *The Grand Trunk Railway of Canada*, 40.

78 Toronto *Leader*, 11 August 1855.

79 RG30, vol. 1000, 20 October 1855; 21 November 1855.

80 *Morning Chronicle*, 20, 22 February 1856; *Leader* (Toronto), 2 March 1857.

81 *Montreal Gazette*, 27 June 1856; J. E. Hodgetts, *Pioneer Public Service: An Administrative History of the United Canadas, 1841-1867*

(Toronto: University of Toronto Press, 1955), 96-117.

82 *Leader*, 12 June 1856; Brown Papers, Montreal, 3 July 1856, L. H. Holton to G. Brown; Currie, *Grand Trunk Railway of Canada*, 46-47.

83 Toronto *Leader*, 16 June 1856; Leo A. Johnson, *History of Guelph 1827-1927* (Guelph: Guelph Historical Society, 1977), 174-176.

84 Toronto *Leader*, 16 June 1856.

85 Adelaide Leitch, *Floodtides of Fortune: The Story of Stratford and the Progress of the City through Two Centuries* (Stratford: Corporation of the City of Stratford, 1980), 52.

86 *Montreal in 1856: A Sketch Prepared for the Celebration of the Opening of the Grand Trunk Railway of Canada by a Subcommittee of the Celebration Committee* (Montreal: John Lovell, 1856), 6.

87 *Montreal Gazette*, 13 November 1856.

88 *Leader*, 13 November 1856.

89 *Globe*, 12, 13 November 1856.

90 *Montreal Gazette*, 13 November 1856.

91 *Pilot*, 14 November 1856.

92 *Leader*, 4 March 1857.

93 *JLA*, 1857, vol. 15, 5 March 1857, 45.

94 *Statutes of the Province of Canada*, 20 Victoria, Cap. 11 (1857); J. M. and Edw. Trout, *The Railways of Canada* (Toronto: Monetary Times, 1871), 75-77.

95 *JLA*, 1857, vol. 15, Appendix VI, Report of the Special Committee of Inquiry on the Grand Trunk Railway.

96 *London Atlas*, in *Leader*, 8 April 1857.

97 *Morning Chronicle*, 4 May 1857.

98 *JLA*, 1857, vol. 15, Appendix VI, Report of the Special Committee of

Inquiry on the Grand Trunk Railway.

99 *Montreal Herald*, 23 May 1857; *Leader*, 13 May 1857.

100 RG30, vol. 1000, 10 June 1857.

101 *Pilot*, 22 May 1857.

102 QRGDC, Canada West, vol. 26, York County, 252. For an account of unprofitable railway building ventures, see Richard White, "Losing Ventures: The Railway Construction Contracts of Frank Shanly, 1860-75," *Canadian Historical Review* 79 (June 1998), 237-260.

Chapter 5
Keeping Up an Active Interest in Public Affairs

1 Montreal, 2 September 1857, L. H. Holton to A. T. Galt, in Oscar Douglas Skelton, *The Life and Times of Sir Alexander Tilloch Galt* (Toronto: Oxford University Press, 1920), 229.

2 Montreal, 14 November 1857, L. H. Holton to A. T. Galt, in ibid., 229.

3 Montreal, 22 November 1857, L. H. Holton to A. T. Galt, in ibid., 229.

4 *Canadian News*, 11 November 1857.

5 *New Era* (Montreal), 8 December 1857.

6 *Montreal Gazette*, 19 December 1857.

7 *Montreal Herald*, 12 December 1857.

8 *Le Pays*, 7 December 1857.

9 A. Coffey Collection, Montreal, George E. Clerk Diary, 12 December 1857.

10 *Montreal Gazette*, 26 December 1857; *La Minerve*, 28 December 1857.

11 *Montreal Herald*, 26 December 1857.

12 *Le Pays*, 31 December 1857.

13 *Montreal Gazette*, 2 January 1858.

14 *Montreal Argus*, 23 December 1857.

15 J.M.S. Careless, *Brown of the Globe, Vol. One, The Voice of Upper Canada, 1818-1859* (Toronto: Macmillan of Canada, 1959), 165.

16 *Montreal Gazette*, 27 February 1856.

17 NAC, Brown Papers, Montreal, 22 January 1858, L. H. Holton to G. Brown.

18 Ibid.

19 RGDC, Montreal, vol. 5, 242.

20 Brown Papers, Montreal, 29 January 1858, L. H. Holton to G. Brown.

21 Queen's University Archives, Alexander Mackenzie Papers, Toronto, 29 January 1858, G. Brown to L. H. Holton.

22 Brown Papers, Montreal, 2 February 1858, L. H. Holton to G. Brown.

23 Registry Office, Brockville, Deed of Transfer, 11 December 1857, from Anner Stafford to Cleveland P. Stafford.

24 *New Era*, 8 December 1857.

25 Brown Papers, Toronto, 31 July 1858, E. Head to G. Brown.

26 *Leader*, 30 July 1858.

27 George E. Clerk Diary, 30 July 1858; *Montreal Gazette*, 7 August 1858.

28 Careless, *Brown of the Globe, Vol. One, 1818-1859*, 266-267.

29 *Globe*, 9 August 1858.

30 NAC, CO42, vol. 614, Memorandum for the consideration of His Excellency the Governor-General, August 3, 1858, by Brown-Dorion Ministry, in Toronto, 9 August 1858, E. Head to E. B. Lytton.

31 Careless, *Brown of the Globe, Vol. One, 1818-1859*, 272-273; *Le Pays*, 5 August 1858.

32 CO42, vol. 614, Toronto, 9 August 1858, E. Head to E. B. Lytton.

33 Careless, *Brown of the Globe, Vol. One, 1818-1859*, 276-278.

34 *Montreal Herald*, 14 August 1858; *Le Pays*, 12 August 1858.

35 Brown Papers, Montreal, 2 September 1858, L. H. Holton to G. Brown.

36 *Le Pays*, 4 September 1858.

37 Brown Papers, Montreal, 17 September 1858, A. A. Dorion to G. Brown.

38 Brown Papers, Brockville, 20 August 1858, J. Morris to G. Brown.

39 Brown Papers, Montreal, 17 September 1858, A. A. Dorion to G. Brown.

40 *Globe*, 25 September 1858.

41 *Globe*, 27 September, 4 October 1858; *Montreal Herald*, 23 October 1858.

42 W. L. Morton, *The Kingdom of Canada: A General History From Earliest Times* (Toronto: McClelland & Stewart, 1969), 309-310; Donald Creighton, *John A. Macdonald: The Young Politician* (Toronto: Macmillan of Canada, 1956), 275-279.

43 Brown Papers, Montreal, 26 October 1858, L. H. Holton to G. Brown.

44 CO42, vol. 614, London, 10 September 1858, E. B. Lytton to E. W. Head.

45 Brown Papers, Montreal, 23 November 1858, L. H. Holton to G. Brown.

46 *Globe*, 11 May 1859.

47 Mackenzie Papers, Toronto, 8 July 1858, G. Brown to L. H. Holton.

48 Brown Papers, Montreal, 10 July 1859, L. H. Holton to G. Brown.

49 Ibid.

50 Ibid.

51 Brown Papers, Montreal, 17 September 1859, L. H. Holton to G. Brown.

52 Brown Papers, Montreal, 28 September 1859, L. H. Holton to G. Brown.

53 Brown Papers, Montreal, 7 October 1859, L. H. Holton to G. Brown.

54 Brown Papers, Montreal, 14 October 1859, L. H. Holton to G. Brown; Yvan Lamonde, *Louis-Antoine Dessaulles: Un seigneur libéral et anticlérical* (Montreal: Fides, 1994), 112-114.

55 Brown Papers, Montreal, 20 October 1859, L. H. Holton to G. Brown.

56 *Pilot*, 26 October 1859.

57 Brown Papers, Montreal, 20 October 1859, L. H. Holton to G. Brown.

58 Brown Papers, Montreal, 28 October 1859, L. H. Holton to G. Brown.

59 *Montreal Herald*, 5 November 1859; *Le Pays*, 29 October 1859; *Montreal Gazette*, 5 November 1859; *Pilot*, 29 October 1859; *Morning Chronicle*, 5 November 1859; *Globe*, 31 October 1859.

60 *Montreal Transcript*, 29 October 1859.

61 Brown Papers, Montreal, 28 October 1859, L. H. Holton to G. Brown.

62 *Montreal Herald*, 5 November 1859.

63 *Le Pays*, 10 November 1859.

64 *Montreal Transcript*, 29 October 1859.

65 *Pilot*, 10 November 1859.

66 Brown Papers, Montreal, 16 November 1859, L. H. Holton to G. Brown.

67 *Pilot*, 26 November 1859; Brown Papers, Montreal, 22 November 1859, L. H. Holton to G. Brown.

68 Brown Papers, Montreal, 30
November 1859, L. H. Holton to
G. Brown.
69 J.M.S. Careless, *Brown of the
Globe, Vol. Two, Statesman of
Confederation, 1860-1880*
(Toronto: Macmillan of Canada,
1963), 6-7, 27-29; Montreal, 14
August 1860, L. H. Holton to G.
Brown, in *Globe*, 16 August 1860.
70 Brown Papers, Montreal, 16 March
1861, L. H. Holton to G. Brown.
71 Brown Papers, Montreal, 4 June
1861, L. H. Holton to G. Brown;
Montreal Herald, 13, 22, 25 June
1861; *Le Pays*, 26 June 1861;
Montreal Gazette, 27 June 1861.
72 Brown Papers, Montreal, 6 July
1861, L. H. Holton to G. Brown.
73 Brown Papers, Montreal, July
1861, A. A. Dorion to G. Brown.
74 Brown Papers, Montreal, 12 July
1861, L. H. Holton to G. Brown.
75 Brown Papers, Montreal, 6 June
1862, L. H. Holton to G. Brown;
Montreal Transcript, 6,21 June
1862.
76 Letter, Cincinnati, 31 August 1967,
John Mullane to the author.
77 *Montreal Transcript*, 5 December
1859; *Pilot*, 5 December 1859.
78 *Montreal Transcript*, 5 December
1859.
79 Robin W. Winks, *The Blacks in
Canada: A History Second Edition*
(Montreal: McGill-Queen's
University Press, 1997), 174-177.
80 *Montreal Transcript*, 10, 19
January 1861.
81 Robin W. Winks, *Canada and the
United States: The Civil War Years*
(Montreal: Harvest House, 1971),
148.
82 NAC, Galt Papers, Montreal, 23
April 1861, L. H. Holton to A. T.
Galt.
83 Brown Papers, Montreal, 24
February 1862, L. H. Holton to
G. Brown.
84 Ibid.

85 Ibid.
86 Galt Papers, Montreal, 4 February
1862, L. H. Holton to A. T. Galt.
87 *Montreal Herald*, 2 August 1862;
Montreal Gazette, 13 August 1862.
88 *Montreal Gazette*, 13 August 1862.
89 *Montreal Gazette*, 12 September
1862.
90 NAC, RG14, C1, vol. 182,
legislative council, immigration
committee, 23 February 1863.
91 RG14, C1, vol. 182, legislative
council, immigration committee,
25 April 1863.
92 Brown Papers, Quebec City, 19
February 1863, L. H. Holton to G.
Brown.
93 Careless, *Brown of the Globe, Vol.
Two, Statesman of Confederation,
1860-1880*, 91-92.
94 CO42, vol. 638, Quebec City, 25
July 1863, Monck to Newcastle.
95 *Montreal Gazette*, 26 August 1863.

Chapter 6
Minister of Finance

1 Bruce W. Hodgins, *John Sandfield
Macdonald 1812-1872* (Toronto:
University of Toronto Press, 1971),
66-67.
2 NAC, Brown Papers, Quebec City,
11 May 1863, George Brown to
Gordon Brown.
3 *Montreal Herald*, 25 August 1863.
4 Ibid.
5 NAC, CO42, vol. 637, Quebec
City, 16 May 1863, Monck to
Newcastle.
6 *Montreal Herald*, 21 May 1863; *Le
Pays*, 19, 21 May 1863.
7 *Montreal Gazette*, 2 June 1863.
8 *La Minerve*, 31 May 1863.
9 NAC, MG24, D16, vol. 19,
Buchanan Papers, Montreal, 19
May 1863, Alexander Campbell to
Isaac Buchanan.
10 *Montreal Gazette*, 24 June 1863.

11 Wendy Cameron, "John Langton," *Dictionary of Canadian Biography, XII, 1891-1900* (Toronto: University of Toronto Press, 1990), 527-529.

12 *Montreal Gazette*, 21 December 1863.

13 Brown Papers, Montreal, 1 November 1863, L. H. Holton to G. Brown; Peter Baskerville, "Imperial Agendas and 'Disloyal' Collaborators: Decolonization and the John Sandfield Ministries, 1862-1864," in David Keane & Colin Read, eds., *Old Ontario: Essays in Honour of J.M.S. Careless* (Toronto: Dundurn Press, 1990), 246-249; A. A. den Otter, *The Philosophy of Railways: The Transcontinental Railway Idea in British North America* (Toronto: University of Toronto Press, 1997), 101-125.

14 NAC, RG1, Canada, State Books, L1, vol. Y, 12 August 1863; *Sessional Papers* (1864), no. 1, Report of the Postmaster General for the year 1863, 67; *Montreal Herald*, 27 August 1863; *Globe*, 17 August 1863; A. Margaret Evans, *Sir Oliver Mowat* (Toronto: University of Toronto Press, 1992), 47-48.

15 *Sessional Papers* (1866), no. 40, Copies of correspondence between the Minister of Finance and the Provincial Agents in England in Reference to the Surrender of the Grand Trunk Railway Bonds, Manchester, 31 December 1863, E. W. Watkin to L. H. Holton; Quebec City, 21 January 1864, L. H. Holton to E. W. Watkin.

16 *Sessional Papers* (1864), no. 2, Public Accounts for the Year 1863, 5.

17 Douglas McCalla, "Railways and the Development of Canada West, 1850-1870," in Allan Greer and Ian Radforth, eds., *Colonial Leviathan State Formation in Mid-Nineteenth-Century Canada* (Toronto: University of Toronto Press, 1992), 192.

18 Canada, State Books, L1, vol. Y, 18 May 1863.

19 Canada, State Books, L1, vol. Z, 10 September 1863.

20 Graham D. Taylor and Peter A. Baskerville, *A Concise History of Business in Canada* (Toronto: Oxford University Press, 1994), 240-242; A. A. den Otter, "Alexander Galt, the 1859 Tariff and Canadian Economic Nationalism," *Canadian Historical Review* 63 (June 1982), 151-178.

21 Canada, State Books, L1, vol. Z, 31 October 1863.

22 *Montreal Herald*, 27 August 1863.

23 *Globe*, 14, 18 August 1863.

24 Brown Papers, Montreal, 24 February 1863, L. H. Holton to G. Brown.

25 AO, John Sandfield Macdonald Papers, Toronto, 25 January 1864, G. Brown to J. S. Macdonald.

26 *Globe*, 2 September 1863.

27 *Statutes of Canada*, 27 Victoria, Cap. 2 (1863); Cap.3 (1863); *Globe*, 10 September 1863.

28 *Sessional Papers* (1864), no. 2, Public Accounts for the year 1863, iv.

29 *Montreal Herald*, 30 December 1863; Robin Winks, *Canada and the United States: The Civil War Years* (Montreal: Harvest House, 1971), 119.

30 *Montreal Gazette*, 8 September 1863.

31 *Globe*, 19 September 1863.

32 *Montreal Gazette*, 21 September 1863.

33 *Montreal Herald*, 19 September 1863.

34 *Economist*, 10 October 1863; *Times*, quoted in the *Canadian News*, 8 October 1863.

35 Michael J. Piva, *The Borrowing Process: Public Finance in the Province of Canada 1840-1867* (Ottawa: University of Ottawa Press, 1992), 224-228.

36 *Montreal Herald*, 18 September 1863.

37 *Parliamentary Debates*, 8 October 1863; *La Minerve*, 10 October 1863.

38 *Montreal Herald*, 18 September 1863; Travis L. Crosby, *Sir Robert Peel's Administration, 1841-1846* (Hamden, Conn.: Archon Books, 1976), 45-78.

39 *Sessional Papers* (1864), no. 2, Public Accounts for the year 1863, iii.

40 *Montreal Herald*, 18 September 1863.

41 *Toronto Globe*, 19 September 1863.

42 *Montreal Herald*, 6 June 1863.

43 *Montreal Herald*, 6 June 1863.

44 *Montreal Gazette*, 20, 21 May 1863.

45 Canada, State Books, L1, vol. Z, 31 October 1863.

46 *Sessional Papers* (1864), no. 3, Tables of the Trade and Navigation of Canada for the year 1863, 14-16; John P. Heisler, *The Canals of Canada* (Ottawa: National Historic Sites Service, 1973), 116-117.

47 *Montreal Herald*, 2 December 1863, Montreal, 1 December 1863, A Merchant and Forwarder to the editor of the *Montreal Herald*.

48 *Sessional Papers* (1864), no. 3, Tables of Trade and Navigation of Canada for the year 1863, 14-16.

49 *Montreal Herald*, 18 September 1863.

50 *Sessional Papers* (1864), no. 2, Public Accounts for the year 1863, 2.

51 *Sessional Papers* (1864), no. 21, Copies of Papers Relative to the Transfer of the Provincial Ac-

counts from the Bank of Upper Canada to the Bank of Montreal, Quebec, 21 November 1863, L. H. Holton to E. H. King.

52 Brown Papers, Montreal, 22 October 1863, L. H. Holton to G. Brown.

53 *JLA*, 1854-1855, no. 9, Appendix EE, Report of Select Committee on the Subject of Public Deposits.

54 Brown Papers, Montreal, 17 December 1863, L. H. Holton to G. Brown; *Le Pays*, 10 November 1863.

55 Canada, State Books, L1, vol. Z, 19 November 1863.

56 NAC, RG19, A1, Finance Minister, Letterbook, vol. 38, London, 27 November 1863, Baring Brothers and Glyn, Mills to L. H. Holton.

57 Finance Minister, Letterbook, vol. 38, London, 17 December 1863, Baring Brothers and Glyn, Mills to L. H. Holton.

58 NAC, Glyn, Mills & Co. Papers, reel A-541, Quebec, 29 May 1863, L. H. Holton to Glyn, Mills and Baring Brothers; Finance Minister, Letterbook, vol. 38, London, 18 June 1863, Baring Brothers and Glyn, Mills to L. H. Holton.

59 Glyn, Mills & Co. Papers, reel A-541, Quebec, 24 July 1863, L. H. Holton to Glyn, Mills and Baring Brothers.

60 *Montreal Herald*, 18 September 1863.

61 J. M. S. Careless, *Brown of the Globe, Vol. Two: Statesman of Confederation, 1860-1880* (Toronto: MacMillan of Canada, 1963), 113-114.

62 Brown Papers, Quebec, 22 October 1863, L. H. Holton to G. Brown.

63 Brown Papers, Quebec, 1 November 1863, L. H. Holton to G. Brown.

64 Brown Papers, Quebec, 6 December 1863, L. H. Holton to G. Brown.

65 Queen's University Archives, Alexander Mackenzie Papers, Toronto, 23 October 1863, G. Brown to L. H. Holton; *Globe*, 12 November 1863.

66 Brown Papers, Montreal, 1 November 1863, L. H. Holton to G. Brown; Peter Baskerville, ed., *The Bank of Upper Canada: A Collection of Documents. Edited with an Introduction by Peter Baskerville* (Toronto: The Champlain Society, 1987), cxliii-cxliv.

67 *Sessional Papers* (1864), no. 21, Copies of Papers Relative to the Transfer of the Provincial Accounts from the Bank of Upper Canada to the Bank of Montreal, Quebec, 11 December 1863, L. H. Holton to R. Cassels; Glyn, Mills & Co. Papers, reel C-1549, Montreal, 11 November 1863, L. H. Holton to Glyn, Mills and Baring Brothers.

68 *Sessional Papers* (1864), no. 2, Public Accounts for the year 1863, iv.

69 *Montreal Herald*, 25 September 1863.

70 *Globe*, 9 June 1864; Morris Zaslow, *Reading the Rocks: The Story of the Geological Survey of Canada, 1842-1972* (Ottawa: Macmillan of Canada, 1975), 79-85.

71 *The Montreal Pocket Almanac and General Register for 1852*, 77; *Montreal Argus*, 27 June 1857.

72 Suzanne Zeller, *Inventing Canada: Early Victorian Science and the Idea of a Transcontinental Nation* (Toronto: University of Toronto Press, 1987), 49.

73 *Parliamentary Debates*, 23 September 1863.

74 Robin W. Winks, *Canada and the United States: The Civil War Years* (Montreal: Harvest House, 1971), 342-343. L. H. Officer and L. B. Smith, "The Canadian-American Reciprocity Treaty of 1855-66," *Journal of Economic History* 28 (December 1968), 596-623, challenge the view that Canada received great benefit from the Reciprocity Treaty of 1854.

75 CO42, vol. 640, Montreal, 8 March 1864, John Young to L. H. Holton; National Archives, Washington, D.C., T-222, Despatches from United States Consuls in Montreal, roll 1, Montreal, 25 September 1857, W. B. S. Moor to L. Cass.

76 National Archives, Washington, D.C., T-222, Despatches from United States Consuls in Montreal, roll 4, Toronto, 26 November 1863, D. Thurston to W. H. Seward; Toronto, 4 November 1863, R. Spence to G. T. Abbott.

77 AO, J. S. Macdonald Papers, Quebec, 21 January 1864, J. S. Macdonald to G. Brown; Brown Papers, Montreal, 24 January 1864, L. H. Holton to G. Brown.

78 J.S. Macdonald Papers, Toronto, 25 January 1864, G. Brown to J. S. Macdonald.

79 Finance Minister, Letterbook, telegram, Quebec, 3 February 1864, L. H. Holton to J. Young.

80 CO42, vol. 640, Montreal, 8 March 1864, J. Young to L. H. Holton.

81 Canada, State Books, L1, vol. Z, 19 February 1864.

82 Cited in Elizabeth Batt, *Monck Governor General 1861-1868: A Biography* (Toronto: McClelland & Stewart, 1976), 89.

83 CO42, vol. 640, Quebec, 15 March 1864, Monck to Newcastle.

84 *Parliamentary Debates*, 25 February 1864.

85 NAC, pamphlet, Arthur Harvey, *First Prize Essay The Reciprocity Treaty: Its Advantages to the United States and Canada* (Quebec: Hunter Rose & Co., 1865).

86 Brown Papers, Quebec, 21 November 1863, L. H. Holton to G. Brown.

87 *Sessional Papers* (1864), no. 2, Public Accounts for the year 1863, iii; Brown Papers, Quebec, 21 November 1863, L. H. Holton to G. Brown.

88 Brown Papers, Montreal, 24 January 1864, L. H. Holton to G. Brown; Peter Baskerville, "Imperial Agendas and 'Disloyal' Collaborators: Decolonization and the John Sandfield Macdonald Ministries, 1862-1864," in David Keane and Colin Read, eds., *Old Ontario: Essays in Honour of J.M.S. Careless* (Toronto: Dundurn Press, 1990), 249; Hodgins, *John Sandfield Macdonald*, 73; J.E. Hodgetts, *Pioneer Public Service: An Administrative History of the United Canadas, 1841-1867* (Toronto: University of Toronto Press, 1955), 106-107.

89 Brown Papers, Montreal, 24 January 1864, L. H. Holton to G. Brown; *Globe*, 30 January 1864.

90 Brown Papers, Montreal, 3 April 1864, L. H. Holton to G. Brown.

91 Radcliffe College Archives, Eliza J. Holton Flint, "School Days," in *Seaview Gazette*, Belleville, Ontario, February 1894, 15-18.

92 Brown Papers, 24 January 1864, L. H. Holton to G. Brown.

93 Brown Papers, 6 December 1863, L. H. Holton to G. Brown.

94 NAC, Baring Papers, Quebec City, 20 March 1864, John Rose to Thomas Baring; *Le Pays*, 5 April 1864.

95 *Montreal Herald*, 22 March 1864.

96 Brown Papers, Montreal, 3 April 1864, L. H. Holton to G. Brown.

97 CO42, vol. 640, Quebec City, 31 March 1864, Monck to Newcastle.

98 *Globe*, 1 April 1864.

99 Ibid.

100 Ibid.

Chapter 7
Continuing Challenge of Politics

1 NAC, Brown Papers, Montreal, 21 April 1864, L. H. Holton to G. Brown.

2 *Globe*, 14 May 1864.

3 *JLA*, vol. 23, 14 June 1864.

4 *Globe*, 14 July 1864.

5 *Globe*, 23 June 1864; *Le Pays*, 23 June 1864.

6 *Globe*, 23 June 1864; *Montreal Herald*, 27 June 1864; *Le Pays*, 27 June 1864; *Montreal Gazette*, 24 June 1864.

7 *Canadian Gleaner*, 1 July 1864.

8 *Canadian Gleaner*, 23 September 1864.

9 Brown Papers, Toronto, 1 October 1864, G. Brown to Anne Brown.

10 Brown Papers, Toronto, 31 October 1864, G. Brown to Anne Brown.

11 *Parliamentary Debates on the Subject of the Confederation of the British North American Provinces* (Quebec, 1865) (hereafter *Canadian Confederation Debates*), 15; *Le Pays*, 16 February 1865.

12 *Canadian Confederation Debates*, 705; *Le Pays*, 9 March 1865; *La Minerve*, 9 March 1865.

13 Brown Papers, Quebec City, 4 February 1865, G. Brown to Anne Brown; Quebec City, 27 February 1865, same to same; Quebec City, 10 March 1865, same to same; NAC, John A. Macdonald Papers, St. John, 13 February 1865, S. L. Tilley to J. A. Macdonald; Quebec

City, 20 February 1865, J. A. Macdonald to S. L. Tilley; *Montreal Gazette*, 9 March 1865.

14 Brown Papers, Quebec City, 17 March 1865, G. Brown to Anne Brown; Ottawa, 26 June 1866, same to same.

15 Brown Papers, Montreal, 19 January 1867, L. H. Holton to G. Brown.

16 Brown Papers, Montreal, 1 May 1867, L. H. Holton to G. Brown.

17 *Montreal Herald*, 26 March 1867.

18 Brown Papers, Montreal, 5 May 1867, L. H. Holton to G. Brown.

19 Brown Papers, Montreal, 1 May1867, L. H. Holton to G. Brown.

20 Brown Papers, Montreal, 16 May 1867, L. H. Holton to G. Brown; *Le Pays*, 1, 4 June 1867.

21 *Montreal Herald*, 3 July 1867.

22 *Montreal Herald*, 2, 3 July 1867.

23 Brown Papers, Montreal, 2 July 1867, L. H. Holton to G. Brown.

24 *Canadian Gleaner*, 5 July 1867.

25 Brown Papers, Montreal, 1 May 1867, L. H. Holton to G. Brown; Montreal, 31 May 1867, same to same.

26 Brown Papers, Montreal, 16 May 1867, L. H. Holton to G. Brown.

27 *Canadian Gleaner*, 5 July, 30 August 1867.

28 *Canadian Gleaner*, 26 July 1867.

29 *Canadian Gleaner*, 30 August 1867.

30 Brown Papers, Montreal, 28 August 1867, L. H. Holton to G. Brown.

31 *Ottawa Times*, 6 November 1867.

32 *Montreal Gazette*, 19 December 1867; *Globe*, 7 November 1867.

33 Canada, *House of Commons Debates*, p. 245, 11 December 1867.

34 *House of Commons Debates*, p. 245, 11 December 1867.

35 *House of Commons Debates*, p. 296, 16 December 1867.

36 *House of Commons Debates*, pp. 586-587, 29 April 1868.

37 *Montreal Herald*, 6, 26 July 1870; *Le Pays*, 29 July 1870; *Montreal Gazette*, 9 July 1870.

38 *Montreal Herald*, 15, 16, 24 June 1871, *Montreal Herald*, 17 January1874; *Montreal Gazette*, 16 June 1871; *Morning Chronicle*, 13 January 1874; Marcel Hamelin, *Les Premières Années du Parlementairisme Québécois 1867-1878* (Québec: Les Presses de l'Université Laval, 1974), 131.

39 *Morning Chronicle*, 14 December 1872; Brian J. Young, *Promoters and Politicians: The North-Shore Railways in the History of Quebec 1854-85* (Toronto: University of Toronto Press, 1978), 23-53.

40 McCord Museum of Canadian History, J. S. Sanborn Papers, Quebec City, 10 December 1871, L. H. Holton to J. S. Sanborn.

41 Quebec, *Legislative Assembly Debates*, p. 63, 16 December 1873.

42 *Montreal Gazette*, 16 May 1872.

43 Queen's University Archives, Richard J. Cartwright Papers, Ottawa, 15 May 1872, L. H. Holton to R. J. Cartwright.

44 *Montreal Gazette*, 16 May 1872.

45 Ibid.

46 *Montreal Herald*, 4 July 1872.

47 *Montreal Herald*, 18 July 1872.

48 *Canadian Gleaner*, 29 August 1872.

49 *Canadian Gleaner*, 5 September 1872.

50 *Montreal Herald*, 3 September 1872.

51 Brown Papers, Ottawa, 7 March 1873, A. Mackenzie to G. Brown.

52 Ibid.

53 *Montreal Herald*, 4, 18 July 1873; Dale C. Thomson, *Alexander Mackenzie: Clear Grit* (Toronto: Macmillan of Canada, 1960), 154.

54 *Montreal Herald*, 6 August 1873.
55 *Montreal Gazette*, 6 August 1873; OA, Blake Papers, Montreal, 26 June 1873, Montreal, L. H. Holton to E. Blake.
56 *Ottawa Citizen*, 13 August 1873; *Montreal Gazette*, 14 August 1873.
57 *Montreal Gazette*, 14 August 1873.
58 *Montreal Herald*, 14 August 1873; *Ottawa Citizen*, 14 August 1873.
59 Canada, *Parliamentary Debates*, 7 November 1873.
60 *Montreal Herald*, 24, 25 December 1873.
61 Brown Papers, Ottawa, 5 November 1873, A. Mackenzie to G. Brown; Ottawa, 13 November 1873, same to same.
62 *Canadian Gleaner*, 22 January 1874.
63 *Canadian Gleaner*, 5 February 1874.
64 *Montreal Herald*, 19 January 1874; *Montreal Star*, 12, 19 January 1874; *Montreal Gazette*, 12 January 1874.
65 Queen's University Archives, Mackenzie Papers, Montreal, 21 February 1874, L. H. Holton to A. Mackenzie.
66 Canada, *Journals of the House of Commons*, p. 279, 19 May 1874; p. 292, 20 May 1874; Canada, *Parliamentary Debates*, 20 May 1874.
67 *House of Commons Debates*, p. 529, 5 March 1875.
68 Canada, *Sessional Papers* (1879), No. 1, Public Accounts of Canada for the year ending 30 June 1878, pp. xvi-xvii.
69 *Sessional Papers* (1879), No. 8, Report of the minister of public works for the year ending 30 June 1878, pp. 6-7.
70 J. M. S. Careless, *Brown of the Globe, Vol. Two, Statesman of Confederation, 1860-1880* (Toronto: Macmillan of Canada, 1963), 312-324.
71 Blake Papers, Montreal, 14 June 1874, L. H. Holton to E. Blake.
72 *Montreal Herald*, 5 December 1874.
73 Ben Forster, *A Conjunction of Interests: Business, Politics, and Tariffs, 1825-1879* (Toronto: University of Toronto Press, 1986), 131.
74 C.W. de Kiewiet and F.H. Underhill, eds., *Dufferin-Carnarvon Correspondence, 1874-1878* (Toronto: The Champlain Society, 1955), 115-116, Ottawa, 8 December 1874, Dufferin to Carnarvon.
75 *Parliamentary Debates*, 30 April 1874.
76 Mackenzie Papers, Montreal, 24 April 1875, L. H. Holton to A. Mackenzie.
77 Ibid.
78 *Montreal Herald*, 14 October 1875.
79 *Montreal Herald*, 1 November 1875.
80 Peter B. Waite, *Canada 1874-1896 Arduous Destiny* (Toronto: McClelland and Stewart, 1971), 78; Forster, *A Conjunction of Interests*, 141.
81 Waite, *Canada*, 78-79.
82 *House of Commons Debates*, p. 903, 8 March 1878.
83 *Parliamentary Debates*, 15 April 1874.
84 *Montreal Herald*, 10 December 1874.
85 Mackenzie Papers, Montreal, 27 January 1875, L. H. Holton to A. Mackenzie.
86 *House of Commons Journals*, p. 70, 11 February 1875.
87 *House of Commons Journals*, pp. 77-78, 12 February 1875.
88 *Globe*, 31 December 1875.
89 Mackenzie Papers, Montreal, 28 January 1876, L. H. Holton to A. Mackenzie.

90 *House of Commons Debates*, p. 48, 14 February 1876.
91 Mackenzie Papers, Montreal, 17 October 1875, L. H. Holton to A. Mackenzie.
92 NAC, Alexander Mackenzie letterbook, Ottawa, 27 January 1876, A. Mackenzie to L. H. Holton.
93 Mackenzie Papers, Ottawa, 22 January 1876, A. Mackenzie to G. Brown.
94 Mackenzie Papers, Montreal, 17 October 1875, L. H. Holton to A. Mackenzie.
95 Mackenzie Papers, Montreal, 24 November 1877, L. H. Holton to A. Mackenzie; Mackenzie letterbook, Ottawa, 3 December 1877, A. Mackenzie to L.H. Holton.
96 *Montreal Gazette*, 6 December 1877; *Montreal Star*, 5 December 1877; *Montreal Witness*, 5 December 1877.
97 *Halifax Morning Chronicle*, 13 September 1878.
98 *News* (Kingston), 8 August 1878.
99 *Montreal Star*, 30 August 1878.
100 *Montreal Witness*, 27, 30 August 1878.
101 *Montreal Witness*, 30 August 1878.
102 *Montreal Witness*, 5, 6 September 1878.
103 *Montreal Witness*, 23 August 1878.
104 Mackenzie Papers, Montreal, 11 August 1878, L. H. Holton to A. Mackenzie.
105 *Canadian Gleaner*, 12 September 1878.
106 *Canadian Gleaner*, 19 September 1878.
107 *Montreal Witness*, 18 September 1878.
108 *Montreal Witness*, 18 September 1878; *Montreal Herald*, 23 September 1878; *Montreal Gazette*, 26 September, 5 October 1878.
109 Mackenzie Papers, Montreal, 1 February 1879, L. H. Holton to A. Mackenzie.

Chapter 8
Financing the
Canada Engine Works

1 Larry S. McNally, "Montreal Engine Foundries and their Contribution to Central Canadian Technical Development, 1820-1870," M.A. thesis, Carleton University, 1991, 152-153.
2 ANQM, I. J. Gibb, 6901, inventory of the estate of Moses Haskell Gilbert, 9 August 1843.
3 "E. E. Gilbert," *Transactions of the Canadian Society of Civil Engineers* 3 (1889), 364-365.
4 NAC, RG11, A1, vol. 62, Board of Public Works Correspondence, Montreal, 16 October 1849, E. E. Gilbert to commissioners of public works; Gerald J. J. Tulchinsky, *The River Barons Montreal Businessmen and the Growth of Industry and Transportation, 1837-53* (Toronto: University of Toronto Press, 1977), 220-223; Brian Young, *In its Corporate Capacity: The Seminary of Montreal as a Business Institution, 1816-1876* (Montreal: McGill-Queen's University Press, 1986), 132-133.
5 *Montreal in 1856: A Sketch prepared for the Celebration of the Opening of the Grand Trunk Railway of Canada* (Montreal: John Lovell, 1856), 43.
6 ANQM, J. H. Isaacson, 1592, contract and agreement between Gilbert & Bartley and George Smith, 19 December 1850.
7 Information on this sale is contained in ANQM, J. H. Isaacson, 1849, dissolution of copartnership of Gilbert & Bartley, 2 July 1851.
8 RGDC, Montreal, vol. 5, 181.

9 ANQM, I. J. Gibb, 14345, contract and agreement between E. E. Gilbert and H. Jones & Co., 10 December 1852; 14437, contract and agreement between E. E. Gilbert and the Montreal and New York Railroad Company, 19 January 1853.

10 ANQM, I. J. Gibb, 14606, declaration and protest, E. E. Gilbert against H. Jones & Co., 6 April 1853.

11 ANQM, J. H. Isaacson, 2785, protest, E. E. Gilbert against the Montreal and New York Railroad Company, 22 July 1853.

12 ANQM, W. Easton, 4849, demand and protest, E. E. Gilbert against Louis A. Sénécal, 19 August 1853.

13 ANQM, J. H. Isaacson, 2662, apprenticeship contract between John Young (for the estate of the late James Inglis, father of William Inglis) and E. E. Gilbert, 21 April 1853. For John Young's involvement in Lachine Canal development, see Tulchinsky, *The River Barons*, 225-226; Young, *In Its Corporate Capacity*, 133-141.

14 ANQM, I. J. Gibb, 14977, articles of copartnership between E. E. Gilbert and D. J. Macfarlane, 4 October 1853.

15 ANQM, I. J. Gibb, 15962, protest, City Bank against E. E. Gilbert, 22 November 1854; 15962, promissory note, E. E. Gilbert on L. H. Holton, 19 August 1854.

16 ANQM, W. A. Phillips, 851, protest, City Bank against E. E. Gilbert, 5 December 1854; 851, promissory note, E. E. Gilbert on L. H. Holton, 2 September 1854.

17 RGDC, Montreal, vol. 5, 181.

18 ANQM, J. S. Hunter, 2788, obligation and mortgage from E. E. Gilbert to L. H. Holton, 15 October 1857.

19 ANQM, W. A. Phillips, 1200, assignment and transfer in trust, E.

E. Gilbert to L. H. Holton, A. Campbell, and T. Workman, 16 May 1855.

20 ANQM, W. A. Phillips, 1200, assignment and transfer in trust, E. E. Gilbert to L. H. Holton, A. Campbell, and T. Workman, 16 May 1855; Douglas McCalla, *The Upper Canada Trade, 1834-1872: A Study of the Buchanans' Business* (Toronto: University of Toronto Press, 1979), 83-84.

21 ANQM, T. B. Doucet, 6421, contract between E. E. Gilbert and Brown, Hibbard, Bourne & Co., 11 November 1853.

22 ANQM, J. H. Isaacson, 3291, contract between E. E. Gilbert and G. & A. Davie, 7 September 1854; W. M. Easton, 5291, contract and agreement between E. E. Gilbert and George Bryson, 16 January 1855.

23 ANQM, W. A. Phillips, 1200, assignment and transfer in trust, E. E. Gilbert to L. H. Holton, A. Campbell, and T. Workman, 16 May 1855.

24 ANQM, W. A. Phillips, 1200, assignment and transfer in trust, E. E. Gilbert to L. H. Holton, A. Campbell, and T. Workman, 16 May 1855.

25 ANQM, W. A. Phillips, 1200, assignment and transfer in trust, E. E. Gilbert to L. H. Holton, A. Campbell, and T. Workman.

26 ANQM, W. A. Philips, 1200, assignment and transfer in trust, E. E. Gilbert to L. H. Holton, A. Campbell, and T. Workman, 16 May 1855.

27 ANQM, I. J. Gibb, 16858, cancellation of deed of assignment by E. E. Gilbert to L. H. Holton, A. Campbell, and T. Workman, 31 October 1855.

28 ANQM, W. A. Phillips, 1200, assignment and transfer in trust, E. E. Gilbert to L. H. Holton, A.

Campbell, and T. Workman, 16 May 1855.

29 *Montreal in 1856*, 43.

30 *Montreal in 1856*, 43.

31 ANQM, I. J. Gibb, 16865, transfer of judgement from E. E. Gilbert to L. H. Holton, 30 November 1855.

32 ANQM, I. J. Gibb, 17166, signification, L. H. Holton to the Montreal and New York Railroad Company, 23 May 1856.

33 RGDC, Montreal, vol. 5, 181.

34 RGDC, Montreal, vol. 5, 181.

35 *Canada Directory for 1857-58*, 1211.

36 ANQM, J. S. Hunter, 2738, contract and agreement between E. E. Gilbert and Henry B. Wales, 19 September 1857.

37 *Canada Directory for 1857-58*, 1211.

38 On the financial crisis of 1857, see Douglas McCalla, *The Upper Canada Trade*, 96-100; Douglas McCalla, *Planting the Province The Economic History of Upper Canada 1784-1870* (Toronto: University of Toronto Press, 1993) 237-238; Michael Bliss, *Northern Enterprise Five Centuries of Canadian Business* (Toronto: McClelland and Stewart, 1987), 188-189.

39 ANQM, J. S. Hunter, 2788, obligation and mortgage from E. E. Gilbert to L. H. Holton, 15 October 1857.

40 ANQM, J. S. Hunter, 2789, sale of machinery, tools, implements, and engine at Beaver Foundry from E. E. Gilbert to L. H. Holton, 15 October 1857.

41 RGDC, Montreal, vol. 5, 46.

42 RGDC, Montreal, vol. 6, 110.

43 RGDC, Montreal, vol. 6, 231.

44 *Montreal Business Sketches* (Montreal: Canada Railway Advertising Company, 1864), 94.

45 John W. Oliver, *History of American Technology* (New York: Ronald Press Company, 1956), 273; Alan I. Marcus and Howard P. Segal, *Technology in America: A Brief History* (New York: Harcourt Brace Jovanovich, 1989), 137-138.

46 "E. E. Gilbert," *Transactions of the Canadian Society of Civil Engineers*, 365.

47 *List of Canadian Patents from the beginning of the Patent Office, June 1824, till the 1st of January 1869* (Ottawa, 1868), 47.

48 W. Inglis, "On Valves and Valve Gearing on Steam Engines," *Transactions of the Institute of Engineers in Scotland* 7 (1863-1864), 116-117; James L. Wood, "The Introduction of the Corliss Engine to Britain," *Transactions of the Newcomen Society*, 52 (1980-1981), 3-5.

49 "E. E. Gilbert," *Transactions of the Canadian Society of Civil Engineers*, 365; Larry S. McNally, "Montreal Engine Foundries and their Contribution to Central Canadian Technical Development, 1820-1870," M.A. thesis, Carleton University, 1991, 68-69.

50 RGDC, Montreal, vol. 6, 231.

51 ANQM, J. H. Isaacson, 13537, deed of sale, E. E. Gilbert to M. Holland & Son, 4 December 1863; 13605, declaration, L. H. Holton and M. Holland & Son, 4 January 1864.

52 *Montreal Business Sketches*, 94.

53 ANQM, I. J. Gibb, 19538, release and discharge from A. Cantin and E. E. Gilbert to General Cuban Steam Navigation Company, 6 December 1864.

54 ANQM, J. H. Isaacson, 15749, loan from L. H. Holton to E. E. Gilbert, 4 August 1865.

55 ANQM, J. S. Hunter, 15489, contract and agreement between E. E. Gilbert and the Canadian

Navigation Company, 16 December 1869.

56 NAC, Manuscript census of 1871, Montreal West, Schedule no. 6, Return of Industrial Establishments; *Lovell's Province of Ontario Directory for 1871*, 1095.

Chapter 9
Savings Banker

1 Laurentian Bank of Canada Archives, Montreal City and District Savings Bank Records, Minutes of the Board of Managing Directors Meeting (hereafter cited as Directors Meeting), 11 April 1846.
2 Laurentian Bank of Canada Archives, "Growth Through Cooperation," undated note on the history of the Laurentian Bank of Canada, 4.
3 *Montreal Herald*, 23 October 1872.
4 *Montreal Transcript*, 7 January 1841.
5 Unitarian Church Archives, Minute Book A, 7 August 1843, 25 December 1844, 29 December 1845.
6 *Montreal Herald*, 23 October 1872.
7 *Montreal Herald*, 23 October 1872; *A Few Words on the Savings Banks in Eastern and Western Canada, and Particularly on the Montreal City and District From its Establishment* (Montreal: John Lovell & Son, 1884), pamphlet, 4-5.
8 Directors Meeting, 11 April 1846.
9 *Montreal Transcript*, 23 May 1846; Montreal *Pilot*, 23 May 1846; *Statutes of the Province of Canada*, 4 & 5 Victoria, Cap. 32 (1841).
10 H. Oliver Horne, *A History of Savings Banks* (London: Oxford

University Press, 1947); Robert Sweeny, *A Guide to the History and Records of Selected Montreal Businesses before 1947* (Montreal: Centre de recherche en histoire économique du Canada français, 1978), 161-163; Peter Lester Payne and Lance Edwin Davis, *The Savings Bank of Baltimore, 1818-1866: A Historical and Analytical Study* (Baltimore: Johns Hopkins University Press, 1956).
11 *Pilot*, 23 May 1846; Brian Young, *In its Corporate Capacity: The Seminary of Montreal as a Business Institution, 1816-1876* (Montreal: McGill-Queen's University Press, 1986), 127; Edward P. Neufeld, *The Financial System of Canada: Its Growth and Development* (Toronto: Macmillan of Canada, 1972), 140-144.
12 *Pilot*, 13 April 1847;10 April 1852.
13 Directors Meeting, 14 April 1846.
14 *Montreal Directory for 1852*, 357; Young, *In its Corporate Capacity*, 127.
15 Directors Meeting, 14 April 1846.
16 Directors Meeting, 20 May 1846.
17 *Pilot*, 13 April 1847.
18 *Pilot*, 9 May 1848.
19 Directors Meeting, 3 April 1848.
20 *Pilot*, 6 April 1848, 4 April 1849.
21 *Pilot*, 4 April 1849.
22 Directors Meeting, 30 June 1848.
23 *Montreal Gazette*, 12 March 1849.
24 Directors Meeting, 17 March 1849.
25 Directors Meeting, 29 March 1849.
26 Directors Meeting, 2 July 1849.
27 Directors Meeting, 28 September 1849.
28 Directors Meeting, 6 October 1849.
29 Directors Meeting, 30 December 1850.
30 Directors Meeting, 31 March 1851.
31 ANQM, T. B. Doucet, 8055, acquittance, François Xavier Trudeau to the Montreal City and

District Savings Bank, 24 October 1854; T. B. Doucet, 4579, acquittance, John Orr and Christina Bower, widow of the late William Robert Orr to the Montreal City and District Savings Bank, 13 March 1852.

32 Directors Meeting, 15 July 1851.

33 Ronald Rudin, *Banking en français: The French Banks of Quebec, 1835-1925* (Toronto: University of Toronto Press, 1985), 28-29.

34 *Montreal Herald*, 23 October 1872.

35 Directors Meeting, 26 February 1856, 18 March 1856.

36 *Pilot*, 7 April 1859.

37 *Pilot*, 5 April 1860.

38 *JLA*, vol. 20, 28 April 1862, 2 May 1862, 13 May 1862, 30 May 1862, 6 June 1862, 9 June 1862; Canadian Library Association, *Parliamentary Debates*, 13 May 1862, 28 May 1862, 7 June 1862.

39 *Statutes of the Province of Canada*, 25 Victoria, Cap. 66 (1862).

40 Directors Meeting, 9 January 1865.

41 *Montreal Herald*, 5 April 1866.

42 Max Magill, "The Failure of the Commercial Bank," in Gerald Tulchinsky, ed., *To Preserve and Defend: Essays on Kingston in the Nineteenth Century* (Montreal: McGill-Queen's University Press, 1976), 169-181.

43 Directors Meeting, 2 March 1868.

44 *Montreal Herald*, 9 April 1868.

45 *Montreal Herald*, 8 April 1869.

46 *Montreal Herald*, 5 April 1871.

47 Directors Meeting, 4 April 1871.

48 *Montreal Herald*, 23 October 1872.

49 Ibid.

50 *Statutes of Canada*, 34 Victoria, Cap. 7 (1871); Neufeld, *The Financial System of Canada*, 153-154.

51 For an account of government savings banks, see Dan Bunbury,

"The Public Purse and State Finance: Government Savings Banks in the Era of Nation Building, 1867-1900," *The Canadian Historical Review* 78 (December 1997), 566-598.

52 Directors Meeting, 15 April 1871.

53 Directors Meeting, 17 April 1871.

54 *An Act Respecting Certain Savings Banks in the Provinces of Ontario and Quebec and the Charter of the Montreal City and District Savings Bank* (Montreal: John Lovell, 1871), pamphlet, 17-23.

55 Directors Meeting, 24 April 1871.

56 Directors Meeting, 24 April 1871.

57 Directors Meeting, 27 April 1871.

58 *Montreal Star*, 23 October 1872.

59 *Montreal Herald*, 10 May 1872.

60 Directors Meeting, 27 December 1871.

61 *Montreal Herald*, 5 April 1871; Montreal City and District Savings Bank Records, Minutes of the Stockholders Annual Meeting (hereafter cited as Stockholders Meeting), 6 May 1873.

62 *Montreal Herald*, 5 April 1871; Stockholders Meeting, 6 May 1873.

63 *Montreal Star*, 23 October 1872.

64 Directors Meeting, 21 October 1872.

Chapter 10
Real Estate Entrepreneur

1 Montreal City Hall Archives, St. Ann's Ward, assessment roll for 1847, 50; assessment roll for 1848, 15.

2 Montreal City Hall Archives, St. Antoine Ward, assessment roll for 1848, 31; assessment roll for 1850, 11.

3 ANQM, J. H. Isaacson, 6572, information in deed of sale, L. H. Holton to Sarah Coates Leeming, 15 June 1859.

4 Montreal City Hall Archives, St. Ann's Ward, assessment roll for 1849,29; assessment roll for 1851, 29.

5 ANQM, I. J. Gibb, 14586, deed of sale, Joseph Savage to L. H. Holton, 30 March 1853.

6 RGDC, Montreal, vol. 5, 81.

7 NAC, Galt Papers, Montreal, 10 April 1853, L. H. Holton to A.T. Galt.

8 ANQM, I. J. Gibb, 15143, lease of farm and premises, L. H. Holton to Michael Corrigan, 30 November 1853.

9 ANQM, I. J. Gibb, 17026, lease of farm and premises, L. H. Holton to Lawrence Quinn, 24 January 1856.

10 *Montreal in 1856: A Sketch Prepared for the Celebration of the Opening of the Grand Trunk Railway of Canada by a Subcommittee of the Celebration Committee* (Montreal, John Lovell, 1856), 14-18; Robert Prévost, *Montréal: A History* (Toronto: McClelland and Stewart, 1993), 262-263.

11 Montreal City Hall Archives, St. Antoine Ward, assessment roll for 1856, 50-59.

12 NAC, Manuscript Census of 1861, Canada East, Montreal, Saint Antoine Ward, Reel C-1239, 34.

13 Galt Papers, Montreal, 4 February 1862, L.H. Holton to A.T. Galt.

14 McGill University, Law Library, Canadiana Room, Torrance-Morris Papers, Letterbook 8, Montreal, 15 November 1862, Torrance & Morris to L. H. Holton. A helpful analysis of the work of Torrance & Morris is G. Blaine Baker, "Law Practice and Statecraft in Mid-Nineteenth Century Montreal: The Torrance-Morris Firm, 1848 to 1868," in Carol Wilton, ed., *Essays in the History of Canadian Law Beyond the Law: Lawyers and Business in Canada, 1830 to 1930* (Toronto: The Osgoode Society, 1990), 45-91.

15 *Montreal Directory for 1872-1873*, 605.

16 *Montreal Herald*, 4 April 1868.

17 *Montreal Star*, 23 October 1872.

18 ANQM, J. S. Hunter, 5116, quit claim of rights in property, David L. Macpherson to L. H. Holton, 19 October 1859.

19 *Prospectus and Rules of the Montreal Permanent Building Society* (Montreal: Starkes Co., 1858), 1-6; Michael Bliss, *Northern Enterprise Five Centuries of Canadian Business* (Toronto: McClelland and Stewart, 1987), 269-271. For a useful discussion of terminating building societies in Quebec City in the mid-nineteenth century, see Donald G. Paterson and Ronald A. Shearer, "Terminating Building Societies in Quebec City, 1850-1864," *Business History Review* 63 (Summer 1989), 384-415.

20 *Statutes of Canada*, 8 Victoria, Cap. 94(1845); *Montreal Directory for 1858-1859*, 539.

21 *Prospectus and Rules of the Montreal Permanent Building Society*, 1.

22 Ibid., 8.

23 *Montreal Directory for 1861-62*, 234; *Montreal Directory for 1872-73*, 630.

24 *Prospectus and Rules of the Montreal Permanent Building Society*, 1.

25 Ibid., 1,9.

26 *Prospectus and Rules of the Montreal Permanent Building Society*, 9.

27 Court House, Montreal, Minute Book, Second Series, B39, 20429, deed of sale, David L. Macpherson to L. H. Holton, 7 March 1856.

28 Court House, Montreal, Minute Book, Second Series, B46, 29937,

deed of sale, L. H. Holton to Charles A. Low, 3 May 1858.

29 ANQM, J. H. Isaacson, 6572, deed of sale, L. H. Holton to Sarah Coates Leeming, 15 June 1859.

30 ANQM, J. H. Isaacson, 6903, receipt and discharge, L. H. Holton to Sarah Coates Leeming, 12 September 1859.

31 ANQM, J. Belle, 20183, deed of sale, L. H. Holton to the Victoria Skating Club of Montreal, 14 July 1862.

32 ANQM, J. Belle, 24334, deed of transfer and assignment, L. H. Holton to the Victoria Skating Club of Montreal, 30 October 1862.

33 Court House, Montreal, Minute Book, Second Series, B65, 33491, deed of sale, A. T. Galt to L. H. Holton, 4 September 1862.

34 Galt Papers, Montreal, 30 January 1862, L. H. Holton to A. T. Galt.

35 Galt Papers, Montreal, 4 February 1862, L. H. Holton to A. T. Galt.

36 ANQM, J. S. Hunter, 13874, deed of sale, L. H. Holton to John Redpath, 27 May 1868.

37 RGDC, Montreal, vol. 5, 24.

38 For a helpful discussion of the life of working families in Montreal in this period, see Bettina Bradbury, *Working Families Age, Gender, and Daily Survival in Industrializing Montreal* (Toronto: McClelland & Stewart, 1993), 39-43.

39 Court House, Montreal, Minute Book, Second Series, B91, 44472, deed of sale, L. H. Holton to John Rankin, 30 June 1866.

40 Court House, Montreal, Minute Book, Second Series, BB10, 47735, donation, L. H. Holton to Mary Eliza Holton Britton, 24 August 1867.

41 *Montreal Herald*, 28 February 1867.

42 Court House, Montreal, Minute Book, Second Series, B98, 47752, deed of sale, L. H. Holton to Médéric Lanctot, 26 August 1867; John Irwin Cooper, *Montreal: A Brief History* (Montreal: McGill-Queen's University Press, 1969), 42, 87.

43 Court House, Montreal, Minute Book, Second Series, B107, 51142, deed of sale, L. H. Holton to Orrin Squire Wood, 8 August 1868.

44 Interview by the author with Mrs. H. Y. Russel, Montreal, 30 May 1966.

45 Russel interview, 30 May 1966; Robert Prevost, *Montreal: A History* (Toronto: McClelland & Stewart, 1991), 256; Brooke Hindle and Steven Lubar, *Engines of Change: The American Industrial Revolution 1790-1860* (Washington, D.C.: Smithsonian Institution Press, 1986), 86-87.

46 Brian Young, *In its Corporate Capacity: The Seminary of Montreal as a Business Institution, 1816-1876* (Montreal: McGill-Queen's University Press), 145.

47 ANQM, J. S. Hunter, 17970, deposit of plan of property by L. H. Holton, 19 July 1872.

48 Patricia Burgess Stach, "Real Estate Development and Urban Form: Roadblocks in the Path to Residential Exclusivity," *Business History Review* 63 (Summer 1989), 356-383, provides a useful analysis of the use of deed restrictions in the Linden area of Columbus, Ohio.

49 *Montreal Gazette*, 14 October 1872.

50 ANQM, J. S. Hunter, 17971, deed of sale, L. H. Holton to Frank Bond, 19 July 1872.

51 ANQM, J. S. Hunter, 17971, deed of sale, L. H. Holton to Frank Bond, 19 July 1872.

52 ANQM, J. S. Hunter, 17971, deed of sale, L. H. Holton to Frank Bond, 19 July 1872.

53 *Montreal Gazette*, 14 October 1872.

54 *Montreal Gazette*, 14 October 1872; *Montreal Herald*, 11 October 1872.

55 *Montreal Gazette*, 6 June 1873; *Montreal Herald*, 9 June 1873.

56 Queen's University Archives, Alexander Mackenzie Papers, Montreal, 19 April 1875, L. H. Holton to A. Mackenzie.

57 AO, Edward Blake Papers, Montreal, 12 September 1875, L. H. Holton to E. Blake.

58 Mackenzie Papers, Montreal, 28 September 1875, L. H. Holton to A. Mackenzie.

59 *Montreal Star*, 4 October 1875.

60 Mackenzie Papers, Montreal, 17 October 1875, L. H. Holton to A. Mackenzie.

61 ANQM, J. S. Hunter, 22677, deed of sale, L. H. Holton to Hannah Davy Holden, 6 February 1877.

62 Court House, Montreal, Minute Book, Second Series, BC 1047, 115287, appointment of guardian, document dated 25 April 1876 appointing Joseph B. Learmont as guardian of Holton Hamilton Learmont.

63 *Monetary Times*, 8 December 1876, 642.

64 ANQM, J. S. Hunter, 23159, deed of sale, David J. Craig to L. H. Holton, 21 July 1877.

65 ANQM, J. S. Hunter, 23036, obligation and mortgage, Ellen M. Schofield Jackson to L. H. Holton, 13 June 1877.

66 McGill University Archives, McGill University, Governors' Minute Book, 156.

67 *Montreal Witness*, 17 March 1880.

68 *London Advertiser*, 15 March 1880.

69 *Globe*, 15 March 1880.

70 *London Advertiser*, 16 March 1880.

71 *Montreal Star*, 16 March 1880.

72 *Montreal Gazette*, 16 March 1880.

73 T. L. Brock Collection, Ottawa, March 1880, Agnes Macdonald to Mrs. Holton.

74 *Montreal Herald*, 18 March 1880.

75 *Globe*, 18 March 1880.

76 McGill University Archives, McGill University, Governors' Minute Book, 313.

77 ANQM, J. S. Hunter, 21365, last will and testament of Luther H. Holton, 22 October 1875; Montreal City Hall Archives, St. Antoine Ward, assessment roll for 1879, 5190-51-91, 5200-5201.

78 *Ottawa Free Press*, 15 March 1880.

79 *Canadian Illustrated News*, 27 March 1880.

A Note on Sources

A problem arises in any study of Luther Holton: his personal papers, and those of Hooker, Holton & Co., have vanished. The extensive National Archives of Quebec in Montreal and the Bank of Montreal Archives do, however, contain substantial material for Holton's forwarding business. He had an important relationship with the railway contracting firm C. S. Gzowski & Co., and the papers of one of his partners, Alexander T. Galt, are extremely helpful. These papers contain correspondence in Holton's hand and are deposited in the National Archives of Canada. The account of Holton's business dealings with Ebenezer E. Gilbert in the Canada Engine Works is largely from the papers in the National Archives of Quebec in Montreal and the R. G. Dun & Co. Collection in the Baker Library, Harvard University, Boston. In the Laurentian Bank of Canada Archives, there is much material on Holton's role in the development of the Montreal City and District Savings Bank. The papers in the National Archives of Quebec in Montreal provide a valuable source of information about Holton's real estate interests. Newspapers, especially the *Montreal Gazette*, the Montreal *Pilot*, and the *Montreal Herald*, are filled with rich factual material on Holton's entire business career.

Since Luther Holton had such extensive contacts, a wide range of manuscript collections contain excellent material relating to his political career. Significant numbers of Holton's letters can be found in the George Brown Papers and the Alexander Mackenzie Papers in the National Archives of Canada, the Alexander Mackenzie Papers in the Queen's University Archives, and the Edward Blake Papers in the Archives of Ontario. The files of newspapers, including the Montreal *Pilot*, the *Montreal Herald*, the *Montreal Gazette*, and the Toronto *Globe*, are chock-full of information on Holton's political activities. This is also true of material in the debates in the Canadian legislative assembly and the House of Commons.

Holton's role in the evolution of Hooker, Holton & Co. is best viewed in Gerald J. J. Tulchinsky, *The River Barons: Montreal Businessmen and the Growth of Industry and Transportation, 1837-53* (Toronto: University of Toronto Press,

1977). Other important books that shed light on the business and social environments in which Holton operated are: Brian Young, *George-Étienne Cartier: Montreal Bourgeois* (Montreal: McGill-Queen's University Press, 1981); Brian Young, *In its Corporate Capacity: The Seminary of Montreal as a Business Institution, 1816-1876* (Montreal: McGill-Queen's University Press, 1986); Paul-André Linteau, *Histoire de Montréal depuis la Confédération* (Montréal: Boreal, 1992); John Irwin Cooper, *Montreal: A Brief History* (Montreal: McGill-Queen's University Press, 1969); Douglas McCalla, *The Upper Canada Trade 1834-1872: A Study of the Buchanans' Business* (Toronto: University of Toronto Press, 1979); Douglas McCalla, *Planting the Province: The Economic History of Upper Canada, 1784-1870* (Toronto: University of Toronto Press, 1993); A. A. den Otter, *The Philosophy of Railways: The Transcontinental Railway Idea in British North America* (Toronto: University of Toronto Press, 1997); Michael Bliss, *Northern Enterprise: Five Centuries of Canadian Business* (Toronto: McClelland & Stewart, 1990); Donald Creighton, *The Empire of the St. Lawrence* (Toronto: Macmillan of Canada, 1956); Bettina Bradbury, *Working Families: Age, Gender, and Daily Survival in Industrializing Montreal* (Montreal: McClelland & Stewart, 1993). Holton's business relationship with Alexander T. Galt can be discerned in Oscar Douglas Skelton, *The Life and Times of Alexander Tilloch Galt* (Toronto: Oxford University Press, 1920).

Holton's political relationship with George Brown is best studied in J.M.S. Careless, *Brown of the Globe*, 2 vols. (Toronto: Macmillan of Canada, 1959 and 1963). For the political environment of the Holton era, see Jean-Paul Bernard, *Les Rouges Libéralisme Nationalisme et Anticléricalisme au Milieu du XIX Siècle* (Montréal: Les Presses de l'Université du Québec, 1971); Jacques Monet, *The Last Cannon Shot: A Study of French-Canadian Nationalism, 1837-1850* (Toronto: University of Toronto Press, 1969); Marcel Hamelin, *Les Premières Années du Parlementarisme Québécois, 1867-1878* (Québec: Les Presses de l'Université Laval, 1974); J.M.S. Careless, *The Union of the Canadas: The Growth of Canadian Institutions, 1841-1857* (Toronto: McClelland & Stewart, 1967); W. L. Morton, *The Critical Years The Union of British North America, 1857-1873* (Toronto: McClelland & Stewart, 1964); Peter B. Waite, *Canada, 1874-1896, Arduous Destiny* (Toronto: McClelland & Stewart, 1971). Indispensable also are the biographies of Holton's contemporaries – see especially Brian Young, *George-Étienne Cartier: Montreal Bourgeois* (Montreal: McGill-Queen's University Press, 1981); Bruce W. Hodgins, *John Sandfield Macdonald, 1812-1872* (Toronto: University of Toronto Press, 1971); Dale C. Thomson, *Alexander Mackenzie Clear Grit* (Toronto: Macmillan of Canada, 1960); Joseph Schull, *Edward Blake: The Man of the Other Way, 1833-1881* (Toronto: Macmillan of Canada, 1875); Donald Creighton, *John A. Macdonald*, 2 vols. (Toronto: Macmillan of Canada, 1952 and 1955); Margaret A. Evans, *Sir Oliver Mowat* (Toronto: University of Toronto Press, 1992).

Bibliography

Manuscript Collections

Quebec

A. Coffey Collection, Montreal
  George E. Clerk Diary
Archives de la Province de Québec, Quebec City
  Edward Goff Penny Papers
Archives nationales du Québec à Montréal, Montreal
  J. Belle files.
  J. Blackwood files.
  C. Cushing files.
  N. B. Doucet files.
  T. B. Doucet files.
  W. M. Easton files.
  I. J. Gibb files.
  H. Griffin files.
  J. C. Griffin files.
  J. S. Hunter files.
  J. H. Isaacson files.
  W. F. Lighthall files.
  W. A. Phillips files.
  W. Ross files.
  Court of Queen's Bench Records
  Partnership Books

Presbyterian Church Register
Unitarian Church Registers
Wills Registers
Bank of Montreal Archives, Montreal
  Bank of Montreal Records
  Commercial Bank of the Midland District Records
Laurentian Bank of Canada Archives, Montreal
  Montreal City and District Savings Bank Records
McCord Museum of Canadian History Archives, Montreal
  David Ross McCord Papers
  J. S. Sanborn Papers
McGill University Archives, Montreal
  McGill University Records
  Torrance-Morris Papers
Montreal Board of Trade Archives, Montreal
  Montreal Board of Trade, Council Minutes
  Montreal Board of Trade, General Meeting Minutes
Montreal City Hall Archives, Montreal
  Assessment Rolls
Montreal Court House Archives, Montreal

Court House Minute Books

Customs Records

Montreal Registry Office Archives, Montreal

Partnership Books

Montreal Unitarian Church Archives, Montreal

Montreal Unitarian Church History

Montreal Unitarian Church Minute Books

Mrs. H. M. Hague Collection, Montreal

Correspondence

National Harbour Board Archives, Montreal

Montreal Harbour Commissioners, Minute Books

Ontario

Archives of Ontario, Toronto

E. Blake Papers

J. Dougall Papers

C. S. Gzowski Papers

J. S. Macdonald Papers

F. Shanly Papers

D. B. Stevenson Papers

Lansdowne and Leeds Assessment Rolls

Lansdowne and Leeds Census Records

Douglas Library, Queen's University, Toronto

Benjamin Tett Papers

Kirkpatrick-Nickle Collection

J. Macaulay Papers

Calvin Company Papers

A. Mackenzie Papers

Mrs. A. N. St. John Collection, Toronto

B. Workman's Journal

National Archives of Canada, Ottawa

Baring Brothers Papers

D. Bethune Papers

G. Brown Papers

I. Buchanan Papers

A. T. Galt Papers

Glyn, Mills and Company Papers

C. S. Gzowski Papers

J. A. Macdonald Papers

A. Mackenzie Papers

John Rose Papers

R. W. Shepherd Papers

Board of Public Works Correspondence

British Military and Naval Records

Canada Land Petitions

Canada State Books

Canadian National Railway Company Records

Colonial Office Records

Finance Minister's Letterbooks

Manuscript Census for the City of Montreal

Montreal Port Records

Montreal Shipping Registers

National Revenue Records

Upper Canada Civil Secretary's Correspondence

War Office Records

Thomas Fisher Rare Book Library, University of Toronto, Toronto

British America Assurance Company Papers

Toronto City Hall Archives, Toronto

City Council Journals

City Council Minutes

Toronto Public Library

R. Baldwin Papers

University of Toronto Library, Toronto

Joseph Workman's Diary

British Columbia

T. L. Brock Collection, Victoria
  Correspondence

Massachusetts

Baker Library, Graduate School of
  Business Administration, Harvard
  University, Boston
R.G. Dun & Company Collection
Radcliffe College Archives, Boston
  Seaview Gazette (Belleville).

New York

New York Public Library, New York
  Phelps Dodge & Co. Papers
Owen D. Young Library, St. Lawrence
  University, Canton
  G. Redington Papers
  C. Ripley Papers

Ohio

Cincinnati Historical Society Archives,
  Cincinnati
  S. Lester Taylor Papers

Pennsylvania

CIGNA Archives, Philadelphia
  Aetna Insurance Company Papers

Washington, D.C.

National Archives
  Despatches from U.S. Consuls in
  Montreal

Government Documents

Lower Canada

*Journals of the House of Assembly of
  Lower Canada, 1830-1840.*
Statutes of Lower Canada, 1830-1840.

United Province of Canada

*Canadian Parliamentary Debates,
  1858-1874*, Canadian Library
  Association.
*Debates of the Legislative Assembly of
  United Canada, 1841-1867*, edited
  by Danielle Blais.
*Journals of the Legislative Assembly of
  the Province of Canada, with
  Appendices, 1841-1867.*
*Parliamentary Debates on the Subject
  of the Confederation of the British
  North American Provinces.* Quebec,
  1865.
*Statutes of the Province of Canada,
  1841-1867.*
Sessional Papers, 1860-1866.

Canada

*Debates of the House of Commons,
  1867-1880.*
*Journals of the House of Commons,
  1867-1880.*
Royal Commission on Banking and
  Finance, *Hearings Held at Montreal*,
  vol. 17A, brief presented by Quebec
  Savings Banks, 17 May 1962.
Sessional Papers, 1867-1880.
Statutes of Canada, 1867-1880.

Newspapers and Magazines

Argus (Kingston)

L'Avenir (Montreal)

British Whig (Kingston)

Brockville Recorder

Canadian Courant (Montreal)

Canadian Economist (Montreal)

Canadian Gleaner (Huntingdon)

Canadian Illustrated News

Canadian Merchants' Magazine

Canadian News (London)

Economist (London)

Examiner (Toronto)

Globe (Toronto)

Guelph Advertiser

Halifax Morning Chronicle

Hunt's Merchants' Magazine

Illustrated London News

Independent (Toronto)

Kingston Chronicle and Gazette

Kingston Gazette

La Minerve (Montreal)

Leader (Toronto)

Le Pays (Montreal)

London Advertiser

L'Union Nationale (Montreal)

Mail (Toronto)

Montreal Argus

Montreal Gazette

Montreal Herald

Montreal Star

Montreal Transcript

Montreal Witness

Morning Chronicle (Quebec)

New Era (Montreal)

News (Kingston)

Ottawa Citizen

Ottawa Free Press

Pilot (Montreal)

Quebec Mercury

Republican (Ogdensburg)

The Times and Daily Commercial Advertiser (Montreal)

Times (London)

True Witness (Montreal)

Victoria Warder

Directories, Pamphlets, and other Printed Materials

A Few Words on the Savings Banks in Eastern and Western Canada, and Particularly on the Montreal City and District From its Establishment. Montreal: John Lovell & Son, 1884.

An Act Respecting Certain Savings Banks in the Provinces of Ontario and Quebec and the Charter of the Montreal City and District Savings Bank Montreal: John Lovell, 1871.

Canada Directory for 1851.

Canada Directory for 1857-1858.

Doige, Thomas, *An Alphabetical List of the Merchants, Traders, and Housekeepers Residing in Montreal.* Montreal: James Lane, 1819.

Dun & Bradstreet Reference Books, 1864-1887.

History of Toronto and County of York, Ontario. Toronto: C. Blackett Robinson, 1885.

Keefer, Thomas Coltrin, *The Canals of Canada: Their Prospects and Influence.* Toronto: 1850.

Keefer, Thomas Coltrin, *The Philosophy of Railroads, Published at the Request of the Directors of the Montreal and Lachine Railroad.* Toronto: Andrew H. Armour and Company, 1850.

Lovell's Province of Ontario Directory for 1871.

Lower Canada Almanack and Montreal Commercial Directory for 1840.

Mann, Moses Whicher, *Glimpses into the Holton Family History.* Mt. Hermon, Mass.: Holton Family Association, 1924.

Minutes of Information Given Before the Select Committee of Council on the Esplanade Contract, Toronto, 17 April 1855, C. S. Gzowski & Co. to the Citizens of Toronto.

Montreal Almanacks, 1819,1823, 1830, 1833, 1837, 1839, 1841, 1842.

Montreal Pocket Almanacks, 1845-1866.

Montreal Business Sketches. Montreal: Canada Railway Advertising Company, 1864.

Montreal Directories, 1842-1880.

Montreal in 1856: A Sketch Prepared for the Celebration of the Opening of the Grand Trunk Railway of Canada by a Subcommittee of the Celebration Committee. Montreal: John Lovell, 1856.

Morgan, Henry J., ed., *The Dominion Annual Register and Review 1879.* Montreal: John Lovell & Son, 1880.

Morgan, Henry J., ed., *The Dominion Annual Register and Review 1880-1881.* Montreal: John Lovell & Son, 1882.

Prospectus and Rules of the Montreal and Permanent Building Society. Montreal: Starke & Co., 1858.

Unpublished Genealogical Materials

Gilbert, Geoffrey, ed., "The Ancestry of Ezra Holton of Northfield, Mass. and Soperton, Ont., 1785-1824," typescript copy, Victoria, British Columbia, 1953.

Gilbert, Geoffrey, and Eva L. Moffatt, eds., "The Ancestors of Moses Haskell Gilbert of Vermont and Montreal, 1790-1843," typescript copy, Victoria, British Columbia, 1954.

Gilbert, Geoffrey, ed., "The Ancestors of William Forbes of Barre, Mass. and Montreal, Quebec, 1788-1833," typescript copy, Victoria, British Columbia, 1953.

Books

Ajzenstat, Janet, Paul Romney, Ian Gentles, and William D. Gairdner, eds., *Canada's Founding Debates.* Toronto: Stoddart, 1999.

Baskerville, Peter A., ed., *Canadian Papers in Business History,* 2 vols. Victoria, British Columbia: Public History Group, University of Victoria, 1989 and 1993.

Baskerville, Peter, ed., *The Bank of Upper Canada: A Collection of Documents. Edited with an Introduction by Peter Baskerville.* Toronto: The Champlain Society, 1987.

Batt, Elizabeth, Monck: Governor General, 1861-1868. Toronto: McClelland & Stewart, 1976.

Beck, J. Murray, *Joseph Howe,* vol. II, *The Briton Becomes Canadian 1848-1873.* Montreal: McGill-Queen's University Press, 1983.

Bernard, Jean-Paul, Les Rouges; libéralisme, nationalisme et anticléricalisme au milieu du XIXe siècle. Montréal: Presses de l'Université du Québec, 1971.

Blackford, Mansel G., *A History of Small Business in America.* NewYork: Twayne, 1991.

Blackford, Mansel G., *A Portrait Cast in Steel: Buckeye International and Columbus, Ohio, 1881-1980.* Westport, Conn.: Greenwood Press, 1982.

Blackford, Mansel G., and K. Austin Kerr, *Business Enterprise in American History,* 3d ed. Boston: Houghton Mifflin, 1994.

Bliss, Michael, *Northern Enterprise: Five Centuries of Canadian Business.* Toronto: McClelland & Stewart, 1990.

Borthwick, John Douglas, *History and Biographical Gazeteer of Montreal to the Year 1892.* Montreal, 1892.

Bosworth, Newton, *Hochelaga Depicta: The Early History and Present State of the City and Island of Montreal.* Montreal: William Greig, 1839.

Bradbury, Bettina, *Working Families: Age, Gender, and Daily Survival in Industrializing Montreal.* Toronto: McClelland & Stewart, 1993.

Broehl, Wayne G., Jr., *Cargill: Trading the World's Grain.* Hanover, New Hampshire: University Press of New England, 1992.

Bruchey, Stuart W., ed., *Small Business in American Life.* New York: Columbia University Press, 1980.

Calvin, D.D., *Saga of the St. Lawrence, Timber and Shipping Through Three Generations.* Toronto, 1945.

Campbell, Robert, *A History of the Scotch Presbyterian Church, St. Gabriel Street, Montreal.* Montreal: W. Drysdale & Co., 1887.

Careless, J.M.S., *Brown of the Globe,* 2 vols. Toronto: Macmillan of Canada, 1959 and 1963.

Careless, J.M.S., *The Union of the Canadas: The Growth of Canadian Institutions, 1841-1857.* Toronto: McClelland & Stewart, 1967.

Chandler, Alfred D., Jr., *Scale and Scope: The Dynamics of Industrial Capitalism.* Cambridge, Mass.: Harvard University Press, 1990.

Chandler, Alfred D., Jr., *The Visible Hand: The Managerial Revolution in American Business.* Cambridge, Mass.: Harvard University Press, 1977.

Clark, John G., *The Grain Trade in the Old Northwest.* Urbana: University of Illinois Press, 1966.

Cooper, John Irwin, *Montreal: A Brief History.* Montreal: McGill-Queen's University Press, 1969.

Cornell, Paul G., *The Alignment of Political Groups in Canada 1841-1867.* Toronto: University of Toronto Press, 1962.

Creighton, Donald, *John A. Macdonald,* 2 vols. Toronto: Macmillan of Canada, 1952 and 1955.

Creighton, Donald, *The Empire of the St. Lawrence.* Toronto: Macmillan of Canada, 1956.

Creighton, Donald, *The Road to Confederation.* Toronto: Macmillan of Canada, 1964.

Croil, James, *Steam Navigation and Its Relation to the Commerce of Canada and the United States.* Montreal: Montreal News Company, 1898.

Crosby, Travis L., *Sir Robert Peel's Administration, 1841-1846.* Hamden, Conn.: Archon Books, 1976.

Currie, A.W. *The Grand Trunk Railway of Canada.* Toronto: University of Toronto Press, 1957.

Darroch, James L., *Canadian Banks and Global Competitiveness.* Montreal: McGill-Queen's University Press, 1994.

De Kiewiet, C. W., and F. H. Underhill, eds., *Dufferin-Carnarvon Correspondence 1874-1878.* Toronto: The Champlain Society, 1955.

den Otter, A. A., *The Philosophy of Railways: The Transcontinental Railway Idea in British North America*. Toronto: University of Toronto Press, 1997.

Denison, Merrill, *Canada's First Bank: A History of the Bank of Montreal,* 2 vols. Toronto: McClelland & Stewart, 1967.

Dent, J. C., *The Canadian Portrait Gallery*. Toronto: John B. Magurn, 1880.

Doucet, Michael and John Weaver, *Housing the North American City*. Montreal: McGill-Queen's University Press, 1991.

Doughty, Howard, *Francis Parkman*. New York: Macmillan, 1962.

Easterbrook, W.T., and Hugh G.J. Aitkin, *Canadian Economic History*. Toronto: Macmillan of Canada, 1967.

Evans, A. Margaret, *Sir Oliver Mowat*. Toronto: University of Toronto Press, 1992.

Forster, Ben, *A Conjunction of Interests: Business, Politics and Tariffs, 1825-1879*. Toronto: University of Toronto Press, 1986.

Greer, Allan, and Ian Radforth, eds., *Colonial Leviathan State Formation in Mid-Nineteenth-Century Canada*. Toronto: University of Toronto Press, 1992.

Hamelin, Marcel,Les premières années du parlementarisme québécois, 1867-1878. Québec: Presses de l'Université Laval, 1974.

Heisler, John P., *The Canals of Canada*. Ottawa: National Historic Sites Service, 1973.

Hill, Robert, *Voice of the Vanishing Minority: Robert Sellar and the Huntingdon Gleaner, 1863-1919*. Montreal: McGill-Queen's University Press, 1999.

Hills, Richard L., *Power From Steam: A History of the Stationary Steam Engine*. Cambridge: Cambridge University Press, 1989.

Hind, Henry Youle, ed., *Eighty Years' Progress of British North America*. Toronto: L. Nicols, 1863.

Hindle, Brooke, and Steven Lubar, *Engines of Change: The American Industrial Revolution 1790-1860*. Washington, D.C., Smithsonian Institution Press, 1986.

Hodgetts, J.E., *Pioneer Public Service: An Administrative History of the United Canadas, 1841-1867*. Toronto: University of Toronto Press, 1955.

Hodgins, Bruce W., *John Sandfield Macdonald 1812-1872*. Toronto: University of Toronto Press, 1971.

Horne, H. Oliver, *A History of Savings Banks*. London: Oxford University Press, 1947.

Ingham, John N., *Making Iron and Steel: Independent Mills in Pittsburgh, 1820-1920*. Columbus, Ohio: Ohio State University Press, 1991.

Inwood, Kris E., *The Canadian Charcoal Iron Industry, 1870-1914*. New York: Garland, 1986.

Jenkins, Kathleen, *Montreal: Island City of the St. Lawrence*. Garden City, New York: Doubleday, 1966.

Johnson, Leo A., *History of Guelph, 1827-1927*. Guelph: Guelph Historical Society, 1977.

Kilbourn, William, *The Elements Combined: A History of the Steel Company of Canada*. Toronto: Clarke, Irwin, 1960.

Lacoursière, Jacques, *Histoire populaire du Québec,* III, *1841-1896*. Sillery, Québec: Septentrion, 1996.

278 • LUTHER H. HOLTON

Lamonde, Yvan, *Louis-Antoine Dessaules, 1818-1895: Un seigneur libéral et anticlérical*. Québec: Fides, 1994.

Leitch, Adelaide, *Floodtides of Fortune: The Story of Stratford and the progress of the city through two centuries*. Stratford: Corporation of the City of Stratford, 1980.

Linteau, Paul-André, *Histoire de Montréal depuis la Confédération*. Montréal: Boréal, 1992.

Linteau, Paul-André, *The Promoters City: Building the Industrial Town of Maisonneuve, 1883-1918*. Toronto: James Lorimer, 1985.

Lowitt, Richard, *A Merchant Prince of the Nineteenth Century: William E. Dodge*. New York: Columbia University Press, 1954.

Martin, Ged, *Britain and the Origins of the Canadian Confederation, 1837-67*. Vancouver: UBC Press, 1995.

McCalla, Douglas, *Planting the Province: The Economic History of Upper Canada, 1784-1870*. Toronto: University of Toronto Press, 1993.

McCalla, Douglas, *The Upper Canada Trade 1834-1872: A Study of the Buchanans' Business*. Toronto: University of Toronto Press, 1979.

McCallum, John, *Unequal Beginnings: Agriculture and Economic Development in Quebec and Ontario Until 1870*. Toronto: University of Toronto Press, 1980.

Monet, Jacques, *The Last Cannon Shot: A Study of French-Canadian Nationalism, 1837-1850*. Toronto: University of Toronto Press, 1969.

Moore, Christopher, *1867: How the Fathers Made a Deal*. Toronto: McClelland & Stewart, 1998.

Morton, W.L., *The Critical Years The Union of British North America, 1857-1873*. Toronto: McClelland & Stewart, 1964.

Morton, W.L., *The Kingdom of Canada: A General History From Earliest Times*. Toronto: McClelland & Stewart, 1969.

Myers, Gustavus, *A History of Canadian Wealth*. Toronto: James Lewis & Samuel, 1972.

Naylor, R.T., *The History of Canadian Business 1867-1914*, 2 vols. Toronto: James Lorimer and Company, 1975.

Neufeld, Edward P., *The Financial System of Canada: Its Growth and Development*. Toronto: Macmillan of Canada, 1972.

Noel, S.J.R., *Patrons, Clients, Brokers Ontario Society and Politics, 1791-1896*. Toronto: University of Toronto Press, 1990.

Norrie, Kenneth, and Douglas Owram, *A History of the Canadian Economy*. Toronto: Harcourt Brace Jovanovich, 1991.

Oliver, John W., *History of American Technology*. New York: Ronald Press, 1956.

Olmstead Alan L., *New York Mutual Savings Banks, 1819-1861*. Chapel Hill: University of North Carolina Press, 1976.

Passfield, Robert W., *Building the Rideau Canal: A Pictorial History*. Toronto: Fitzhenry & Whiteside, 1982.

Payne, Peter Lester, and Lance Edwin Davis, *The Savings Bank of Baltimore, 1818-1866: A Historical and Analytical Study*. Baltimore: Johns Hopkins University Press, 1956.

Piva, Michael J., *The Borrowing Process: Public Finance in the Province of Canada, 1840-1867*. Ottawa: University of Ottawa Press, 1992.

Prévost, Robert, *Montréal: A History*. Toronto: McClelland & Stewart, 1993.

Romney, Paul, *Getting It Wrong: How Canadian Forgot Their Past and Imperilled Confederation*. Toronto: University of Toronto Press, 1999.

Rose, Mary B., *The Gregs of Quarry Bank Mill: The Rise and Decline of a Family Firm, 1750-1914*. Cambridge: Cambridge University Press, 1986.

Ross, Eric, *The Canadas in 1841: Full of Hope and Promise*. Montreal: McGill-Queen's University Press, 1991.

Rudin, Ronald, *Banking en français: The French Banks of Quebec*. Toronto: University of Toronto Press, 1985.

Scheiber, Harry N., *Ohio Canal Era: A Case Study of Government and the Economy*. Athens, Ohio: Ohio University Press, 1969.

Schull, Joseph, *Edward Blake The Man of the Other Way 1833-1881*. Toronto: MacMillan of Canada, 1975.

Segal, Howard P., *Technology in America: A Brief History*. New York: Harcourt Brace Jovanovich, 1989.

Skelton, Oscar Douglas, *The Life and Times of Sir Alexander Tilloch Galt*. Toronto: Oxford University Press, 1920.

Skelton, Oscar Douglas, *Life and Times of Sir Alexander Tilloch Galt*. Edited with an Introduction by Guy MacLean. Toronto: McClelland & Stewart, 1966.

Smyth, T. Taggert, *The First Hundred Years: History of the Montreal City and District Savings Bank, 1846-1946*. Montreal: Montreal City and District Savings Bank, n.d.

Stilgoe, John R., *Borderland: Origins of the American Suburb, 1820-1939*. New Haven, Conn.: Yale University Press, 1988.

Storey, D. J., ed., *Small Firms in Regional Economic Development: Britain, Ireland and the United States*. Cambridge: Cambridge University Press, 1985.

Sweeny, Robert, *A Guide to the History and Records of Selected Montreal Businesses before 1947*. Montreal: Centre de recherche en histoire économique du Canada français, 1978.

Taylor, Graham D., and Peter A. Baskerville, *A Concise History of Business in Canada*. Toronto: Oxford University Press, 1994.

Thomson, Dale C., *Alexander Mackenzie Clear Grit*. Toronto: Macmillan of Canada, 1960.

Triggs, Stanley, Brian Young, Conrad Graham, and Gilles Lauzon, *Victoria Bridge: The Vital Link*. Montreal: McCord Museum of Canadian History, 1992.

Trout, J.M. and Edw., *The Railways of Canada*. Toronto: Monetary Times, 1871.

Tucker, Gilbert Norman, *The Canadian Commercial Revolution, 1845-1851*. New Haven, Conn.: Yale University Press, 1936.

Tulchinsky, Gerald J.J., *The River Barons: Montreal Businessmen and the Growth of Industry and Transportation, 1837-53*. Toronto: University of Toronto Press, 1977.

Wade, Mason, *Francis Parkman: Heroic Historian*. Hamden, Conn.: Archon Books, 1972.

Waite, Peter B., *Canada, 1874-1896, Arduous Destiny*. Toronto: McClelland & Stewart, 1971.

Waite, P. B., *The Life and Times of Confederation, 1864-1867: Politics, Newspapers, and the Union of British North America*. Toronto: University of Toronto Press, 1962.

Walker, Frank, *Daylight Through the Mountain: The Life and Letters of Walter and Francis Shanly.* Montreal: The Engineering Institute of Canada, 1957.

Ward, James A., *J. Edgar Thomson: Master of the Pennsylvania.* Westport, Conn.: Greenwood Press, 1980.

Ward, N., *The Public Purse: A Study in Canadian Democracy.* Toronto: University of Toronto Press, 1962.

Warner, Sam Bass, Jr., *Streetcar Suburbs: The Process of Growth in Boston, 1870-1900,* 2d ed. Cambridge, Mass.: Harvard University Press, 1978.

Weiss, Marc A., *The Rise of the Community Builders: The American Real Estate Industry and Urban Land Planning.* New York: Columbia University Press, 1987.

Welfling, Weldon, *Mutual Savings Banks: The Evolution of a Financial Intermediary.* Cleveland: The Press of Case Western Reserve University, 1968.

White, Richard, *Gentlemen Engineers: The Working Lives of Frank and Walter Shanly.* Toronto: University of Toronto Press, 1999.

Winks, Robin W., *Canada and the United States: The Civil War Years.* Montreal: Harvest House, 1971.

Winstanley, Michael J., *The Shopkeeper's World, 1830-1914.* Manchester, England: Manchester University Press, 1983.

Young, Brian, *George-Etienne Cartier: Montreal Bourgeois.* Montreal: McGill-Queen's University Press, 1981.

Young, Brian, *In its Corporate Capacity: The Seminary of Montreal as a Business Institution, 1816-1876.* Montreal: McGill-Queen's University Press, 1986.

Young, Brian, *Promoters and Politicians: The North-Shore Railways in the History of Quebec, 1854-85.* Toronto: University of Toronto Press, 1978.

Young, Brian, and John A. Dickinson, *A Short History of Quebec: A Socio-Economic Perspective.* Toronto: Copp Clark Pitman, 1988.

Zaslow, Morris, *Reading the Rocks: The Story of the Geological Survey of Canada, 1842-1972.* Ottawa: Macmillan of Canada, 1975.

Zeller, Suzanne, *Inventing Canada Early Victorian Science and the Idea of a Transcontinental Nation.* Toronto: University of Toronto Press, 1987.

Articles

Armstrong, Frederick H., "John Torrance," *Dictionary of Canadian Biography, IX, 1861-1870.* Toronto: University of Toronto Press, 1976, 792-794.

Baker, G. Blaine, "Law Practice and Statecraft in Mid-Nineteenth Century Montreal: The Torrance-Morris Firm, 1848 to 1868," in Carol Wilton, ed., *Essays in the History of Canadian Law Beyond the Law: Lawyers and Business in Canada 1830 to 1930.* Toronto: The Osgoode Society, 1990, 45-91.

Baskerville, Peter, "Donald Bethune's Steamboat Business: A Study of Upper Canada Commercial and Financial Practice", *Ontario History* 67 (September 1975), 135-149.

Baskerville, Peter, "Imperial Agendas and 'Disloyal' Collaborators: Decolonization and the John Sandfield Macdonald Ministries, 1862-1864," in David Keane and Colin Read, eds., *Old Ontario:*

Essays in Honor of J.M.S. Careless. Toronto: Dundurn Press, 1990, 234-256.

Bunbury, Dan, "The Public Purse and State Finance: Government Savings Banks in the Era of Nation Building, 1867-1900," *The Canadian Historical Review* 78 (December 1997), 566-598.

Cameron, Wendy, "John Langton," *Dictionary of Canadian Biography,* XII, *1891-1900.* Toronto: University of Toronto Press, 1990, 527-529.

Cooper, John Irwin, "Some Early Canadian Savings Banks," *Canadian Banker* 57 (Spring 1950), 135-143.

Cooper, John Irwin, "The Origins and Early History of the Montreal City and District Savings Bank 1846-1871," *The Canadian Catholic Historical Association Report 1945-1946,* 15-25.

Cornell, Paul, "John Ross," *Dictionary of Canadian Biography,* X, *1871-1880.* Toronto: University of Toronto Press, 1972, 631-633.

Craven, Paul, and Tom Traves, "Canadian Railways as Manufacturers, 1850-1880," Canadian Historical Association, *Historical Papers,* 1983, 254-281.

Cruikshank, Ken, "Sir David Lewis Macpherson," *Dictionary of Canadian Biography,* XII, *1891-1900.* Toronto: University of Toronto Press, 1990, 682-689.

Davison, George A., "The Hincks-Brown Rivalry and the Politics of Scandal," *Ontario History* 81 (June 1989), 129-151.

den Otter, A. A., "Alexander Galt, the 1859 Tariff and Canadian Economic Nationalism," *Canadian Historical Review* 63 (June 1982), 151-178.

Désilets, Andrée, "Sir Hector-Louis Langevin," *Dictionary of Canadian Biography,* XIII, *1901-1910.* Toronto: University of Toronto Press, 1994, 567-572.

Dubuc, Alfred, "William Molson," *Dictionary of Canadian Biography,* X, *1871-1880.* Toronto: University of Toronto Press, 1972, 517-526.

Dyster, Barrie, "John William Gamble," *Dictionary of Canadian Biography,* X, *1871-1880.* Toronto: University of Toronto Press, 1972, 299-300.

Eadie, James A., "David Barker Stevenson," *Dictionary of Canadian Biography,* VIII, *1851-1860.* Toronto: University of Toronto Press, 1985, 836-837.

Farr, David M.L., "Sir John Rose," *Dictionary of Canadian Biography,* XI, *1881-1890.* Toronto: University of Toronto Press, 1982, 766-772.

Goheen, Peter G., "The Struggle for Urban Space: Disposing of the Toronto Waterfront in the Nineteenth Century," a paper presented at the 78th Annual Meeting of the Canadian Historical Association, 6-8 June 1999, Sherbrooke, Quebec.

Gundy, H.P., "Edward Jackson," *Dictionary of Canadian Biography,* X, *1871-1880.* Toronto: University of Toronto Press, 1972, 379.

Hague, G., "The Late Mr. E.H. King," 4 *Journal of the Canadian Bankers Association* (September 1897), 20-29.

Hamelin, Jean, "Médéric Lanctot," *Dictionary of Canadian Biography,* X, *1871-1880.* Toronto: University of Toronto Press, 1972, 420-426.

Hanna, David B., "Creation of an Early Victorian Suburb in Montreal," *Urban History Review* 9 (October 1980), 38-64.

Ingham, John N., "Iron and Steel in the Pittsburgh Region: The Domain of Small Business," *Business and Economic History*, Second Series 20 (1991), 107-116.

Inglis, W., "On Valves and Valve Gearing for Steam Engines," *Transactions of the Institute of Engineers in Scotland* 7 (1863-1864), 115-120.

Kesteman, Jean-Pierre, "Sir Alexander Tilloch Galt," *Dictionary of Canadian Biography, XII, 1891-1900*. Toronto: University of Toronto Press, 1990, 348-356.

Klassen, Henry C., "Luther Hamilton Holton," *Dictionary of Canadian Biography, X, 1871-1880*. Toronto: University of Toronto Press, 1972, 354-358.

Klassen, Henry C., "Luther Holton: Mid-Century Montreal Railwayman," *University of Ottawa Quarterly* 52 (July-September 1982), 316-339.

Knight, Russell M., "Determination of Failure in Canadian Small Business," in *World of Small Business: Problems and Issues. Proceedings 24th Annual Conference, International Council for Small Business, Laval University, Quebec City, June 23rd to 26th 1979* (Ottawa: Federal Business Development Bank, 1979), Paper 40, 1-11.

Legault, Réjean, "Architecture et forme urbaine: L'exemple du triplex à Montréal de 1870 à 1914," *Urban History Review* 18 (June 1989), 1-10.

Lewis, Robert D., "The Development of an Early Suburban Industrial District: The Montreal Ward of Saint-Ann, 1851-1871," *Urban History Review* 19 (February 1991), 160-180.

Livesay, Harold C., "Entrepreneurial Dominance in Businesses Large and Small, Past and Present," *Business History Review* 63 (Spring 1989), 1-21.

Magill, Max, "The Failure of the Commercial Bank," in Gerald Tulchinsky, ed., *To Preserve and Defend: Essays on Kingston in the Nineteenth Century*. Montreal: McGill-Queen's University Press, 1976, 169-181.

McCalla, Douglas, "Joseph Davis Ridout," *Dictionary of Canadian Biography, IX, 1881-1890*. Toronto: University of Toronto Press, 1982, 735-736.

Morgan, H. R., "Steam Navigation on the Ottawa River," *Ontario Historical Society, Papers and Records* 23 (Toronto, 1926), 370-383.

Nelles, H.V., "Introduction," to *The Philosophy of Railroads* by T.C. Keefer. Toronto: University of Toronto Press, 1972, ix-lxiii.

Nelles, H.V., "Sir Casimir Stanislaus Gzowski," *Dictionary of Canadian Biography, XII, 1891-1900*. Toronto: University of Toronto Press, 1990, 389-396.

Obituary, "E.E. Gilbert," *Transactions of The Canadian Society of Civil Engineers* 3 (1889), 364-365.

Officer, L.H., and L.B. Smith, "The Canadian-American Reciprocity Treaty of 1855-66," *Journal of Economic History* 28 (December 1968), 596-623.

Paterson, Donald G., and Ronald A. Shearer, "Terminating Building Societies in Quebec City, 1850-1864," *Business History Review* 63 (Summer 1989), 384-415.

Pietersma, Harry, "Samuel Crane," *Dictionary of Canadian Biography,* VIII, *1851-1860.* Toronto: University of Toronto Press, 1985, 181-183.

Platt, D.C.M., and Jeremy Adelman, "London Merchant Bankers in the First Phase of Heavy Borrowing: The Grand Trunk Railway of Canada," *Journal of Imperial and Commonwealth History* 18 (May 1990), 208-227.

Robert, Jean-Claude, "Horatio Gates," *Dictionary of Canadian Biography,* VI, *1821-1835.* Toronto: University of Toronto Press, 1987, 277-280.

Romney, Paul, "The Ten Thousand Pound Job: Political Corruption, Equitable Jurisdiction, and the Public Interest in Upper Canada 1852-6," in David H. Flaherty, ed., *Essays in the History of Canadian Law,* Vol. II. Toronto: University of Toronto Press, 1983, 143-199.

Scranton, Philip, "Small Business, Family Firms, and Batch Production: Three Axes for Development in American Business History," *Business and Economic History,* Second Series, 20 (1991), 99-106.

Soltow, James H., "Origins of Small Business and the Relationships Between Large and Small Firms: Metal Fabricating and Machinery Making in New England, 1890-1957," in Stuart W. Bruchey, ed., *Small Business in American Life.* New York: Columbia University Press, 1980, 192-211.

Stach, Patricia Burgess, "Real Estate Development and Urban Form: Roadblocks in the Path of Residential Exclusivity," *Business History Review* 63 (Summer 1989), 356-383.

Ste. Croix, Lorne, "Charles Joseph Coursol," *Dictionary of Canadian Biography,* XI, *1881-1890.* Toronto: University of Toronto Press, 1982, 206-207.

Story, Norah, "William Gamble," *Dictionary of Canadian Biography,* XI, *1881-1890.* Toronto: University of Toronto Press, 1982, 332-333.

Sylvain, Philippe, "Francis Cassidy," *Dictionary of Canadian Biography,* X, *1871-1880.* Toronto: University of Toronto Press, 1972, 153-155.

Tal, Benny, with Derek Jones and John Clinkard, "Small Business in Canada," *CIBC Observations* (April 1994), 1-5.

Tulchinsky, Gerald, "John Redpath," *Dictionary of Canadian Biography,* IX, *1861-1870.* Toronto: University of Toronto Press, 1976, 654-655.

Tulchinsky, G., and Brian J. Young, "John Young," *Dictionary of Canadian Biography,* X, *1871-1880.* Toronto: University of Toronto Press, 1972, 722-728.

Waite, P.B., "Thomas White," *Dictionary of Canadian Biography,* XI, *1881-1890.* Toronto: University of Toronto Press, 1982, 919-921.

Waterston, Elizabeth, "David Kinnear," *Dictionary of Canadian Biography,* IX, *1861-1870.* Toronto: University of Toronto Press, 1976, 429-430.

White, Richard, "Losing Ventures: The Railway Construction Contracts of Frank Shanly, 1860-75," *Canadian Historical Review* 79 (June 1998), 237-260.

Wood, James L., "The Introduction of the Corliss Engine to Britain," *Transactions of the Newcomen Society,* 52 (1980-1981), 1-13.

Young, Brian J., and Gerald J.J. Tulchinsky, "Sir Hugh Allan," *Dictionary of Canadian Biography,* XI, *1881-1890.* Toronto: University of Toronto Press, 1982, 5-15.

Unpublished Theses

Allen, Gene Lawrence, The Origins of the Intercolonial Railway, 1835-1869. Ph.D. thesis, University of Toronto, 1991.

Brouillard, Pierre, Le Développement du Port de Montréal, 1850-1896. M.A. thesis, Université du Québec à Montréal, 1976.

Cross, Michael, The Dark Druidical Groves and the Commercial Frontier in British North America to 1854. Ph.D. thesis, University of Toronto, 1968.

Davison, George A., Francis Hincks and the Politics of Interest, 1831-1854. Ph.D. thesis, University of Alberta, 1989.

Dever, Alan R., Economic Development and the Lower Canadian Assembly, 1828-1840. M.A. thesis, 1977.

Index

as whipping boys, 89; Woodstock &
Lake Erie Railway and Harbour
Company, 89
Rambler (steamboat), 195
Ramsay, T.K., 163
Ranger (steamboat), 195
Rankin, John, 227
real estate, ix, 99; deed restrictions, 230;
property, administration of, 159;
property taxes, 150; rental property
income, 217; resale of property, 224
Rebellion Losses Bill, 51–52; and the
burning of parliament house, 52
Rebellion of 1837, 17, 51
Reciprocity Treaty, 81, 85–86, 147–49,
177; abrogation, 1866, 150;
American senate, 177
Redpath, John, 50, 225
Redpath's Canada Sugar Refinery, 94, 178
Reform victory, 83
repeal movement, 166
representation by population, 102–4,
107, 115–16, 158
Richards, Albert N., 150
Richardson & Co., 29
Rideau Canal, 15, 30, 42, 47; tolls, 33–
34
Riel, Louis, 179–80
Rielle, Joseph, 230–31
Robert Watson (ship), 28
Robertson, Masson & Co., 29–30
Robinson, John Beverley, 122
Rose, John, 101, 120, 130, 152
Ross, Alexander M., 71, 74
Ross, John, 70, 84–85, 88–90, 95, 108,
111
Royal Commission, Pacific Scandal, 171–
72
Rupert's Land, 165
Ryan, M.P., 183

Salaberry (steamboat), 195
Sandfield Macdonald-Dorion cabinet,
129, 140
Sandfield Macdonald-Dorion government, 147, 149, 152; militia, 136;
precarious majority, 137
Sandfield Macdonald-Dorion ministry,
150

Sandfield Macdonald-Sicotte government,
126, 133, 140; defeat of, 127
Santoire, John, 174
Sarnia land scandal, 72–74, 97
Sarnia (schooner), 41
Savage, Joseph, 218
Savage farm, 218, 229; capital for, 224;
developments in Montreal and, 219;
middle-class neighbourhood, 233;
subdividing, 229
Savage farm property: deed restrictions,
231; depression of mid-1870's, 234;
middle class people, 231; plan, 232;
St. Antoine suburb, 229; subdivision, 220, 235; subdivision plan,
230
savings bank services: market for, 202,
204
Scott, Thomas, 179
screw propellers, 42–43, 45; safety, 42
seat of government, 83, 90, 105;
Kingston as, 24; Montreal as, 100,
106; Quebec City as, 83; Toronto as,
90
sectionalism, ix, 83, 102–3, 107, 111,
119, 121, 145, 152, 156, 160. *See
also* English-French relations;
representation by population
Seers, Louis A., 183
Sellar, Robert, 158, 163
Sénécal, Louis A., 190
separation, 104
Shanly, Francis, 71, 78
Shanly, Walter, 71, 78, 133
Shanly brothers, 71–72
Sheffield's Corners, 3, 5
Shepherd, Robert H., 31
Sherbrooke St. home, 218–19, 221, 229
Sicotte, L.V., 85, 121, 128, 131, 137
Sir Charles Bagot (schooner), 41
slavery, 96, 122
Smith, George, 189
Soper, Levi, 3–5
Soper, Lois, 3
St. Andrew's Society, 36
St. Anne's Rapids: lock, 30–32
St. Lawrence canals, 42, 139–40; toll
regulations, 57
St. Lawrence Cotton Mills, 94